Final Notes from the Field

Northbound on the Appalachian Trail

Kirk Ward Robinson

HIGHLAND
HOME

Nashville, Tennessee

BOOKS BY KIRK WARD ROBINSON

NONFICTION

Founding Character:
Documents that Define the United States of America and its People

Founding Courage:
Courage and Character in the United States of America

Hiking Through History:
Hannibal, Highlanders, and Joan of Arc

Notes from the Field:
A Diary of Journeys Near and Far

More Notes from the Field:
Southbound on the Appalachian Trail and Other Journeys

Final Notes from the Field:
Northbound on the Appalachian Trail

FICTION

August Roads
Novellas

Life in Continuum
Stories

The Appalachian
A Novel

The Latter Half of Inglorious Years
A Novel

Timewall Speaks
A Novel

A Robin Waits
Short Fiction

Final Notes from the Field
Northbound on the Appalachian Trail

A Highland Edition

Photographs used with permission

Designed by Victoria Valentine
PageandCoverDesign.com

Printed in the United States of America

HighlandHome Publishing
Nashville, Tennessee
37215

ISBN 10: 0-9996042-8-7
ISBN 13: 978-0-9996042-8-1

Visit www.kirkwardrobinson.com

Watch the mountain turn to dust and blow away

Tommy James & the Shondells
Sweet Cherry Wine

Through shining eyes the landscape lies
To be walked
To be felt
To be breathed deeply.
Through intrepid eyes the Trail abides
Mountains climb high
Tall trees sigh and cry in the wind.
Through weary eyes the hiker sighs
A journey ends but life begins
It seems
On a mountain top.

CONTENTS

A GLOSSARY OF THRU-HIKER TERMS

AWOL – Trail guide published by David "Awol" Miller, a 2003 thru-hiker.

banana blaze – Girl chasing boy on the Appalachian Trail. (I guess boy chasing boy, too)

blowdown – Trees that fall across the trail. Roots are shallow in the rocky Appalachians, forming large root mats that can rip out of the soil to create veritable caves or overhangs. So many trees can fall after storms—especially winter storms—that the trail can become completely engulfed for miles, forcing hikers to duck and climb and sometimes wend through tangled limbs.

blue blaze – A side trail to a view or other feature, sometimes a shortcut through a difficult section, and sometimes a bad-weather bypass. There are many fewer blue-blazed trails now than there used to be.

bog logs – Narrow footbridges over bogs or other wet sections. The Maine Appalachian Trail Club used actual logs for this purpose, hence the name, while trail clubs farther south used boards.

cowboy camp – To sleep out in the open sans tent.

croo – The staff—or crew—who work at the huts in the White Mountains. The term has evolved to include the staff at hostels and elsewhere.

flip-flop – Hiking a portion of the Appalachian Trail and then returning to hike the other portion. Most commonly, flip-floppers will hike north to Mt. Katahdin from Harpers Ferry, then return to Harpers Ferry and hike south to Springer Mountain. The purpose of this is to relieve crowding on the trail, and to take better advantage of the seasons. This practice has become popular. In 2018 there were more flip-floppers than southbounders.

free-hike – Hiking naked, which is becoming more popular in Europe. There are no rules against hiking naked in America's national parks, and the Appalachian Trail is, in essence, a national park. Local authorities often look at this askance, however.

Guthook (now *FarOut*) – A phone app with detailed, mile-by-mile information about the Appalachian Trail and other trails. Users can leave reviews of everything from the flow rate of springs to the quality of service at hostels and hotels—to the benefit (and chagrin) of many.

hiker box - Boxes most often found in hostels in which hikers deposit unwanted food, clothing, and gear. These are their fullest down south, where northbounders are still trying to determine their needs. It is possible for a time to completely feed and clothe one's self from these boxes, and collect some surprisingly good equipment.

hiker brain - An addled state that occurs as a result of dehydration and low blood sugar. It becomes difficult to focus one's attention, process what others are saying, and act with restraint.

Hiker Hilton - Refers to the several multi-story shelters located mainly in Virginia and Pennsylvania. Some of these shelters have internal stairs, verandas, porches, and skylights.

hiker hunger - A state of extreme calorie deficit. Depending upon age, gender, and terrain, thru-hikers might expend upward of 8000 calories per day, which exceeds two pounds of bodyweight, and this while most would struggle to carry enough food to be able to replenish more than 2000 to 3000 calories per day. As stomachs shrink, it becomes practically impossible to eat enough to compensate for the deficit, which leads to constant, starvation-level hunger.

hiker midnight - 9:00 p.m. Everyone should quiet down so that thru-hikers can sleep. This is not an arbitrary time as it allows eight hours of sleep until hiker sunrise.

hiker sunrise - 5:00 a.m. Perhaps mostly defined by southbounders and based upon the springtime sunrise in the higher latitudes. I never met a northbounder who was aware of this term.

lash - Long-ass section hike.

nero - Near zero.

nobo - Northbound thru-hiker.

pink blaze - Boy chasing girl on the Appalachian Trail. (Ditto)

platinum blaze - Shuttling out to a hotel or other comfortable accommodation most nights, made more common by smart phones.

PUD - Pointless up and down.

relo - Trail relocation or reroute. This is often necessary to prevent erosion. Sometimes the trail is relocated from private land to public land, and sometimes the trail is relocated just for the heck of it.

ridgerunner - Sometimes a volunteer but often an employee of the Appalachian Trail Conservancy who hikes back and forth through a designated section in order to educate hikers and monitor conditions.

section hiker - Someone hiking the entire Appalachian Trail in sections and over time. The term is often used to describe anyone on the trail who isn't thru-hiking, although this application is inaccurate.

slackpack - An evolving term but usually refers to someone hiking with a mostly empty backpack and expecting to be shuttled back to a hostel in the evening where the majority of their gear awaits.

sobo - Southbound thru-hiker.

Springer fever - Originally referred to a visceral need to get back to Springer Mountain, Georgia in the spring to begin another thru-hike. For southbounders, Springer fever represents the overwhelming urge to race the final few hundred miles to Springer Mountain to complete the thru-hike.

stealth - To hike, stay, or otherwise comport one's self in defiance of rules, such as to sneak through a national park without obtaining a permit.

stealth camp - To camp outside of a designated camping area.

thru-hiker - Someone hiking the entire trail from end to end.

trail angel - A person who helps and supports hikers without any expectation of reimbursement.

trail legs - A state in which the plodding pace of early on becomes quick and seemingly effortless. I believe that the onset of this state occurs when all the fat around the quadriceps has been burned off. Onset varies by age and physical condition. I generally acquire my trail legs after about 500 miles.

trail magic - Generally, food and drinks left beside the trail in coolers for hikers—first come, first served. Once upon a time, sodas and beers were often left floating in the cold streams up north by trail angels. Concerns about litter and raids by wild animals now discourage this practice. More and more we now encounter trail angels at the trailheads, with tables, chairs, and elaborate offerings of food and drink. Also refers—although decreasingly—to any moments of enchantment on the trail.

Trail-runner / trailrunner - Someone running the trail as an extreme sport akin to an ultramarathon. Also refers to a lightweight trail shoe.

trail telegraph - The uncanny way that information travels up and down the trail via word of mouth and through the trail registers.

tramily - A group of hikers who come together as a tightly-knit trail family.

tramline - The long, stretched out line of a tramily on the move.

Triple Crown - Successfully thru-hiking each of the three major U.S. long trails: Appalachian Trail, Continental Divide Trail, and Pacific Crest Trail. Can also refer to the Virginia section that includes Dragons Tooth, McAfee Knob, and the Tinker Cliffs.

vitamin I - Ibuprofen.

white blaze - For the purist, the only blazes on the Appalachian Trail that count.

yellow blaze - To skip a section by hiking a road, or most often, by car.

yogi - The art of acquiring food or other items without asking for them directly. Otherwise we would be begging.

yo-yo - To reach the terminus of the Appalachian Trail and then turn around and go back the other way.

zero - A day on the Appalachian Trail in which no miles are hiked.

TRAIL ETIQUETTE

- First and foremost, leave no trace of your passage on the trail.
- Downhill hikers should yield and step aside for uphill hikers. This is because uphill hikers acquire a momentum to carry them to the top. Being forced to stop sheds this momentum. Downhill hikers also have an easy view of the coming trail, while uphill hikers are either subsumed into the effort, watching where they place their feet, or else the climb might be too steep for them to incline their necks high enough to see ahead.
- Hikers should never set up their tents inside shelters. Shelters are designated for a certain number of people, and tents will decrease that number, leading to harsh words and perhaps more, especially in poor weather. Hikers should also not spread their gear out and occupy more space than is appropriate.
- Inflatable mattresses should not be used in shelters. These scrunch and make noises that are magnified by hard wooden floors.
- Large groups should tent out and reserve the shelters for individual hikers.
- Never burn plastic or foil in the fire rings. These items will melt or become charred, but will never go away.
- Close and latch the privy doors when finished, and avoid urinating in the privies.
- Don't listen to loud music or have phone conversations while hiking. This only cheapens the experience for everyone in earshot.
- Don't feed the wildlife.
- Stay on the trail. Jumping up on the verges or cutting switchbacks leads to erosion.

- Behave well in towns. Your behavior leaves a legacy for those to come.
- When coming up behind another hiker, announce yourself well in advance.
- Observe hiker midnight.
- If you come into a shelter after dark, be quiet, respectful, and use your red headlight.
- Last, and perhaps the most important item of etiquette: Don't be a dick.

PROLOGUE

SUNDAY, DECEMBER 19, 2021

Smith County, Tennessee

Is this a depression of incipient gray winter, or is it of the lingering post-trail variety?

It's been eighty-seven days since I summited Baxter Peak on Mt. Katahdin, the first few of those days in muddled apathy, the remainder kept full of farm work and elective projects in a frenetic race ahead of a winter that now lurks beyond a bare pair of days. These are eighty-seven days that passed in a falcon's blink, Sunday to Sunday to Sunday until now I am here and I cannot recall the hours that brought me.

Eighty-seven days prior to my fog-whipped summit of the great mountain, on a day blistering above the sheltering canopy, I reached Dragons Tooth in Virginia and paused with my hiking partner Ultra Burn to take photos of that monumental geologic incisor. Beyond Dragons Tooth, we endured the merciless sun of a seemingly endless rocky ridge, descended forever to reach Virginia Route 624, and after 21.3 profanity-strewn miles, sun-basted and as parched as Arizona leather, we were completely, totally, absolutely spent.

It was marvelous, I tell you. Marvelous.

I can recall every day that came after, a lifetime of them if not several lifetimes, miles underfoot, elevations gained and given back, biting bugs and stinging rain, great conversations and some less so, larger than life people and those smaller than life as well, all while that summit of Baxter Peak was as yet so far in the gauzy future that it seemed more rumor than eventuality; and now the eighty-seven days since, purposefully kept full to slow this march but nothing can compete with the Appalachian Trail. Time has sped by just the same. It *is* post-trail depression then, still there after these winged months. I should have expected it—I've done this four times, after all.

In the aftermath of an Appalachian Trail thru-hike, whether having passed every white blaze or not, the mind stirs in the heady sense that nothing is unachievable. Every fleeting idea lands with gravity. The perplexing issues of life seem trivial, the days ahead so promising and engorged with potential that greatness must lay but a few breaths away. And then a day passes, and then another. For a time you wake up each morning and still think with relief, "I don't have to hike today;" and then some unremarkable weeks run together and you wake up and think, "I wish I were hiking today;" and then it's all gone, like a vaporous dream in the small hours, and you wake up and think, "I have to hike again or I'll be lost."

This is what happened to me, in 2001, 2008, 2018, and now in 2021. I went southbound on my first three hikes, northbound on this last. I said my fourth would be my final thru-hike of the Appalachian Trail. I said it repeatedly and I meant it. That trail is a mean bull that twists and bucks between your thighs, sparing no opportunity to gore you with its horns. It's a stony, slippery, serpentine test of endurance beyond enduring. I said I would never do it again. God help me but I want to.

Writing this down will help, I hope. I thought so last time, too, but May 16, 2021, the date I began my fourth thru-hike, proved that hope irrelevant because once begun I would certainly see it through. My fourth must be my last, though, it has to be. It's not the physicality of age that holds me back, but acceptance of the very real lightness of the years ahead against the weight of that which I must still accomplish. Time is a pitiless predator in waiting, prepared to pounce without provocation, and thru-hikes take time no matter how quick your feet.

So this will be the final installment in my *Notes from the Field* series, a trim trilogy of my travels, a fitting legacy. Since this volume will contain only the one journey, I will deviate from my previous format somewhat. I will still include my diary entries and posted field notes, as always edited for accuracy and clarity and grammatical competence, but this time I'll also add deeper observations and a bit more opinion than might be wise. Because the Appalachian Trail is not the utopian jaunt we would have it be, I intend to change some people's names here and there. I haven't decided yet if I'll apprise the reader of this. We'll see.

If you have a hankering to thru-hike the Appalachian Trail, I advise you to take up golf instead. If you make us proud and decline time on the links in favor of this other, more intensive endeavor, I think this book will be a good place to start.

PRELUDE

I have described my first Appalachian Trail thru-hike in 2001 as a soul-searching mess. Yes, it was a mess. It was a glorious mess, an exultant mess, a mess that changed everything. What weighed wearily on my mind, what drove me to the Appalachian Trail in the first place, was within days ground beneath the soles of my boots as my mind turned to more immediate concerns, those being pain and dehydration and unrelenting insects; equipment mismatched for the task, sixty pounds on shoulders that were no longer as young as they once were, short miles that made little impact when compared to a map, uncertainty, indecision, and how I would live with myself if I quit.

As have many others, and despite ample literature to the contrary, I had enjoined that peculiar dissonance of mind, I had idealized the Appalachian Trail as a bucolic walk through pastoral scenes of serene green, where a day's journey would conclude with a satisfying dash in a pure stream, followed by a rustic meal, a crackling fire, and a downy-snug sleeping bag, none of which is the reality of a thru-hike but these maladies of mind and moment lead us onward regardless, until we're finally forced to face the reality of what we have undertaken and must now find a way to make peace with it or else go home.

Don't make the same mistake, don't be lulled into this idealized mindset. I will state it clearly, right now: Thru-hiking the Appalachian Trail is *not* a walk, let alone a walk in the woods. It is scarcely even a hike, at least as we might define what that is. It is mostly a scramble over rocks, through rocks, and around rocks, rocks that most often must be climbed and descended and climbed again. There are still a few farm fields to cross, a few barbwire fences to swing a leg over, the odd cow patty to sidestep, some short sections of road to plod along, and a scattering of quaint towns with no way around, but for the most part the Appalachian Trail follows the ridgelines, which require climbing—a lot of climbing—sometimes within a screen of trees, often within the full brunt of whatever weather happens along. At first this will seem like a betrayal of trust, of what we swore the Appalachian Trail was supposed to be, but as reality sets in (if we stick with it), as the backpack grows lighter from discarded equipment, as heavy boots are unceremoniously tossed over a line and replaced with fleet trailrunners, we come to understand that *of course* the Appalachian Trail follows the high ridges, otherwise it would be more akin to an Atlantic Coastal Trail.

I was still innocent of these thoughts on a damp and gloomy May 21, 2001 as I trudged into Katahdin Stream Campground to begin my first southbound thru-hike. I was fresh out of Alaska, where I had spent three years in Anchorage's surprisingly cosmopolitan surrounds, followed by two years in a remote cabin near Denali National Park, certain of my competence as an outdoorsman as evidenced by my many subarctic perambulations, which had prepared me in no way for a thru-hike but I didn't know that yet.

In appearance I was emulating the cover photo of a book I'd read some thirty years before, *The High Adventure of Eric Ryback*, the story of a teenager thought to be the first to thru-hike the Pacific Crest Trail. Young Eric wore jeans and khaki and leather boots in the photo, and carried an external frame backpack quite similar to the one that was currently digging into my shoulders. To this assemblage I added an Alaska Willow hiking staff, a gift from my employees up there. It was Ryback's book that had set this decades-old idea in my mind in the first place, carried from childhood fantasy to middle-aged imperative. I was on the Appalachian Trail rather than the Pacific Crest Trail because, in truth (if not in back-slapping irony), I thought the Appalachian Trail would be easier.

Things were different in May 2001. The September 11 attacks hadn't happened yet, ubiquitous security cameras were still a creepy peculiarity of the British, phones either flipped or lay like bricks, and the rangers at Baxter State Park in Maine were less than harried.

"Where'd you come from?" the sole ranger asked me. "We haven't seen anybody up here in a week."

I explained my purpose. If he eyed me skeptically I now know why, considering that I stood bowlegged because my damp jeans were hitching up and crowding my junk, and I needed his help to heft my backpack off my shoulders.

"The mountain's closed," he said after that. "Too bad." And then with a wink, "It would have been a solo ascent, and that don't happen too often."

I looked around. The weather was dreary, clouds down into the trees, a fine mist lingering in the air, and with a chill that was raising goose bumps on my arms now that I was standing still. "Yeah, too bad," I agreed, not as crestfallen as I might have been on a more inspiring day. "So what do I do then?"

"So I'll write you down for today anyway. Got a trail name?"

"Naw." I hadn't given that any thought at all, just figured I'd wind up going by one of my teenage nicknames, *The Goat*, from my hot-rodding GTO days, or *Doc* from my earlier medical studies, maybe even *Cheechako* or *Sourdough* from my time in Alaska.

"Let's call you..." he paused to think. "*Solo*. Yeah, I like that." He wrote *Solo* on the register, then: "Give it a few days." Another wink, which I was beginning to suspect was some kind of facial tick. "The weather will get better and then you can go up." Wink.

He helped me re-shoulder my backpack, which required me to squat and then lift as if under barbells. There was a trail to Daicey Pond Campground somewhere in the mist. I saw only brooding shapes in the gloom, greens made gray. "Where's Daicey Pond?" I asked, shivering now in the chill.

"That way," he pointed. Wink. "And you might wanna stash that big backpack in the woods." Wink.

What followed was more than four months through which I could count pleasant, pain-free days in the single digits. I came off the trail at Atkins, Virginia on September 27, weak, broke, dispirited, and rattled by the calamity in New York City. After a few days of soul-seeping depression, I went on down to Georgia, climbed up Springer Mountain and sat, lips trembling. It's shattering to be confronted so starkly with your frailties, with nowhere to put them but in the front of your mind. That's what the Appalachian Trail does to you, it gives you no place to cower from who you are.

I eventually made up those lost miles, but even before then I had put away that shame. I had, after all, lived on the Appalachian Trail for more than four months, long enough to immerse myself into the somewhat Bohemian culture of the thing. I had subsisted on noodles and instant potatoes and honey buns, battled peak after peak, poison ivy and pestilent bugs, ground blisters into oozing sores, shed fifty pounds...and I had discovered trail time, that uncanny elongation of life. My mind became startlingly clear, renewed goals and a focus. I might not have completed the Appalachian Trail in a single season but I was a thru-hiker just the same. I could feel it in the core of myself, which is why I have since granted so much latitude to others who have skipped a section here and there, sometimes even an entire state. It's not the miles, dammit, but the journey that makes the experience whole. That journey, that soul-searching mess, brought me to where I am now, and I would not trade what I have gained to a tech entrepreneur for his billions.

I abandoned corporate life soon thereafter, surrendering my fate to the vicissitudes of trail and time, come what may. By 2008 I had published my first two books, finished a third and was at work on a fourth. I had cycled cross-country, hiked all over Europe, and was now fit and financially able to give the Appalachian Trail another go. And I had learned much. My backpack was this time a Go-Lite, my gear ultralite. I wore trailrunners from Denmark, and held trekking poles from the Czech Republic. I began my second southbound thru-hike on May 20, 2008. The weather hadn't improved in the interim.

My first weeks were tentative as I recalled the pain and misadventure of my first thru-hike, still not wholly confident that I wouldn't suffer equally this time. There were nights, especially in the Whites, when I slapped myself for the idiocy of putting myself through this again. Then, in Vermont, my trail legs arrived from one morning to the next and I pulled a near thirty-mile day, the biggest miles I had ever achieved, and from then on I shrugged off my doubts and rocked that trail. I finished on September 27, 2008, a fitting anniversary. Standing alone as the sun set on Springer Mountain, after a thirty-plus-mile push from Neel Gap, gazing at what I call the *view that never changes*, a new book swirling in my mind and desperate to be written, my spirit was charged with heady energy. I set a lofty goal right then, before post-trail depression could come along to tamp it down: to thru-hike the Appalachian Trail every ten years as long as I was physically able.

That book became my first novel, a monster at nearly 750 pages. It was titled *The Appalachian*, and remains my best seller. There were—I don't know—three or four more books in the following years, more cross-country bicycle rides, more travels around the world, and then with a snap of aging fingers a decade had passed.

I brooked no denial, sought no way to evade it. At the chosen time I gathered my gear, along with the ashes of a friend I'd never met, and made my way to the state of Maine to begin my third Appalachian Trail thru-hike.

The date was May 16, 2018. The weather hadn't improved in the interim. There were changes, though: there were people, a lot of them, and this time there were no winks from the rangers. The mountain was closed, and to violate that rule could lead to repercussions far beyond the interruption of my journey. I did the Hundred-Mile Wilderness through conditions that would have claimed my life on Hike 1, then shuttled back to Katahdin for the climb, which I made through veritable crowds of jocular students and others out for the day. The weather had finally improved, if only marginally. Of thru-hikers there were surely some, albeit lost in the throng.

Despite turning sixty in the state of Maine—having crossed a blustery cold Saddleback Mountain as well as the prior peaks the day before—Hike 3 exceeded Hike 2 in every way except one: the trail was crowded, always, from one end to the other. I had never heard of flip-flopping, and section hiking had previously not been a thing. Where once I would hike alone from Pennsylvania south to Georgia, well ahead of the sobo bubble and able to spread out in luxurious solitude in the shelters, I now had to squeeze into those same shelters most nights—that is if people were willing to make room. That old adage, *you can always get one more hiker in*, had been lost to societal narcissism. I wasn't carrying a tent, a lesson in weight-saving I had learned during Hike 1, so I soon entered into an anxiety that I called *where will I sleep tonight*, which found me, more often than not, racing through the rain and cold to reach shelter before the others so that I could claim a place out of the weather.

Trail relocations warred with my memory. The once gentle swells of Shenandoah National Park were now rocky from the erosion of over use. I arrived at shelters full of surly old men, indifferent young men, dismissive young women, and aloof flip-floppers of all ages and genders. That I was a 6000-miler gathered no curiosity at any time. One suspiciously overweight section hiker in Tennessee actually showed me his gun, *his freakin' gun*. And phones...for fuck's sake! Everyone had a smart phone. They would make video calls as they hiked, you could hear them way down the trail, overwhelming any sounds of nature that might be; or they would be listening to music, blaring it tinnily and gratingly over their speakers—and they would watch videos in shelter, everyone secluded behind barricades of their own self-importance, the fraternity of the trail, the commonality of experience, rendered obsolete. With their devices, playlists, apps &c., everyone's hike had become bespoke.

On Hike 1 a sobo named Devon, eighteen years old, was the only person we ever encountered who carried a cell phone, which we sobos thought was the nuttiest, most aberrant thing to do. The Appalachian Trail was meant to detach us from routine life, after all. Young Devon explained sheepishly that his parents wouldn't allow him to hike otherwise, which redeemed him a bit, and from Pennsylvania all the way to lower Virginia, the last time I ever saw him, he never took that phone out of his backpack as far as I could tell. To do so would have been too humiliating, as if he weren't tough enough to hike untethered. Sure, I carried a phone on Hike 3, but mainly because my phone was lighter than my digital camera. I never used it for anything else, and I seldom had reception anyway, which bothered me not.

In spite of these annoyances, I crushed the trail in 2018, making bigger miles and with the prospect of beating my time from Hike 2 even though I was now, undeniably, a senior citizen. The young man whose ashes I carried had been given a fitting trail name way up in Maine, *Freewind*. Scattering his ashes at prominent places along the trail, and signing his name into the registers along with mine, had added an extra spiritual depth to the hike. Because of inclement weather during my final week, I slowed my pace in order to ensure good weather on Springer Mountain, which I reached after a 31.1-mile push on a sunny September 29, 2018.

Twilight was encroaching on the view that never changes, mine and Freewind's final entries were in the trail register, I was lean and fit and feeling fine even after having made such big miles, and I felt a tug that I'd never experienced before. I turned to look back over my shoulder at the trail, my lips atremble. I didn't want it to end. I didn't want it to end. Depression came down in a darkening cloud. I shouldered my backpack, took a step, hesitated. I can yo-yo, I told myself. I have all I need. I have food left over, a full water bottle, and Freewind is with me. I can go, right now, Neel Gap by sunrise. Just do it!

Post-trail depression is a common phenomenon, but I suspect that we don't all experience it for the same reasons. For me it's that loss of uncluttered freedom, where for months, long enough to leave an imprint, our concerns are only primal. There is no pandering to petty personalities. If you encounter a jerk on the trail, you simply hike on. Politics becomes something that engages only the smallest minds, paying bills only a necessity to maintain a more common life. The only thing we are responsible for on the trail is to make the next mile, complicated life reduced to a mind-clearing minimum. When you lose that, believe me, you feel it. That's what my post-trail depression derives from.

And that's what I felt on Springer Mountain in the lowering light of September 29, 2018. I was also astounded by my physical resiliency. I was sixty years old—*sixty years old*—and yet I could still keep pace with the younger hikers, even pass them from time to time. Turning sixty is something that lands with a shock. In my youth, sixty-year-olds were ancient, toothless and used up, sitting in their easy chairs watching daytime dramas and waiting for the end to come. That would eventually be my fate too, barring misadventure, but for now I felt strong, virtually indestructible, and I tell you without reservation that the Appalachian Trail is why. Who would want that to end?

Responsibilities, though...at sixty they can be deferred but not abandoned. And I had responsibilities: an ancestral farm to tend, dusty archives to curate, a family legacy to preserve. If not me then no one. That legacy would perish on my watch and I couldn't allow that to happen. I sniffed and wiped my nose, took the trail listlessly down to U.S. Forest Service Road 42 to await my shuttle to Gainesville, Georgia and a motel room that I had gotten to know well over the years. Tomorrow would come but the trail wouldn't be in it. The tears were real.

I returned home to find the gardens overgrown and become jungles, the orchards crying for intensive care. The fields had been mowed but looked rough, and the old house needed urgent repairs. I was back to a busy life more common, the trail tugging ever harder as I labored, and then I learned that my mother had a cancer, which took her life two years later. In the absence of her guiding strength, impetuous siblings rent what remained.

As all of this embroiled, Covid came along. Hale people whom I knew succumbed. Petty personalities proliferated, unavoidable even in my secluded patch of Tennessee. Why not wear a mask? Maybe it works, maybe it doesn't, but so what? At least you would be showing some sense of civic responsibility to other people. The Appalachian Trail Conservancy was encouraging thru-hikers to leave the trail, which occurred in the hundreds. With the virus raging and siblings warring, and with an Appalachian Trail now depopulated into a condition that perhaps only the earliest era of thru-hikers had enjoyed, what better time could there be to begin another thru-hike? Why wait until I was seventy? Patience is for people who think they're going to live forever. How could I even know I would make it to seventy? Covid might catch up to me by then, or cancer. These were not morose thoughts, death is the price of having lived, but death does tend to put a finale on things.

The trail tugged like a rope winding around an arm with each pull.

I began to lay plans for a northbound thru-hike, that aspect of the trail I had only ever encountered as a head-on wave. But with Covid there would be no crowding. This was not a once-in-a-lifetime opportunity, this was an *only* opportunity, a chance to experience the trail as close to the way it was than it would ever be again.

But then Great Smoky Mountains National Park closed, and Shenandoah National Park, and Massachusetts, and North Carolina. While I was prepared to take on shuttered stores and hostels, I was not prepared to stealth two national parks and a hodgepodge of states, all of which would probably take over-reactive governmental umbrage to a guy simply hiking in the woods. So I stayed home, and worked the farm, and wrote three more books, the need to return to the trail never less than an urgent yank at my core.

And then they came out with a vaccine.

I rushed to the pharmacy, bared my shoulder and pointed. "Stick it right here," I said, "right next to my smallpox vaccination scar," and it was done. I began gathering my gear the moment I got home. It was now April 2021.

WEDNESDAY, APRIL 14, 2021

Smith County, Tennessee

I turned forty-three on the Appalachian Trail; I turned fifty on the Appalachian Trail; I turned sixty on the Appalachian Trail. The Appalachian Trail has come to define my philosophy as well as my worldview, and now appears regularly as an element in my written work. In spite of (or perhaps because of) the debacle of my first thru-hike, the Appalachian Trail has become a dominant theme in my life.

After my second thru-hike, my plan had been to return to the trail every ten years as long as I was physically able. I had met hikers in their seventies then, bent under the weight of their backpacks and shuffling onward with aching joints and gritted teeth, determined to complete their hikes, and no few of them did. Through their example I could look forward to two, possibly three more hikes before my body eventually gave out, a worthy endeavor.

Armed with this as a life goal, I returned ten years on for my third thru-hike, turned sixty in lower Maine and, if not for several frustrating weather delays, would have beat my second thru-hike by a week or more. This was a startling accomplishment, not only because I had experienced extraordinary stamina during my second thru-hike, but also because ten years on I could feel the effects of encroaching age with painful certainty. Something about that third thru-hike had sequestered those aches and pains into a place where they could be ignored. I hiked long. I hiked fast. I left hikers young and old well behind. I was transfixed.

All of my thru-hikes have been southbound; northbound is a different experience, an experience I am anxious to undertake. Were I to keep to my plan, I wouldn't hike again until 2028. From the moment I reached Springer Mountain, Georgia on September 29, 2018, though, I knew I wouldn't be able to wait. Regardless best health practices, there could be no guarantee that something wouldn't go wrong in the interim, something that would force me to miss that northbound experience—not to mention that we suddenly find ourselves living in fraught times. There is too much else that could go wrong besides my health.

So, freshly vaccinated against Covid, I'm returning for my fourth thru-hike this year—2021—going northbound for the first time and (hopefully) girded for the crowding. I could call this a twentieth anniversary hike, although that's not my reasoning at all. I would be going anyway. Still, an anniversary hike does have a novel sound to it, and will certainly come up in conversation from time to time. If other hikers puzzle why I could possibly want to endure the Appalachian Trail for a fourth time, this will provide a ready explanation.

Physically I feel no worse off than I did three years ago, with the exception of my right shoulder. While climbing Mt. Katahdin in 2018 (which is a climb, by the way, not a hike), I slipped while reaching up for a handhold, twisted above the void, and wrenched that shoulder, probably a rotator cuff tear. The burning, stabbing pain accompanied me all the way to Georgia, such that I could seldom lie on my right side in shelter at night, and sometimes had to sling my backpack over my left shoulder to take the pressure off my injury. That shoulder has mostly healed, although I still feel a sharp twinge from time to time. This is the only health concern I have.

I'm starting in May on the same date that I began my 2018 thru-hike, this so I can compare southbound versus northbound side by side. I'll be leaving late by usual northbounder tradition, but I suspect that I'll make a good pace, arriving at Mt. Katahdin, Maine in mid-September or thereabouts (assuming, of course, that I don't break along the way).

I have expanded my rules for this hike, hoping to recreate something of that first hike two long decades ago:

Always forward, never backward

Bear the weight I chose to carry on the A.T.

Avoid paid shuttles

Pass every white blaze

A BRIEF HISTORY OF THE APPALACHIAN TRAIL

Before I take to the trail, perhaps I should interject here a few words describing what the Appalachian Trail is and what the Appalachian Trail is not...no, instead I should recount a brief history of the trail and let the reader decide what the Appalachian Trail is supposed to be.

The geological origins of the Appalachian Range are fascinating beyond measure. Older by magnitudes than the oldest dinosaurs, once rising as high as the Himalayas, they were then riven by tectonic drift, parts of the range becoming stranded in what are now Africa and Europe. This history alone could fill a hefty book, so I'll advance by a couple of geologic eras and begin in the antebellum nineteenth century with what I call *The Progenitors*.

The Progenitors arose from an emergent New England philosophy called Transcendentalism, which covered a lot of philosophical territory but pertains to the Appalachian Trail in that the Transcendentalists, who counted among their number Massachusettsmen Ralph Waldo Emerson and Henry David Thoreau, believed that spiritual fulfillment could be better derived from independence and self-reliance out in nature, away from the distractions of society. Perhaps you've read Emerson and Thoreau (not light reading nowadays), if not then you might still be aware of the romanticized natural world they described, where noble natives and intrepid pioneers once ventured, and where the color of a pond could occupy a page or two of ponderous prose.

A rapid shift from yeomanry to industrialization in the northern states in the decades following the Civil War lent a moral imperative to sojourns out in nature, not necessarily for purposes of spiritual renewal but because urbanized (white) men in the north were coming to be seen as effeminate, having succumbed to lives of ease. Theodore Roosevelt, as governor of New York and with his eyes on higher office, gave a speech in 1899 that he called *The Strenuous Life*, in which he railed against ignoble ease and in favor of ruggedness and bitter toil as a means of elevating one's manly qualities. He had been raised by his father under the doctrines of muscular Christianity, which expounded athleticism and untarnished manhood over the more placid practices of the mainstream church.

Roosevelt did lead by example. He had been a sickly child, and was not completely hale as an adult, but he never allowed his afflictions to deter him from adventure and physical strain. His outdoor exploits were well known—especially his time as a rancher in the Dakota Territory—because he had published several popular books that described his life in the West, which made it clear that Western men were vigorous and virile while Eastern men were known to...well, often share unmanly duties with their wives.

In a couple of short years, Theodore Roosevelt would be president of the United States and would launch a dizzying era of progressive reform. It's through his efforts that the National Park Service was created, and with it a wider recognition of nature as a necessary ingredient in a healthy life. History was now set for the arrival of what I call *The Visionaries.*

Of The Visionaries there were many, notwithstanding Muir and Burroughs, but of particular importance to the Appalachian Trail was a man named Benton MacKaye (pronounced ma-Ky). Born in Connecticut in 1879, MacKaye's formative years occurred during Roosevelt's efflorescence. MacKaye studied forestry and conservation, and made extensive forays onto the trail systems in New England. In 1921, after having been rocked by a personal tragedy, MacKaye wrote an article titled *An Appalachian Trail: A Project in Regional Planning*, which envisioned a continuous trail running the length of the Appalachian Range by means of connecting existing trail systems and for the purpose of inciting a restorative return-to-nature movement that would help curb the more deleterious effects of urban life, themes than reach back to the Transcendentalists and with a good dose of Roosevelt's strenuous life as well.

An Appalachian Trail Conference (ATC) was created to coordinate the activities of myriad trail clubs and land managers, and after sixteen years of dedicated work, aided by ready labor during the Great Depression, the original Appalachian Trail, 2050 miles long and with extensive sections along roadways, was completed. It's important to understand that it was no one's intention that the Appalachian Trail would be thru-hiked from end to end, but rather that sections of vigorous trail would be accessible from almost anywhere along the east coast. It was by no accident that the trail was routed close to major urban areas and near so many small towns. This provided urban dwellers with ease of access up and down the trail, as well as places to obtain food and supplies and park their vehicles.

Another Visionary, Myron Avery, became chairman of the ATC in 1931. An avid hiker from the state of Maine, and still in his energetic early thirties,

Avery was the first to hike the entirety of the trail in sections. He then turned his focus toward improving and accurately mapping the trail corridor, an endeavor that was interrupted by World War II. After the conclusion of that war, the entire philosophy of the trail would be altered with the arrival of what I call *The Searchers*.

The first Searcher was twenty-nine-year-old Earl Shaffer, whose home in Pennsylvania lay but twenty miles from the newly completed Appalachian Trail. Battling what we would now call PTSD after his service in the Pacific war, where his close friend and hiking partner had been killed, he set out in 1948 to "walk the war out of my system," and became the first documented Appalachian Trail thru-hiker, a sensational exploit considering that many of those involved with the trail weren't certain that a thru-hike was even possible.

In succession after Shaffer were Gene Espy and Chester Dziengielewski in 1951 (Dziengielewski completed the first southbound thru-hike that year, and met up with Espy in passing), Peace Pilgrim in 1952, whose affected name lends her the ultimate personification of *Searcher*, followed in 1955 by Emma "Grandma" Gatewood, whose stoic multiple thru-hikes of the Appalachian Trail brought her national attention and, hopefully if not probably, a sense of peace after the hard life she'd endured as an abused farm wife.

By now the future was set. People would still venture in droves to the more popular points along the trail, for hearty day hikes up grueling inclines in order to reach commanding views but, in defiance of MacKaye's original concept, the lure of the Appalachian Trail would not become the strenuous two-week getaway for dispirited urban dwellers he had envisioned. It would instead become a soul-reviving journey from end to end, which could be achieved by only the hardiest few. This contradiction in purpose is what led Grandma Gatewood to say, "This is no trail. This is a nightmare. For some fool reason, they always lead you right up over the biggest rock to the top of the biggest mountain they can find."

Grandma Gatewood said it succinctly. For much of its length the Appalachian Trail is less a trail than it is a *route*. As a trail—or as we might define a trail—it has no utility. Contrary to some post-apocalyptic science fiction books I've read, armies at march could never use the Appalachian Trail except for the odd short section here and there. The trail is simply too steep, too narrow, and too rocky to accommodate massed soldiery. Livestock could never be herded along it for the same reason. Any survivors in that post-apocalyptic world would eschew the trail as well. As a means to go from one place to another, it would be too difficult, too slow, too inefficient—those survivors would blaze their own easier, more common-sense routes.

This is the contradiction that confounds first-time thru-hikers, and no few multiple thru-hikers either considering the rants I've heard and have personally leveled at the roots and rocks. Even Earl Shaffer had something to say about this during his third and last thru-hike in 1998. During my own third thru-hike in 2018, I came across a group of 1998 thru-hikers who were throwing a twentieth anniversary jubilee. Some of those guys had hiked with Shaffer. They recounted to me his grumbles, his lament that, through land acquisition and trail relocations, the trail had become too difficult, too isolated from the country hamlets he'd hiked through in 1948. He especially missed the spontaneous interactions with local people, of whom he wrote fondly in his book, *Walking with Spring.*

Most of us come to terms with this contradiction eventually—that is if we stay on the trail. The excruciating physical toll the trail takes on us does tend to heighten our senses of triumph at the end of the journey, but that doesn't mean we don't wish that the latest trail relocation had blazed a less aggressive grade more in line with what the trail has become rather than what it was envisioned to be a century ago, or that we could—from time to time—simply *hike*, as one can do on the prettily-groomed Pacific Crest Trail. What an absolute joy that would be.

The goal of the National Park Service and the ATC is laudable, that is, to make every mile of the Appalachian Trail lie across public land by means of purchasing private land that the trail now crosses or else relocating entire sections onto public lands. As this occurs, though, the new sections of trail are made, if anything, even more aggressive. I have climbed to 9000-foot passes in the Alps and have expended fewer calories than I would climbing many of the 3000-footers on the Appalachian Trail. When Earl Shaffer thru-hiked in 1948, the Appalachian Trail was approximately 2050 miles long. When I hiked in 2001 it was 2168.1 miles long, 2176.2 miles long in 2008, and 2190.9 miles long in 2018, each increase in length representing a series of new climbs. The trail does and should follow the peaks and ridges, but with better routing when the width of the trail corridor allows it, climbing those peaks and ridges wouldn't be more akin to an extreme sport than a spiritual journey. I could linger longer and enjoy the view if I didn't know that I had five or more excruciating climbs to make before day's end, or that all of those climbs might take place through driving rain over deadly slippery rocks.

Nevertheless, the trail is what it is and history continues apace (although as regards the Appalachian Trail we might want to coin the word *aclimb*).

The Searchers carried on in twos, threes, and fours into the sixties, their trail a world of solitude and simplicity of which we simply cannot conceive today; and then in 1968 Congress passed the National Trails System Act, which among other things designated the Appalachian and Pacific Crest Trails as National Scenic Trails with federally protected corridors. As a result of this recognition, the numbers of thru-hikers each year began to increase markedly. (I have a theory that hippies and Vietnam-era draft dodgers also contributed to this increase.) A thru-hiker culture was codified during the seventies, propelled by the greater number of hikers and with an evolving counter-culture aspect. It is in this era that much of our trail lingo originated.

Continuing on from The Searchers, from the late sixties through the present day, I identify five eras of thru-hikers—not meant to define every thru-hiker and with plenty of overlap between each—beginning with *The Venturers*, such as Ed B. Garvey, who loved hiking for the sake of hiking, and sought adventure on the Appalachian Trail; followed through the seventies by *The Hippies*, who were fleeing The Establishment and perhaps the Vietnam War, and who brought with them some of the more colorful aspects of trail culture; leading into the eighties and *The Woodsmen*.

The Woodsmen (Woodswomen, too—I've met them) were motivated by the resurgent back-to-nature and ecology movements of the seventies, and were perhaps inspired by the folk music of John Denver. The Woodsmen were square-jawed and pragmatic, uncomplaining and undeterred by hardship. Many of the older trail volunteers I've met were of this generation. Carlton Jeffries, the protagonist of my novel *The Appalachian*, is a Woodsman.

The late eighties and then into the nineties introduced *The Enthusiasts*, thru-hikers who loved trail life so much that they couldn't stay away. Dan "Wingfoot" Bruce, who thru-hiked seven times during this era, is an example, as is "Baltimore Jack" Tarlin, who also went seven times beginning in the later nineties. It's also during this era that ultralite gear came into wide use, and the trail was routinely thru-hiked in less than four months.

And finally *The Technicians*, from the mid-2000s on. The Technicians have tech, they have phones, solar chargers and satellite trackers. They use apps instead of maps, can pinpoint themselves precisely and so are less reliant on blazes. Through their phones they can read reviews of shelters and forthcoming sections of trail, know in advance if a spring is flowing or not, locate and claim the best stealth sites, call for shuttles—or, quite often, *Ubers*—and reserve hostel space well in advance. The Technicians have not made the Appalachian Trail physically easier (commentary on this later in the book), but they have made the trail easier to endure. The Appalachian Trail has not become crowded because of Bill Bryson's 1998 book *A Walk in the Woods* (as many believe), but because of Steve Jobs' iPhone.

As for myself, I am an amalgam of eras, I think—certainly an Enthusiast and a Venturer, possibly a Searcher, but by no means a Hippie or Technician; and my 2001 thru-hike proved I was no Woodsman.

That's a brief history of the Appalachian Trail as I interpret it. Now it's time to go and make miles on that trail, 2193.1 of them this time.

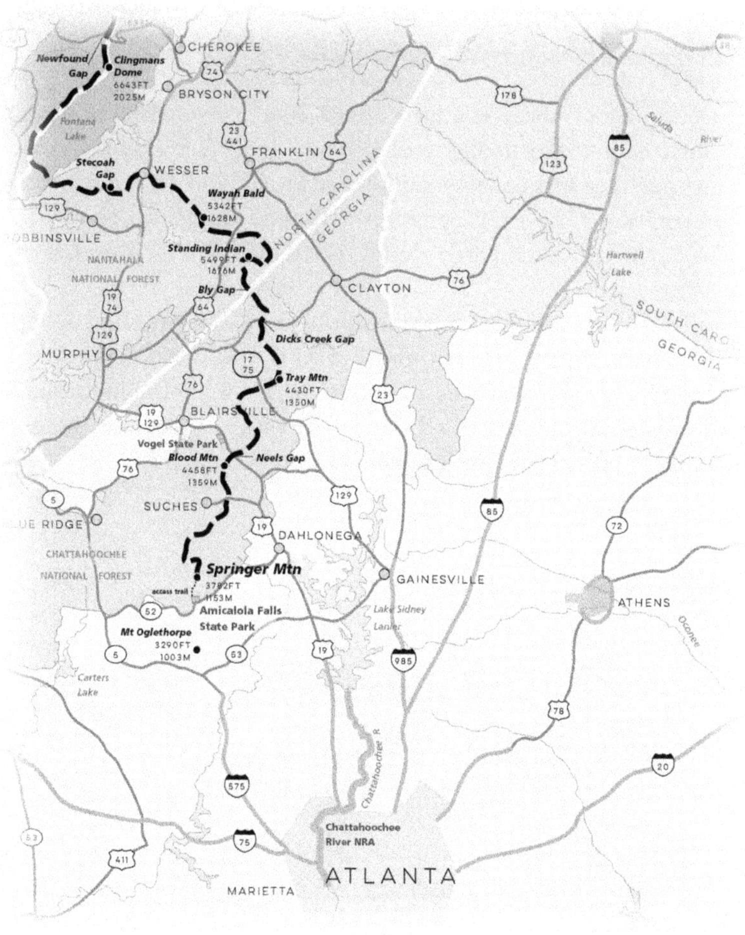

GEORGIA

78.1 MILES

+ 8.8 MILES OF

APPROACH TRAIL

SATURDAY, MAY 15, 2021

Springer Mountain, Georgia - 8.8 Miles

Left Cousin Sam's house at a little after 8:00 a.m., but made slow time to Amicalola. Didn't start hiking until 3:30 p.m. local. Sam hiked with me for half an hour, then we said our goodbyes and I turned on the speed, impatient to make miles as if this were September 2018 and I was doing a yo-yo after all.

The day is warm and partly cloudy, perfect weather for the start of the hike. What a contrast!

Passed a lot of young guys, made Springer by 7:00 p.m., and set up my tent. Now it's 8:15 p.m. and I'm turning in for the night. No cooking because Sam and I had a big lunch. This is a condition that won't last long, that's for sure. I wonder if I can make Neel Gap in one pull, the way I do on a southbound hike. I guess I'll find out tomorrow.

Here I am on the Approach Trail

—

While traveling to the state of Maine to begin my southbound thru-hikes, whether on rails or runway, I have always transited through Boston. I discovered by accident in 2001 that connecting with regional transportation is so easy in Boston that I have never even considered an alternate itinerary. One has to simply walk off the train or plane, go through the glass doors, and within an hour or thereabouts a Concord bus bound for Bangor, Maine will pull up, no reservations necessary, no poking at the phone, no frenetic interpretations of confusing roads and routes, it just arrives. Pay the driver and take a seat. This is one of the most efficient systems I have encountered anywhere in the world. My hat's off to the Bostonians.

At Bangor, a Cyr bus will pull up by and by and then it's onward to Medway. An easy hitch from Medway gets me to Millinocket, and the sun hasn't even set yet! I camped in 2001, stayed at hostels in both 2008 and 2018, and each time I was on the Appalachian Trail the next morning.

Easy, easy, easy.

Getting to Amicalola Falls State Park in Georgia from middle Tennessee to begin a northbound thru-hike would have to be even easier. Mapping the directions, I found that Amicalola is only 218 miles from my home. *Only 218 miles!* Gee whiz, we'd drive that far in Texas just to enjoy awesome fajitas. I simply needed a ride. With a departure time of about five in the morning, I could be hiking by nine—well, ten in that time zone but still early enough to put on a solid twenty-plus miles before the sun set.

Because of this later start, I wasn't expecting to make Neel Gap in one pull, mirroring my southbound thru-hikes. When I do those 31.3 miles (previously 30.7), I leave from Neel Gap at about four in the morning, climb Blood Mountain in the dark, and just haul ass in the southbound version of Springer fever. (By the way, the dedication plaque says *Neel Gap.* It sounds weird, but there it sits.)

For this hike I had decided to take the 8.8-mile Approach Trail up to Springer Mountain, a trail I'd never hiked. On a southbound thru-hike, Springer Mountain is it, the weary end. Additional miles would intrude on nightfall as well as any sense of closure, so I have always retraced the mile down to the Forest Service road and shuttled out from there, drinking beer and eating pizza long before I would have made it to Amicalola. But this northbound hike was my chance to take the Approach Trail in the light of day, to get the entire experience. I expected to camp somewhere near Gooch Mountain. What a juxtaposition that would be, waking in my own bed in middle Tennessee, eating a hearty breakfast followed by a swift journey on the interstate, burning through some not unrespectable miles on the trail, and then camping on Gooch Mountain by nightfall.

I started down my list of friends, fishing for a ride at first subtly and then bluntly as I neared the bottom. It turned out that the good folks of middle Tennessee interpret distance on a different scale than their Texas kin. *Georgia? You cain't be serious. Why, that's even further than Chattanooga!* Chattanooga lies on the state line, actually. I think the Georgians still claim the place as their own. The city center is only 130 miles from mi casa. I sometimes drive there when I want a lunch out somewhere other than Nashville.

I exhausted my list, and in disbelief came to realize that getting to Amicalola Falls State Park in our neighboring state might be more difficult than the journey to far Maine. I went down my list again, this time marketing the trip as a weekend getaway, possibly even an opportunity to hike a few miles of the illustrious Appalachian Trail with a soon-to-be 8000-miler, something to talk about when they got home. *I love readin' 'bout all the crazy walkin' you done, but it ain't are thang.* I sighed when I reached the bottom of the list once again, reminding myself that if a branch went through my roof during a storm, most of them would be out with tarps and chainsaws within an hour.

I could fly to Atlanta, catch a shuttle from there. I still had the phone number for a shuttle driver I used on Hike 3. This would require a ride to the Nashville airport, though, an easier favor to ask–but damn! That would mean having to deal with Homeland Security and Covid prices for tickets, and more time involved waiting in lines and in the air than the actual drive would take, not to mention coordinating things on the other end. That shuttle driver I knew had either met his maker or quit the area, and Atlanta is no Boston. It wouldn't be as easy.

Or I could rent a car. Why not? Well, the same problems. I would need a ride to the nearest rental car outlet, about an hour away, and I would have to turn that car in at Gainesville, Georgia and then pay for a shuttle to Amicalola, which would use up the entire day and a not insignificant bit of my budget as well. So, yes, getting to Maine is definitely easier. Not too late to go southbound instead, but in my mind it was northbound or nothing.

I continued laying my plans despite these setbacks. There would be a way, or as we say, *the trail provides*. That providence arrived as a reply to a hopeless email I'd sent to Cousin Sam Smith, one of many recipients of that email and the only person who got back with me. Sure he would drive me, he wrote. He hadn't been to Amicalola in years. He'd love to go.

I had to put on my glasses and read his reply again, certain that I had grazed past a negative somewhere in his missive, but no, he plainly stated: He'd love to go.

It's like when you receive those Publishers' Whatever announcements in the mail, the ones that say *You Have Won*, but upon closer scrutiny you find the all-important *if* and then toss the thing with disgust into the recycle bin. I looked for the *if* in Cousin Sam's reply and did not find it. He was serious. Problem solved. Yea!

Cousin Sam Smith (we share a pair of great grandparents) is a retired Tennessee Historical Archaeologist. His delivery is measured and academic. You can engage in fascinating conversation with him but you'd better be able to support your position with facts. Flying loose doesn't fly with him, which puts me in treacherous territory since I'm prone to hyperbolize if that's what it takes to make a story interesting.

We set out at around eight o'clock on a sunny Saturday morning, three hours later than I would have preferred but there was no way I would ask him to rouse as early as I arise. My first thru-hike turned me into an early riser, changed my circadian rhythms somehow. Prior to that thru-hike I could routinely sleep past eight o'clock; since then (with the exception of jetlag during my international travels) I never have. I'm awake between five and six regardless the time zone and regardless how late I go to sleep, perhaps subconsciously expecting to break camp in the cool of morning and start making miles. Over the years I've become somewhat self-conscious about disturbing other people who can still sleep more or less normally.

The route I intended was to shoot down to Chattanooga from Cookeville, but Sam knew some alternate roads that would link us up with Interstate 24 by and by, so that way we went, proceeding at a sedate 55 mph as the sun rose higher and as my right foot pressed a depression in his floor mat. We passed farms, discussed invasive species and historical points of interest. I learned that deer and wild turkeys had been wiped out in middle Tennessee and not reintroduced until the eighties, an historical error in my novel, *The Appalachian*. Oh well, I said. When you finish a book you move on to the next, and I had written four more since then, maybe five, but that would be hyperbole.

I sighed in relief when we reached Interstate 24, as the sun neared the noon hour, ready to put the hammer down and push the speed limit envelope to its safest maximum in order to make up time. We shot up onto concrete made for flying, and then settled into a stately 65 mph, which kept us assuredly moving forward if not with urgency, and then we reached Chattanooga and traffic came to a standstill. I shot glances at my watch. We crept forward a few feet. Another glance at my watch. I did the math and ground my teeth. There was no question: were I heading to Maine for a southbound thru-hike I would be well on the way to Bangor by now.

It took maybe an hour to clear Chattanooga, and then we shot onto Interstate 75 as if we'd found a hole in a net. I was ready for 75 mph, maybe 80, but Sam settled in at his comfortable 65 mph and we proceeded on toward the town of Resaca and Highway 136, what looked like the most direct route to Amicalola.

It was past noon now, any hope of camping on Gooch Mountain dashed as if by design. Goal-setters should be careful what goals they set, and I'm a goal-setter, too often pushing myself beyond reasonable bounds to achieve the ambitions of the day. Age and the Appalachian Trail have given me some perspective on this, though, so I relaxed my right foot and yielded to the whims of the journey. It was Saturday, May 15. I didn't need to start the hike until tomorrow, which would surely come. Maybe that's what the trail was trying to tell me: *Just settle down. You're not supposed to start hiking until tomorrow anyway.*

The exit at Resaca had nothing but a hazy truck stop off a ways, which came as a surprise. Here was the highway to the vaunted Amicalola Falls State Park, gateway to the Appalachian Trail, and there wasn't even a diner at the exit? We were both starving by then, having spent what seemed all day in the car, so we went on past the exit until we spied a chain restaurant, whipped in there and had lunch. I ate until I ached, knowing full well that this would be a luxurious memory in mere days. We doubled back, exited onto Highway 136, and proceeded to go on...forever.

I'd never been to Amicalola Falls State Park, but I'd heard enough about it during my thru-hikes to picture it as a place almost too easily accessible from Atlanta, so much so that I never even scrutinized a map in advance. Highway 136 winds and twists and intersects, defying speeds much higher than about 40 mph, a nice country drive except when you have an agenda, and we had lingered long over lunch. The day was getting on.

After fifty interminable miles and perhaps another ninety minutes, frustration now affecting the tones of both our voices, we entered the park–and found it jammed with more cars than a pre-Covid Super Bowl parking lot. We crept with the flow, went past the visitors center, and searched in futility for a place to park. Finally, in absolute exasperation, I asked Sam to drop me where we were. I would hoof it back to the visitors center, take care of business, and he could circle around or else meet me in the middle if he found a place to park.

The visitors center was as packed as the parking areas. I spotted a sole young woman at the registration desk, an enthusiastic smile on her face despite the column waiting in line for her attention. I have never registered any of my thru-hikes but I had intended to this time. I quashed that idea, though.

There were simply too many people in line. I grabbed a park map instead, which was hand-drawn on white copy paper, and beat it back out into the sun. I studied the map, couldn't work out where I was supposed to go to find the arch and the onset of the Appalachian Trail.

The crowds and the kids were so visually distracting that I couldn't focus on anything. I thought there would have been a blue blaze right around there, but damn if I could see it. Sam walked up then, looking a little warm in the brow. He had found a parking place about a quarter mile up the road. "I have a map," I said. "Let's go."

He sighed, turned, and we retraced his steps to the car. "Just keep going up this road," I told him. "There's gotta be a sign or something."

The road wound up looping us back around, and Sam's frustration finally broke through. "I thought you had a map," he growled, or not really growled but stated as if he had. I glanced at the map, which showed a hand-drawn line that did loop back, like a shepherd's hook, no scale of miles, dotted lines showing the various trails.

"I do have a map," I said defensively. "It just doesn't have any detail. I thought there would be a sign."

Sam eyed a parking place and dove into it. "Let's just get out here and look around."

This place was as promising as any, lots of dotted lines on the map. One of them had to be the Approach Trail. I shouldered my backpack, extended my trekking poles, we spotted a trail, tossed mental coins, and took it—and the trail provided. We were on the Approach Trail! The time was half past three.

Sam stayed with me until about four o'clock, but as the day continued to descend, and a drive ahead that might not get him home until midnight, we stopped and shook hands. I felt awful, having roped Sam into a drive that took hours longer than I had anticipated, and now he was having to cut his hike short because of it. When I spoke with him after my thru-hike, though, he said he hadn't felt put out at all. It had been a good outing on a nice day. But I still feel a little guilty about it.

When Sam turned back, I turned on the speed. The urgent need to make miles is an impulse I can't explain, although over beers, boxes of wine, and plastic bottles of whiskey I have tried. It wasn't until Hike 2 that I first sensed this urgency, perhaps arising when I made my first big miles on that thru-hike and was so astounded that I wanted to keep doing it. It's the dichotomy of the trail, which is not a race but many of us race through it anyway, sprinting toward an end that we don't want to arrive even as we are desperate for it to. *Det er mer filosofi i et glass vin enn i alle bøkene i verden*, the Norwegians say. There is more philosophy in a glass of wine than in all the books in the world, but if Jack Daniels hasn't been able to crack this conundrum then Merlot certainly won't.

I felt marvelous shooting up that trail, planting my poles, a bead of sweat like an old friend. In contrast to the crowding below, there was no one else on the trail. I rounded the bushes into the little clearing on Springer Mountain as the sun still softly hovered above the layered horizon, feeling as if that hike had simply gone by too quickly. I wasn't going to push on, there was no need. The official hike could begin tomorrow, on May 16 the way it was supposed to. I took in the woodsy view that never changes, then went to both plaques, brushed my fingers across them and signed the register: *Solo, Headin' north this time. MEGA '01, MEGA '08, MEGA '18, GAME '21.*

There were about eight other guys already on top with their tents set up, all young. One said he was a thru-hiker (if so, I never saw him again after that night), the rest were out for the weekend. One of them had a pistol on his hip, to ward off bears, he said. I tried not to let him see my eyes roll. Otherwise they were a good group of guys, sharing their food, respectful and in awe of my hikes. None made snide remarks about my kilt.

Yes, I was wearing a kilt, Blackwatch tartan, and if the Scotsmen say never to ask a Highlander what he's wearing under his kilt it's because he's not wearing anything under his kilt. I got the idea for the kilt on Hike 3 after meeting many hikers who swore by them. In the cold rain of Kinsman Notch on that hike, I watched the rain bead and run off a guy's kilt, leaving his nether parts as dry as a day in the desert. I had been intrigued, decided to give it a try myself, and after some day hikes back home I came to love the thing. Kilts really are quite practical up to a point, but more about that later.

As for that night, I pitched my tent and watched the view that never changes turn to dusk, a gentle wind soughing through the trees. I felt as if I'd finally made it home.

SUNDAY, MAY 16, 2021

Gooch Mountain Shelter - 15.7 Miles

Up at 5:00 a.m., out of the tent by 6. It took a while to boil water with my new ultralite alcohol stove. I'm a little disappointed with it.

Good weather. Started out strong but began to bonk after only ten miles or so, not sure why. This trail is pretty easy, I mean, I always fly through here. Met a lot of section hikers, and one thru-hiker named Fisherman.

Nope, no Neel Gap today. I don't get it, I'm really beat. Threw down early, in the tent by 7:00 p.m. Maybe I'm only adjusting, my three-day theory. I hope that's all it is.

—

I was on the trail before any of the guys camping on Springer Mountain had even gotten up to pee, making miles in the gentle light and feeling invincible.

The weather was wonderful, a bit cool in the morning but warming nicely. My first hour, what I call the *magic hour*, was the best. It's during the magic hour that songbirds find their morning voices, chippering first here and then there and then in a growing chorus. The woods are deep and still and dreamily lit. Other hikers have yet to rouse, so the trail is your own, a personal pathway of solitude and reflection. This is when I make my best miles and feel my greatest gratitude for being alive. There is an entire day ahead in which anything can happen, those far dusky hours as far away as an ocean's horizon. Hikers who sleep late miss out on this.

Other hikers began to pop up as the morning progressed, as if they had spontaneously generated from the woods. I passed them singly and in groups. Section hikers? Thru-hikers? It was much too soon to tell. I would announce my approach well in advance so as not to startle them out of their shoes, although they were most often startled anyway, their focuses ahead rather than behind. We would exchange pleasantries in passing and then I would be around a bend and gone.

I began to fatigue after only ten miles, a state I simply couldn't explain to myself. First-time thru-hikers get their first rude awakening on Hawk Mountain, barely six miles in but I had blazed over that. Sassafras Mountain would be next, a bit more of a climb for a northbounder than a southbounder but nothing that I expected to be hindered by. Nevertheless my pace slowed. I took Sassafras Mountain neither winded nor sweating, although not at the exhilarated pace I was accustomed to. There was no lightness left in my steps as I cleared the top, and it wasn't until late afternoon that I reached Gooch Mountain Shelter, far short of the miles I thought I would make, and the place I had expected to spend last night if I'd had an early start. I had some reckoning to deal with here.

This was not my three-day theory, the amount of time it takes to acclimate to new surroundings. This was something else. Consider how many calories we burn while hiking. This varies by weight and gender and how heavy our backpacks are, but in rough numbers, hiking with a backpack of moderate weight burns between 400 and 600 calories per hour. For comparison, walking at a moderate pace will burn about 240 calories per hour. Climbs while hiking can increase this to 630 calories or thereabouts, while intense climbs can push this burn as high as 900, probably settling in at around 750 for most of us—and most of the climbs on the Appalachian Trail are intense.

Now consider that a pound of bodyweight, generically, represents about 3500 calories. Hiking for eight hours on the Appalachian Trail, therefore, can burn between 3200 and 6000 calories, probably weighted toward the upper end of that range, which means we burn between one and two pounds of bodyweight per day. *Per day*. Hikers with low body mass indexes will burn fewer calories and lose less weight, but for hikers with high body mass indexes, this much weight loss coupled with significant fluid loss can be catastrophic, which is why so many would-be thru-hikers throw in the towel between Sassafras and Blood Mountains, and totter on into Suches, Georgia looking for salvation.

Those who stick with it, though, are operating at a calorie deficit from their first step off Springer Mountain to their last step up Baxter Peak. I have not known any thru-hiker who could carry and ingest 6000 calories per day extended over the months it takes to thru-hike the Appalachian Trail. Most of us do well to put in 2000 to 3000 calories per day, and most of these in the form of fast carbs that metabolize quickly and burn off just as quickly. This deficit leads to the insatiable hunger that we call *hiker hunger*. Despite gorging ourselves on pizza and beer in the trail towns, we cannot make up this deficit. We condition our bodies into this state, and it takes a while post-trail for our bodies to equalize again.

Stated simply, hiker hunger does not go away once we climb Mt. Katahdin, so if you keep eating for the trail you will put on weight—fast.

I kept myself fit after Hike 3. For the first time, with determination, self-discipline, and gnawed knuckles, I fought off hiker-hunger post-trail, confining myself to 2400 calories or less per day (this on account of my age; younger hikers would need between 2400 and 2800 calories, perhaps more). My hunger pangs dissipated after a few weeks, and my weight stabilized at a comfortable 160 pounds, up from the 148 pounds I weighed when I finished the hike. On previous hikes I had quickly ballooned into the fleshy190s. I maintained my muscle tone with light weight work, and my cardiovascular health through cycling and farm work such that my blood pressure settled consistently into the lower part of the healthy spectrum, with my resting heart rate generally in the high forties. I hadn't felt this fit since I'd been a teenager.

In other words, I began Hike 4 lean and fit and expecting to fly. I was still burning calories, though, quite a few of them in proportion to my weight;

and hiker legs evolve independently of any other activity one might pursue save long-distance running. Cycling is an extraordinary activity for the maintenance of cardiovascular health, but muscles contract and retract differently between cycling and hiking. I know this with certainty because whenever I have first gotten back on the bike after a thru-hike, the pain in my quads is alike being bitten by a bear. It takes a while for new muscle memory to form, and that's what was happening to me now.

These are the thoughts that distracted my mind as I picked my way toward Gooch Mountain Shelter. Southbounders are faced first with Mt. Katahdin followed by the Hundred-Mile Wilderness, a terrain that guarantees short miles for most of us so we come to expect and accept it. Now here I was on Day One making peace with the fact that I would not fly through a northbound hike as I had anticipated. My trail legs wouldn't arrive until I'd burned off most of the fat from around my quads, and that probably wouldn't happen until about Damascus, Virginia. In the meantime, I might hike stronger than a first-timer because of my experience and low backpack weight, but thirty-mile days were going to elude me for a while. That's just the way it was.

I trudged up to Gooch Mountain Shelter, found a place to pitch my tent and did so. The shelter was full of people, and tents dotted the site like colorful mushrooms. Fisherman, a young guy I'd met along the way, lumbered in and I smiled. He wore garish shorts and a hat that a fisherman would wear, the kind you can set your hooks and lures into. He greeted me cheerfully if wearily.

"Hey, Solo."

"Hey Fisherman. You did better than you thought you would. I just got here."

"Really?" he exclaimed with a grin.

"Really."

He stood a little taller as he went to pitch his own tent. The picnic table was overrun with scattered gear, with stoves and water bladders and whatnot, so I boiled my noodles out front of my tent, alarmed by how much alcohol my little stove consumed.

Later in the twilight, I lay in my tent, alone with my thoughts. So I wouldn't be able to make big miles after all. I discovered that this didn't trouble me. I was enjoying these miles in Georgia, on a lovingly maintained trail that I'd never known except at a sprint. This time I could savor those miles, and that was okay. Neel Gap tomorrow, Blood Mountain in the light of day. I would really be seeing it all for the first time. Those were good thoughts to spend a good night with.

MONDAY, MAY 17, 2021

Neel Gap - 15.6 Miles

Up early and hiking before sunrise. Made a good pace, but was sore in the shoulders by the time I reached Blood Mountain, my old injury acting up and aggravated by the way this backpack hangs on me. Not enough support where I need it.

I smiled going through Jarrard Gap, where on my last hike I passed Ridley still asleep in her tent.

A lot of the hikers from last night bailed in Gooch Gap and went into Suches. I've never been there, never even paid attention to the place.

Arrived at Neel Gap at 1:30 p.m., ate a pizza then decided to buy a new backpack. I love my Go-Lite but it's just not working out. I let Bill talk me into a ULA pack. I remember Bill from my 2012 Tour de Virginia. He had been working at Mt. Rogers Outfitters then, and gave me what turned out to be pretty good directions to avoid some traffic. Apparently Pirate is long gone, enjoying life with a woman somewhere in the area. I doubt he'd remember me anyway.

This ULA pack was pricey, but it's pretty nice. The trouble is that all of my stuff won't fit in it. My bear resistant food container (BRFC) won't fit inside, and my synthetic sleeping bag won't compress enough. I spent the rest of the day and evening trying to figure all of this out. I'll probably have to buy a new sleeping bag as well.

Met some section hikers from Wisconsin who drove me into Blairsville to buy a few things. Fisherman came in. I didn't expect him to make it, but he's a stronger hiker than he thinks.

The hostel here is closed due to Covid, so I'm sacking out under the awning.

Day Two was a good day, Blood Mountain brilliant in the sunlight, the stone shelter on top fashioned by grateful hands during the Great Depression. But I had some nagging concerns that wouldn't let go.

I had wanted this thru-hike to be as old-school as I possibly could make it. I would not rely on my phone except as a camera (my BlackBerry is so old that no apps will run on it anyway), I would reenlist my older, dated gear, and I would fabricate a few things as well. For backpacks I had some choice. There was my classic Go-Lite Gust backpack, the one described in its day as the *grocery sack*. I had never used it for backpacking but instead more as a duffel bag during my international trips. On Hike 3 I used my Kelty Moraine, my favorite all-time backpack but, threadbare after two decades and thousands of miles, I wistfully retired it after that hike. On Hike 2 I used my Go-Lite Breeze backpack, the ultimate in ultralite but no way would all of the stuff I was carrying this time fit in there. On Hike 1 I used a Kelty Super Tioga external frame, seven pounds dry and empty. A Navajo man in Page, Arizona owns that backpack now, bought it from me at a garage sale and got a good deal on it, too.

So I went with the Gust because of its interior volume, and I needed the space. I have a policy that I adhere to, which is to *never* attach things to the outside of my backpack. I have come across too many bandanas, camp shoes, water bottles and pack covers along the trail, where they lay until a ridgerunner comes by or else another hiker finds a need. Things snag and fall off backpacks, the hiker completely unaware. I also prefer a neater, more contained look, and the ability to duck under blowdowns without scraping off the bark.

My first nagging problem was that no matter how I packed the Gust, it pulled back on my shoulders rather than down onto them, causing pain in my injured shoulder. And then there was my sleeping pad. I had fashioned my own out of a length of shiny attic insulation. It compressed to nothing, weighed nothing, but in defiance of its purpose, did little to insulate me from the ground. My first two nights were uncomfortably cold, and this during unseasonably warm weather. I would clearly lie freezing in the Smokies, not to mention the White Mountains and the entire state of Maine.

My BRFC was also going to be a problem, even though I'd made it myself and was proud of it. The container was originally a very large protein powder canister that I reinforced and had attached straps and a carabiner after painstakingly removing every trace of the label. It could be easily hung from a tree or a hook in shelter, weighed nothing, kept my crunchy snacks from crumbling, and would frustrate mice as a bonus. But bulky BRFCs are meant to be strapped above or below the backpack. Keeping it inside meant that it pressed uncomfortably into my back, which would eventually leave a bruise.

Ironically, the only item working well was my cheap $49.95 pup tent, which was roomy, set up quickly with trekking poles, and only weighed about two pounds. Having formerly hiked without a tent, I was in no state of mind to spend hundreds of dollars on one, and I particularly dislike having to fool with collapsible poles and so on. So I bought a pup tent, old school, the kind I used when I was in the Scouts. It was doing its job better than I hoped, and would continue to serve me well all the way to Mt. K.

I was going to have to give up on the Gust for sure, possibly my homemade sleeping pad and cleverly constructed BRFC as well. To continue with improper gear because it fulfilled an idealized notion would be foolish. The Appalachian Trail is not an idealized notion, it's an uncompromising reality.

I was in Neel Gap by about half past one, crossed the highway and went into Mountain Crossings searching first for pizza and a cold drink. There would be plenty of time afterward to address my equipment problems. A trail-wizened guy named Bill slid my frozen pizza into the oven.

"Hey bra, I know you," I said.

Bill looked me up and down. "You seem kinda familiar, too."

I searched my memory, which contains quite a few memories these days and quite a few faces to go along with them. Bill's face and demeanor fit into a particular era, so I zeroed in on that and then I had it. "Did you ever work at Mount Rogers Outfitters?" I asked.

"Sure did."

"Maybe in 2012?"

"Yeah, I was there in 2012."

"So it *is* you!" I smacked the counter. "I was doing a cross-country bike ride that summer. I went into Mount Rogers Outfitters looking for directions to the TransAm and you came out and showed me a way around some traffic. Then we started talking about the A.T."

"Oh, yeah," he rubbed his whiskers, "I remember you. Dude on a bicycle who'd done the A.T. a couple of times."

"Yeah. Wow. Small world."

"Not so small when you're hiking."

"I hear ya, bra."

I inhaled my pizza and sipped a cold coke. Try as I did, I simply could not yogi a personal beer out of Bill. Afterward I asked him about backpacks. Go-Lite is my go-to brand, but Go-Lite is gone now. I wasn't up on the latest thing.

"I know what you need," he said. "C'mon over here."

He had a wall of the more popular brands of backpacks, and a smaller section that housed a brand called ULA. I wasn't familiar with them but that's where Bill went, disregarding all the others.

"What color?" he asked.

"Black if you've got it."

"Hmm." He pulled out a solitary black backpack. "Only one I got in black," he said, "but...I need to measure you."

"Measure me?"

"Yeah, stand still."

I've never been measured for a backpack—old school, remember—I always went with what felt right, but Bill was going at this like science, which I thought was pretty cool.

"Man, you wear a small," he said, astounded. "I wouldn'ta thought it. Put this on."

I slung the pack and then Bill started fiddling with a confusion of straps. I could already tell that I wanted the pack, though. It fit so snugly, right up against my center of mass, and it had the lean, trim profile that I really love. He started tossing in gear from the shelves.

"How much do you carry?" he asked.

"Twenty, twenty-one pounds. Base weight fifteen, maybe sixteen."

"Okay." He tossed in more stuff then fiddled with the straps some more. "How does that feel?"

I have to tell you, it felt great. I was sold. I more than wanted that backpack, I was coveting the thing. "How much is it?" I asked. He told me and I gulped. As backpacks go these days this one was actually reasonably priced, but compared to what I'd spent on backpacks in the past, this one was beyond extravagant. It's the Appalachian Trail, I reminded myself, 2161.8 miles to go and this backpack could make those miles a lot more pleasant. "I'll take it," I said then.

I went out into the sun with my brand new backpack as if it were a shiny new car, went around the side where the showers are and started laying everything out on a picnic table. The hostel was closed because of Covid, but there were still plenty of places to tent out. Looking around, though, I thought I might just sack out right there.

Other hikers started coming in, one of them Fisherman. I figured we'd probably be seeing each other on and off from then on, although I never saw him again after that night. I don't know what happened to him.

A family from Wisconsin came in. They had an adorable young daughter who took to the trail as if it were in her blood, undeterred by any hardship while her parents winced at their various aches. I had passed them earlier and had paused to complement their daughter, which had drawn smiles from them and a beam from the girl. They were finishing their section here and they had a car, so I sidled on over to yogi a ride into town. I could use a few things if an opportunity presented itself. They graciously made room for me in their crowded car and we were off to Blairsville.

I bought the things I needed, took advantage of the outing to eat as much food as I could cram in my stomach, and then we all piled in for the drive back to Mountain Crossings. By the time we got there, Bill was just closing up shop. I wanted to mail the Gust home and needed his help to do it. "I'll be back at nine in the morning," he said, which meant that there would be no magic hour for me in the morning. I would be up for four hours before he turned the key in the door, but that's the way it goes. I still had a few hours of daylight, though, so I went around to see about making all of my stuff fit into my new backpack—and could not do it no matter what I tried. The BRFC was the problem. There was a length of strap on top of the backpack, which is where bulky things are supposed to be attached, but that was no solution for me. I would not have things visible outside of the pack, nor did I want that bulk rising above my shoulders. I would look like a Sherpa, and I would bang every blowdown between here and Maine. That was it, then: my BRFC was going home. I could use a stuff sack as I always had, not as pretty but at least my food would fit inside the pack.

Then came my sleeping bag, which I'd used on and off since Alaska. It was olive green (I dislike garish-colored gear), was super light even though synthetic, and was no longer manufactured. It was irreplaceable, in other words, a true classic, but it wouldn't compress deeply enough into that slim ULA backpack to leave enough room for everything else. I made the decision pragmatically: my sleeping bag was going home, too. After another cold night on my homemade sleeping pad, I decided in the morning that it, too, would be going home.

TUESDAY, MAY 18, 2021

Low Gap Shelter - 11.5 Miles

A loud night from the road traffic, but I did get some sleep. Now to wait four hours for the place to open so I can sort out this gear problem and mail stuff home.

Did all of that! Now I have a nifty new food bag, sleeping bag, and an inflatable mattress as well. Hopefully I'll sleep better and it will all have been worth it.

Didn't start hiking until 11:00 a.m., the others long gone. One of my toes is swollen and that is worrisome. Took some vitamin I. Hope it helps.

Pitched my tent here next to the trail. This site is really full of people, all good people, though. No dicks. I don't feel as beat up today as I did yesterday. Maybe I'm acclimating, or maybe the new backpack has made that much difference.

Looking forward to a restful night.

—

I couldn't make enough coffee to while away the hours until Mountain Crossings opened, but when it did I was the first inside. I moved quickly to get what I needed so I could get out and still make some miles. I started with the better coffee brewing inside Mountain Harbor, and enough breakfast biscuits to placate my grumbling stomach.

I soon learned that sleeping bags have gotten expensive, too. I quailed at the prices of the down bags, while the synthetics were simply too heavy. I had about given up on the idea when I spied a forlorn bag liner in a dusty corner. It was a down bag liner, not fleece or silk. The package had been opened, the thing obviously examined and rejected by many customers previous, but it was marked down to a reasonable price, it compressed to the size of a softball, and I liked the way it looked. It was a bag liner, though, not a sleeping bag. Nevertheless I thought it would do for now—I could always replace it later. As providence would have it, I used that bag liner all the way to Mt. K, enduring some very cold nights in it. It now serves as a throw over the couch in my sitting room, and is probably the wisest purchase I have ever made.

Next was a sleeping pad. I very specifically wanted a Therm-a-Rest Z Lite foam pad. I had one at home that I'd used on all my hikes, and had left behind only because I thought I'd been clever in making a less bulky pad out of attic insulation. The problem was that because of Covid and its attendant supply interruptions, Mountain Crossings didn't have any in stock (this problem would precede me all the way to Maine), which left only the inflatable pads, and I despise those things. They invariably spring leaks, and they crunch and scrunch every time a sleeper moves, particularly translating their noise through the hard wooden floors of shelters, waking everyone but the sleeper, who is always unapologetic in the gritty-eyed morning. Hikes are now bespoke, after all. Who cares about other people?

With no choice I bought one anyway, fully intending to replace it with a Z Lite at my first opportunity, which never came. I even tried to trade my pricey inflatable to other hikers for their Z Lites, but found no takers. As providence would have this piece of equipment, it also wound up serving me all the way to Mt. K—and never sprung a leak.

I said goodbye to my discarded gear, which was now boxed and ready to ship, stepped out into the morning light with my new stuff, found that it packed neatly and trimly, slung that beauty of a backpack, and at about eleven o'clock, started making miles.

It was a perfect day, a few climbs but nothing taxing. The new backpack felt great, liberating even. One of my toes was swelling, although not causing me any pain. I worried only because I couldn't explain it. I downed some vitamin I and then shrugged it off.

I sprung into Low Gap Shelter still feeling energetic, but I'd made enough miles in a shortened day. Fisherman was probably at least a half day ahead, so I pitched my tent and set about trying to make some new northbounder friends, a novel concept for me.

WEDNESDAY, MAY 19, 2021

Around the Bend Hostel - 26.4 Miles

What a day!

It started early. I was out of the bag by 4:30 a.m. (very snug and soft, this new bag), packed and ready to go by 6:00.

Made great miles on a mostly easy trail, 14 miles by noon. Met a PCT thru-hiker named James and shared a few anecdotes.

Began to slow after the noon hour, but reached Tray Mountain Shelter by 1:00 p.m. This was the goal for the day at 15.4 miles, but too early so I pushed on to Deep Gap Shelter for a 22.8-mile day.

Reached Deep Gap Shelter at 6:00 p.m., tired and sore after that long climb over Kelly Knob, and found the shelter full of a bunch of dicks. I kept a distance, started boiling noodles, then overheard that the former Top of Georgia Hostel was now the Around the Bend Hostel, and only 3.5 miles away!

Anything to get away from those dicks. I inhaled my noodles, packed in a hurry, and hauled ass.

Made it to the road at exactly 8:00 p.m. The hostel has changed for the better. A youngish guy named Gordon owns the place now, and he was very helpful. No word what happened to Vagabond, who was the caretaker here on my last hike.

Pizza, beer, a shower—I feel great. Pitched my tent around back because the hostel is full, met up with James, who's been here for a while (I wish I were that fast), and had a great night.

—

My fist big miles of this hike came unexpected and without too much physical strain, my three-day theory at work again. This was now Day 4, three days of acclimation behind me and on the fourth day I made miles. Wide awake at half past four after having slept well on my scrunchy new pad, I was up while the others snored, excited—actually *excited*—to get on the trail and put in some miles.

I went through my morning routine with impatience. Coffee is a must regardless, which tried my patience even further because my little titanium alcohol stove simply was not performing as I had expected. Sure, it weighed nothing, and sure, I would eventually learn how much alcohol to squirt in it without wasting any excess, but even with that knowledge it took much too long to boil water.

I had bought this little stove from Uncle Johnny in Erwin, Tennessee on Hike 2. I didn't need the stove, especially that close to the end of my hike, but I was simply intrigued by the look of it, as if it were a titanium part out of a jet engine, and I was entranced by the feather-weight of it.

The stove I'd been using since my debacle at Poplar Ridge Lean-to in Maine on Hike 1 was a Trangia alcohol stove that I bought a day or so later at Ecopelagicon in Rangeley. While there is some weight to the Trangia (not that much, really), the trade-off is worth it because the Trangia will burn just about anything that's liquid and combustible and it has a screw-on lid, which means there is no waste and also that you can carry extra fuel in it. I used that stove on Hikes 1, 2, and 3, and all over the world. I've made morning coffee with it in Spanish pensions (do you have any idea how *late* those people sleep over there?), I even used witch hazel as fuel when I was in the French Alps (try translating methyl alcohol to a Frenchman, or *dry gas* for that matter). The Trangia is a versatile stove.

Before the Trangia, I used an MSR WhisperLite, old school, the kind where you pump the separate fuel bottle with a plunger in order to build up pressure. That stove had followed me from Alaska, where it had seen service from the Kenai Peninsula to the Arctic National Wildlife Refuge and then beyond to the Highlands of Scotland. That stove was versatile too, and served me well until Poplar Ridge.

I was sitting on the porcupine step, facing into the lean-to with my feet in the well, the WhisperLite set up on the floor in front of me. I had been hiking with The Dude since West Carry Pond. He and I were the only ones there. We were at the end of a cold, pitiless day, and The Dude was already curled up in his bag. The Dude was nineteen years old, with Viking red hair and a matching beard that made him look fierce, although he was actually a gentle young man from Wisconsin, still in awe that he could carry hard cheddar in his backpack and the stuff didn't turn to goop.

I wearily pumped the fuel bottle the recommended number of times, and as I lowered my lighter to the burner—before I even turned the valve—the whole thing exploded in my face, blowing me backward out of the lean-to, where I landed with a hard crack to the back of my head. I jumped up, swimming in stars, to find the inside wall of the lean-to awrap in flame, the WhisperLite roaring its fury as if it were a flamethrower, and The Dude slapping at the wall with his sweat-dampened shirt.

With panic-induced poor judgment, I reached into the inferno, grabbed the WhisperLite, and tossed it back-handed into the stream, where it hissed and spat and eventually settled down. The Dude, meanwhile, had stifled the flames within and was looking at me bedazed, his newly ventilated shirt still tight in his hand and with a spot of soot on his nose.

"What the fuck, Solo?" he blurted.

"I don't know what happened," I muttered defensively while trying to soothe my burned fingers.

"I'm gonna start callin' you *Flamer*, man," to which I groaned. Trail names can stick, and I was afraid that one might.

It turned out that the WhisperLite's fuel line had somehow been punctured. It was a small puncture, so small that I couldn't see the fuel jetting out as I pumped the fuel bottle, but still large enough to produce the conflagration that followed. The WhisperLite went back to MSR in the mail (MSR graciously sent me a free replacement), and while in Rangeley taking care of all this I discovered the Trangia. No more bombs in my backpack, I was sold.

But while gathering my gear for Hike 4 I came across that little titanium stove in the bottom of a foot locker, where it had rested unremarked all these years. It reminded me of irascible Uncle Johnny, who passed away between Hikes 2 and 3, and I decided that I needed to use that little stove, if only in memory of Uncle Johnny. So here I was now, my beloved Trangia stove languishing back home, and my nifty titanium stove wasn't working out.

Nevertheless, the miles called and I made them, fourteen miles by noon. I met a good-natured young PCT thru-hiker named James, who overtook me from behind but paused long enough for us to share some PCT anecdotes.

"The A.T. sure isn't the PCT, is it," he stated.

"Nope," I said, not going further to say that this section was actually pretty easy as the A.T. goes. He had the hiker legs of a gazelle, though, so I knew he would crush the A.T., maybe even come to enjoy it once he accepted that the A.T. and PCT do not compare in any way. He said his goodbyes and sprinted ahead, and I doubted I would ever see him again.

The afternoon brought on some heat, which slowed me but I still reached Tray Mountain Shelter by one o'clock, my goal for the day at 15.4 miles, but one o'clock was much too early to throw down so I pushed on for Deep Gap Shelter. I should note here that while I *was* carrying a tent this time, I hadn't yet adapted to the concept of stealth camping. In my mind I was still going shelter to shelter as I always had. It would be a while before the flexibility of tenting finally took hold.

I reached Deep Gap Shelter at six o'clock, weary after 22.8 miles and the inevitable last big climb before reaching shelter, ready for some noodles and to lay my head and to get an early start on tomorrow. I hiked in and announced myself, and was ignored by a grizzled old guy who was holding forth to a passel of young guys around the picnic table. I shrugged, took out my stove, set up on a stump and went about boiling my ramen. A young guy with the eager face of a hound came over.

"Love your kilt, man," he said.

"Thanks."

"When did men start wearing dresses?" the grizzled old guy asked. I shot a menacing look his way and found him still holding forth to the guys, as if that comment had arrived on the wind and came not from him.

The young guy gave me an apologetic look and returned to the group, my water and ramen were finally boiling, and then I heard, *"Yeah, Around the Bend Hostel. It used to be Top of Georgia but it's got new owners now."*

I perked up. I'd stayed at Top of Georgia on Hike 3. The caretaker then, Vagabond, had gone out of her way to cater to me, the only thru-hiker in a gaggle of section hikers who occupied every flat surface in the place. Vagabond had thru-hiked in the eighties, during the Woodsmen (Woodswomen)

The Tramily

(l-r) Spreader, Tortilla, Cockadoodle, Sheila, Donnie Brasco, Jersey, Hoosier Daddy, Brooklyn, me

era. I liked her at once, and was saddened when I didn't find Top of Georgia Hostel in the latest AWOL. But now I had just inadvertently learned from a dick that Top of Georgia was of late called Around the Bend which, after quickly consulting my AWOL, was only 3.5 miles away!

I slurped noodles that were still hot enough to burn my tongue, tossed everything haphazardly into the ULA, grabbed my trekking poles, and took off without a further word to the dicks behind me.

The sun wasn't setting until after eight so I could do this in the daylight, I just had to *move*, which I did as if I were sprinting for Springer. I reached the road at exactly eight o'clock, had to invert myself from southbound to northbound so I didn't turn the wrong way, and was walking up that long sloping driveway a half mile later.

The place was packed with hikers, who were gathered in a circle of camp chairs around a pit fire in front of the bunkroom. Every hand held a cold beer or a glass of wine. I smacked cracked lips and proceeded toward the throng. A youngish guy who was definitely not a hiker detached himself and came up to me. The sun had just set and we were standing in the dark now. His name was Gordon. He was the owner and the place was full. If I could have wilted I would have. I snapped to attention, though, when he said I could take a shower and tent out, and that he had frozen pizzas in a cooler by the office door.

"And beer?" I asked gravelly.

His look went furtive. "I'll give you one," he said, *sotto voce*, "but don't tell anybody."

"Thank God," I exhaled.

After some food and a shower, and a beer to hydrate my desiccated throat, I joined the group in the camp chairs and found them to be good people. James was there—what a surprise—and was kind enough not to steal the limelight when the others ogled that I'd just pulled 26.4 miles, more like twenty-seven with the road walk (James probably pulled thirty-plus miles that day). These guys were truly in awe, and I was astounded. One of them, a thirty-something red-headed guy with a flaming beard that reminded me of The Dude, offered me a beer, which I accepted with gratitude. Another guy, middle-aged and good-looking, with an earring and exuberant white teeth, offered me a hit from his reefer, which I declined with gratitude.

I settled in to listen to their talk. It would be a few days before I would remember all of their names, but some of those people were to become my first-ever tramily.

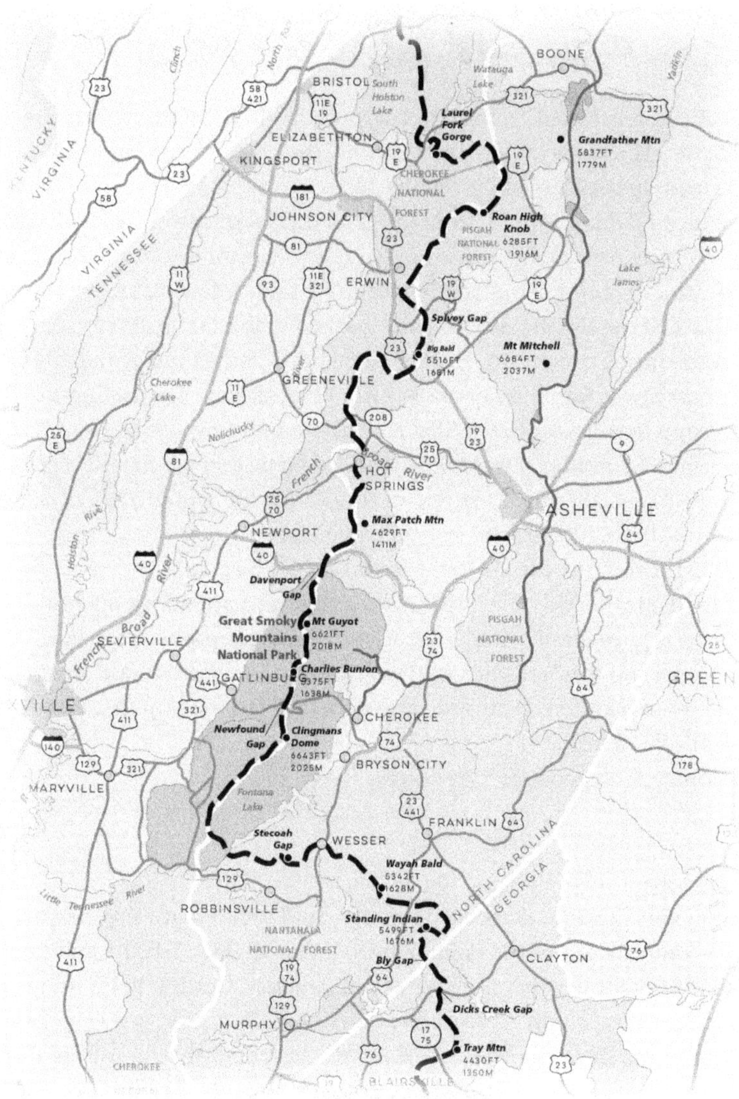

NORTH CAROLINA

96.4 MILES

THURSDAY, MAY 20, 2021

Whiteoak Stamp Campsite - 12.6 Miles

Up early to get started on the day. Had laundry done before sunrise, then got a ride into Hiawassee to buy a new stove. Now it's 10:30 a.m. and all I need to do is load up the ULA and get going.

Which I did at about 11:15. Made good time despite the climbs, and some of them were pretty long and steep, especially Buzzard Knob and Courthouse Bald, the latter being the obligatory big climb right before making it to shelter.

Reached the North Carolina state line and took a photo. Some of the guys from the hostel caught up with me then, but I pushed out ahead and never saw them again. Ran into an old guy from Florida who was leading a strung-out group to Muskrat Creek Shelter, where I and a few others from Around the Bend were headed. I was taken aback when he told me that he'd sent two younger hikers ahead to "reserve" campsites for the group. That's bound to go over well, could even lead to harsh language.

When I reached the shelter, I found it occupied by a surly dad and his two loud, erratic kids. The dad made a snide remark about my kilt. There was bad juju at that shelter, what with the Florida group "reserving" their campsites, and this jerk with his noisy kids, so I pulled out and went about a mile to a primitive campsite, where I was able to set up in solitude and bathe in the creek.

Hoping for a good, bear-free night.

—

A little rain overnight dampened my tent, but I found that I slept very well to the rhythmic patter of the rain. I was up before the sun, left the tent pitched so that it might dry out, and went to do laundry. Gordon had told me last night that this wouldn't disturb the other hikers.

I used my little titanium stove for the last time that morning, to boil coffee on the porch while I awaited my laundry and the coming day. The sun was well up before the other hikers roused, all looking eager if not a little hungover. Gordon came out eventually, and now it was time to sit for a full breakfast, which one comes to appreciate more and more with each additional day on the trail.

Once that was cleared up and cleaned up, Gordon shot me into Hiawassee to buy a new stove. Two nights before, at the sprawling and crowded Low Gap Shelter, I'd met a section hiker from Raleigh, North Carolina named Sheila who was searching somewhat despairingly for an available tent site, as was I.

We wound up pitching our tents side by side right off the trail, then proceeded to the next important duty, which was to make food.

I lit my stove and set water to boil while the sound of a jet engine came from Sheila's cooking area. She was using a canister stove, had heated one of those nice, pre-packaged camp meals, and had all but finished eating it before my water had even begun to bubble.

"Man, that's fast," I said jealously.

"Yeah, I'm surprised you don't have one."

I had never been attracted to canister stoves. My reasons sound silly, especially now, but they were: What happens if you run out of fuel and can't find a new canister? Sure, I could run out of alcohol, but in that case I could easily substitute something else, even rubbing alcohol. With a canister stove it's canisters or nada. And what about the empty canisters? Can they be recycled or do they wind up in landfills by the thousands?

Be that as it was, the powerful sound of Sheila's stove, and the speed in which it boiled water, had me yearning. Sheila let me examine her stove. The four-ounce canister weighed less than I thought it would, and the valve assembly was a wonder of engineering, what with its ingeniously-folding pot holders and valve adjuster. With the canister unscrewed, the valve assembly rested as lightly in my palm as a song sparrow. That did it, I was sold. I would find a way into Hiawassee, and if the outfitter there didn't have a Trangia stove then I was going to become a convert and go with a canister stove.

Gordon dropped me out front of Trailful Outdoor Co. at a little after nine o'clock. I went to the door, gave it a fruitless yank, and discovered that the place didn't open until ten. With nothing else to be done, I paced, tracing a path from the front of the store and then along the side, adjacent to the road. The sun was laying heat already, no shade, so I kept my eyes down and paced my thoughts away from the present and toward a cornucopia of issues: my mother's recent death, the book I'd just published, *A Robin Waits*, whether or not things were going well back home on the farm. Thus distracted, I didn't see the copperhead until I was practically on top of it, and when it did intrude into the corner of my eye, I jumped about as high as a man my age possibly can.

"Holy shit!"

I came down and backpedaled so quickly that I tripped and fell on my butt, spread-eagled and certain that a copperhead was about to sink its fangs into my junk. I crabbed away on heels and elbows as if I were on the ship in that movie, *Alien*, and about to suffer the same fate.

The copperhead lay there, as disinterested in me as I would be a guppy in a stream. I stilled my breath. It was a pretty big freakin' snake, partially coiled so I couldn't tell how long it was but I swear it was as big around as my lower arm. And it lay there unmoving in the morning heat, plenty hot enough at this hour to have gotten its blood circulating, and then I realized that the copperhead was dead, recently dead at that since flies hadn't even found it yet. It must have been hit by a car in the lethargic morning, retained enough life to slither into the narrow grassy patch between the road and the sidewalk, and there expired.

Now I felt bad for the copperhead. I'm no fan of snakes—I've had my share of encounters with them on the Appalachian Trail—but this had been a magnificent snake, surviving years to achieve its size, its life ended because it dared venture onto concrete. I've been hit by cars, too. I can relate.

I was the first customer in the store at exactly ten o'clock. A young woman greeted me and I got right to it. She was unaware of Trangia stoves, but led me upstairs and into a corner where the canister stoves were displayed. There were so many models, so many mysterious features. I grabbed the least expensive one, an MSR Pocket Rocket, along with a small can of fuel, then paid up and called Gordon.

"By the way," I said to the young woman as I was leaving, "there's a big dead copperhead just outside your store."

Her eyes went wide. "Really?"

"Yeah."

Back at Around the Bend, my tent had dried fully in the sun. I got everything packed away and went to settle up with Gordon. I handed him my titanium stove and the fuel bottle.

"This is too nice to leave in the hiker box," I told him. I could have mailed it home from Hiawassee, but that thought hadn't occurred to me in time. Gordon held the practically weightless stove and seemed to find it fascinating. "Give it to someone worthy, would you? Or keep it if you want it."

From the captivated way Gordon was gazing at that stove as I left his office, I have a feeling he held on to it for himself.

The guys were loitering out front of the bunkroom as I started down the driveway toward the road. I enjoy a stay in a hostel, but it's terribly hard to leave sometimes, especially when you're clean and well fed. Each procrastinating hour just slips into the next until you realize that half the day is gone. It wasn't noon yet, only a little after eleven, but for me the day was practically over; for people who sleep later it was only just beginning. We agreed to meet up at Muskrat Creek Shelter, and then I left them and started making miles.

I was making a good pace until Buzzard Knob, which is not a bad climb compared to what lies ahead but I'm always pitifully slow on climbs until I get my hiker legs, and even then I slow to a pace that finds me being passed by hikers young and old. After 8000 miles, I'm still not sure why I perform so poorly the moment gravity turns against me. I'm the same way on a bicycle, flying—I mean *flying*—until even the slightest upgrade comes along, and then I plod. I don't pant, my heart doesn't race, but my legs become leaden anyway.

Because of this, some of the others were able to catch up to me at the North Carolina state line, including the red-headed guy, whose name I learned, would forget, and then learn again, was Jeff. We took photos and then I pushed on and didn't see them again that day.

Somewhere on the other side of Courthouse Bald I met an old couple sitting on a rock resting and taking in the view. They seemed approachable enough so I stopped to talk with them. It turned out that they were part of a mixed group from Florida, most of their members people I had passed on my way up (despite my plodding pace), one of them an old Asian lady I'd met struggling on the climb and who was not having fun. She'd asked in a rattled voice if I'd seen her daughter, whom she described. I said no, but that I would pass along her concern, which I did now.

"Oh, yeah," the man said. "Her daughter's behind her. We must have people strung out for a couple of miles back there. It's impossible to keep 'em together. I had to send some kids ahead to reserve our campsites at the shelter."

I took a step back in shock. "*Reserve* your campsites? That's not—" But then I held my tongue, which did not need to lash this guy because surely someone else would do it before the day was done. I left them—glad to have them behind me—and dropped down to Muskrat Creek Shelter.

I could hear a booming ahead as I neared the side trail to the shelter, a deep, concussive booming that was too low for a gunshot but I couldn't come up with another explanation. I approached the shelter warily, prepared to drop to the ground in case some redneck was firing off rounds, and came upon two boys hard at work on a large branch that they'd drug across a campfire ring bordered with stones. One of the boys was an early teen, the other perhaps ten or so. The branch was actually a small blowdown, its dead roots canted upward on the other side of the fire ring. The teenager hefted a big rock and slammed it into the trunk just above the roots. *Boom*. The younger boy cackled and then the teenager lifted the rock once again. *Boom*.

"What are you boys doing?" I asked in incredulity.

"We're trying to make firewood," answered the younger boy. *Boom*.

"I told you that wouldn't work," said a severe-looking man who appeared as if from nowhere.

"I don't wanna do this anymore," said the younger boy, who then jumped up into the shelter and started banging on the walls.

Boom, went the rock.

"Nice skirt," the man said with a sneer my way.

"Actually," I said with surprising reserve, "it's a kilt. Scottish Highlanders wear them, pretty much known all over the world. A skirt is a garment that a woman wears under a blouse."

The man eyed me as if I had just delivered an insult, which I had, and I was ready to give him more than he could give me, and right there in front of his kids, if he took this any further. The younger boy was in the shelter bouncing off the walls as if he were possessed. The man, their father I assumed, looked away. Good thing. *Boom*.

Sometimes you get to a shelter (or even a hostel) and can just sense that things are off. I call this *bad juju*, and Muskrat Creek Shelter had plenty of it, not only these nutty people but also a gaggle of Floridians on the way who thought they could Airbnb their campsites in advance.

Boom.

I spun on my heels and returned to the trail. There was a campsite about a mile farther on. Hell, I'd cowboy camp on a ledge before I'd spend a night with those people, who made the obstreperous Boy Scouts I encountered at Blackrock Hut in Shenandoah on Hike 2 seem like well-behaved model citizens.

A bit less than a mile brought me to Whiteoak Stamp, where I was able to pitch my tent in solitude and with enough daylight left to go down to the creek to bathe. One of the advantages of the kilt is that you can go right to the edge of the water, drop the kilt and hop in without needing to take off your camp shoes or pull shorts or underwear over muddy feet. I had a refreshing splash, and then I smiled deviously. This was Muskrat Creek, the water source for the shelter down below. All of those dicks would soon be drinking my funk.

FRIDAY, MAY 21, 2021

Long Branch Shelter - 20.4 Miles

Spent a pretty good night, it was just windy as hell.

Up at 4:30 a.m., broke camp by 6:00. Beautiful and cool in the morning, got hot later. Met quite a few people, some I really liked although I've forgotten their names.

The climb up Albert Mountain is tougher for nobos than sobos, wore me out. I have a sizable blister on my right little toe, and this pisses me off.

Passed 100 miles today. Six days of hiking and I made no better pace than the 100-Mile Wilderness.

Arrived at this shelter at a little after 5:00 p.m., prepared to pitch my tent and do what I have become accustomed to doing, but at 6:30 no one else has come in to stay so I'm using the shelter. This is a nice, fairly new double-decker. Looking forward to a good night's sleep up above the varmints and crawling things. Might go into Franklin tomorrow after all, last trail town before the Smokies.

SATURDAY, MAY 22, 2021

Franklin, North Carolina - 7.2 Miles

Wow, had the shelter all to myself all night. Quiet, cool, clean from my bath in the stream—I slept well. Everyone else pushed on the 3.4 miles to Rock Gap Shelter so that they would be closer to Winding Stair Gap and the road to Franklin. 3.4 miles still seems like a long way to them. Rock Gap Shelter is a half century old, while this shelter is new and clean. Well, I tried to tell them.

Woke up at 5:00 a.m., on the trail by 6:00 and passing the tents of sleeping hikers the entire way. Met a really weird couple in Wallace Gap. Enough said about them. I was out and alone in Winding Stair Gap by 9:00, thumb out for a hitch and then out came the late sleepers, one after another until there was a dozen of us trying to hitch at the same time, which is futile with those numbers. I edged away from them and tried to make myself look like someone's weary grandpa, playing the sympathy card.

A nice lady with a suburban and trailer took four of us, dropping me at the library, where I posted field notes for an hour then walked the mile or so to Three Eagles Outfitters, where I scored a beer and bought some new socks and insoles. That should head off any further blisters.

Met Solace, a three-time thru-hiker who works at the place. He drove me to Gooder Grove Hostel after I finished shopping. Zen is off pink-blazing somewhere, but his caretaker Myrtle (I think that's how he spells it) set me up in style.

Ate a pizza, drank another beer, then modified and reconfigured the new backpack to make it easier to work with. Shortening some straps, removing a few others, I think this will do nicely.

Went out with the group to a couple of brewpubs. Drank too much and didn't get back to the hostel until 11:30 p.m., but had a good time.

—

I had only been on the trail for five days, but already trail time had taken hold. I felt as if I'd been at this for a month. My memories of Around the Bend were already recessing into a distant past, and I would have been pressed to accurately affirm what day of the week it was.

It felt wonderful to be in this state again.

In those simultaneously short and indefinitely long five days, I had already reestablished my pattern, which was to wake early and break camp early so I could get out and enjoy the magic hour.

This was now Day 6, although I wouldn't have guessed that if someone had asked. The magic hour was even more magical, cool, stonily quiet, and with the rising mist gradually revealing details of the forest, like a cover pulled slowly from a painting. I made miles in a state of grace, and as the heat came up I began to encounter hikers I hadn't met before: a young guy with a beautiful black and well-behaved dog; a nice young couple lashing to Harpers Ferry; another young couple who swore they would make it all the way. I liked those people and looked forward to seeing them again and again as the miles progressed. This was the northbounder experience, what I had never known as a southbounder, and I found to my surprise that I looked forward to meeting even more people who were sharing this experience with me.

I took Standing Indian Mountain, our first 5000-footer, while I was still in the magic hour, clambering to the summit without a drop of sweat and rewarded with an Impressionist's view of layered colors. By the time I reached Albert Mountain—our next 5000-footer—some twelve miles later, the heat was up and the magic was only a dreamy memory from a lifetime ago. I rested on top at the fire tower, the valley below now washed of color in the heat haze, then dropped down to Long Branch Shelter.

It was still early enough that I could easily make the 3.4 miles farther on to Rock Gap Shelter, which would place me within 3.8 miles of Winding Stair Gap and the road to Franklin, North Carolina, but pushing for those extra miles was simply not necessary. I would make Winding Stair Gap during the magic hour tomorrow regardless where I stopped today, and Long Branch Shelter was a nice site. It had good juju. The shelter was a double-decker and was fairly new, the tent pads were flat and clean, the woods around the shelter looked full and healthy, and the cascading stream had plenty of private spots for bathing.

And, to my further surprise, there was no one around.

I claimed a tent site—there would surely be others along by and by—then set up my new stove and marveled at how uncomplicated cooking had suddenly become. Now briskly bathed and with a full stomach, and after a further hour of quiet solitude, a young couple named Jersey and Brooklyn came bouncing in. I'd met them previously and liked them. Brooklyn was from Brooklyn, a statuesque young woman of about twenty who had a razor wit and a beaming smile to deflect it, and who towered over her partner Jersey, a closely-bearded twenty-something with a cappuccino complexion, enthusiastic smile, street-wise dark eyes, and an accent that confirmed he was from New Jersey.

"Hey Solo."

"Hey guys."

"You staying here?"

"Yeah."

The two looked around as if sizing the place up.

"I think we're gonna push on," Jersey said.

"Why?" I asked.

"We wanna be closer to Winding Stair Gap, you know?" Brooklyn said.

"Those miles won't make much difference in the morning."

"Maybe not to you, Solo," Jersey said. "You're too damn fast, man."

"I am not fast," I objected, and not for the first time. I'm not fast–not really. I just get an early start every day. I didn't want to find myself in some kind of undeclared competition with other hikers, so I had to tamp down this kind of talk.

"Well, you're faster than us," Jersey said as they planted their poles and turned back toward the trail. "Maybe we'll see you in Franklin."

"Maybe."

Silence returned once they were gone, and as deepening dusk began to drape the forest floor, no other hikers had come in. I rolled out my pad and bag in the upper deck of the shelter, lay there listening to the night sounds and the gurgling of the stream, thinking all the while that the Appalachian Trail might be crowded, but not tonight.

I'd been to Franklin, North Carolina twice. On Hike 2 I stayed with Ronnie Haven at his Budget Motel; on Hike 3 I stayed with Zen at his Gooder Grove Adventure Hostel. At some point, Ronnie had started his own hostel, which he called Baltimore Jack's Place in honor of the beloved multiple thru-hiker who passed away in Franklin in 2016. I met Baltimore Jack in New Jersey on Hike 1, and remember him as being open and friendly and ready with sage advice. He was also the first multiple thru-hiker I'd ever met, on his fifth or sixth thru-hike at the time. We sobos were in awe. Hero worship, truly.

I'd hitched a ride late in the day on Hike 3. The guy who picked me up was a tractor mechanic on his way home to Holly Springs, a nice guy with a console full of beers that he was happy to share. When I asked him if he could drop me at the hostel in town, he said sure and dropped me at Gooder Grove.

So I didn't see Ronnie on Hike 3 but I did meet Zen, who was an interesting if peculiar guy. I liked him and looked forward to seeing him again.

I was on the trail during the magic hour, making wraith-like progress through the dreamy woods and passing the tents of yesterday's hikers one after another. It was nine o'clock when I came out into Winding Stair Gap. I wasted no time, but went straight to the median and stuck out my thumb.

Cars flew past, a half hour flew as well, and I began to wonder if some dire trail event had occurred in the area since my last thru-hike. Standing right where I'd stood twice before, where I'd caught hitches in minutes or less, this time the drivers wouldn't even make eye contact.

And then the other hikers began to pile out of the woods, a dozen of them eventually, as well as a dog or two, all bunched together with a dozen thumbs in the air and with dogs drizzling saliva off lolling tongues. No one would stop amid that kind of crowd.

I edged away from the group, patted down what hair I had, and made myself look as much like a lovable grandpa as I could. Who wouldn't want to stop for an old grandpa? Well, no one, but then a lady in a Suburban pulling a trailer, both loaded to bursting with goods bound for a flea market, pulled in and rumbled up next to me. "I have room for you and three others," she said.

By then the entire gaggle had skittered on over, eyeing the assemblage and wondering how they could squeeze themselves in. When I explained that the lady could only take three of them, they fell into a debate about who should go. Minutes passed as the lady idled, although she showed no impatience whatsoever. Eventually three people separated from the rest, one of them a guy with a dog, who beseeched a place for himself and his dog in the trailer. The rest of us squeezed in. The other hikers were now off with hunched shoulders, thumbing their phones, and we were on our cramped way to Franklin.

I asked the lady to drop me at the public library so I could use the library's computers to post field notes, the first notes I would post on this hike. With that task completed, I set out for Three Eagles Outfitters, about a mile away. The day was still young, plenty of time to resupply and then make my way to see Zen. At Three Eagles Outfitters, I wanted to buy some insoles that would give me better support and hopefully do away with any further problems with blisters. Whatever had caused my toe to swell a lifetime ago had gone away on its own, no explanation.

It took a while to do that mile. Larger towns in the south are simply not conducive to walking. A quick mile took the better part of an hour of skirting culverts, climbing over rusty chain-link fences, and dodging cars. The sun was high now, it was pretty damned hot, but there at last was Three Eagles

Outfitters. I went inside wishing desperately that outfitters sold beer, and almost toppled when the young woman behind the counter reached into a cooler and handed me one.

When it comes to thirst and recovery, a single cold beer is an elixir for me. Sports drinks make me gag. Cokes are passable, but are sugary and sticky. But a beer is just right, cold liquid with some carbonation and a clean finish, and plenty of complex carbs that don't rush straight into my bloodstream. The rule is one beer, though. More than one in a dehydrated state makes me drunk almost immediately. Others laugh at my preference, but I have shared more than once—to let them know that I'm serious and not just boozing my way up the trail—that in earlier times, when one could still come across beers floated in the cold streams by trail angels (a practice that's frowned upon these days), I discovered that drinking a cold beer toward the end of the day could propel me another five miles.

I made my purchases and then gave Zen a call. No answer at his place. Hmm. I gave Ronnie a call, but got no answer there either. Where the hell was everyone? I worked out a route to Zen's place and was about to head out the door and hoof it along pedestrian-unfriendly roads when a guy named Solace came sweeping in.

"Solace might give you a ride," the young woman behind the counter suggested.

"Really?"

I've never fully understood Solace's relationship with Three Eagles Outfitters. He seemed to have the run of the place. At first I thought he was the owner; later I came to understand that he helps out seasonally—sometimes. Solace said he was in his forties, although he looked much younger. He was a hyper-energetic guy, well built, and with a running story for any situation. He'd thru-hiked three times, he said, which bonded us on the spot. I liked him, even though his stories seemed to contain more hyperbole than mine.

He took care of some business while I walked over to the supermarket to resupply, then he drove me to Gooder Grove.

"You doing anything tonight?" he asked as I climbed out of his SUV.

"No," I shook my head. "Probably just sleep."

"There's a cool band playing tonight at the Lazy Hiker. Some of us are going. Hikers, you know? Wanna come with?"

"Sure," I said hesitantly. The night life doesn't appeal to me as much anymore, and staying out too late might preclude an early return to the trail in the morning, but this was the nobo experience in its purest form and I didn't want to miss out. "Yeah," I confirmed. "I'm down."

"All right, then. I'll swing by at six."

"I'll be here."

I had never seen Gooder Grove in the daylight, so I now found myself a little disoriented. It was definitely Zen's place, though, lots of plants and rules and a rack for leaving shoes and poles outside. I went to the door and knocked. It was strange that no one was around. A portly, bearded and barefoot guy answered. This was the caretaker, Myrtle (his elocution could have delivered this as anything from *Marple* to *Merle*, but I didn't press).

"I'm looking for Zen or Stickman," I said, a little bewildered.

"Zen's pink-blazin' in the Grayson Highlands, and Stickman ain't here no more."

Pink-blazing? Zen?

"No one answered the phone or returned my calls," I said. Solace had assured me that the place was open.

Myrtle shrugged. "I ain't got the password for the voicemail."

This all sounded about as weird as it could get, but there I stood, and Ronnie still wasn't answering his phone. "Are y'all open?" I asked uncertainly.

"Sure. Drop your pack, take off your shoes, and c'mon in."

Things settled down after that. The kitchen was where the kitchen had been, the big table in the main room was still cluttered with mail drops, hiker boxes still crowded the back door, and the bunks were still downstairs. "I got two down there," Myrtle said, "a big guy and his girl. She ain't feelin' well."

I groaned. I knew who he was talking about. "I'll take a room, then."

I ordered a pizza, took a shower, and then sat down out front to do some work on my backpack. The ULA was overburdened with straps of all kinds for securing all kinds of things to the outside, which I don't do, so with a lighter and a pair of scissors I was shortening those straps and fusing the ends. A young, good-looking guy wearing a crisp short-sleeved button-down shirt and an ultralite backpack came up then and settled into a chair. I learned that his name was Lynx and that this was his third thru-hike. I was eager to share anecdotes but Lynx seemed aloof, as if he were as ephemeral as mist on the wind. He asked about the rates at Gooder Grove, then stood.

"I'm going to head out," he said.

"You aren't staying here?"

"No, I just wanted to check it out." He walked off as quietly as he'd arrived.

I finished with my backpack, inhaled my pizza, and six o'clock finally came. Solace pulled up promptly at six, his SUV full of the people I'd been hiking with on and off for the past couple of days. Some of them were staying in a motel, others had managed to get ahold of Ronnie, and all had met Solace at Three Eagles Outfitters. I squeezed in and we were about to leave when Myrtle came out and spoke to Solace.

"That girl down there's in bad shape," Myrtle told Solace. "I think she needs to go to the hospital but she won't do it."

"I'll go talk to her," Solace said, and then to us: "This won't take long."

The couple downstairs, whom I will call Gamer and Sparky, were a pair I'd met earlier in Wallace Gap while I was on my way to Winding Stair Gap. They'd been sitting on a log by the narrow road, and said they were waiting for a shuttle into Franklin, which seemed awful early to be waiting for a shuttle, and an odd and expensive place to be doing it considering that Winding Stair Gap—and a potential free ride—was only 3.1 miles farther on. I made the mistake of stopping to talk with them, and then found myself roped into some of the most bizarre conversation I've ever endured.

Gamer was big. He wore a black Matrix T-shirt and an undershirt of tattoos. I couldn't have lifted his backpack, and his department-store shoes were large enough to ferry hikers across the wider rivers on the A.T. Sparky was short, unhealthily thin, and had teeth that betrayed some substance abuse in her past. She wore a blue T-shirt with a dolphin on it, and had tattoos on her arms that hadn't been inked with skill. Gamer assured me that they were going all the way to Maine. It was with stoic control that I didn't let my skepticism show.

"Well, maybe only to Virginia," Sparky interjected. "My mama ain't doin' too good, an' I might have ta go help her. She had her gall bladder taken out and now her stomach kinda goes the wrong way and there's somethin' else wrong because she cain't sit the toilet right no more an' sometimes she misses an' that can make a mess so she might need me."

I suppressed my nausea at this excess of information, offered my condolences and turned for the trail.

"But if that don't happen we're goin' all the way," Gamer said with conviction. "Whaddaya think? Can we do it?"

"Sure you can, guys," I said hastily. "See you around." The trail was there, *right there.*

"I don't know," Gamer said, conviction displaced in an instant. "I got this big sore on my foot. Let me show you."

My stomach is usually pretty solid, but not enough for that. "Uh," I stumbled. "I wouldn't really know what to do about it."

"Did you get the vaccine?" Gamer asked out of absolutely nowhere.

"Uh, yeah, I did."

"We didn't." He smiled proudly. "That's all a conspiracy—you can read about it online. Here, I'll show you." He started thumbing at his phone.

"No, that's okay." I waved him off. The trail was *right there.*

"The NSA put 'em up to it. They let the virus out on purpose so they could put trackers in everybody. Now you got one, too."

"But we don't," Sparky gap-grinned.

"That's why we're on the A.T.," Gamer explained. "Ta get away from that shit."

I was raised to be Southern polite. Even at my age I still have a hard time just brushing people off, but if this conversation went on any longer I would need a hot shower to be rid of it.

"Well, good luck then," I said in motion, and then there were trees between us and I was saved.

And now the two were in the hostel I'd thrown down in, and Solace seemed to know something about them and felt compelled to help.

"Are you an EMT?" I asked Solace.

"No, but I help people if I can."

And then he was into the house and we were all realizing how uncomfortable we were, crammed together mostly bare-legged with mostly a bunch of strangers. The minutes ran to five, then ten, and that's when our patience ebbed and we all got out. Myrtle was outside the front door smoking a cigarette, so I went on over.

"What's going on down there?" I asked him.

He exhaled a puff. "Don't know. The girl's hysterical. I think it's just cramps or somethin'."

"I saw her on the trail this morning and she seemed fine."

"Well," his brows bounced, "what do I know about this stuff? She was a little wacky when they got here, and they've been down there ever since."

"Hmm." I returned to the group.

The red-headed guy who'd given me the beer at Around the Bend—Jeff—quietly asked, "So what's going on?"

I told him what I knew of Gamer and Sparky, and left him to draw his own conclusions.

Fifteen minutes.

Twenty minutes.

I watched the day wane, and grew impatient. "Does anyone know where this place is?" I asked the group. "Can we just walk there?"

"I'm not sure," Jeff said. The rest were as equally noncommittal.

"It's a little far," Myrtle piped over.

Thirty minutes.

Solace emerged from the house to sighs of relief, but then went straight to Tortilla and Spreader. These two young women had just graduated from medical school and were doing a little trail time together before their residencies took them to opposite sides of the country. They were only hiking as far as Stecoah Gap, about another forty miles, which was too bad because we all liked them a lot. Solace made as if to huddle with them in private, but of course most of us sidled over to hear what was going on.

"I think it's just hemorrhoids," he told the young doctors, "but she thinks her rectum has prolapsed." Gulps were heard. Someone stifled a gag reflex. Tortilla and Spreader, to their credit, were professionally focused.

"We'd better go see," Tortilla said.

We all settled in for another wait.

"Why won't she go to the hospital?" I asked Solace.

"She says she's too embarrassed."

The girl was in a hostel bunkroom, hysterical, while strangers went up and down the steps and were possibly examining her between her legs—and she was too *embarrassed* to go to the hospital?

"Can we walk to this place and maybe meet you all there later?" I asked him.

He shook his head. "It's kinda far. This shouldn't take too much longer."

Twenty minutes.

It was now pushing seven thirty and the sun was getting low. I was about to give up and go to my room when Tortilla and Spreader emerged, their expressions tentative.

"She'll go to the hospital," they told Solace. "Can you taker her over there?"

"So what is it?" just about everyone asked at once.

"Yeah, I can do that," Solace said.

"Look guys," I said. "It's gotten late. I think I'll just go turn in."

"No, Solo, it's cool," Solace countered quickly. "I'll run you all over there and then come back for her."

"Cool," said Jeff and a few others, while I thought we could have done the same thing an hour and a half ago. This was a free ride, though, I reminded myself. Solace didn't have to do anything for any of us.

We all piled in, and minutes later we were in a downtown that had long since pulled the shades on the day. Solace walked us into the Rock House Lodge, introduced us around, then took off on his mission of mercy. We all held bewildered looks on our faces.

"This isn't the Lazy Hiker," Jeff said.

I looked around. There were only two other people in the place besides us. The Rock House Lodge was a nice pub, a great place to hang, but it wasn't where we thought we were going.

"They've got local brews and food," I said, heading for the bar. "That's good enough for me."

By the time Solace returned, we had all taken station at a long table, nibbling and drinking and getting to know one another. Because I'd been having such a difficult time remembering names on this hike, I wrote each in my diary. There were Tortilla and Spreader—Natalie and Polly—the two bright young residents who had me wishing I'd produced a daughter of my own; Jersey—off-trail name Ron—and Brooklyn—off-trail name Katy—who hadn't known each other until meeting in Atlanta on their way to Amicalola. Katy, as it turned out, was only eighteen years old while Ron was twenty-four. Both were thru-hiking all the way. Jeff—known as Hoosier Daddy because he was from Indianapolis and had recently become a father—was lashing to Hot Springs, North Carolina from Springer Mountain, a 275-mile outing that he would have extended if not for his nascent paternity; and the exuberant ganja guy with the earring, Don—Donnie Brasco—an attorney from Florida who led rafting trips on the Nantahala River every spring and had decided to hike there this time rather than drive. This was my tramily. We weren't all heading for Mt. Katahdin, but that was a destination too far in the nebulous future to consider. At the moment, we were all hikers.

It was dark beyond the windows now. Solace swept in with his indefatigable smile, as if he were a booster club of one. We all spit it out at the same time: "So what's up with Sparky?"

"She's staying in the hospital overnight," he said. "That's all I know."

"So when are we heading to the Lazy Hiker?" I asked.

"Pretty soon," he answered noncommittally, and then he took a seat and held center while everyone peppered him with questions. We learned that he alternated between here and New York, that he had a twin, and that he wasn't intimidated by a fifty-pound backpack. "You know how it is, Solo. You gotta tough it out, man."

His shoulders were definitely stronger than mine.

As this went on, I'd already had too many beers if this was only our first stop. "Can I walk to that place from here?" I asked Solace. Maybe I could walk off some of my wooziness.

"Sure."

He gave me directions and I got up, kilted and unsteady. "Okay, I'll see you all there."

I made my way along quiet streets, following Solace's directions, walking mainly in the roadways but there wasn't much traffic to worry about. The night had become cool and somehow expectant, as if something monumental were in the waiting. I turned toward a boisterous sound, saw lights beyond a bank of darkened warehouses, and went that way. Passing through a copse, as if the very Appalachian Trail were here in the town of Franklin, I emerged onto a manicured lawn of drinking patrons and with the sound of twanging music coming from inside the building. This was it, the Lazy Hiker, but no, this place was called Currahee Brewing Company.

I must have made a wrong turn somewhere. I'd lost my new tramily. But I was a thru-hiker, this place had beer—great beer, as it turned out—and we'd all meet up on the trail again tomorrow anyway. I'd find a way back to Zen's place, the trail would provide, so I took a high-top, ordered a beer, and sat back to watch a surprisingly good country duet twang out some tunes.

Sometime later—not too much later—the entire tramily came streaming in, led by Solace.

"Solo!" they waved.

Solace herded them to a table and got them all seated, and then I went over.

"How did you all find me?" I asked, dumbfounded.

"This is where we were coming," Solace answered over the din.

"I thought we were going to the Lazy Hiker."

"That didn't work out," he said enigmatically, and then turned his attention to the group, recommending various beers as if he'd brewed them himself and intimately knew their inner workings. The group was all smiles and cheer. We had time for about one beer each before the place closed, and then we trundled back to the SUV and our return ride to our various lodgings. Back at Gooder Grove, I asked Solace the best way for me to get back to the trail.

"Can I hitch from town?" I asked. Towns always confused me. It was hard to know which road to hitch from.

"Naw, don't worry about that, Solo. I'll take you."

"I appreciate it, Solace, but I want to get an early start."

"How's nine o'clock sound?"

I'd rather be hiking by the magic hour, but you can't ask a free ride to get up that early. And besides, my stomach was heavy with beer. I would still wake up early, but I doubted I'd feel like hiking that early. Nine o'clock wasn't bad. I would still be able to make some good miles.

"Sounds great," I said. "See you at nine."

SUNDAY, MAY 23, 2021

Wayah Bald Tower - 10.1 Miles

Up at 6:30 a.m., not feeling bad at all. Coffee, breakfast, and then after a confusing period of hours trying to find a way back to the trailhead, Solace got me there at 12:30 p.m. So a late start, but I made Wayah Bald by 5:00 p.m. in great weather.

Donnie Brasco was already there, having shuttled up because of a painful blister on his heel. Brooklyn, Jersey, and Hoosier Daddy came in later. Some other hikers we knew came through but pushed on to the next shelter. Of Tortilla and Spreader, no word. They were staying in a hotel somewhere, and no one had seen them since last night.

We all camped up there, watched a magnificent sunset and then an equally magnificent moonrise. We drank boxed wine to celebrate, and had a great evening. I wanted to sack out in the tower but it was too cold and windy at that height. We all wound up pitching our tents in the grassy area beside the walkway to the tower. I didn't know if we were allowed to camp there, but I didn't care. The view was gorgeous, and that's all that mattered right then.

MONDAY, MAY 24, 2021

Nantahala Outdoor Center - 17 Miles

Had an up and down night, but did sleep for a few hours. It was unexpectedly cold and windy throughout.

Got out of the bag at 4:45 a.m. Made coffee at the tower, not only to get out of the wind but also for the morning view. The moon was still up, big and surreal and casting enough clean silver light that I could have hiked all night without my headlight. Broke camp as the others were waking, and hit the trail at 6:30.

Made quick time at first, ups and downs, but at about mile nine I tripped and went over the side then down the mountain about twenty or thirty feet. Tumble tumble, scratch scratch, poke poke, and me yelling to myself "Stop! Stop! Stop!" as I tried to arrest my fall, throwing out arms and legs every which way to catch on something. I eventually crashed into some dead limbs, which left a mark but held me from falling farther. I clawed back onto the trail scratched and punctured and scraped. No serious damage, but my pace was off from then on.

Lynx went by me minutes later, while I was still working to regain my composure, shared a few words, and then he disappeared ahead.

Made it (very tired) to the N.O.C. at 2:00 p.m. Had a beer and a burger and then ran serendipitously into No Rush and his young son Crazy Nut, whom I'd met eons ago while taking a break at Tray Mountain Shelter. Amazing. No Rush hikes through here often, and knows the area pretty well. He showed me a place to stealth camp since the N.O.C. charges a minimum $80.00 for a small room with four bunks. With showers and a community kitchen, this is a good deal for four people, not as affordable if you're alone.

I took a brisk shower (hopefully removing any poison ivy oil I might have contacted while tumbling), and now I'm waiting to see if any of the others make it. Seventeen miles is still a big day for them.

Hoosier Daddy and Jersey came in at 6:30 or so. Wound up sharing a bunkroom with them and an old guy named John, so only $20.00 each. Ran into Lynx again at the restaurant, entertaining some section hikers and being treated to free beers. With his speed, I figured he'd have been in the Smokies by now.

TUESDAY, MAY 25, 2021

Stecoah Gap - 13.6 Miles

Woke up early after sleeping very soundly for at least seven hours. Scavenged food from the community kitchen, although no coffee this time. It's amazing the odds and ends you can make a filling meal out of when you're this hungry.

On the trail by 6:30 a.m., made great time on that long climb, but began to falter by noon. Felt sleepy, weary.

Got into the Gap about 1:30 p.m., feeling not strong. It was blazing hot, and there was little water in that section. Some other hikers lounging in the only shade were out of water as well, chuckling when I tried to yogi some from them. Lonnie from Stecoah Wolf Creek Hostel came to pick me up, and dropped off boxes of bottled water for the other hikers at no charge. What a gesture.

At the hostel, I showered, did laundry, and took a nap for two hours. The nap was what I needed. Now I feel great. I should probably carve out time to take naps on the trail, but I simply don't have the patience for that when I'm making miles.

The caretaker here is Shadow, who reminds me of Tollbooth Willy on Hike 1, what with his pronounced Boston accent. There is also Pope, a groggy guy who looks like Tommy Chong.

More hikers came in, but no one in my tramily. At 5:00 p.m., we all went to dinner at a diner, and while there Lynx came in. What is it with this guy? He's good-looking, as agile as a springbok, but there's something clever and calculating in his eyes. He centers attention in every group, and is deft at massaging egos. He also keeps turning up when he could be miles and miles gone by now.

Looking forward to a restful night. Fontana Dam tomorrow, and then the Smokies.

WEDNESDAY, MAY 26, 2021

Fontana Marina - 14.2 Miles

Woke up at 5:00 a.m., packed up, and ate ten fried cheese sticks for breakfast. On the trail by 7:00. Cleared Brown Fork Gap Shelter within an hour, where it turns out Hoosier Daddy, Jersey, and Brooklyn were still breaking camp. I sped past and didn't learn of this until later.

Reached Fontana Marina at 2:00 p.m. I went in for a beer and a sandwich, and then Lynx came in. How many days in a row now? Maybe my miles aren't as short as I thought they were. It has been damned hot the past few days.

Later, Hoosier Daddy, Jersey, and Brooklyn showed up. They had reservations at Fontana Resort, so I went with them and yogied a place to sleep indoors once again. We had a great dinner on a terrace as the sun was setting, although we spent way too much. Turns out Hoosier Daddy and Jersey appreciate a good single malt as much as I. I'm invited to go rafting with them at the N.O.C. tomorrow, which means I would be taking my first zero—and unscheduled at that—but I think I'm going to go.

THURSDAY, MAY 27, 2021

Fontana Marina - Zero

What a day!

I did decide to zero and do the Nantahala float with the others, which began with a big breakfast here at Fontana Resort followed by a shuttle back to the N.O.C.

We met up with Donnie Brasco, who was to be our guide, then waited as one by one everyone else showed up. There was Cockadoodle, whom I hadn't seen since Low Gap Shelter. He looks odd with his ungainly backpack, guitar and fishing rod protruding, but he's an interesting, good-natured guy. Tortilla and Spreader came, and even Sheila, the woman at Low Gap Shelter who turned me on to canister stoves. It was extraordinary to see them all again.

The raft trip took several hours, but was enjoyable if not also cold. I wore the wrong clothes and shoes, but had a great time just the same.

We finished late in the afternoon and set up a beer and pizza bash down by the river. Solace drove up from Franklin with the beers. What a gathering. Cockadoodle threw out a fishing line and caught a fish. We woozily missed our shuttle back to Fontana Resort. Solace wound up driving us, which was long in the dark and ever longer for him to get home afterward. I felt guilty about that, but I was with others so they could share some of that guilt.

What was really touching were the sincere hugs from all as we parted for the last time. Donnie Brasco and Sheila had reached their destination, Tortilla and Spreader had finished at Stecoah Gap, and Cockadoodle was living the trail life, uninterested in making miles. Now our tramily was just the four of us: myself, Hoosier Daddy, Jersey, and Brooklyn.

By taking this unscheduled zero, I will now be catching the Smokies over the weekend and will have to deal with the weekend crowds. It's worth it, though. Today's experience is why I'm hiking nobo this time, after all.

—

Getting out of Franklin became more of a challenge than I'd anticipated. I woke up early that next morning, all those beers metabolized, and felt well enough to start making miles right then. I had to wait until nine o'clock, though, which came and went without an appearance by Solace. The call I made to him went to voicemail.

I was well aware of my impatience, my conscious need to make miles. During the course of the hike I would explain more than once that I hadn't been this driven on my southbound hikes, and conjectured that perhaps this was because of Mt. Katahdin. Rationally, I knew I had ample time to make it to Maine but I still couldn't shake the notion that at some point in autumn that mountain would be closed. What if something happened and I got there too late, the pinnacle of my goal foiled because of dragging feet? Southbounders never have to worry about someone coming along and closing Springer Mountain. Going southbound, there's time for anything and everything: short days, long days, side trails along the way; a nero here, a nero there, a cluster of zeros at a hostel that has good juju, or in a trail town that boasts authenticity and culture—the worst that would happen from a late finish would be to catch some snow at elevation, but Springer Mountain would still be there waiting.

Sitting at Gooder Grove with my backpack against my knee, my need to make miles absolutely *right now* became intolerable. I started making calls to shuttle drivers, prepared to break one of my rules and pay for a shuttle if that's what it took to get me moving again. Fortunately—although I didn't feel that way at the time—all the shuttle drivers were out with other hikers. I offered Myrtle money if he would take me to the trailhead. He chuckled and shook his head. I stood and shouldered my backpack.

"Where's the best place to hitch?" I asked Myrtle. He seemed a little confounded by the question.

"You have to go down here and turn left," he pointed. "Go across a parking lot, then across another road..." And then down a way, take a right then a left, then another right, and on and on and on. I couldn't keep all of that in my head. I needed a map, but my phone wouldn't run that app anymore, while paper maps seemed to be a thing of the past. I was about to go for it anyway, just to be going *somewhere*, when Solace pulled in.

"Thank God," I exclaimed.

"Sorry, Solo. I've been shuttling hikers all morning. Get in and I'll get you there."

He reversed with a screech out of Gooder Grove, straightened out on the road and then put the pedal to the floor. I double-checked my seatbelt.

"It's been a crazy day," he said while whooshing through a yellow light. "Hikers going all over the place. I've been to Winding Stair Gap five times already." He made a hard left that I leaned into as if I were in a tight turn on my fastest carbon bicycle. "I've gotta make a quick stop if that's okay." Suddenly we were at Three Eagles Outfitters, Solace shooting up the steep driveway like a bullet from a barrel. Holy cow but we were going to hit the wall! Instead we jerked to a stop. "This won't take a minute," he said, and then he was unbuckled, out, and on his way into the store.

I followed him at a more sanguine pace, went inside to find Brooklyn hugging a down sleeping bag as if it were the teddy bear of her childhood. Jersey was in the store too, a canister of fuel in one hand, a couple bags of trail meals in the other.

"You buying a new bag?" I asked Brooklyn.

"Yeah," she breathed with excitement. "This one is so much *lighter* than my other one."

So she was learning. Good. Brooklyn was a strong young woman, but why carry extra weight if you don't have to? I used to do backpack shakedowns for people, who inevitably balked when I recommended they toss the three extra fuel canisters or the full roll of duct tape, the four pairs of socks or the bulky winter coat, not to mention sets of laminated A.T. maps, flares, hatchets, saws, trenching tools, umbrellas—and deodorant (for God's sake). Their rationalizations for all this excess would often descend into the testy defensive. I don't offer shakedowns anymore because of this, but my basic guidance on the A.T. is: barring a first aid kit and rain gear, if you don't touch it every day get rid of it. A.T. hikers are seldom more than a couple of days from a trail town and resupply, so carrying pounds of extra food, fuel, and clothing is simply unnecessary. Take a length of duct tape and wind it around your toothbrush handle. That's the most you'll probably ever need for patching holes or securing soles, but if need does arrive then a town or store will usually be a short hike away.

Solace swept out of a backroom with a harried expression, went to Brooklyn and began demonstrating how to compress her new sleeping bag into a stuff sack. Other hikers came in, other sales to be made. The young woman from yesterday wasn't there. Solace seemed to be running the place alone.

Jersey and Brooklyn went off to the supermarket to resupply, someone came in to help Solace, and at last we were on our way to Winding Stair Gap. It was twelve thirty. We said hurried goodbyes—Solace in as much of a rush as I—and then I got on the trail and felt sheltered again from the chaos of civilization.

The day went well, a satisfying hike that took me above 5000 feet, much cooler at that elevation. I reached Wayah Bald at five o'clock.

There's a stone lookout tower on Wayah Bald, a magnificent edifice that I had always passed early in the day on my southbound thru-hikes but which had left me wishing each time that I'd been there for a sunset. I'd wanted to camp in that tower from the first time I'd seen it years ago. And now here I was at the end of the day, finally able to fulfill that wish. I'd mentioned this to the others back at the Rock House Lodge. What I didn't realize was that they'd taken this to heart.

Donnie Brasco was there when I climbed the steps to the top of the tower, a reefer cupped in his palm against the wind. He smiled and offered me a hit, but I waved that off.

"What are you doing here?" I asked, surprised.

"You said you always wanted to camp here, so here I am. The others are coming, too."

"Really?" I was touched deeply enough for a lip to quiver. On none of my hikes had anyone ever made a gesture like this. "But," I sputtered, "how did you get here ahead of me?"

"I got a ride up or else I wouldn't have made it in time." He limped closer. "I've got a blister that hurts like hell. Didn't you say you had some magic fix for blisters?"

No, it's not a magic fix, just a realization that came to me on Hike 2. Some blisters form because many of us proceed from our adolescent years wearing the same size shoes we wore in high school, which are generally too small. They compress our heels and eventually deform our toes. By the time we recognize this (if we ever do) the damage is done. I learned between Hikes 1 and 2 to wear shoes a half size larger than my measured size, which reduces pressure on the heel as well as friction in the toe box, but those toes trained over time to roll on their sides are still a problem. Despite the larger shoes, I was still getting blisters.

I tried all the usual fixes—bandaids, moleskin, petroleum jelly—but none of these worked. The bandaids and moleskin would sweat off within minutes of strenuous hiking, sometimes bunching between my toes to rub their own blisters. Petroleum jelly sweated off quickly as well, and would require a stop every half hour or so to reapply it (by the way, powders are likewise overwhelmed by sweaty hiker feet). What I needed was a lubricant that would stick and stay, and then I thought about my boys when they were babies, the diaper rash cream their mother and I used on them, and how that stuff would still be smeared all over the next day despite multiple changes of wet diapers. So why not try diaper rash cream on my feet?

I bought some, tried it, and it worked! I had no further blisters on Hike 2, and none on Hike 3. I developed a blister on this hike because I'd gotten lazy and hadn't applied the cream. (I corrected that behavior and suffered no more blisters for the remainder of the hike.) An additional benefit of using diaper rash cream with zinc is that it soaks into your socks and shoes, killing bacteria. This not only keeps your feet, socks, and shoes from reeking, but helps prevent blisters from becoming inflamed if you do develop one.

Another discovery in blister care was to not pop them but to let them shrink and harden into callouses. If a blister did pop on its own inside my shoe, it tended to not become infected (because of the diaper rash cream) and would therefore not cause me any pain.

I told all of this to Donnie Brasco, who then slipped a bare foot out of a comfortable camp shoe and asked, "Do you think it would work on this?"

I cringed. The back of Donnie Brasco's heel had been rubbing so hard and so long that he had what looked like an ulcer about the size of a quarter. This wasn't a blister, this was a *wound*. I couldn't believe he could walk at all, and wondered how he'd stayed on the trail as long as he had. His tolerance for pain must have been extraordinary.

"No, Donnie," I told him, "the cream's not going to work on that. You're going to have to let it heal. The next time you do a hike, use the cream then and you should be okay."

Donnie Brasco was pretty much done making miles on this hike; nevertheless, in pain as he was, each step a tortured raw nerve, he'd still made the effort to come up here and spend the evening with us. I knew right then that we'd remain friends well beyond the trail.

The evening came on in splendid layers of color that wept with beauty. Hoosier Daddy, Jersey, and Brooklyn soon arrived to join us. No one had seen Tortilla and Spreader all day, so we assumed they were still in Franklin. Other hikers we knew stopped in for a quick look and then pushed on to Wayah Bald Shelter, barely a mile away, leaving us with only a few lingering day hikers, who filtered away after sunset, and then we were alone on that high bald. I wasn't sure that camping was even allowed on the site, but I saw no signs to the contrary and I doubted any ranger or ridgerunner would be out this late to run us off.

We passed around a box of Merlot as the sun set, Donnie Brasco alternately cupping and brandishing his reefer as day hikers came and went, and then a waxing moon rose behind us, fluorescent in a crystalline sky. I wanted to sack out in the tower for the night, but the wind was strong, cold, and would grow colder. Instead we all went down and pitched our tents in a patch of manicured grass along the paved walkway, and then one by one turned in for the night.

It became a raucous night of cold gusts that rattled the walls of my tent as if I were camping on a glacier high in the Alps. My down bag liner kept me warm and snug, to my surprise. That arrestingly luminous moon arced above me then behind me, lighting the inside of my tent as if a dozen hikers were standing outside with their headlights singling me out. I roused at a quarter till five and went out to watch the moonset, casting long, firm shadows back toward the tower. It was as if an ocean-going searchlight were slipping beyond an inky horizon. It was magic.

I went up into the tower to retrieve my food bag, which I'd left hanging in the rafters in case there were any stray bears in the area (even though I'd seen no sign yesterday—no scat, no tipped rocks, no rubs on the trees). I made coffee in the lee of the tower, sipped that warmth as the moon at last shimmered away and as the glow of the coming day slowly engulfed the horizon behind me. The others had slept through this, but there would be other moonsets for them to experience, other sunrises. Of these, the Appalachian Trail provides plenty.

I was packed and hiking by six thirty, only Hoosier Daddy up to give me a parting wave. I passed Wayah Bald Shelter as those hikers still slept, climbed Copper Ridge Bald in the magic hour, then started down as the day's heat quickly rose around me. My thoughts were all within, solemn solitude, the miles passing unnoticed beneath my feet, and then my left foot snagged a rock at the edge of the trail and over I went.

Over I went. I'd had plenty of falls on the Appalachian Trail, but I had never tumbled *off* the trail. Suddenly from an internal reverie I was cartwheeling down an open mountainside of desiccated brush and briars and sticks perfectly primed for the next wildfire. "Stop!" I hollered at myself, not quite believing what was happening. "Stop!" My trekking poles were elsewhere, good thing because otherwise I might have been impaled by one or both. In one moment my kilt was wafting in my face, my nether parts taking in the sun; in the next my knees were scraping across a sun-dried log. I threw out alternately arms and legs, as if trying to brace myself in a spinning airplane. "Stop!"

With a crunch and an "ouch," I spindled into a pile of dry brush, most of my weight on my left shoulder and my legs splayed above me. Anyone hiking by would have had to laugh—I laugh at it now, this completely undignified posture, but in that moment this was nothing less than a fiasco. Gingerly—if that's possible in this position and with sharp thorns at every point of grasp—I righted myself and looked up to the trail twenty or thirty feet above. I tried to stand but the mountainside was too steep, so I scrabbled on all fours back onto the trail, adding more scratches and punctures, and damned glad I wore gloves on this hike.

Back on the trail, a white blaze just ahead, my thru-hiker world returned to the reassuring familiar. I retrieved my trekking poles—one had been slightly bent I know not how—dropped my backpack, and bent to inspect the damage, which wasn't as severe as it felt. I had a gash on my right shin—the scar is still there as I write this—but the rest were just scratches and scrapes that would heal quickly enough, along with some punctures that really hurt but would take care of themselves by and by. My biggest concern was poison ivy, to which I am deathly allergic. Poison ivy turns me into an oozing zombie. I have encountered it on every hike, which is why this time I was carrying some prescription-strength steroid cream.

I searched below with foreboding, saw no poison ivy and prayed I'd gotten lucky. It took a few minutes to pick the sticks and briars out of my backpack and kilt. Once that was done I shouldered my backpack, grabbed my trekking poles, and just then Lynx came trotting around the bend, all long legs and strong knees.

"Hey Solo," he said as he passed.

"Hey Lynx."

"How's it going?"

"Oh, it's going great."

"See ya up the trail, man."

"Yeah, see ya."

I breathed a sigh of relief that he hadn't seen me inverted and spread-eagled in the brush below. The way we kept encountering each other, that story would have plagued me all the way to Mt. Katahdin.

I was rattled from then on, as if I couldn't find my center, my eyes always probing far ahead for rocks or other trip hazards. I went over Wesser Bald in searing heat, and then down, down, down to Nantahala Outdoor Center. It was only two o'clock but felt as if a decade had passed since moonset on

Wayah Bald. After a cold shower—cold water is best for removing the urushiol oil of poison ivy; hot water opens your pores to let the stuff in, while soap emulsifies it and spreads it even farther—I went into one of the restaurants for a much needed beer as well as a burger to pacify my stomach.

While there I ran into No Rush and his young, precocious son Crazy Nut. I'd met them days ago—ages ago—while I was taking a break at Tray Mountain Shelter. No Rush so resembled a man named Jason whom I'd worked with years back that when I first saw him at Tray Mountain I had exclaimed, "Jason, is that *you*?"

What followed was a long and interesting conversation that ranged from the doppelgangers we meet on the trail to the current state of the Appalachian Trail Conservancy. No Rush agreed with me that the ATC had taken a wrong turn somewhere during the past few years, and no longer resembled our once beloved Appalachian Trail Conference. What this meant for the future of the Appalachian Trail neither of us could speculate. I was just relieved that I wasn't alone with these concerns.

Father and son lived in the region and were section hiking, retracing lengths of trail that No Rush had hiked many times. Crazy Nut was inquisitive and curious, rare traits for kids these days. The boy was fascinated by thru-hikers, loved to hear trail names, and was definitely proud of his own. No Rush, with his knowledge of the area, showed me a great place to stealth camp right up the river from the N.O.C. The lodging at the N.O.C. consists of dorm-style rooms of four bunks each at a price of eighty dollars. For groups of four this is a great deal since it comes with free showers and the use of a community kitchen, but for a single person it's a little pricey. I stayed at the N.O.C. twice before, arriving after dark and after thirty-plus-mile days. In those circumstances I paid the price and was grateful for the accommodation, but this hike was different. I was happy to stealth camp this time.

No Rush and Crazy Nut took off, I went into the restaurant for another beer, and there was Lynx, holding court with a group of section hikers who were plying him with beer and baskets of french fries while he told his trail stories. I approached to join the group, possibly yogi some beer and food for myself, but was dissuaded by a look from Lynx that seemed to say, "This is my show, go find your own."

So I went outside with my beer, where I met John, a hobbling old man who made my age look like a portrait of youth. John was section hiking, spent, and looking for a place to collapse for the night. I told him about the stealth site, and that others of my tramily might be along. If so we might be able to split a room, we'd have to wait and see.

Hoosier Daddy and Jersey popped out of the woods at six thirty. Brooklyn had thrown down at A. Rufus Morgan Shelter a mile back, apparently after some kind of spat with Jersey, I didn't pry. But that left three of us, plus John, so we pitched in for a room that was now affordable. The trail provides.

We weren't sure in the morning if John had survived. He lay still in his bunk, not a breath of movement to indicate life. In a huddle next to his bunk, we three debated whether or not we should go shake his shoulder, our voices low so as not to disturb him if he were sleeping, reverent in case he was dead. The sun was up but barely. I had been up for more than an hour, treated myself to another shower and foraged for food in the community kitchen. If the food isn't labeled then it's a free-for-all, and there was plenty of it. The only downside this time was that there was no coffee. There was coffee before. I was now packed and ready to make miles, just this to attend to.

I slept well that night, so deeply that I didn't even have to get up to pee, and apparently deep enough to sleep through John's moaning and braying and nocturnal tumbling, which Hoosier Daddy described in detail and of which Jersey nodded his corroboration.

"He fell out of his bunk," Hoosier Daddy said. "It was like he was dying."

"Yeah," Jersey seconded. "And you *slept* through that?"

"Well, I was tired."

"So now what?" Hoosier Daddy asked.

"Hmm. If he's asleep he'll wake up, and if he's dead it doesn't matter. I'm gonna get going. It's a long climb out of this hole. You guys can decide what to do when you're ready to leave."

With that I walked out into the magic hour and began my climb.

The N.O.C. is in a gorge between two long and steep climbs, what I call a *hole*. The climbs are tough whether northbound or southbound, but in the magic hour I could lope up this with seemingly little effort. It would be a different story were I to catch either side in the heat of day. On my southbound thru-hikes I'd reached the N.O.C. after dark, then departed before dawn the next morning, making big miles.

The climb was gorgeous, Cheoah Bald spearing 5000 feet into the new sun, but then the heat came up and I began to drag. The northern slope of that mountain was in a rain shadow, as dry and stifling as a busy kitchen with ovens ablaze. There was no water anywhere that I could find. When I reached Stecoah Gap at one thirty, after only 13.6 miles, I was out of water and at my limit. A cluster of section hikers was sprawled in the only available shade, as listless as dogs on a dusty Tucson street in August. I went over to see if I could yogi some water from them but they only laughed.

"We don't have any," one of them said. "There's supposed to be a water source here but we couldn't find it."

Nor could I. I'd gotten off trail earlier, beating through the bush trying to find this alleged water source but without success. This hole wasn't as deep as the N.O.C., but it was still too steep of a climb to make in the heat and without water.

"Do any of you have bars?" I asked. My phone was useless in that hole.

"I do," a woman said.

"There's a hostel," I told her. "Stecoah Wolf Creek. Let's give 'em a call."

She handed me her phone, I made the call and reached a man named Lonnie, who said he'd be by shortly to pick me up. I spared a moment of guilt, realizing that lately I'd been going hostel to hostel, but in that heat it was easy to push my guilt aside.

"Tell him we'll pay if he'll bring a few bottles of water," someone hollered before I hung up. I did as asked, returned the woman her phone, then stood in the small shade of a tree awaiting Lonnie.

Lonnie, an older gent but not outwardly cynical, arrived within twenty minutes and waved me over. "I got four cases of water in the back," he said. "Pass 'em out, would ya?"

The section hikers ambled over, gratitude if not also salvation on their faces. I downed a bottle before I even climbed in beside Lonnie, had another one at my lips as I searched for the seat belt. One of the section hikers pulled out a wad of cash but Lonnie waved this off. "Just leave what you don't use by the trailhead," he said.

Lonnie dropped me out front of his hostel, said there was a caretaker inside, that he'd be back at five to ferry us to dinner if we wanted, and then he was gone. I had never stayed at Stecoah Wolf Creek Hostel. On previous thru-hikes I was flying through here, racing over the peaks and balds toward the N.O.C. Every hostel has its own culture, its own rules, so I proceeded tentatively until I knew what the rules were here. There weren't many, leave shoes and poles outside, that was about it.

The caretaker was a guy named Shadow whose pronounced Boston accent reminded me of Tollbooth Willy from Hike 1, the Tollbooth Willy who'd had the conjugal visit with his girlfriend at Kirkridge Shelter in Pennsylvania while the rest of us slept elsewhere to give them privacy. Shadow had a sidekick, a sleepy guy named Pope who resembled Tommy Chong in both detail and demeanor. The guy was so stoned that all he could do was sit on the sunken couch, smile blankly, and utter absolute nonsense in the form of earthly wisdom.

I set about my business, food first, a shower, then I lay down for a nap. When I awoke it was five, other hikers had arrived (none from my tramily), and it was time to go to dinner. The prospect of food will rouse a thru-hiker in an instant. I was the first outside to meet Lonnie.

Lonnie dropped us at a family diner up the road, a meat-and-three place that was apparently popular with the local folks. The place was packed. We had to wait for a table, so I went outside into the air while the others stood waiting inside trying to stay out from underfoot of the sole, harried waitress. Lynx came walking up while I was out there, looking dapper and collected in his hiking attire, the button-down shirt and khaki shorts, with not a drop, stain, or any other indication of sweat. His blondish wavy hair was perfect. There was a young woman at his shoulder, and both were being trailed by an older woman. I didn't know whom to focus my surprise on first.

The women were mother and daughter. I'd met them both on the trail an hour or so before Stecoah Gap. I'd met the mother first, came upon her sitting on a log looking not well, and not sweating in that heat.

"Are you all right?" I'd asked her.

"Yes," she answered, but her voice was hoarse, I imagined from dehydration.

"Do you have any water?" I asked then, a little concerned. I had about half a liter left and would share it out if she were in as bad a shape as she sounded.

She waved a small water bottle. "It's okay," she said as if her throat were lined with sandpaper. "My daughter's up the trail, not too far."

"Okay, then," I said uncertainly. "Maybe I'll see you later."

I pushed on, hoping the old lady was really all right and wondering if I should have pressed the matter further. Soon I overtook an athletic young woman who was poking along although she could clearly have been going faster. We were on a thickly wooded down grade that went a long way toward fending off the worst of the heat.

"Is that your mother back there?" I asked.

"Yeah," she answered casually.

"I think she might be dehydrated," I said. "She looked flushed and her voice was hoarse."

The young woman smiled as if at some joke. "She's had plenty of water. I wouldn't let anything happen to my mom. The reason she sounds hoarse is because she just had surgery on her vocal cords. She's tough enough for this trail, I promise."

Now I felt embarrassed. "I guess I should have just minded my own business," I said in a self-deprecating voice.

"No, it's cool," the young woman said. "It's nice to know that some people still care about other people."

I gave her a nod at that and then I pushed on, and now here they were with Lynx, whom I'd run into now more times than I could remember and who deftly placed a proprietary hand on the young woman's shoulder. I see, I said knowingly to myself.

"Hello again," said the mother with a gracious smile, her voice unimproved from earlier.

"Hi."

"Thank you for your concern today. My daughter explained it to you, didn't she?"

"Oh, gosh," I said, flushing. "I should probably learn to mind my own business."

"That's all right," she said. "People need to look out for one another."

I held the center at that moment, and out the corner of my eye I could see Lynx subtly nudging the young woman forward. I yielded to the attention he craved, said a quick goodbye to the trio and walked off a way, feeling no rancor. If I were his age and had his good looks I'd yogi a meal and maybe more with the same alacrity.

Later, crammed around a corner table and with our meals finished, I entertained the group with stories of the Appalachian Trail, the Pacific Crest Trail, and other journeys afoot that I'd made around the world. Lynx came over and joined us. In an instant he commanded the center, my last sentence cut off and left hanging. I laughed to myself and pushed my chair back a few inches so I could observe Lynx at work. This was an art and he was a master. I had to give him credit for that.

Lonnie got me back to the trail early enough the next morning that I could still enjoy the last glimpses of the magic hour. I sped past Brown Fork Gap Shelter, where it turns out that Hoosier Daddy, Jersey, and Brooklyn were even then breaking camp. I wouldn't meet up with them and learn this until later. The day went quickly along serrated ridges, and then the long descent to Fontana Dam, another section I'd only ever known in the pre-sunrise dark.

I made it to Fontana Marina at two o'clock, parched but not as bad as the previous day. The worst of the heat had broken and a peculiar chill wind sometimes wafted across my arms, buffeted by warmer air out of the south. Still, a beer was what I needed. It was early enough that I could cross the dam and get up into the Smokies but I'd decided to join the group for a raft trip on the Nantahala River tomorrow. The marina is where we'd agreed to meet.

I walked down the long dock and into the air-conditioned store, selected a beer and a sandwich, then went outside to the dining area and sat at a table under an umbrella. There were only a few other people out there, who soon got up to leave, and then Lynx walked up.

Gazing at the empty tables and chairs, he looked misplaced, out of his element. Eventually, if not reluctantly, he took a chair at my table. I had just finished my beer and half my sandwich. Lynx had come out of the store with empty hands, but then of course he would have expected some gratis largesse beyond. He eyed my sandwich. I didn't offer.

"Hey Lynx."

"Hey Solo."

He drummed his fingers on the table, looked around as if someone might have materialized in that moment. I resisted asking him what kind of night he'd had. After a period of strained silence, he stood.

"See you around, Solo."

"Yeah, see ya."

I never saw Lynx again.

Hoosier Daddy, Jersey, and Brooklyn showed up an hour later, pleased that I'd decided to go with them on the raft trip tomorrow. Hoosier Daddy brought me up to date on the saga of John, who was not dead as feared but not lively enough to make the climb out of the N.O.C. hole. After a grumpy, indecisive hour of passing gear in and out of his backpack, John had climbed back into his bunk without a word and pulled his sleeping bag over his head. His fate since then was anyone's guess.

Regarding arrangements for tonight, Hoosier Daddy and Jersey had reserved rooms at Fontana Resort, which made my brows arch. That couldn't have been cheap. I yogied a place with them, although I didn't have to work hard for the invitation. A shuttle pulled up after a while and carried us to the resort.

Jersey and Brooklyn shared a room, all handsy and smiles now after whatever spat they'd endured earlier. I crashed with Hoosier Daddy, sacking out on the floor. After showers, we all met at a restaurant, took a table on the terrace, and watched the sun graze the mountain tops beyond. It was a surreal juxtaposition, everyone clean, with city manners and within these luxurious surroundings. I ordered a single malt that also wasn't going to be cheap. Hoosier Daddy and Jersey did the same, which surprised me, Scotch being an acquired taste that has appealed to few people I know. At eighteen years old, Brooklyn was underage so ordered a coke.

The restaurant was out of their top-of-the-line single malt, so we dropped down the whisky list to the next best selection, a Macallan that had been aging for as long as Brooklyn had been alive. The restaurant proved to be out of the Macallan as well, but our eager young waiter was undeterred. He would sprint down the hill to their other restaurant and secure a bottle for us. We all looked over the rail and down that steep hill, examined the whisky list for the next, next best selection but then chose to take the kid up on his offer. It would be a long climb back out of that hole but the kid was game and he'd be burning the calories, not us.

It was half an hour before he came sweating back with prize in hand. In the meantime we snacked on appetizers and got to know one another better. Jersey and Brooklyn were reticent about much of their backstories, but I gleaned that Brooklyn had done a semester at Northern Arizona University, studying what I am not sure, then cut out abruptly to thru-hike the Appalachian Trail for reasons inexplicable and with no previous experience and no gear whatsoever, leaving behind a pair of bemused parents.

Jersey's backstory was similarly vague, some of his youth spent in rural Pennsylvania, the rest on the Jersey Shore. He was a deliberate young man, not prone to idealistic distractions. Before making the journey from distant Jersey to the Deep South, he'd researched every aspect of a long hike. He selected only the best equipment, from his backpack to the hiking shirt he wore, some customized to his personal specifications when manufacturers would accommodate him, and all well-reviewed with glowing online comments. He was an encyclopedia of specifications. He knew the capacity in liters of each pocket of his backpack, the UV rating for his shirt, and the density of the down in his sleeping bag.

But—and here things took a twist—he had originally intended only to hike the Benton MacKaye Trail, the three-hundred-mile precursor to the Appalachian Trail. What his motivation was he never said, and why the Benton MacKaye Trail as opposed to any number of trails closer to home he was likewise nebulous. He and Brooklyn hadn't known each other previously. They met at the R.E.I. in Atlanta, where she was buying all the gear she would be carrying when I first met her. From a planned few weeks on the Benton MacKaye Trail to months and months on the Appalachian Trail, Jersey found himself, well, perhaps distracted.

Hoosier Daddy and I did most of the sharing. I learned that he was going through much of the mid-life turmoil that had driven me to the Appalachian Trail in 2001, and was looking for a similar clarity of mind. He'd quit his job in sales, sensing a stupefying future on that path, and would probably have gone all the way to Mt. K if not for the arrival of his new daughter, whom we dubbed Hoosier Baby. His wife—we called her Hoosier Mama, of course—supported him in this time away from his family, but still he ached for them daily. He only hoped that the distance to Hot Springs would give him enough of what he was looking for, make this separation from his family worthwhile.

Despite his flaming beard, Hoosier Daddy was clean-cut, a model of maturity. He was gregarious, his mild mid-western accent soothing to even the most frayed nerves on the trail. He spoke of music with the enthusiasm of first love, describing himself a decade previous as being fully immersed in that culture. It was hard to envision him in sandals and a tattered Jerry Garcia T-shirt under the sun at Bonnaroo, a beer or a reefer in his hand, but that's the way he described his earlier times.

As for me, I reiterated my belief that the Appalachian Trail was a journey of discovery, not an extreme sport, and that everyone hiking was in search of something whether they knew it or not. I cast astute looks at Jersey and Brooklyn as I made that statement. All I knew for sure, I asserted to the group, was that by the end of their hikes they would have learned something fundamental about themselves.

Silence settled in after that. We sipped our single malts as connoisseurs do, completed a meal that was an evolutionary leap from trail food, left a generous tip for our waiter, then turned in for the night.

The next morning, gathered around our decadently-laden breakfast table, I could have easily concluded that the week I'd spent on the trail so far (Two weeks? Maybe three? I wasn't sure anymore.) had been an illusion. I poured another glass of orange juice, craving vitamin C, ate another pancake, aw heck, and another one after that. More eggs? Why not? Love those sausages.

We met a shuttle out front that carried us back to the N.O.C. We each gazed at the woods as we went, alone in our thoughts, yearning for a reassuring glimpse of a trailhead, knowing that we'd spent two hot days crossing those woods and would now cover that distance in minutes. Life seemed diminished in the face of that.

Donnie Brasco met us at the N.O.C., his engaging smile as inviting as ever. Whatever pain he was experiencing from the wound on his heel was subsumed into his enthusiasm. There would be a wait, he informed us. Others were coming.

Over the course of half an hour, Tortilla and Spreader arrived, all smiles and excitement. Then came Cockadoodle, cheerful under his bulky backpack, glittering things attached all over it as if he were a refugee on the move. And finally Sheila, whom I'd lost touch with back in Georgia. Donnie Brasco had somehow arranged all of this, staying in touch with people, helping organize their shuttles from points all along the trail. It promised to be a fine day, well worth the zero.

And it was. Outfitted with personal flotation devices and careful instructions from Donnie Brasco, we loaded our two rafts atop an N.O.C. bus and shuttled upriver. I'd been on a raft only once before, five years previous on the river Guil in the French Alps. That experience had been unnerving, not from any perceived danger in the whitewater but because I don't like to appear incompetent at anything I attempt. That float had been a last-minute thing that swept me along unsure of the outcome. By my own devices I would have practiced first—alone—until I was sure I knew what I was doing. This time I felt no such trepidation.

We dropped our rafts, splashed in, took up our oars, and paddled along through a mostly gentle flow. Donnie Brasco stopped us in various places to take in the scenery or else jump into the water and let the current sluice us along for a few exhilarating minutes. I declined that invitation, but Jersey and Spreader made the most of it, shrieking in the cold water but grinning all the way. At last we reached the N.O.C. and the end of our day on the water. It was not to be the end of our celebration, however.

In a picnic area along the river, Donnie Brasco had arranged food and snacks. Solace showed up by complete surprise with a car-load of beer. The party was, as they say, on. The revelry was authentic, the companionship and commonality sincere. Cockadoodle was at the bank, gazing at the river in the late-day light, his bulky backpack leaning against a tree. Some kind of guitar protruded from it, as well as a fishing rod. I sidled up with sage advice.

"I've met a lot of hikers who wanted to fish and forage their way down the trail," I told him, "and it never worked out for any of them."

He looked at me, not taken aback but with a confident smile, tugged out his fishing rod, cast, and within a few breaths reeled in a fish.

"I stand corrected," I said in awe.

"I'm not in a hurry," he told me in an easy tone. "The trail's not going anywhere."

There it was, the philosophy I advocated but couldn't practice myself, that it wasn't about the miles but the journey. Cockadoodle's hike could end tomorrow if he felt it was time, that he'd found what he came for. The miles meant nothing, only his experiences along the way. I completely empathized but I had to reach the goal, get to the end no matter the cost. If Cockadoodle's journey were available in pill form, I would have taken the prescription without hesitation.

Donnie Brasco joined us, the harsh odor of his reefer announcing his approach well in advance.

"You said you would do it," he said with a grin.

Back at Wayah Bald, thinking I would never see him again, I had deflected one of his offers with the promise that if we met again I'd give it a go. I hadn't held a reefer to my lips in fifty years, *half a freakin' century!* I remembered that last time well. I was sitting on a street corner in Houston, Texas in 1971 with a pretty girl named Artie Johnson. Nixon was president, we all might get drafted and sent to the Nam in a few years, possession of any amount of cannabis was a felony with stiff consequences, and I didn't care. I only knew that

Artie was paying attention to me and that she had a reefer in her little leather purse, one she was adamant to share. It only took a few hits to send my head spinning, which is why I'd never touched the stuff since. I don't like to lose control of my head. And while I enjoy a good Scotch as often as possible, I indulge in moderation. I don't like to be drunk. Same thing.

Donnie Brasco's gaze was expectant. I looked toward the group, who were all staring my way with various heights of grins, except for Sheila, who wore the matronly look of a disappointed mom. So they were all in on this.

"It's been fifty years, you guys," I whined. Any two of them added together wouldn't have equaled a half century. Still they grinned. "Aw, hell, Donnie. Just make sure I do it right, would ya?"

Clapping and cheers accompanied that first hit, as if I were a virgin at a frat party coming down the stairs with a dreamy look, on the arm of a girl draped in a sheet and with bedroom eyes. Donnie Brasco laughed and slapped me on the back, the reefer made the rounds, and my head soared.

The rest is woozy. We packed up in the twilight, missed our shuttle, then sat on some steps with our swollen heads in our hands. We'd said our good-byes earlier, to Spreader and Tortilla, who'd hugged us each with affection; to Cockadoodle, who wandered off afterward and was never seen again; to Sheila, prim and with that same disapproving look but she still passed out a few light hugs. This was our tramily at the ends of their trails, now only the four of us to carry on and we'd missed our shuttle while screwing around with inebriants.

Solace came over with a box of unclaimed beers that would go far to gain him favor with his next group of thru-hikers. "I can give you a ride," he said.

We all perked up at that. My head was now firmly enough resettled that I could recognize the enormity of his offer. Driving us back to Fontana would take him miles and miles out of his way. He probably wouldn't make it home until after midnight, and then he'd be up early the next morning running shuttles. We took him up on his offer and were glad for it, but I felt bad all the way. Partying is fun, but it does often tend to affect other people one way or another.

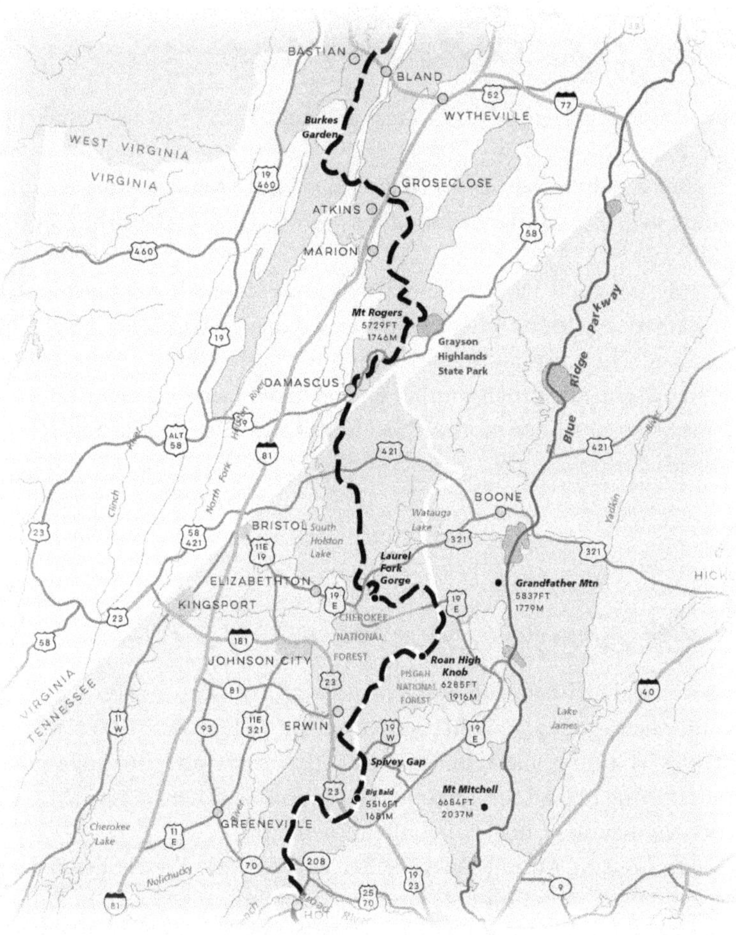

TENNESSEE/ NORTH CAROLINA/ TENNESSEE

292.5 MILES

FRIDAY, MAY 28, 2021

Mollies Ridge Shelter - 13 Miles

Slept straight through to 6:00 a.m. Amazing. Today will be a challenge, I think. Rain is on the way.

Didn't get underway until 9:30, but made good time despite the rain. Everything wet. Thankfully the rain did slack off once I started the climb into the Smokies.

A gray and chilly day of climbs. Arrived at Mollies Ridge Shelter at 4:10 p.m. Wanted to push on, but the rain started up again and there were storms on the way. There was already a section hiker in the shelter. Hoosier Daddy showed up soon after, then another section hiker, then four more, then Jersey and Brooklyn, then two more section hikers and more on the way. It will be a crowded shelter tonight.

SATURDAY, MAY 29, 2021

Double Spring Gap Shelter - 19.5 Miles

It wasn't a bad night after all, everyone respectful of everyone else. It was pouring rain when I got up, so didn't get started until a little after 7:00 a.m.

This was a long, hard, wet and cold day. Jersey and Brooklyn got out ahead, starting to find their legs now. I was proud of them. They take a lot of breaks, though, so I caught up to them by and by.

Made stops at Russell Field Shelter and Derrick Knob Shelter just to warm up. A lot of section hikers on the trail and in the shelters, throwing down early because of the weather, which is dripping continuously and has become much colder.

Not much else to say. I have always pulled Double Spring Gap Shelter to Fontana in one hike, but not this time. The trail really wore me down today.

Made Double Spring Gap Shelter at 6:00 p.m. Lots of section hikers, so many that I'm tenting. Some of those section hikers have been here since noon, their sleeping pads laid out and their territories claimed while we did three times their miles in the rain. One lady is wearing pink pajamas. She barked at me when I sat to rest out of the rain next to her sleeping pad, as if she owned the floor of the shelter.

The rest of the tramily crowded into the shelter. I bet I have the better night.

SUNDAY, MAY 30, 2021

Newfound Gap - 10.5 Miles

Damn freezing cold this morning, so cold that my fingers were too numb to operate my stove. I am astounded that this bag liner is keeping me warm. I was fine while curled up in it, using my kilt as an extra blanket, but my fingers went numb the moment I exposed them to the air.

After muddling through a late start, took off for Newfound Gap and a new plan from the tramily to resupply and overnight in Gatlinburg. I guess I could have objected since I have always avoided Gatlinburg while hiking. Short miles, too. My Smokies transit plan is blown, but I like hiking with these people. We'll make up the miles later.

I hiked most of the day with Hoosier Daddy. Went down twice on slippery rocks and roots. In one fall I felt a sharp burning in my right shoulder and was terrified that I'd torn my rotator cuff again. Curiously though, after some minutes, the pain went away entirely, including the nagging ache I've been nursing all along.

Reached Newfound Gap at 2:00 p.m. and met trail angel No Hitch, a 2017 nobo, and his friend Laf. The two were handing out beers and food in the parking area. A section hiker (and former thru-hiker) named Monkey Man drove us down to the N.O.C. in Gatlinburg, where we all bought a few things.

Later, ate dinner at a brewpub—good food and beer—then set out for resupply. Now it's 9:00 p.m., I'm showered and very tired. We are all crammed into this room, including Monkey Man, who has a long drive home to Ohio, I think, and wants to get a little rest before he pulls out after midnight.

Jersey and Brooklyn are in one bed—what are their hands doing under there?—and Hoosier Daddy and Monkey Man are in the other. I'm sacked out on the floor.

MONDAY, MAY 31, 202

Tri-Corner Knob Shelter - 15.1 Miles

Woke up at 5:00 a.m. feeling well rested. Monkey Man left at 2:00 a.m. Used the morning hours to dry my tent on the railing outside. Got everyone up at 6:00 a.m. then went for breakfast. Dodged a bear that was rooting in a dumpster, the only bear we've seen in the Smokies so far.

Unable to get a hitch with this many people, we finally called a taxi to take us up. Started hiking at 12:30. Moved out fast in perfect weather, and stayed ahead all day. The trail was uncrowded after Charlies Bunion, where I stopped in to pay homage to Freewind. Gorgeous views finally, in weather that had become inspiring. I didn't even sweat much.

Arrived at Tri-Corner Knob Shelter at 6:30 p.m., full of section hikers, weekenders, &c. Hoosier Daddy, Jersey, and Brooklyn showed up about an hour later. I passed out a lot of trail names today. Everyone seems to approve of my choices.

Turning in at 8:30. Standing Bear Hostel tomorrow.

—

The Great Smokey Mountains were next. With some of the highest peaks on the Appalachian Trail, the Smokies are the bugaboo, or *boogerbear* in southern slang, of the northbound thru-hiker. I had boogerbears too, but all in the state of Maine. The Smokies for me were familiar and unintimidating. I'd been hiking in and out of them since I was an early teenager. On southbound thru-hikes I got across them in two and a half days. Not so on this thru-hike but I hadn't got my trail legs yet. And I enjoyed hiking with my tramily, making their miles to keep us all together.

The bonding we'd experienced over the past few days was new for me on the Appalachian Trail. The social aspect of the trail had always eluded me, but now I was in it and I cherished the experience. From Fontana until mid-Virginia I would hike with one or more of these people. I wouldn't pull away. I wouldn't make the big miles unless they did too, and I found I was satisfied with that, perhaps even grateful. For a time, which seemed an eternity then but poignantly brief in retrospect, I was able to temper my impatience.

Our diminished tramily shuttled back to Fontana Marina the next morning at a little after nine o'clock, just as spits of rain evolved into a chill, lazy drizzle. This was a miserable way to begin our ascent into the Smokies, when minutes before we had been loitering around a resplendent breakfast, warm and dry. I'm certain that some of them were rethinking an excursion in this weather, the first rain of the hike so far. It's too easy to rationalize another zero day, especially in gloom like this.

"This won't be our last rain," I let them know. "Or the worst." Beads of water were skirting off my kilt, dry underneath, just as I had hoped.

We all shouldered our backpacks, took to the short wooded section of trail that parallels the road between the marina and the dam, and within the first few steps had returned to trail mentality, Fontana resort already receding into distant memory.

Shuckstack Mountain was the first climb, 2000 feet in about three and a half miles. Every time I'd come down this I'd stood aside for nobos making the climb, thinking to myself as I watched them huff and puff that I was sure glad I wasn't a nobo. But now I *was* a nobo, making that climb, and it wasn't that bad after all. I felt the old juice while going up that mountain, light on my feet, unstoppable. The rain had let up although the woods were misty and dripping. My kilt, to my continued satisfaction, remained dry.

There had been a ridgerunner parked at the trailhead beyond the dam, a sight that caught me off guard. In all my miles I'd never seen a ridgerunner staking out a trailhead. He was a young, outdoorsy guy, missing a leg but in no way hobbled. However long that leg had been gone, he'd adapted, looked as if he could have taken off up Shuckstack right then if he'd had a mind to. He hopped off his tailgate, the bed of his truck jammed with camping gear, and gestured me over. Now I had that itchy feeling I get in national parks.

On thru-hikes, the trail becomes a green tunnel that seems endless and borderless, trees merging into trees, a rocky top here and there, but a continuum regardless, a place where one can dissolve into an unregulated expanse. "There are no rules on the Appalachian Trail" is a mantra voiced by many, but there are rules, especially in national parks. I've worked at national parks, I admire the National Park Service, but their mission is to preserve their park, their resource, not to pander to an annual parade of adventure seekers; and while park rangers are almost uniformly courteous and professional, they remain representatives of the United States government, a government that is too often inflexible and capricious. At a word, a trail could be closed. I've never experienced it but I've read about it. I didn't want to become the next thru-hiker who had to shuttle around a section because of bureaucracy.

It wasn't as bad as all that. This ridgerunner was a remnant of the Covid closures, inquiring about vaccination status and health awareness. By now, those of us on the trail felt so far removed from Covid as to give it no thought whatsoever. All of my tramily had been vaccinated, as had everyone I'd met. To us the crisis was, if not over, at least far away. The president had relaxed restrictions just recently, his directive simply hadn't filtered through the bureaucracy to this ridgerunner yet, which was okay. He got to be paid to work outdoors. I would have ridden that rail as far as I could, too.

It remained gray and chilly all day, growing colder toward the later afternoon. I reached Mollies Ridge Shelter a little after four o'clock and with plenty of light left in the day to go farther, at least to Russell Field Shelter another 3.1 miles on. There was a section hiker in shelter already, sleeping pad and bag laid out, wet clothes hanging from every nail. I stopped in to talk with him, and then the sky opened in a deluge, putting an end to any more miles that day.

Hoosier Daddy came dripping in shortly thereafter, chipper despite the conditions. For him, he'd just made a grueling series of climbs in wicked weather, and he'd endured, something to be proud of. We emptied our backpacks and laid out our sleeping bags. More section hikers came in, then more, then Jersey and Brooklyn. We had a full shelter, a damp, close night ahead, but these section hikers were all open and enthusiastic, intrigued by thru-hikers and also in a little awe of us. We spent a good night together.

The next day was a Saturday. One of the section hikers informed me of that. Somewhere in my mind I knew it was a weekend, but I couldn't have pinpointed the actual day without looking it up. Saturday meant that there would be a lot of people on the trail, which meant that our evening bivouac would probably be uncomfortable.

The tramily were finding their legs now, or at least the confidence to push themselves a bit more. Hoosier Daddy wanted to make for Derrick Knob Shelter at 12.1 miles away, while I held out for Double Spring Gap Shelter at 19.5 miles. Such a distance, a functional twenty miles, seemed unreachable to them, but I encouraged them on, reminded them that on southbound thru-hikes I was able to pull Double Spring Gap Shelter all the way to Fontana in one hike. Once achieved, I told them, miles would never intimidate them again. Why not give it a go?

It didn't help that it was pouring rain in the morning. I will hike in rain—we all do, it's a fact of trail life—but I'm loathe to walk out into it first thing. If it catches me on the trail so be it, but to choose to be soaked through before even a first step is a different matter. I loitered in shelter hoping for a break in the rain. At seven o'clock I gave up and hiked into it. The others followed soon after.

It was a miserable day, cold and getting colder, drizzling on and off throughout. There is no magic hour in the rain, only hollow breath in the hood of a rain shell and splash after splash on a trail now running like a stream. Jersey and Brooklyn caught me from behind, the first time they'd ever been able to do that, which infused me with a sort of pride laced with melancholy. They were gaining confidence, pushing themselves harder, hiking faster, and I thought my mentoring played a part in that; but at the same time this meant that one day, perhaps soon, their youth would get them too far ahead and I wouldn't be able to stay with them. These melancholy thoughts dissipated when I caught up to them later. They were boiling noodles under a spruce that was shedding the rain like a teepee. They stopped often for breaks, while I only took short breaks every two to three hours. There was time, then. We would still be together for a while.

Section hikers had kindled fires in the fireplaces at Spence Field and Derrick Knob Shelters. I stopped at each to warm up. Drying out wasn't going to happen. At Derrick Knob Shelter I was practically numb. Hoosier Daddy came in while I was at the fire, an unexpected show of stamina from him. He shouldered next to me and held pruned fingers toward the warmth.

"Wanna throw down here after all?" I asked him. The shelter was a little crowded but there was still room for all of us if Jersey and Brooklyn were getting a move on. We were miserable and I'd pushed them into this. I'd call it a day if Hoosier Daddy agreed.

"Naw, man," he said. "It's still early. Let's keep going."

There was that pride again, Hoosier Daddy wanting to push for miles when only days ago he would probably have called it quits right here. We shouldered our backpacks and turned for the trail, the section hikers looking at us as if we'd lost our minds, if not also relieved that there might be more room for them in the shelter that night. There were 7.4 more miles ahead, with climbs to near 6000 feet, but I knew without reservation that we would make them.

When you set that goal, really embed it in your brain, the last few miles can seem interminable. Distance defies you. Surely you should be there by now. A fallen tree way up the trail resembles the pitch of a shelter roof, so you breathe a sigh and kick it up a step, only to deflate abjectly when you realize your error. Mirages materialize in the mist, canted shapes of shelter that dematerialize as you draw closer. You swear you hear the voices of people under a dry roof, round a bend and discover that what you heard was only the tinkling chime of water.

I reached Double Spring Gap Shelter at six o'clock, stumbled into it out of the mist before I realized it was there. I hurried under the eave. A father-son pair of section hikers were struggling to get a fire going. Sleeping pads and bags filled the bottom deck, two or three guarded feet between each, and with a few already laid out on the upper deck as well. I dropped my backpack and sat wearily, too numb to know what to do first. A woman in—I kid you not—pink pajamas and furry slippers paused to confront me. I was in her way, this was her space. Would I move please? (Not asked politely.)

There is often animus between thru-hikers and section hikers, two tribes in constant friction. Section hikers might assume that thru-hikers are lordly prima donnas who demand an entitled place on the trail. Thru-hikers might assume that section hikers are amateurs who make short miles and take up more than their share of resources. For my part I have most often tried to ameliorate this disparity. When we encounter another hiker on the trail, our first question is generally, "Are you a thru-hiker?" Many section hikers will feel inferior when meeting a thru-hiker, and will answer with a deprecating, "No, I'm only a section hiker," to which I will always reply, "Well, you're *only* hiking the same trail I am." Whether this makes them feel better I don't know, but I do try.

At the core of it, the more people there are out in the woods—the closer we come to MacKaye's vision—the better it is for all of us, the better for advocacy, and for the appreciation of wilderness. Problems arise because thru-hikers have held sway for seventy years on a trail originally designed for section hiking, long enough to establish a culture and etiquette, violations of which can lead to hard feelings. An example is a section hiker going five miles and then crowding into a shelter at noon, seven or eight hours of daylight remaining, while thru-hikers are pushing the big miles they must make in order to reach Mt. K before its closing date in October. Many thru-hikers arrive near dusk, weary, often addled by low blood sugar, and are confronted with full shelters of surly and proprietary attitudes. I've witnessed near-fistfights when thru-hikers are in this state, and have almost been drawn into them myself.

In Great Smoky Mountains National Park it doesn't help that section hikers make reservations to stay in the shelters, which gives them that proprietary air, and that thru-hikers must yield the space to them even if the section hiker arrives well after dark. I've listened to thru-hikers grouse about this. It should be just the other way around, they say. Section hikers are lightweights, after all, incapable of big miles and they really don't know what they're doing anyway.

While I've had my own testy moments, I still can't sanction this philosophy. Hoosier Daddy was a section hiker, as were the rest of the tramily we left at the N.O.C. They were and are dedicated hikers, serious about their outings and making the most of their time on the trail.

The distinction is really in definition. Section hikers, as defined by the ATC and others, are people who intend to complete the Appalachian Trail eventually but are doing it in sections. Who we are grating against are not section hikers, but day hikers or weekenders, people with no or only a limited knowledge of trail culture and etiquette. These are the people who shoulder-check you when you're making a climb, set up their tents in shelters, stop and unload for breaks in the middle of the trail, refuse to step aside when you come up behind them, burn plastic or foil in the fire pits, scrunch and crunch on their inflatable mattresses, toss food to the bears, claim enough space in shelter for three people, and prance around in pink pajamas and furry slippers as if they were booked into a B&B. There will always be dicks on the trail, but most of these people would probably alter their behavior if they were educated in trail etiquette, which must be provided by a governing authority such as the ATC, not by the weary, addled thru-hiker on the spot.

If they weren't thru-hiking, it was easier to refer to them as section hikers, but pink pajama lady was no section hiker. I found that I loathed even the idea of her out on the trail with us. Great Smoky Mountains National Park, as a balance for the section hiker reservation system, allows thru-hikers to tent near the shelters *at discretion*, which is what I chose to do right then rather than spend a night with someone as ridiculous as pink pajama lady. I wasn't concerned about bears, my backpack and food bag would be hung high in the bear cables before I turned in for the night.

The rest of my tramily arrived, then went about the business of heating food, hanging things up to dry (which would never happen in that kind of weather but we go through the motions anyway), and getting to know the people they'd be sleeping next to. I was in my tent by then, not so far away that I couldn't hear their voices. The rain eased and then stopped, just a melodic pattering of drips from the trees. Darkness deepened around us, I began to nod off, and then I heard from the shelter in a voice I didn't recognize, "*Dude! Your shoes are on fire!*" I didn't have time to contemplate what that meant because soon thereafter I was fast asleep.

The next morning was my coldest yet. It wasn't freezing, but nearly so. For the first time, I'd found the limit of my down bag liner. Awoken and cold in a deep, still night, I'd draped my kilt around my shoulders, which provided just the extra insulation necessary for me to sleep through the remainder of the night in comfort.

I lay in the pre-dawn dark, eyes wide, reluctant to break the warm seal around my body. It was the need to pee that finally drove me from this state. Even clothed as I was, the frigid air assaulted me. My fingers were numb before I'd even finished venting into the bushes, so stiff by the time I got back to my tent that I couldn't operate my stove. Hot coffee might have revived me, but I simply couldn't make it happen. I gave up in frustration and began packing up, my lifeless fingers an impediment to that task as well. It took a while.

Hoosier Daddy eventually wriggled out of his bag to confront the cold. The others were curled up fetal in theirs. Brooklyn, I noticed, had drawn a spot next to pink pajama lady. I wondered with a laugh how their night had gone. Brooklyn wasn't visible, just a bulge in her bag, like a torpid snake that has swallowed a rabbit whole. Pink pajama lady's bag was quivering as if in Brownian motion, the woman inside shivering. Perhaps this would teach her to wear appropriate outdoor clothing next time.

Hoosier Daddy had control of his hands, so he made coffee for the both of us. The protein bar I ate for breakfast was so hard that it hurt my teeth, but

I did get it down thanks to Hoosier Daddy's coffee, and with that it was too cold to just stand around so I got going.

Last night's extreme cold promised a clear day ahead. I paused to bathe in the first rays of morning, coaxing warmth from those few photons that filtered down to me. My fingers were still numb, too stiff to bend around my trekking pole handles, so I held the poles in the crook between thumb and index finger. My feet were leaden, and my pace couldn't be called a pace at all, just forward momentum. Hoosier Daddy caught up to me, as resilient in the cold as I might have been at his age.

"They were still in their bags when I left," he said with a chuckle, referring to Jersey and Brooklyn. "And get this: last night somebody knocked Jersey's shoes into the fire."

"Really?" So that's what the commotion had been about.

"Yeah, and I mean it melted the heel totally out of one of them."

"Man, that's too bad."

This is the reason I never try to dry my things near a fire. After the worst of weather, the sun will eventually come out, and when it does it will dry things quickly and thoroughly. I prefer to wait for that rather than risk what had just happened to Jersey. Now we were going to have to go into Gatlinburg so Jersey could buy new shoes.

I've been to Gatlinburg more times than I can remember, but I'd never gone there during a thru-hike. It's a gaudy place, we all know that. My friends and relatives who come to visit always want to go there, and I have accommodated their wishes even though the crowds in Gatlinburg make my skin crawl. I can attest that I first visited Gatlinburg an almost even fifty years ago, another memory in a half-century increment, and that it looked pretty much the same then. There have been efforts, especially after the fire in 2016, to bring a bit more authentic culture to the place. There are some nice brewpubs now, some restaurants worth visiting even if you aren't thru-hiking, but the crowds remain, and for a solitary thru-hiker just out of the woods this can be disturbing, unnerving.

But Jersey needed shoes. This was the decision and I intended to stay with my tramily. So Newfound Gap would be our destination today, where one can get an easy hitch into Gatlinburg. This would mean short miles at 10.5, but so be it.

The sun continued to rise, broken by billowy cotton clouds that seemed close enough to grasp and keep. My fingers thawed, although a chill gust when the sun was occluded by a cloud would threaten to stiffen them again. Hoosier Daddy and I hiked together at a leisurely pace, in no hurry now that the day would be short and with no idea how far back Jersey and Brooklyn were. We were just going along, the trail damp but no longer running as it had been yesterday, when my feet went out from under me for reasons of which I am still not sure, and down I went toward a face-plant on a slick gray rock.

I got my right arm out in a stiff-arm to absorb the blow, impacted hard and felt a burning, numbing jolt shoot through my shoulder. I lay on the trail with gritted teeth as the waves of pain coursed, knowing with dread that I'd done serious damage to my already damaged rotator cuff, and still present enough in mind to fear that this might be my hike-ending injury, right here in the Smokies, two hours from home and only two hundred miles or so into the hike.

I lay there with these thoughts, Hoosier Daddy at a loss what to do, retreating into myself at certain failure. I should have worn a brace, the way I do on the right ankle I permanently damaged on Hike 2. I should have done something to forestall this. I'd known I'd fall sooner or later, possibly impact that arm at just the right angle to destroy the shoulder. The pain from Hike 3 had never really gone away. It had lessened, for sure, but there was always a twinge deep inside to remind me that my shoulder would never be strong again. I couldn't throw overhand anymore, I couldn't reach back to scratch my neck without that twinge stabbing deeper.

"Solo, are you all right?" Hoosier Daddy's look of concern was simultaneously genuine and helpless.

I grimaced, pushed myself up on my forearms. "Walk it off," that's what The Dude would say. He'd laid his leg open to the meat in Vermont on Hike 1. I wanted to get him out to a doctor, but he just tied a bandana around his wound and then limped on, leaving sprinkles of blood on the rocks. "It's cool, Solo," he said. "I'll walk it off."

Now on my knees, Hoosier Daddy gave me a pull and I got to my feet. The pain in my shoulder was fading quickly, amazingly, startlingly. I rolled that shoulder a few times and then the pain was gone—*all gone*, even the twinge that had plagued me since Hike 3! "What the hell?" I exclaimed. Whatever damage I'd done to my shoulder on Hike 3 to cause my chronic pain, a shoulder that had been X-rayed, MRIed, and diagnosed as everything from bursitis to an actual tear, was completely gone and remains so to this day. I'd been cured not by modern medicine, but by an Appalachian Trail mishap.

My grimace turned into a grin. "I'm good, man." I said. "Let's go."

So we went. A dozen steps, maybe two dozen, and down I went again, this time falling backward. My backpack took the impact but rolled me in such a way that my legs were splayed in the air above, the way they'd been when I fell off the mountain in North Carolina, and I couldn't right myself, just flopped around like a turtle on its back while Hoosier Daddy saw what he'd rather not have seen and I couldn't do a damn thing about it.

"Aw hell," I muttered in disgust.

"Here, Solo." Hoosier Daddy got me to my feet again and was kind enough to pretend he hadn't seen what he'd just seen.

"That's it!" I spat in frustration and anger. "I am *not* going down on this trail again."

Would it were so.

We reached Newfound Gap at two o'clock, sprinted across the road to avoid being hit, then passed through the long file of cars circling for a place to park. Newfound Gap was packed as always. This was a crowd I didn't mind, though. On every hike, even in the worst of weather, I'd been able to yogi just about anything I wanted from the visitors at Newfound Gap, who stop for the view but are then treated to tales of the renowned Appalachian Trail. They are aware of the trail because they saw Redford's movie.

"And it's right here?" they ask in serendipitous disbelief.

"Yeah. See that white mark on that rock over there?" I'm pointing back across the road. "That's the Appalachian Trail."

"It's so *close*."

"Uh, huh."

"Are we allowed to walk on it?"

"Sure."

"Is it safe?"

"Pretty much."

"You look hungry. Would you like a sandwich and a coke?"

"Sure I would."

"We have some beer but you probably don't want that."

"No, a beer would be great. How many sandwiches do you have, anyway..."

We didn't need to yogi this time. A trail angel named No Hitch, a 2017 nobo, was passing out food and drinks from the back of his SUV. He had drawn a crowd of hikers, who were sitting against their backpacks or else flopped out to soak up the warmth from the pavement.

"Check it out, Solo," Hoosier Daddy said with glee. I think this was his first trail angel experience. We joined the throng and got to work on the goodies, which included beer, of course.

We spent an hour of camaraderie and conversation before Jersey and Brooklyn showed up. No Hitch and his buddy Laf were giving back, the insatiable gratitude most thru-hikers continue to feel even long after their hikes. That file of cars was still circling, some of the same faces giving us the same curious looks as they went by. Eventually it was time to go. Monkey Man, a slim young guy Jersey and Brooklyn had befriended a while back, had a car parked at Newfound Gap. He offered us a ride into town so we all piled in.

Monkey Man was an interesting guy. A former thru-hiker, he was out this time doing a section, needing the trail but without enough time to thru-hike again. I understood his emotions intimately. I've section-hiked the Smokies a few times myself, and for the same reason.

The others didn't understand my reservations about Gatlinburg. Dodging, elbowing, and shouldering through the crowds didn't rattle them the way it rattled me. For them, Gatlinburg was a plush oasis, a place to get food, a shower, and for Hoosier Daddy, CBD oil. For a time they could be normal again. For me the trail was normal, all the rest of this just a waypoint of confusion and noise. If I could live on the trail and still do the things I needed to do in life, I probably would. By the ends of their hikes, they would finally come to understand this.

For now, Jersey bought his shoes. I advised him again to buy a shoe a half size larger. He had been dubious of this earlier in the hike, but now, he said, after hiking in a shoe that didn't have a heel, he could feel the benefit of not having so much pressure on the back of his foot. He went for the larger shoes and stuck with that size in every pair of shoes he bought from then on.

Then it was time for food, and for resupply, and all the things a thru-hiker has to do when in town. It wasn't until nine o'clock that we all crammed into our motel room, deferring gallantly to Brooklyn for the first shower. I was exhausted, more from the town than the trail, and sacked out on the floor by the front window while the others carried on. Jersey and Brooklyn jumped playfully into one bed, while Hoosier Daddy took the other. Monkey Man was still with us. He knew that the sixty-odd miles of highway between Gatlinburg and Interstate 40 would be jammed bumper to bumper on a Sunday, thousands of tourists turned for home. He had a long drive home himself, to Ohio. He wisely assumed that it would be better to get a few hours of sleep and then depart in the still of the small hours rather than sit in traffic for a good part of the day, and he assumed correctly. When I drive to Gatlinburg, I never come in via I-40 anymore, haven't in a decade or two. I sneak in the back way via Maryville and Townsend. That route would have taken Monkey Man a hundred miles or more out of his way, though, so his plan was the best.

I awoke when Monkey Man departed at two in the morning, bumped fists with him and wished him well, recognized the longing in his eyes even in our darkened room. He was desperate to stay, to keep hiking, but his life was calling him elsewhere.

Dawn rose cerulean over Gatlinburg, chilly but not uncomfortably cold, the promise of great hiking ahead. I was up at five o'clock, watched a bear rooting in a dumpster across the way, draped my tent over a rail to dry, made coffee outside with my stove, then set about to rouse the others, drawing mumbled protests and sighs of indignation. I wasn't impatient, that wasn't it. If we'd been on the trail I would have just taken off, leaving them to sleep in and catch up when they would, but we were in town, our fates were bound, and this rising morning was too remarkable to waste.

At six o'clock they reluctantly roused. At seven o'clock we were waiting in line at a popular breakfast joint. At eight o'clock we were finally eating. At nine o'clock we were finally finished. At ten o'clock we were out of the room. At eleven o'clock we were standing along Highway 441 at the park entrance, thumbs out for a hitch back to Newfound Gap. The day was brilliant but ebbing all around us, our first clear and dry day in the Smokies ticking away as car after car whooshed past without a sidelong glance. At noon we gave up and called a taxi.

I didn't dally at Newfound Gap, just shouldered my backpack, took up my trekking poles, and got moving. It was twelve thirty, a ridiculously late start but I still held on to the fantasy that I could cover the twenty-four miles through Davenport Gap to Standing Bear Hostel by sunset. I have been fond of Standing Bear Hostel since Hike 2, when Curtis Owen, the founder, put me in a plush cabin at no extra charge well after dark after I'd pulled another of my thirty-plus mile days. That comfort was restorative after a long, hard hike. I have always appreciated Curtis's sincerity and concern. I learned on Hike 3 that Curtis had passed away, which shook me even after the ten years between those thru-hikes. I paid my condolences to his wife, Maria, who was keeping the place going. It was possible she might remember me. I would certainly remember her.

The trail was crowded with all manner of people humping up to Charlies Bunion. There were the typical day hikers with their fluorescent day packs, babbling foreigners of every stripe, and a parade of peculiar people dressed in nineteenth-century wool and cotton. I went through them, around them—at one point at a blowdown I went *over* them, a leap no less agile than O.J. Simpson's in those 1970s Hertz commercials, long before he disgraced himself.

Well ahead of the throng, I had Charlies Bunion and its magnificent views to myself. This had been Freewind's favorite place in the Smokies, where a hawk had ridden the thermals close enough for Freewind to see into its eyes. I'd scattered some of Freewind's ashes there on Hike 3, so stopped to reminisce and pay my respects. I had maybe ten minutes of reflection before voices began to sound behind me. I quickly collected my pack and poles, then slipped out while the solitude still held.

The day went long, the views too gorgeous to pass at speed, so it wasn't until six thirty that I reached Tri-Corner Knob Shelter at 15.7 miles. An early start and I would have made Standing Bear Hostel without difficulty, but

Tri-Corner Knob Shelter was far enough on this particularly inspiring day. The others would make it here feeling as equally enervated, and then we could all go together to Standing Bear Hostel tomorrow, the Great Smoky Mountains behind us.

The shelter was full, some of the people a little surly. I pitched my tent and waited for my tramily, who came in together about an hour later. We all tented, Hoosier Daddy saying he'd carried a tent all this way and had never used it. I gathered them together for an important ritual.

Jersey and Brooklyn—Ron and Katy—had never been given proper trail names. Their default origins had served until now, but they had both hoped to eventually receive original, more descriptive trail names. They were adhering to the tradition of receiving their trail names from someone else, another point of pride for me. I went to Brooklyn first. She was sitting on a rock, looking up at me with quizzical brows.

"Your trail name," I said in a voice of pomp and moment, "will now be K-Bar until someone comes up with something better."

"*K-Bar?*" she questioned, clearly confused. "What does *that* mean?"

"K-Bar is a razor-sharp knife to match your razor-sharp wit." She grinned prettily at that. "It could also mean Katy Bar the Door when you finally figure out what a strong hiker you are."

This observation did prove prescient. K-Bar would eventually pull successive thirty-mile days, and she would complete the forty-plus-mile Four State Challenge from Virginia to Pennsylvania, and tack on a few extra miles for good measure.

K-Bar let her new name roll off her tongue a few times until it felt right, and then she accepted it. I'm proud to write that she kept that trail name all the way to Mt. K.

Next was Jersey.

"Your trail name," I said with matching pomp, "will now be Ultra Burn until someone comes up with something better.

"*Ultra Burn—?*"

I went on to explain before he could say more. "Ultra Burn is from your shoe in that fire, and *Ultra* Burn sounds better than *Altra* Burn." He wore Merrell Altra shoes. "But it can also mean what you're going to start doing to this trail pretty soon, which is to burn ultra miles."

This too proved prescient. Within a week, he'd consistently hike at over four miles per hour, overtaking me by noon despite my earlier starts, holding that lead all the way to wherever we were camping that night.

"Ultra Burn. Hmm. I like it," he said. And as with K-Bar, he kept that trail name all the way to Mt. K.

Ultra Burn, K-Bar, and me

There were also some section hikers and lashers who needed names. I passed out Argo, Delphi, Poison Ivy, and Darth that night. Darth was the guy with the dog, and the dog's name was Vader, so, well...easy choice. These were people we'd been hiking with on and off since Georgia, but I suspected we'd start pulling ahead of them soon, which did eventually prove to be the case so I don't know if they kept their names.

We spent the rest of the evening talking about—what else?—gear. I liked the hell out of Ultra Burn's backpack. My ULA was serving me well, but his Gossamer Gear Mariposa had a long outside pocket for his tent, which allowed him to set up camp without having to empty his backpack first. This was especially useful in rain, where he could pitch his tent and then pull his loaded backpack inside where everything was dry. His backpack also had some nifty clips for storing trekking poles out of the way, a feature that would come in handy for the rock scrambles ahead. He'd done his research well.

Then he pulled out something I'd never seen before.

"What is that?" I asked. "An enema—?"

"No," he spat with a look of impatient disgust. "It's a portable bidet."

"*Bidet?*"

"Yeah."

"So what do you do with it? Stick it up your—"

"No, Solo. Damn, man. You don't stick it anywhere. It sprays water."

"Really?"

"Yeah. They don't cost much. You should get one."

A lesson I would never be able to get across to Ultra Burn was that it wasn't just about the weight you carried in your backpack, but the amount of stuff you carried as well. A lot of lightweight stuff might not add up to much but it was still bulk, clutter, things to lose or break or just generally get in the way. I kept the contents of my backpack to the essential minimum.

And besides, I already had that situation under control.

I have avoided scatological discussions in my previous books because the subject is, well...intrinsically indelicate. There are things we simply do not discuss, but as we are here, in Great Smoky Mountains National Park, a park well known for its dearth of privies, perhaps the time has come.

The standard guidance for defecating while on the trail is to dig a cat hole six to eight inches deep and bury the poop. There are special lightweight trenchers for this, sometimes made of bright orange plastic and sometimes of titanium. I have seen chrome garden spades with heavy wooden handles abandoned in shelters, so people are at least starting out with this in mind.

The trouble is, few people actually dig to the required eight inches, and I'm not sure it would help even if they did. Most often, they scrape away a layer of loam, kick sticks and soil over the deposited poo, and then move on, which leaves the merde easily excavated by varmints, which then run off unfurling wads of scented toilet paper through the woods.

The problem is not the poo, it's the paper.

A thousand if not a million species of beetles exist in the ecological spectrum to deal with bæsj, not to mention a similar panoply of flies. After all, bears go number two in the woods. So do rabbits and coyotes, bobcats and foxes. Birds do it *on* the woods, and moose do it on the trail itself. All this gets cleaned up by beetles and by time, but that unfurled toilet paper, which supposedly breaks down in my septic tank, turns to paper mache in the woods, clinging to trees and bushes for an improbably long time, and looks just nasty.

So I don't use the stuff on the trail, nor do I bury my scheisse.

A peculiarity of the human species is that we tend to concentrate our caca in one place, in a privy for instance, where it makes a malodorous mess that someone has to deal with sooner or later. Well, I guess bats do this too. Peeing in the privy is actually what makes that god-awful smell. So, except on rare occasions, I avoid the privies. Instead I walk into the woods, well away from trail and shelter, and fertilize at will. For clean-up (and when practicable) I will perform what I call a *downstream bidet.* Wearing a kilt is especially helpful in this regard. In lieu of that, a lightweight sports bottle will serve the same function as Ultra Burn's portable bidet.

I explained none of this to Ultra Burn, who would continue to try to sell me on his system for weeks and weeks to come.

Enough said on this topic.

TUESDAY, JUNE 1, 2021

Standing Bear Farm & Hostel - 18.4 Miles

Woke early and cold. It took a while to get moving, but I was on the trail by 6:30 a.m.

Made quick time to Davenport Gap, and then slowed in the few extra miles to Standing Bear Hostel. As cold as it was up in the mountains, it was uncomfortably hot below. Ultra Burn went by me and got there first, I think taking his new trail name to heart. Hoosier Daddy and K-Bar arrived shortly after I did.

Beer, pizza, shower, laundry, long talks around the campfire—I'm feeling pretty well, although sleepy. A hiker named Gandalf who looks like Gandalf gave me his digital watch. My venerable Timex Expedition, which I've had since Anchorage, broke and threw a tiny spring, irretrievable in the duff of the trail, so I left that watch in a discreet place as an offering to the Smokies. I'm lost without a watch, though, unable to time my pace and therefore my miles. I'm grateful to Gandalf for helping me out.

WEDNESDAY, JUNE 2, 2021

Walnut Mountain Shelter - 20 Miles

Slept surprisingly well and late. Apparently there was some kind of drama in the bunkroom last night, someone ejected, but I slept right through it.

Got up a little after 6:00 a.m., coffee, breakfast, another shower (never pass up the opportunity), visited with the others, then got on the trail at 8:00.

Overcast and cool, made quick time to Max Patch, crowded with day hikers and all tracked up now—too bad. Reached our goal shelter at 3:00 p.m. then pushed on for the twenty to here.

Trail conditions excellent and fast despite the climbs, which shows what good trail routing can do. Met a volunteer trail maintainer—Carolina Mountain Club—who was doing trail magic. We thank these folks for their service the same way we thank soldiers for theirs. We talked for a while about the trail, the way the trail is changing. This guy had been a member of the ATC since the 80s, said he missed the old Appalachian Trail Conference, and wasn't sure where the Conservancy was heading.

I pushed on, alone most of the day and at a near 3-mile pace.

Reached this shelter at 5:00 p.m. just as a cold rain was letting loose. The shelter was full of nobos, but cool ones. They squeezed me in so I wouldn't have to tent in the rain, tight but at least dry and warm. Their names: Groot, Mountain Goat, Cinderella, Disco, and Hagrid. They are a tramily. I took the narrow space between the unchinked wall and Hagrid, who was a mild-mannered giant of a guy.

Shared stories and a little whiskey, in the bag for the night at 7:30 p.m. Looking forward to Hot Springs tomorrow. The others didn't catch up today, so I'll see them in town.

THURSDAY, JUNE 3, 2021

Hot Springs, North Carolina - 13.1 Miles

What a windy, raucous night it was. Spattering rain and gusts of chill wind that cut through the shelter. I slept poorly, and Hagrid snored in gusts that rivaled the weather outside.

Woke up—or rather, got up—just before 6:00 a.m., stumbling in the cold fog. Through all the confusion of scattered gear and sleeping thru-hikers, I didn't start hiking until 7:15. The gray morning went fast, faster for the others since they passed me one by one. Afterward I was alone all the way to Hot Springs, which I reached at noon.

I'm staying at Sunnybank Inn again. Elmer is still getting along, although he didn't remember me or the book I sent him after Hike 3. I went for food and beer, overindulged, then was joined by Disco, Groot and the rest. While sharing beers with them, Ultra Burn came in, and then Hoosier Daddy and K-Bar.

After a nap, had a farewell dinner with the Hoosiers, including little Anna Piper, just three months old. Now it's early evening. I'm in my room, tired, and with still a lot to do. If it rains tomorrow I will zero. If nice weather I will nero 10 miles or so.

FRIDAY, JUNE 4, 2021

Hot Springs, North Carolina - Zero

Up at 6:00 a.m. I don't think I've ever slept better, solid for nine hours, no dreams. It's always hard to leave when one feels this well rested, so the hell with it, I'm going to zero.

—

It dawned another cold morning. My fingers were as stiff as the morning before, but with extra urgency I managed to set coffee to boil, urgency because today I would hike out of Great Smoky Mountains National Park and could finally shed that pestering itch.

I was out long before the others, hiking through a chilling fog that was actually the clouds lowering onto the mountain tops. My watch quit working, which left me lost, not lost for my way—the blazes take care of that—but lost for my location on the trail. I could have gone five miles or only two, without my watch I simply couldn't tell. I don't use GPS, I don't use my phone. My watch is my most valuable navigation tool. An analog watch will even double as a compass. When I'm heckled about this by other hikers, I point out all the places I've been where phones don't work: at the bottoms of many a slot canyon in Arizona and Utah, some islands in the Atlantic, some alpine valleys in France and Italy, the hills where I live, swathes of the Appalachian Trail, a big county in West Virginia, and on and on endless. A map and a watch will work in the presence or absence of technology, while technology only works in the presence of itself. The choice seems straightforward to me.

I stopped in a clearing to fiddle with my watch, the crown came out, and the tiniest of springs shot into the leaves and needles, which brought an abrupt end to our journey together right then. I'd worn that watch since Alaska. It had been around the world with me several times, from hiking across the Highlands to biking across Hopi. It had guided me on all of my thru-hikes, and now it had found its end on one. Perhaps this was fitting. I went up into the woods, fastened it around a small limb, and left it as an offering to trail and time.

Soon I began that long, five-mile descent of Mt. Cammerer, the day growing warmer with each downward step, the clouds back up in the sky where they belonged. Ultra Burn went by me on fleet feet, a smug smile on his face. Trail legs do not come on gradually, they miraculously arrive from one day to the next. Ultra Burn had either woken up this morning with his trail legs or else he was trying to live up to his new trail name. Either way, I would be hard pressed to keep up with him from then on.

He was the first in to Standing Bear Hostel, showered and bare-chested in the sun before I arrived.

"Hey Solo," said with barely concealed glee.

"Hey Ultra Burn."

I went first to see Maria, who was feeling unwell at the moment so I put off a visit until later. There had been changes at Standing Bear Hostel, either that or I was again confused in a place I had only ever seen at night. Little by little the layout came back to me. I took a bunk, took a shower, took a beer from the commissary, then joined a diverse collection of hikers around a fire pit: a South African couple, a guy from Jamaica, Ultra Burn, and a man named Gandalf who looked like Gandalf. Hoosier Daddy and K-Bar joined us not long after.

I asked the group if anyone had a watch they would sell to me. My next best opportunity to buy a watch would be in Hot Springs, only two days away but those two days felt infinite in the moment. Gandalf took a digital watch from his wrist.

"Here, you can have this one."

"How much do you want for it?"

He waved that off. "Nothing, it's yours. I can't figure out how to set it anyway."

I thanked him profusely then began to poke at the buttons. I'm an analog guy, I couldn't figure them out either. When this happens to people my age, we pass the project off to the nearest young person. "Here, K-Bar, set this watch for me, would ya?"

She looked at me as if I were asking her to knap flint into a knife. "I don't know anything about watches," she said.

I'd skipped too many generations. "Here, Hoosier Daddy, set this watch for me, would ya?"

Hoosier Daddy had it done in a blink. With a sigh of relief, I fastened my new watch around my right wrist as I had been taught as a youngster by my Army Airborne uncle. Gandalf's watch saw me to Mt. K, and is on my wrist even now.

Conversation turned toward the trail and trail life. "This is where we live now," K-Bar said with a bit of reverence. There was a confidence growing in her. The Great Smoky Mountains, I suspected, were a transition point for nobos, the way the White Mountains were for sobos. Once beyond that Rubicon you'd proved your grit, you owned your hike. Nothing would scare you anymore, except maybe the White Mountains, but I dispelled that fear whenever it was voiced to me. "By the time you get there," I always said, "the White Mountains won't be anything you haven't already done, so don't worry about them."

The evening shaded into the cool of night, the fire now something to inch closer to rather away from. I never did get to see Maria, who remained garrisoned in her rooms behind a screen of protective family and friends. She had a devoted caretaker staff to look after things, so any supervision from her wasn't necessary. I wondered if she was really unwell, or if she had simply grown weary of thru-hikers. With those thoughts, I turned out the lights and climbed into my bunk.

Ultra Burn did not catch me the next day. Our rendezvous was to be Roaring Fork Shelter at 15.2 miles, with Snowbird Mountain and Max Patch in between. The day had become overcast, cool but not gloomy. I made a quick pace on climbs that were routed with a sense of humanity, comfortably taking in views above the cloud layer that would have seen me beaten and weary on other sections of the trail.

Max Patch shone in scattered sunlight, uninterrupted lines of day hikers making their way up as if they were picking along the narrow trail to Machu Picchu. It wasn't easy to get around those people, who possessed no trail savvy at all. Many coming down would jerk to a halt at my feet and eye me for the impudence and temerity of not getting out of their way. Tedious.

The top of Max Patch, that broad grassy expanse, was as tracked up as I'd been told, social trails weaving in and out of one another like tangled string. Max Patch was now closed to camping because of these impacts. Red tape was strung to keep people on the trail, but day hikers hopped over this for their selfies, catching the tape on their ankles and pulling it down. Ribbons of red tape lay twining in the grass, marking newly established social trails. Commenting on this to the day hikers would be futile. I hurried through instead.

Coming down the other side, I met a Carolina Mountain Club volunteer at a trailhead, loading clippers and saw and other tools into his truck after a day of trail maintenance. He was doing magic as well, passed me a beer, took one for himself, and then we sat on a log to talk.

He was about my age, shook his head at the condition of Max Patch. "We've got to educate people," he said. My thoughts exactly.

Our conversation turned, somehow, to the ATC. "I've been a member since '86," he said, "but I don't really recognize them anymore."

"What do you mean?"

"I don't know. It used to be about the trail and the thru-hikers. Now it feels corporate, like it's only about money."

He mentioned a payoff for a pipeline that I'd been unaware of. The way he described it, I told him I didn't think I could blame the ATC for the debacle or for taking the money. What else were they supposed to do? Get steamrolled by lobbyists and conservative politicians? I really didn't have enough information, though.

"So what do you think, then?" he asked.

"We always loved the ATC, but I agree—something's changed, I'm not sure what." As a writer and a thru-hiker, the ATC seemed a logical place for some of my books. I had always been greeted with enthusiasm at the ATC office in Harpers Ferry, but when I called about my books I was brushed off and ignored. After more than a year of unreturned calls and emails, I had finally given up.

"That's what I mean," he said with a sigh. "They didn't used to be like that. I wish we could get our old Appalachian Trail Conference back. Things were better then."

Our conversation had turned morose. I complimented him for the quality of the trail in Carolina Mountain Club country, thanked him for his hard work and assured him that we all appreciated it. With people like him, I said to lift his spirits, whatever was going on at the ATC would only be a passing phase.

That beer powered me to Roaring Fork Shelter by three o'clock, much too early to throw down so I left a note in the register for the others and pushed on to Walnut Mountain Shelter and a twenty-mile day.

The dappled sun of earlier occluded during those next 4.8 miles, the wind piercing cold through the trees, and with splatters of rain that left chill pinpricks on my neck. "Damn, damn, damn," I muttered. I could have been dry and snug in Roaring Fork Shelter if I hadn't pushed on, a shelter that was still closer behind me than Walnut Mountain was ahead but that would mean going backward, which I don't do, so I leaned into the coming weather and surrendered to fate.

Walnut Mountain Shelter is one of the older ones, small, not in great shape. I reached it at five o'clock, just as the sky was getting serious, and found it jammed with hikers. Standing under the eave as the rain and wind picked up in earnest, I dreaded trying to pitch my tent. "Come on in," one of the hikers said. "We'll make room."

I wound up between a big, big guy named Hagrid, and a wall that let the rain through if the wind came in just right. There was a floorboard missing beneath me, but I was able to wedge my hip into the gap and not fall through. I rethought my tent. This promised to be a night as nasty as Eliza Brook Shelter in New Hampshire on Hike 3, when two sobos, myself and Chipmunk, squeezed in with at least a dozen rank nobos as the wind howled and the rain came in as bullets of sleet. We wound up spooning each other to squeeze in another hiker or two who draggled in, and the guy I was spooning, a humorless man from Alaska, had a bout of gas that wouldn't go away.

I looked dejectedly at Hagrid, wondered with dread what he'd had for breakfast, and then just resigned myself to the situation.

The night wound up being not that bad. There were five of them, a tramily of good-natured thru-hikers with no chips on any shoulders. Mountain Goat, their main guy, I assumed, passed around a bottle of Jack Daniels. Groot—from Minnesota, I believe—was a tree of a guy with a permanent smile and a gift for gab. Cinderella was really pretty, and Disco reminded me of Tri-Pad from Hike 3, the guy who taught me how to hike the way I hike now, which is to screen ahead and anticipate every footfall. Tri-Pad got me from two and a half miles per hour to a consistent three and a half on that hike, a respectable pace at any age.

There might as well have been a storm out there the way the wind carried on all night. I will say that Hagrid was warm, and that compensated for a lot. The next morning was dripping and dreary but I got out into it early and carried on toward Hot Springs. Mountain Goat's entire tramily passed me one by one, but this left me alone from then on. Where my tramily was I couldn't guess, but they'd be along sooner or later.

I made Hot Springs by noon and went straight to Elmer's Sunnybank Inn. Elmer is a trail treasure whose knowledge of Appalachia is boundless. His old Victorian inn is full to the ceiling with books and trail memorabilia. Earl Shaffer stayed there and has a room named in his honor. I think most thru-hikers stay elsewhere these days. There were certainly no other thru-hikers in the place when I arrived, although Ultra Burn and K-Bar came in later. Perhaps Covid had something to do with this or perhaps a page was turning on the Appalachian Trail, either way I was glad to find Elmer still getting along even though he didn't remember me.

I met up with the others later at a restaurant, where the day that had always seemed to lie in the infinite future had at last arrived—Hoosier Daddy was going home.

"This is the greatest thing I've ever done," he said with a faraway look, but then caught himself and added, "except for her." He meant his daughter, Hoosier Baby—little three-month-old Anna Piper—and with a nod to his wife, Hoosier Mama. Also in their entourage was Hoosier Mama-in-law. The family would stay a day in Hot Springs, then drive back to Indiana.

For us this was bittersweet. Hoosier Daddy had achieved his goal—we all toasted that—but now there would be just the three of us to carry on. Donnie

Brasco still texted me every few days: *Are you keeping the kids together?* So far I was, but I wondered how long that could last.

I had originally planned a zero in Hot Springs but had pushed that back after the zero at the N.O.C. I woke up the next morning feeling fine and with good weather but—the hell with it—decided to zero anyway. Hot Springs is a nice trail town, good food, good beer. Plus there was laundry to do, resupply, a visit to the library, and the Hoosier family, still in town for one more day. I was finding it hard to let go of that trail friendship. Ultra Burn and K-Bar decided to zero as well. Mountain Goat and his tramily would also be in town until later in the day. They had a ride to Asheboro arranged, where they were going to pub-crawl for a few days.

Ultra Burn, K-Bar, and the Hoosiers sought out the springs for which Hot Springs is named, while I lazed through the day doing chores and browsing Elmer's books. We all met for dinner, where we reprised our good-byes of the night before. This was it then, the somber end. We'd all be pulling out in the morning.

SATURDAY, JUNE 5, 2021

Little Laurel Shelter - 19.4 Miles

Up at 5:00 a.m. Coffee across the street at the diner at 6:00, then off for the trail in the early light.

Got off on social trails above the French Broad River twice, which cost me some unnecessary climbs and quite a bit of time, but otherwise I moved out well in excellent weather. Passed some weekenders, but otherwise alone all day.

Arrived at Little Laurel Shelter at 3:45 p.m. to find it overrun with Scouts. A pair of thru-hikers scowled at this and pushed on, but I went ahead and pitched my tent. Ultra Burn came in at about 6:00 and pitched his tent as well.

Almost 8:00 p.m. and K-Bar hasn't shown up yet. Hope she's okay. Maybe she's camping with that couple she met, Breezy and Midnight, no telling.

Finally, a warm night. I remember this shelter from my last hike, the bear dog and Tropical Storm Florence. Much different this time.

I really miss Hoosier Daddy. No signal here or I would text him.

SUNDAY, JUNE 6, 2021

Laurel Hostel - 17 Miles

Woke up early but didn't break camp until 7:15 a.m. This section of trail was mostly smooth, with rock climbs and nice views on Big Butt and elsewhere.

Moved out fast and well. Reached the hostel at 2:45 p.m., 15 minutes behind Ultra Burn. Hatchett and The Gods came in, a pair of peculiar but likeable guys. Drank beer, ate pizza, rehashed conversation until near 8:00 p.m., and K-Bar had yet to show. Turning in now. Maybe K-Bar will show, maybe not, but if she doesn't I doubt we'll see her again. This makes me sad, but what can I do?

Big Bald tomorrow, then Erwin.

MONDAY, JUNE 7, 2021

Mile 337.7 - 26.2 Miles

Up before 5:00 a.m., hiking by 6:00.

K-Bar, Breezy, and Midnight came in right before hiker midnight last night then stayed up late. I had to get up and give them the "hiker midnight" talk, which sobered them more than I expected. They did quiet down after that. I had a talk with K-Bar. I think she's starting to figure out her hike now.

Made quick, magic hour miles, cool, breezy. Met Argo, Delphi, Darth, and Vader on Big Bald. Beautiful weather and incredible view, although sprinkles of rain would come down from seemingly nowhere off and on all day.

Reached Bald Mountain Shelter, our goal at 16 miles, by 1:30 p.m., so decided to keep going. Before I knew it, it was 7:30! I spotted a stealth site right off the trail, so took it. Ultra Burn came up some time later, asking why I was tenting only .3 from No Business Knob Shelter. I'd been in the zone for so long that I'd lost track of my miles and didn't realize how close I was. I felt stupid, but I was all set up for a good night, water bottles full, food bag up in a tree. I told Ultra Burn I'd see him in the morning, and congratulated him for his first big-miles day.

Only 6 ½ miles to Erwin tomorrow, a nero but so what? Tomorrow's my birthday.

TUESDAY, JUNE 8, 2021

Erwin, Tennessee - 6.5 Miles

Slept well, woke up at 5:00 a.m., broke camp and then hiked the .3 to the shelter in the dark.

Met a Mt. Katahdin sobo named Corn Nut, who was of course the only one up at the shelter. We talked about southbounders, problems with northbounders, &c. Ultra Burn finally got up, and we were on our way by 7:00.

6 ½ miles to Uncle Johnny's, where Charlotte did not remember me. I'm starting to get a complex about this.

Shower, laundry, some beers and snacks. Mailed some cold weather gear home to save weight.

K-Bar hitched out from Spring Gap to be here for a surprise birthday dinner they've planned for me. Very touching that they all thought of me.

Rain in the afternoon and forecast for the week. Gakk! Looking for bigger miles, but K-Bar is 11 miles behind. Afraid we'll lose her.

All in all, an excellent and memorable 63rd birthday. Even Hoosier Daddy showed up! How they managed to organize all of this I do not know. This will be a birthday I won't forget.

63rd Birthday Party
(l-r) Hoosier Daddy, me, K-Bar, Ultra Burn

—

After a zero day, Hoosier Daddy's end-of-trail party, and a lot of eating and drinking, I was again ready to make miles. I walked out of Elmer's Sunnybank Inn and into the enfolding dark of early morning, crossed the street to the diner for coffee and food, and after waiting a while as the staff gradually arrived, learned that the place didn't open until eight o'clock on weekends. Crestfallen is the appropriate adjective.

A woman inside informed me of this through a cracked window, observed my look of despair and then offered to bring a cup of coffee out to me. That perked me up. When she came out she also brought a couple of doughnuts, waving off my attempt to pay. "Don't worry about it," she said. "Happy trails."

So, with renewed optimism I made my way down Hot Springs' darkened and deserted main street toward the trailhead across the bridge, enough caffeine and sugar in my system to see me past sunrise. This was going to be a great day, and it mostly was.

Dawn rose as I paralleled the French Broad River, tufts of mist high in the hollows, a fairytale scene of quiet beauty that I paused to take in and hoped I could faithfully remember. But then I encountered social trails going off to discreet fishing spots or other fulsome views, all amid trail blazing that had become sporadic. Suddenly I was making a steep climb, steep even by Appalachian Trail standards, and then the upward trail melded into the chaos of the woods and I realized I was on a social trail. This is probably one of the most frustrating situations for a thru-hiker. With over two thousand miles to put under our feet, paying for the same real estate twice chafes in a visceral way.

I doubled back, found a mottled blaze that resembled little more than lichen, and proceeded on, only to find myself once again off on a social trail that came to an abrupt end at an unsanctioned viewpoint. The view of the river, the hollows, and a still-slumbering Hot Springs was nice, but I again had to backtrack. Frustration stole the beauty from the moment. Once beyond the river, the blazing became consistent again and I was able to pick up the pace.

It did become a gem of a day, over a trail that gave more than it took. I passed a few weekenders early on but was luxuriously alone with my thoughts for the rest of the hike. My destination was Little Laurel Shelter at 19.4 miles. I was eager, even excited, to reach it.

I spent a memorable night in Little Laurel Shelter on Hike 3. Tropical Storm Florence blew in that night and continued through much of the following day. I had become embedded within a group of flip-floppers who were shuttling up and down the trail, hiking sections in reverse, and following such confusing itineraries that I never knew where they were in their hikes or when I might run into them. Somehow, they managed to show up wherever I was just about every day. Flip-floppers, I discovered, had evolved a tribalism of their own, and there were a lot of them now. On Hike 3, there were more flip-floppers than southbounders.

This left me odd and isolated at any gathering, but the flip-floppers were leaving the trail en masse because of Tropical Storm Florence, which meant that for twenty-four hours or so I had the trail to myself, like the old days of Hikes 1 and 2. This was the evening I arrived at Little Laurel Shelter after 19.6 exhilarating miles under a roiling, pre-storm-blackened sky. I was alone. The forest was absolutely still. My ears were popping as the mercury fell.

Sitting on the shelter floor while eating a high-calorie oatmeal bar, my legs dangling over the edge, I heard a snuffling from underneath. I leapt away in a panic, thinking a bear might have taken shelter below, but what I found instead was an emaciated bear dog curled up under there, snuffling and scratching at its radio collar. The dog made eye contact and thumped its tail, the way miserable dogs do when a human is near. God, I felt bad for that dog. If I were on a day hike I would have removed its collar and taken the dog home. I had nothing it could digest but possibly the half-eaten oatmeal bar in my hand, so I tossed that under the shelter and the dog gobbled it down. I had a few more oatmeal bars in my food bag, so I tossed the dog another, which he gobbled down just as jealously. Those few calories were enough to revive the dog. He crept closer to me, allowed me to pet him. I gave him water straight from my bottle. That dog never would come all the way out from under the shelter but he did take a new position right beneath the edge, where he could poke his head up and see inside.

Little Laurel Shelter rocked as the storm came in, like a house on stilts in the Mississippi Delta during a Category 1 hurricane. Lightening wracked the sky in cascading rips of elemental fury, one after another. Thunder crashed close and concussive. Wind raged through the darkness. Trees, lit in flashes of primordial light, creaked and cracked. Rain sliced into the forest at a driving slant, and all the while that dog kept its place, peering into the shelter from time to time as if to check up on me.

The storm still howled the next morning. I left the bear dog where he'd lain all night, his sad eyes following me for a time, and hiked through the gale, wind-whipped and wet, what hair I have pasted against my neck. The lightening had expended itself in the night, although I believe I would have hiked out regardless. I was buffeted by powerful gusts, tossed sometimes off my feet. I don't think I have ever felt more alive. By the time I reached Hot Springs, the storm had passed, the sun even breaking through in places.

These were my memories as I reached Little Laurel Shelter to find it overrun with Boy Scouts. I shook off my disappointment and went to pitch my tent. Ultra Burn arrived later and pitched his tent as well. The Appalachian Trail is not static, it can't be and shouldn't be. Special moments belong to their own place and time. Trail-runners who set the next speed record on the Appalachian Trail set that record for only themselves. By the time the next trail-runner embarks, the trail will have changed, a different race. There's no way to compare any two.

K-Bar didn't show up that night. There was something going on between her and Ultra Burn. Ultra Burn dropped crumbs here and there, of K-Bar's backstory, an allusion to some darkness in her past. I tried to stay a step back from this. I'm not a gossiper and never have been. People's personal business is their own unless they choose to share it, and even then I will strive to keep a distance. But now I found myself in conflict between the role of a mentor and that of a confidant. I couched my discussions with him in the context of story. If K-Bar were a character I'd created for one of my novels, I told Ultra Burn, her backstory would be this, her motivations that. I tried to nudge him away from a fixation on her without casting her as anything other than a sympathetic character, the protagonist of her own story, but I was pretty sure that Ultra Burn was irrevocably smitten already.

Hiking the next day was another joy, exceptional views from Camp Creek Bald and Big Butt Mountain, both near 5000 feet. The afternoon heat came on as I descended into the hole at Devil Fork Gap, drawing real sweat for the first time in what felt like forever. There was a hand-painted sign at the trailhead for a hostel nearby, Laurel Hostel. I didn't know the place but I was suddenly desperate for a cold beer so I turned that way, and when I arrived I found Ultra Burn there. He'd passed me earlier, saw the sign and had made the same decision I had. His beer was already in his hand. It was only two forty-five, but in that heat we decided to stay. Seventeen miles was enough for today.

The day eased along with no sign of K-Bar. A pair of young hikers came in, Hatchett and The Gods. I didn't know what to make of them. They were the 1960s transported to now, either stoned or natally addled, and as out of place on the Appalachian Trail as a pair of fishes with backpacks. It was obvious they would never make it to Mt. K, but I liked them, I truly did. Authenticity counts, no matter how odd. I informed The Gods that his trail name would offend in this part of the country, perhaps with indignant consequences, so renamed him in the Norwegian, *Gudene*, which means exactly the same thing but it was doubtful anyone else would know that. Gudene seemed intrigued by his translated name and said he would keep it.

Our lazy afternoon eased into a lazy evening, and still no appearance by K-Bar. Ultra Burn had gotten some texts from her, but went ambiguous when I asked him about them. The four of us sat at the picnic table out front, using up all of the conversation we were capable of, numbingly repeating stories while we (or at least I) waited and worried about K-Bar. At eight o'clock I resigned myself to the situation and went inside to sleep.

I was awoken an hour and a half later by spirited revelry outside, punctuated punch lines, the crushing of beer cans, and flights of laughter. Looking out the window, I saw that K-Bar had arrived, along with Breezy and her putative boyfriend Midnight. That K-Bar was with us again filled me with unexpected relief. Perhaps I had called this wrong. I certainly hoped so. The noise though, all those young people making the most of their evening... in other circumstances this was as natural as adolescence but we were on the Appalachian Trail now and there were rules, rules they needed to learn because the time would come when the person they woke up might be less understanding than I was.

I went out, a little groggy but not grumpy, and leaned onto the middle of the table. Every voice trailed off and every smile fell, as if I were a dad who'd caught his kids in the middle of some mischief. I smiled inwardly. Having chosen to hike with young people, my role was preordained.

"Do you all know about hiker midnight?" I asked them levelly. A couple of them offered desultory nods, the rest stared on in apprehension as if I possessed some power to vanquish them where they sat. "You all are having a good time, and that's fine. I know you so I don't mind, but pretty soon we're going to start running into southbounders, and by the time southbounders get down here they're all business. So keep hiker midnight in mind. At nine o'clock, lower your voices or else go off where you won't disturb other hikers. Okay?"

I thought I had kept my tone of voice even and thoughtful, but Hatchett and Gudene looked as if they were withering in place. Ultra Burn and K-Bar were giving me looks of dutiful compliance, while Breezy and Midnight were eyeing me with knives. I smiled. "See you all in the morning." And then I went back inside.

K-Bar came in not long behind me and began laying out her sleeping bag. I took advantage of this private moment to probe a little bit.

"So K-Bar," I said softly. "What's going on with you?" She shrugged and continued stowing her things for the night. "C'mon," I said, "it's okay. Talk to Uncle Solo."

I thought that line might draw a smile but it didn't. "It's nothing," she said, as confoundingly reticent as ever.

"Do you still want to hike with us?" I asked.

"Yeah."

"Okay, good, because I like having you with us."

"Me too."

"Okay..."

These abbreviated responses weren't revealing anything. There was no way I would probe her relationship with Ultra Burn, whatever that relationship might be, but I suspected I knew what the conundrum was. I've dated eighteen-year-olds, after all. Of course I was eighteen myself at the time, as confused and disjointed as Ultra Burn was now, but then I've had a few decades since to work it all out.

"So listen K-Bar, I really want us to stay together...but you have to hike your own hike. Have you figured out why you're hiking yet?" She shrugged, and I deflated a bit. This was something I'd repeated over and again since I'd first met her, met them—hike your own hike, don't hike someone else's. I thought by now she might be comfortable enough on that particular topic to give me some insight "Well, you will," I said paternally. "I promise. So hike your own hike, no matter what it is, okay?"

"Okay."

That was the sum of our talk, frustratingly truncated but I really didn't need to know more. If K-Bar were a character I'd created for one of my novels, her backstory would be this, her motivations that. Fiction does sometimes venture close to reality. Eighteen-year-old K-Bar had not found her hike, but like any perceptive teenager peering into a confused and uncertain future, she was getting glimpses of it. I had an idea what it was but it wasn't my place to tell her, it was for her to find. Trail time decompressed around me. I was only weeks on the trail, with months to go, these friendships as fleeting as an airport encounter, sweet in the moment but broken by the next flight announcement. Still, I'd miss her terribly. K-Bar was not lost from our hike, we'd see her now and then, even dare to hope she would rejoin us, but we would never hike together again.

I texted Donnie Brasco, let him know that I'd failed—I couldn't keep the kids together. He replied that all fellowships eventually come to an end. I agreed, but why so soon? Why so damned soon?

I was hiking by six o'clock the next morning, leaving the others to snore soundly in their bags. The magic hour was especially vibrant in the heights heading toward Big Bald. The sky held cotton clouds, backlit by the sun and glowing in their own islands of fire. The freshening breeze was cool and soothing. I made quick miles to Big Bald, an expanse that dwarfs Max Patch and has endured the hiker influx in much better condition. Tall grass waved in the breeze as if this were a mid-western prairie, all dotted with the confetti colors of flowers. Spare spatters of rain would defy the bright sun, as if they had traveled from a far cloud on the horizon.

Bald Mountain Shelter was to be our destination for the day, short at sixteen miles but that's what the others had agreed to. I reached the shelter at one thirty having not sweated a drop and feeling not in the least bit weary. I didn't even feel the need to take a break, so enervating had the day been, so I didn't linger. I left a note in the trail register for the others, then pushed on with no final destination in mind.

This was the day that the plot of a new book entered my mind, first the story, then the characters coming to life. It wasn't long until I was lost to it, enabled by the grace of the trail through that section. The miles went by, the hours, the sun swinging overhead and then lowering over my left shoulder. I paused with a start and checked my watch. It was seven thirty, dark would fall soon, and I had no idea where I was! Dusky shadows were filling the forest as I caromed into the first stealth site I found. I quickly set up my tent, hung my food bag, then crawled inside. Footsteps pounded by and then halted.

"Solo!" It was Ultra Burn's voice. "What are you doing camping only three tenths from shelter?"

"Shelter?" I hollered through the tent wall. "What shelter?"

"No Business Knob Shelter. It's right down there."

"Oh, man." I was scrambling for my AWOL guide now, flipping through the pages, and there it was. I'd gone 26.2 miles and I hadn't even realized it. I couldn't have felt more foolish. "I didn't know where I was. What are you doing here, anyway?"

"I read your note."

"Is K-Bar coming?"

"I doubt it. She was mad that we didn't stop at Big Bald."

"I got there too early to stop."

"I know."

"So you're going to the shelter?"

"Yeah."

"Well, I'm all set up here so I guess I'll see you in the morning."

"Sounds cool."

"Cool. And by the way, congratulations on your first big miles."

"Thanks, man. It was awesome."

There were a lot of hikers at No Business Knob Shelter the next morning, some snoring in the shelter itself, many others in tents scattered all about. I came in well before sunrise, the red of my headlight reflecting off the candy-striped lines that lofted food bags to high branches. I spotted Ultra Burn's tent, much too early to wake him, so I went to the picnic table and set up for coffee and breakfast.

A young, weathered guy came up out of the darkness. Corn Nut was his name and he was a Mt. Katahdin sobo, the first I'd met on this hike. I call him a *Mt. Katahdin* sobo because he had begun his hike on Mt. Katahdin. Whenever I met a hiker coming toward me on the trail, I would always ask if they were a sobo. They would consistently reply that yes they were until I enthusiastically started peppering them with questions and reminiscences of the Hundred-Mile Wilderness and the Whites, at which point they would demur that they were only doing a section, or they were flip-flopping, or something of the like. They didn't understand that *sobo* meant *southbound thru-hiker*. After many of these misencounters I began asking if they were a *true* sobo, which inadvertently invalidated their hikes, so I had taken to asking if they were a *Mt. Katahdin* sobo instead, which got me the answer without causing offense. Corn Nut was the first sobo I met who answered in the affirmative.

Keeping our voices down (even though it was well past hiker sunrise) we discussed the experience of hiking southbound. That I'd done it three times amazed him. That he was all the way down here so early in the season amazed me. "Well, I did a lot of it on snowshoes," he said.

Equally amazing if not reassuring was that he'd had scores of issues with northbounders. He'd penetrated the big bubble up in northern Virginia, had struggled for shelter space, had longed for camaraderie but had been rebuffed, all the minor chafing and grating I'd experienced on my southbound thru-hikes. This was reassuring because now I knew it wasn't just me, some quirk of my personality that put the northbounders off. Apparently nobos were aloof and dismissive of everyone.

I asked him if he had Springer fever yet.

"Oh yeah," he said knowingly.

Springer fever originally referred to a veteran northbound thru-hiker's driving need to get back to Springer Mountain and on the trail in the spring. For southbounders, though, it meant the culmination of a long thru-hike, Springer Mountain on the near horizon and the overwhelming drive to compress that distance with miraculous miles.

"You'll be able to make big miles all the way," I told him. "You'll be there in no time."

With some coercion and passive aggression, I got Ultra Burn up and hiking by seven o'clock. Six and a half quick miles brought us down the mountain and to Uncle Johnny's Nolichucky Hostel, not exactly in Erwin, Tennessee but close enough to call it so. Uncle Johnny's widow, Charlotte, ran the place now, and she did not remember me. This panged in my belly a little because, firstly, I thought of myself as a memorable person; and secondly, because Charlotte had helped me carry out a joke on the flip-floppers during Hike 3.

I had pulled 24.3 miles that day on Hike 3 after a late start from Greasy Creek Friendly because Cee Cee and Gadget had kept feeding me and pouring coffee as if they were prepping me for a run straight through to Springer Mountain. Later on the trail, I met up with Ridley, a young woman from Canada who was doing the southbound portion of her flip-flop hike. Ridley was a pleasant and pleasing young woman but she had remained aloof up until then. I'd met her on and off during the past week, tried to engage her in conversation each time and was each time rebuffed. I'd come to think that she was simply rude.

This time, though, she opened up and wound up hiking with me for a good part of the day. She explained her earlier behavior obliquely, but the crux of it was that as a single woman hiking alone, she had to be careful how she interacted with men she didn't know. Of course, I thought. If I'd had a daughter I probably would have known this. She'd seen me often enough by then that she felt comfortable now, so we had some good conversation over the length of about ten miles. She stopped for a break by and by, I pushed on, and that ended our time together. I liked her, though, and hoped to hike with her again.

Because of my late start and some trail relocations that added some miles, I didn't reach Uncle Johnny's until after six o'clock, late in the day in that season. The sun had all but set. To my surprise, Ridley was there. She had hitched out from a road a ways back, and had been at Uncle Johnny's long enough to shower and order food from town, which arrived shortly after I did. She had taken up station with three or four other flip-floppers, all men I had met at one time or another. The group ignored me completely, not even a wave of hello. When their food was delivered they dug in heartily as my stomach growled. It took an hour or more for food to be delivered from Erwin, it was already late, and I was dizzy from hunger and from pulling miles none of them had ever come close to. Besides food, I wanted nothing more than to take a shower and go straight to sleep.

I thought if Ridley's and my roles had been reversed, knowing she was burning miles for Uncle Johnny's, I would have ordered some food for her so it would be waiting when she arrived. In lieu of that, I thought, I would at least offer a slice or two of pizza. She offered nothing, none of them did. In a similar situation up north I would have even shared my food with nobos. These flip-floppers were a different breed, insular and all too self-centered. They needed a lesson in trail culture.

Charlotte agreed to go along with the joke even though we'd never met up to that time. There was a birthday party going on for one of her family members. Charlotte walked a big—and I mean *big*—piece of cake out to me and exclaimed in a voice that carried: "Solo is famous at Uncle Johnny's, y'all. Here Solo." She passed the cake to me. "And I got a nice cabin for you tonight with a real soft bed."

The flip-floppers looked over with dripping jealousy. They were in the bunkhouse, not the most comfortable of accommodations. I laughed, and was then surprised when Charlotte actually did lead me to a cushy cabin, a cabin with a well-stocked kitchenette, where I ate my fill, showered in splendor, and slept like a king of the trail.

This is what I thought Charlotte would surely remember, but she didn't. Sigh.

Ultra Burn and I got busy with the usual chores, showers, laundry, and resupply. I mailed my cold weather clothes home to save weight. To my surprise (and delight) K-Bar came walking in. She had hitched out at Spring Gap. Why? Because they were throwing a surprise birthday party for me. I thought I would tear up. Really. We shuttled to an Italian restaurant in nearby Elizabethton, and when Hoosier Daddy met us at the door I did tear up.

All of my birthdays on the Appalachian Trail have been memorable. I was at the Stratton Motel in Maine with The Dude on Hike 1 for my 43rd birthday. The owners at the time surprised me with a birthday cake that said in letters of red icing: *Happy Birthday Solo. You Outlived Elvis.* I was on Eddy Pond in Maine on Hike 2 for my 50th, where some Mainers in a fish camp plied me with hot dogs and moonshine well into the night. And I was at Hiker Hut in Maine on Hike 3 for my 60th. Steve, the proprietor, cooked me a dinner of spaghetti with enormous meat balls, and kept the beers coming. All special birthdays for a man who has had few birthday celebrations in his life, but my 63rd was the best.

Afterward, we said our goodbyes again, Hoosier Daddy for good this time and perhaps K-Bar as well. She was eleven miles behind us and didn't seem pressed to make up the difference. We pushed on the next morning, just Ultra Burn and me, the last of our tramily.

WEDNESDAY, JUNE 9, 2021

Greasy Creek Friendly - 24.4 Miles

Slept very well. Broke a fever and now I feel much better.

Started hiking at 6:15 a.m. Made my usual good time in the magic hour, reaching Beauty Spot at 11:00. Stopped for a break and a phone call to Greasy Creek Friendly. Cee Cee sounded distraught, and described her predicament to me. She said she had to close the hostel, but I could stop in if I wanted to visit.

Some climbs today, but not too bad. Ultra Burn caught up and passed me. I guess this is how it will be from now on.

Pushed hard for Greasy Creek Gap, arrived at 6:20 p.m. Ultra Burn's backpack was there against a tree, some of his stuff scattered on the ground, but he was not. I became worried, calling for him. Turned out he was off looking for water, which wasn't close by.

Took the side trail in light rain to Greasy Creek Friendly, where Cee Cee and Gadget were their same colorful selves despite their woes. I loaned them some money to keep the hostel open. They were effusive, and now here we stay. This is going to push the envelope of my budget, but it will have been worth it if they can get the hostel going again.

—

I'd hiked out of Hot Springs with a sore throat. By the end of that day this had evolved into a full-blown head cold. It seemed comically ironic that, amid a pandemic, maladies as common as colds had been all but forgotten. Or perhaps I had a mild case of Covid, how could I know? Regardless, I hiked through it, never missing a mile.

When I awoke in a sweat-soaked sleeping bag the next morning at Uncle Johnny's, my fever had finally broken and I felt startlingly well. It was as if I'd been on an airplane and had finally been able to clear my ears, that crisp, clarifying return to sounds that had been numbed for so long that what did get through had come to seem natural. I packed up, eager to start making miles in my reinvigorated condition.

The climb out of the Erwin hole did not tax me at all. I had twelve miles under my feet by eleven o'clock. I was on Beauty Spot, which was beautiful, but of more interest at the moment, I finally had cell reception and could make a call.

I called Cee Cee at Greasy Creek Friendly to find out what was going on with her and Gadget and the hostel. I'd been hearing since Georgia that

Greasy Creek Friendly had closed, and now I was close enough to inquire in person.

My fondness for Cee Cee and Gadget derives from Hike 3 when, in the gloomy evening after a 26.7-mile day, I pulled in wet, weary and starving, and with nowhere else to go. I wasn't carrying a tent on that hike, remember. The weather was the worst, cold rain for most of the day, practically freezing on Roan Mountain's 6000-plus feet. Night was coming on fast, the next shelter, Cherry Gap, was still 7.2 miles ahead over a series of climbs, and I was certain that I didn't have the strength to get there. I'd read in AWOL that there was a hostel near Greasy Creek Gap, a place I'd never noticed before, so I took a chance and did the half mile of the side trail in the quickening evening, praying the place was still open this late in the season.

I was met at the door of an aged house by Gadget, who was gregarious, welcoming, and looked like a cross between Frank Zappa and Jerry Garcia. He got me inside by the fireplace, brewed hot coffee, and then when Cee Cee got home, the two cooked dinner for me.

Cee Cee was an interesting woman, middle-aged or perhaps more, with a fondness for boxed wine, an authentic look of the South about her, and an accent to match. She was vocally religious, although of what denomination I never learned. The two were kind to me, that's what I remembered the most, and I slept that night in a warm bed while cold rain drummed on their metal roof.

They were as equally gracious the next morning, bringing out food and then more food, my coffee cup always full. I thought of them often as I went on to finish that hike, and now I learned on the phone that they'd had to close the hostel and might even lose the place.

Cee Cee said she remembered me, although I think she was just being nice. She explained that they'd been forced to shut down because of Covid, the inability to observe social distancing in their tight house, and that the loss of income had caused them to miss some payments. Gadget had been ill as well but was on the mend now. So the hostel was closed. I could stop in for a visit if I wanted to but I couldn't stay there. She was sorry about that but what could she do? I told her it was okay, that we'd tent in Greasy Creek Gap, but I did want to stop in for a visit. I was twelve and a half miles out and would see her that evening.

I left Beauty Spot for the climb up Unaka Mountain (pronounced yoo-Nay-ka) with its beautiful spruce forest, my mind fixed on Cee Cee and Gadget's plight, wondering how deep their debt really was and whether or not I had the funds to help. By the time I reached the peak I had made my decision. There was a sum I could afford to part with. If their debt was no more than that, I was going to help them.

Ultra Burn caught and passed me, which would now occur daily from then until well into Virginia. I had timed his miles to find that he was pushing four miles per hour, a pace I wouldn't be able to match even after my trail legs finally came. I told him the plan in passing, that we would camp in Greasy Creek Gap and that I wanted to drop down the side trail to see Cee Cee and Gadget. He said okay and sprinted on.

I continued to mull the situation at Greasy Creek Friendly as the miles went by. Cee Cee and Gadget were nice people, but I really didn't know them. And they expected nothing from me. Ultra Burn and I could camp in Greasy Creek Gap, push on over Roan and Hump Mountains tomorrow, and within a week a year would seem to have passed, my concerns about Greasy Creek Friendly just a relic of an earlier time and them none the wiser. But Cee Cee and Gadget had been kind to me, not just nice, but *kind*. Thru-hikers don't get a lot of that. There are people along the trail who are sincerely helpful, others who are helpful as long as it profits them, but *kind?* That was rare.

And then there was this: Greasy Creek Friendly was located almost half way between U.S. Highway 19E and Erwin, fifty-one miles with three big mountains and a lot of smaller climbs. There were shelters, but none located in just the right place to split that distance. And in unfriendly weather those highlands could be taxing, even dangerous. Greasy Creek Friendly was not just a hostel, it was an important Appalachian Trail resource. Yeah, I would help—no doubt about it.

I made it into Greasy Creek Gap at six twenty, just as the sky became heavy enough to starting loosing a few drops. I spotted Ultra Burn's backpack beside a tree, open and with some of his things scattered around. As for the young thru-hiker himself, he was nowhere to be seen. I called his name several times. When he didn't answer I began to worry. After about five minutes of this I really began to worry. His bidet was lying on the ground so I knew that wasn't what he was doing.

The woods suddenly looked sinister, gnarled and dark, able to hide hillbillies or a body. Or perhaps he'd had an accident. I started looking around, examining the ground for footprints, peering into gullies in case he'd fallen there, into thickets in case he'd been dumped there. I hollered his name louder anon, louder and louder in rising anxiety. I was a breath from racing down to Greasy Creek Friendly to call the police when Ultra Burn came down the trail with a bulging water bag in his hand and a look of annoyance on his face.

"That water source is *not* two tenths from here," he spat. "It's more like half a mile."

"Damn," I exhaled in relief. "I thought something happened to you."

"What would've happened to me?" he asked innocently.

"Aw, nothing, I guess." I didn't want to share my concerns about the hillbillies I'd encountered in that section during hikes past. Why plant that worry in his brain? Anyway, I hadn't seen any hillbillies so far on this hike. Maybe they only came out in autumn.

Ultra Burn packed up. We took to the side trail just as the rain began to patter with purpose. It wasn't long before we were damp, not drenched, not yet, but heavier rain was certainly on the way. We had a soggy camp to look forward to after our visit with Cee Cee and Gadget.

"I bet they ask us to stay," I said to Ultra Burn as we went along.

"I thought the place was closed."

"It is, but if I remember Cee Cee and Gadget the way I think I do, they won't let us go back in the rain. Wait and see if I'm right."

We reached the house, went up onto the covered porch and knocked. I looked around. The chairs and couch on the porch were piled with household items, as if the two were moving out in stages. A Class C RV, one of the shorter ones, was parked nearby.

Gadget answered the door, holding it only partly open. He looked identical to the last time I'd seen him three years earlier, perhaps even wearing the same T-shirt.

"Hey Gadget," I said. "Do you remember me?"

He slipped through and pulled the door closed behind him. "I'm not sure," he said hesitantly, as if afraid to give offense and not sure what a better answer would be short of lying.

"I was here going southbound three years ago. You and I talked about making a card with trail etiquette on it, like those Leave No Trace cards. You were really excited about the idea."

"Oh, yeah," he said, dawning. "I remember that. Yeah, Solo. I do remember you."

"That's great. This is Ultra Burn. We're hiking together."

"Hey, man."

"Hey, man."

"So I just wanted to stop in and see how you all are doing."

"We're doing okay. I had another problem with my heart, but it's better now. We're packing up that RV. I think we'll head down to Florida, and why not? Lots of people do."

"So you really are losing the place?"

"Yeah. Can't be helped. We'll make out all right, though."

Ever optimistic, that's something else I remembered about Gadget. He was of the Cuban diaspora, raised in the United States but from a family that had struggled against Castro for their very lives. He wasn't going to feel sorry for himself or let anyone else do it for him.

"So how's Cee Cee?"

"She's doing okay. Hates to leave, you know, but Florida's nice. She'll like it there."

"I hate that you all had to close the hostel."

"Me, too. I'm gonna miss the hikers. I wish you could stay with us but we've got stuff stacked all over the place."

"That's okay, Cee Cee told me on the phone. We're going to camp in Greasy Creek Gap." I looked around again. It was light, but barely. The rain was a steady drizzle now. We'd be soaked before we made it back. "I just wanted to stop by to see you all. I'm glad you were here."

The door parted and Cee Cee poked her head out. "Solo?"

"Hey Cee Cee."

"What are y'all doin' out there in the wet? C'mon inside."

We dropped our backpacks and went inside. Gadget cleared some boxes off the couch, and then Ultra Burn and I sunk into it. Cee Cee padded to the kitchen and began poking around in a cabinet.

"We still have a lot of food for the hikers we're tryin' to use up. I can heat you some Spaghettios if you're hungry. I have some with meatballs, too, but if you want those you have to heat 'em yourself because they got pork in 'em and I don't touch that."

Both our mouths were watering at the thought of hot food, but neither of us possessed the ambition to get up and make it in someone else's kitchen.

"I'm good with regular Spaghettios," I said.

"Me too," Ultra Burn seconded.

"Okay. This won't take a minute."

Cee Cee began to rattle pots, pausing occasionally to sip from a glass of wine. "Y'all want a glass of wine?" she asked then.

"Sure," we both piped.

Cee Cee brought out a box and poured two glasses. "I like my box wine," she said with a twinkle.

One might be a connoisseur of fine wine, but even aged grape juice will suffice on the Appalachian Trail, while boxed wine is a fantasy.

Gadget cleared space for us at the table, and we sat to our Spaghettios, sipping wine and feeling indulgently sated as only the Appalachian Trail can deliver. Cee Cee sat across from us, fiddling with her wine glass while Gadget poked at a tablet. "Y'all can take a shower if you want. I'd let you stay but the bedroom's full of stuff...Gadget, go clear out that stuff." And then to us, "Why don't y'all go ahead and stay here tonight. It won't be much but it's better than out in the rain."

I nudged Ultra Burn in the side and threw him a surreptitious smile as if to say, *I told you so.*

With our fates for the evening now secure, I risked broaching a topic that was really none of my business.

"So what is the situation with you guys?" I asked Cee Cee, prepared to divert to another topic in an instant if I'd exceeded my bounds, but Cee Cee went on unoffended, candidly, reciting their woes with regular reinforcement from Gadget.

I got the gist of it. It was complicated, but the way things stood they'd be homeless by the end of the month. That rankled for all the reasons I've already mentioned, but on top of that was pure indignation that an aging couple would be tossed out of their house, a house that reminded me a lot of my maternal grandfather's former house in Cumberland County, Tennessee, country people who lived simply and did no harm but still had to fight a system they were unequipped to fight, and at a time in their lives when they should be able to relax and enjoy the seasons to come.

"So how much would you need to keep the place?" I asked her. She told me, frankly, and I winced. The figure was more than I'd anticipated. "So if you had that," I went on, "you could keep the place? Rock solid? No small print, no surprises?"

"Yeah."

"You're sure?"

"Yeah."

I mulled it, crunched numbers in my head. I could possibly do it. "So...if I gave you that money right now, would you be able to stay?" Cee Cee looked up with a start. Gadget set his tablet down and put on a serious face. "And do you really want to stay?" I added.

"Yes," Cee Cee said, hope rising visibly in her face.

"Okay then," I said.

I went out to my backpack, retrieved my diary and the single blank check I kept in it. Sitting at the table, I began writing out the check. Ultra Burn's eyes went wide when I filled in the figure, while Cee Cee seemed to be having a hard time catching her breath and Gadget looked as if he'd just been rescued from a mountain ledge.

Cee Cee took my check as if it were an aged and delicate bible, her eyes moist. Gadget seemed to have grown ten years younger. We discussed fiscal matters. The two promised to have the hostel back open in time for the southbounders. After that, and showers, and the last of Cee Cee's wine, Gadget cleared the bedroom and Ultra Burn and I turned in for the night.

THURSDAY, JUNE 10, 2021

Mountain Harbor B&B - 26.7 Miles

What a day! Cee Cee made us a biscuit breakfast with lots of coffee, and then we were on the trail by 9:00 a.m.

It was a damp day with scattered showers, but still went relatively fast. Pulled in at Stan Murray Shelter at 3:30 p.m., Ultra Burn there waiting. We decided to push on to Yellow Mountain Gap and camp there. Got there at 4:30 p.m. and decided to go the distance to U.S. Highway 19E and Mountain Harbor B&B.

Roan Mountain was wet, muddy, and slow, and Hump Mountain was a bald trek in cold wind and spattering rain. Thought I would never get over it, but then by 6:10 I was heading down, and I made Highway 19E in the last light of day at 8:57 p.m.

Mountain Harbor has really changed. Many improvements since Hike 3, and unrecognizable from Hike 2. There are section hikers here, but no obnoxious ones. One of them is a young guy who's been hiking the A.T. in sections for a few years, and who swears he will finish it someday. He's getting married next week. I think he's settling his head on this hike in preparation for the big leap. I gave him the trail name Eventually, because he will eventually finish the trail. He seemed to like that name.

Looking forward to a restful night.

FRIDAY, JUNE 11, 2021

Kincora Hostel - 24.7 Miles

I have finally met Bob Peoples! He's an ebullient fella with a Snoopy-white mustache and a hearty chuckle, and enough stories of the old days on the A.T. to fill several books.

The day started lazily at Mountain Harbor, waking up at 7:00 a.m. after a good sleep, laundry and then breakfast in the main house at 8:30. It was an elaborate and filling breakfast.

I finally got on the trail at 9:30, barely making it a mile before the sky opened with the heaviest rain we've seen yet. It was brutal getting over the balds, with the trail running like a fast stream. Everything soaked, even the kilt, which began to chafe painfully.

The day went dully and slow in the rain. It stopped mid-afternoon, the sun even came out for a time. My clothes began to dry, then the rain started up again.

Ultra Burn finally caught up, so miserable that we decided to quit early at Moreland Gap Shelter. Trouble was it was already full of section hikers, so at 4:37 p.m. we decided to push on the final 6.3 miles to Kincora, where we arrived at 8:00 p.m. The place is interesting. Lots of cats. Ultra Burn is allergic to cats, it seems. Anyway, we're showered and dry, and tomorrow Bob will drive us into town for resupply.

Too tired to write more.

SATURDAY, JUNE 12, 2021

Kincora Hostel - Zero

Slept pretty damned well. Woke up at 6:45 a.m., made coffee, &c.

Bob drove us into town for resupply at 8:00, and afterward we spoke about history and hiking for several hours.

The weather was miserable, so the decision to take a zero wasn't hard. Napped through the afternoon, spoke with Mudhawk, an outdoorsy boy whom Bob is looking after. Later, Eventually came in. We think K-Bar might be near, but as of 7:00 p.m. she hasn't arrived.

Bob drove us back into town for Mexican food. Now it's evening and I'll be in the bag soon for an early departure tomorrow.

SUNDAY, JUNE 13, 202

Mile 411.4 - 21.5 Miles

Got up early and got an early start. Hiking by 6:00 a.m. Saw Bob on the way out, promised to mail him a copy of my book *Hiking through History*, then had a not too strenuous climb of Pond Mountain. It did take four hours to get over it, but at 10:00 a.m. it was still cool and I wasn't tired, so I didn't go up to Boots Off Hostel for a coke or a beer.

Soon I was at Watauga Lake, where I yogied water and a coke, then I was over the dam and back into the woods. I arrived at Vandeventer Shelter before 3:00 p.m. Ultra Burn arrived soon after. He had taken an hour to go splashing in the lake, otherwise he would have been there waiting for me.

We pushed on 3.8 miles farther to this campsite, first time I've pitched tent or used my stove in a while. Tomorrow is a conundrum with Damascus close enough to reach with a big pull, bear closures and no water sources in a shorter pull. We'll decide what to do when we see how tomorrow goes.

—

Cee Cee and Gadget were up early the next morning preparing breakfast for us, obsequious now and I regretted that. Their improved circumstances were due to the people they were, the person I was, and the importance of their hostel, a simple confluence of interests. They were still Cee Cee and Gadget, I was still Solo, and I didn't want that to change in any way. I told Ultra Burn that I'd made up my mind long before we arrived. They were going to get my help whether we stayed there or not.

"I've never known people like them before," he said to that, "people who'll help you even when they need help themselves. I mean, all those cans of food? That's not hiker food, Solo, that's what you get at a food pantry. Believe me, I know. And Cee Cee was burning paper to stay warm. They've had it bad, but they still give. I never would've met them if not for you."

"There's a lot of people like them in the South," I said ruefully. "But not a lot on the A.T."

We weren't able to say our goodbyes and get underway until nine o'clock. It soon proved to be one of those days you simply have to resign yourself to, dull, sloshy, sporadic bouts of rain, and bitingly cold at elevation. Roan Mountain was clotted in cloud and wisps of wet, without a view beyond the next few feet of muddy gray trail. I sighed at that. I'd crossed that mountain in almost identical conditions going southbound last time, while on an earlier hike I'd taken in those heights on a day that could draw tears at the beauty of it.

In defiance of all this, we still made good miles, arriving at our planned stops early and deciding each time to push on. By the time we reached Little Hump Mountain late in the featureless day, there was no question any longer: we would push on all the way to U.S. Highway 19E and Mountain Harbor B&B.

Hump Mountain was our final obstacle at about 5500 feet, a bald, undulating plain aloft in the sky, an ancient highland realm where one might expect to encounter the stones of a keep or the bones of a dragon. As if by our very nearness to the sun, a few rays broke through, turning lifeless greens into dappled islands of emerald.

Ultra Burn took this at his new-found pace while I watched his figure on that rolling bald recede to a point in the distance. The chilling wind razored through every layer I wore, while my feet fell clumsily into and out of that muddy groove of a trail. Balds can be beautiful but they share with farm fields a trail gone narrow due to encroaching grass, a trail that becomes rutted with use until it's more a drain for rain than a path for feet. I stumbled through this, but once into the cover of the far trees I found my pace again, and then it was a race with the sun, which I won but by only minutes.

I reached the highway at eight fifty-seven, still light enough to see but not enough to throw a shadow. Turning left on the shoulder, I made a quick half mile to Mountain Harbor.

I first stayed at Mountain Harbor on Hike 2 after twenty-four-plus miles, when the hostel was in the loft of the barn, snug and rustic. It was late in the season so I had the place to myself. I remember that night as being one of the most restful and satisfying nights of that hike. Terry Hill, who founded Mountain Harbor with his wife Mary in 2003, greeted me when I came in late that day, set me up, got some food for me, and made me feel welcome. I was saddened to learn on Hike 3 that Terry had passed away just two years before, as have so many others I've known on the Appalachian Trail. His wife Mary now ran the place, keeping it going, improving it, ever improving it.

I found Ultra Burn inside the expanded and refurbished barn, showered, of course, and fed. I'd arrived too late for the last meal. I settled instead for a microwaved pizza, which was feast enough, and a beer that Ultra Burn had somehow secreted into the place.

I passed out another trail name before I turned in for the night, this time to a young man on a section hike, one of many hikes for him but with still many to go before he would eventually complete the Appalachian Trail. He was set to be married the following week, an event that coursed excitement in his cheeks even while revealing a hint of apprehension about his future. I thought this hike might have been his way of reconciling those emotions. I called him Eventually because he would eventually get there, and he took this to heart.

The next morning rose slowly under a heavy sky. I did laundry, mostly to dry out my kilt and clothes, then went to the main house at eight thirty for an elaborate breakfast in which there were so many choices it was hard to decide where to begin. Pancakes, sausage, omelets, crepes, scrambled eggs, potatoes...I sampled them all while I would have felt wealthy to have indulged in only one. At nine thirty the air was damp but there hadn't been any rain so I took off for the trail, leaving Ultra Burn to complete his own chores.

A half mile back up the road, turn left onto the trailhead, through a patch of woods, across a farm field, my newly dried socks already soaking wet from the grass along that narrow, rutted trail, not a mile from Mountain Harbor, always forward, never backward, and the sky opened up biblically.

In less than an instant even my kilt was soaked through, hanging heavily on my hips and sluicing runnels of water down my thighs. After some miles of this my kilt began to chafe indelicately, which required some application of diaper rash cream more in line with the way I'd used it on my boys when they were babies. As I climbed I fought not only gravity but also the rush of water down the trail, which parted around my ankles as if I were a rock in a stream.

The sun came out in mid-afternoon, and for a time I dared hope I'd seen the last of the rain. My clothes were beginning to dry, even my socks, and my kilt now felt more like a damp towel than a wet blanket. I had just gotten used to this new state when the sky opened again, again biblically, and this time it didn't stop, not once for the next twenty-four hours or so.

Ultra Burn finally caught up to me just short of Moreland Gap Shelter after 18.4 miles of the purest misery, looking like a cat caught in a well. This was the worst rain he'd experienced, the worst rain I'd experienced since a nineteen-mile slosh in Vermont on Hike 3. Ultra Burn was a Technician, but unrelenting rain had reduced his technology to useless. He was more miserable than I'd ever seen him, as if mortally wounded by the effrontery of nature against his meticulous planning. It was not up for debate as far as he was concerned. Enough of this, and the hell with big miles, he was pulling in at Moreland Gap Shelter.

He didn't need to twist my arm. I was as miserable as he, I just didn't express it as visibly. And besides, my chafed nether parts were crying for another application of the cream. We both lit up when the shelter came into view, surcease at last, safe for the night, then we rounded the corner and found a tuna can of a shelter, in both smell and contents. The shelter was jammed full of section hikers or weekenders, surly, rank, bedraggled guys whom I would not spoon if the parted sea were about to close upon us and that alone would stop it.

The life seemed to go out of Ultra Burn right then. We stood ineffectively under the eave as chill rainwater ran down our backs. Not a soul in that shelter moved to make room for us, to give us an extra inch out of the rain. Ultra Burn looked crazed as he took in the shelter, his mind whirling, surely a place within where he could wedge himself, surely some release from the onslaught of the rain, surely *something*. At the same time, some part of him recognized the futility of it. I swear I saw the essence of him drain out of his eyes.

"Listen, Ultra Burn," I said, ignoring the others as if they were no more than flotsam astern. "It's only six point three miles to Kincora. We can do it, man. We can do it."

Some of the section hikers looked up with such dubious looks that I couldn't fail to notice them, which reinforced my determination. "I'm a thru-hiker, you amateurs," I wanted to say. "This isn't my first rodeo."

Ultra Burn went numb at the thought, spiritless, his knees trembling, but perhaps that was just the cold. "We can do it," I said again, placing a reassuring hand on his shoulder. "Here, man." I wrestled a little bottle of Jack Daniels out of my backpack. "Drink this."

Lips smacked inside the shelter but I dismissed them as irrelevant. Ultra Burn took that little bottle and downed it in one gulp, handing it back to me as if there were more to share. "Are you ready, man?" I asked. He nodded absently. "Okay, man, let's do it!"

"Yeah, man, let's do it!" he said with alcohol-charged verve.

We turned our backs on those guys without another thought, and Ultra Burn leapt into his four-mile pace, leaving solid splashes that faded as he disappeared ahead.

I went on at my own pace, teeth gritted, nether parts screaming, my rain shell all but useless but at least it did keep in some warmth. At the bottom of White Rocks Mountain, at a ponding trail junction, I found Ultra Burn sitting in the mud, his knees up, his backpack swimming nearby, a sodden cigarette paper in his pruned fingers as he tried abjectly and futilely to roll a cigarette in the deluge. It was the most miserable I would ever see him, worse even than before. He resembled nothing less than a Dickensian orphan on the muddy Thames bank, forlorn, with neither sou nor sanity to sustain him.

"Ultra Burn!" I took him by the shoulders and stood him up, felt a paternal pang pounding in my heart. "It's only one point seven more miles," I hollered over the rain. "Only one point seven!"

He didn't answer. He seemed as if he were somewhere else far away.

"C'mon, man. Let's stay together. Let's do it together, both of us."

I retrieved his backpack. He slipped it on as if it were an afterthought, I gave him a light push in the right direction, and we plodded ahead, one splash at a time. I talked about everything, a running chatter that finally began to stretch even my imagination, afraid to pause for even a single syllable and risk losing his focus; but then, in the middle of one bawdy story, we stepped onto pavement. From one footfall to the next, Ultra Burn revived as if saved from the gallows. When we walked up the steps to Kincora he was fully himself again, the master of his fate.

I'd never met Bob Peoples, a personage on the trail who could perhaps rival Earl Shaffer for affection. Bob was a trail maintainer with the Tennessee Eastman Hiking and Canoeing Club, and had been since the 1990s when he moved to the area from Massachusetts. He established his rustic Kincora Hostel in 1997 and has been a trail treasure ever since. I tried to meet him on Hike 2 but he was away when I got to his place. On Hike 3 I threw down at Boots Off Hostel late in the evening, with not enough energy left to get over Pond Mountain to Kincora. Now on Hike 4 I was determined to meet Bob, and I did.

Bob gave us a tour of the place, and then later, in dry clothes and with some food in our bellies—and as always on the Appalachian Trail—our struggles all day seemed as far removed from our memories as our births.

Bob seemed reluctant to be drawn into conversation, but once I nudged him there he was a fount of history and information. I could understand now why he was so beloved on the trail. He had a glottal, bobbing chuckle that translated any humor without the need for accompanying words, and from his stories, he knew or had known just about everyone of note on the Appalachian Trail.

The aging hostel needed repairs, though, more than one old man could handle, something I knew firsthand from my century-old homestead. I could see with a practiced eye where wood was rotting, where water was getting in, how the forest was encroaching closer, the way honeysuckle was climbing walls and through opened windows. Bob's wife had passed some years earlier, leaving him alone with the place. It was a wonder that a dozen grateful young thru-hikers weren't even then at work with hammers and nails and clippers and tubes of caulk, but then maybe this was the way Bob preferred it, Kincora being slowly reclaimed by the very nature it had displaced.

And beyond the hewn rail, the rain still fell through the dark of night.

The next morning dawned in silty hues, the rain a thrum that had lulled me comfortably to sleep last night but now invited just the opposite. Another zero received no argument from me.

Bob drove us into Hampton for resupply. Afterward, he and I spoke on the weathered porch for hours as rain dripped from the eave in a wet wall beyond. We spoke about history, the Appalachian Trail, and his hikes of the various Caminos in Spain. I felt that my three thru-hikes and my journeys around the world paled in comparison.

Bob had a young ward named Mudhawk, an eager boy who romped through the puddles beyond the rail as if not inconvenienced in the least by the rain. The boy scampered into the woods, circled round and round the hostel, pausing at each pass to inform us of some new discovery, some new observation. When I asked the boy how he'd gotten his trail name, he applied his hands to the hair pasted against his forehead, combed upward with his fingers, and produced a respectable Mohawk. His first Mohawk, he grinned, had been held aloft with mud.

It was a wonder to watch Mudhawk out in the rain, oblivious of any discomfort. I had been like him as a child, the rain nothing more than another adventure. When had we grown so intolerant of it? At what age? What had been that transition? I searched clear memories all the way back to my very early childhood and could find no answer. I thought, not for the first time, how different life would have been if I could have been exposed to the Appalachian Trail at his age, and how effortless the rigors of the trail would be if it were hiked only by children.

I napped through the rest of the day. Ultra Burn sat on the porch poking at his phone, his shoulders seeming to harden as the day wore on. K-Bar was in the area.

"Tell her where we are," I said excitedly.

"I did," he said with less enthusiasm. By early evening she hadn't arrived.

Eventually came in, though, dripping but with a smile of accomplishment. Kincora was at the end of his section. He'd be going home in the morning, soon to be married, a new life. We congratulated him, went with Bob to a Mexican restaurant to eat and celebrate. As we finished our beers and our refried beans, a ray of sun broke through, angling low between the hills. By the time we returned to Kincora there were stars in the sky.

I stepped off the porch at six the next morning, back into a magic hour I'd missed these past days. Bob saw me off. He and I were the only ones up, either because of age or trail or both. I took Pond Mountain with a hearty stride, three miles up and then three miles down, four hours in between and without a drop of sweat. Pond Mountain was one of my least favorite PUDs on the Appalachian Trail, one I had always reached late in the day where it served as nothing but a barrier to progress, but that morning it was magic and I loved it.

On the other side of Pond Mountain, Boots Off Hostel was up a driveway to my left, beer or a cold coke only minutes away. But I felt fine and it was only ten o'clock, so I pushed on. I reached Watauga Lake a mile and a half later. During that interval, and in complete defiance of the preceding few days, the sun was out, full and hot. I successfully yogied a bottle of water and a cold coke from a family picnicking near the trailhead, then pushed on over the dam into an ever-warming afternoon.

Vandeventer Shelter was our goal for the day at 17.7 miles. I was there before three, and Ultra Burn showed up about ten or fifteen minutes later. He'd stopped at the lake for a swim, showed me photos of him on a tire swing and letting go out over the water, his signature grin back on his face. If not for that diversion he would have passed me an hour or so earlier.

Reinvigorated by his swim, and with me wanting to push on for at least a twenty, we went on for 3.8 more miles and stealth-camped beside a nice stream. We both tried to recount in our minds the last time we'd pitched our tents, and couldn't form an answer. It seemed we'd been going hostel to hostel for weeks, perhaps months. To be out in the woods again, heating our food and sleeping in our tents, was curiously comforting.

We weren't sure what we'd do tomorrow. Damascus, Virginia was almost thirty miles away through a section I remembered as being pretty fast, but Ultra Burn was more reserved about attempting a thirty-mile day. There were few water sources along the way, though, and several shelters were closed because of aggressive bear activity. We might find ourselves in the middle of that if we didn't go for it. I was prepared to make it happen, but Ultra Burn couldn't shed his caution. Let's just see how the day goes, he said, and with that we turned in for our last night in Tennessee.

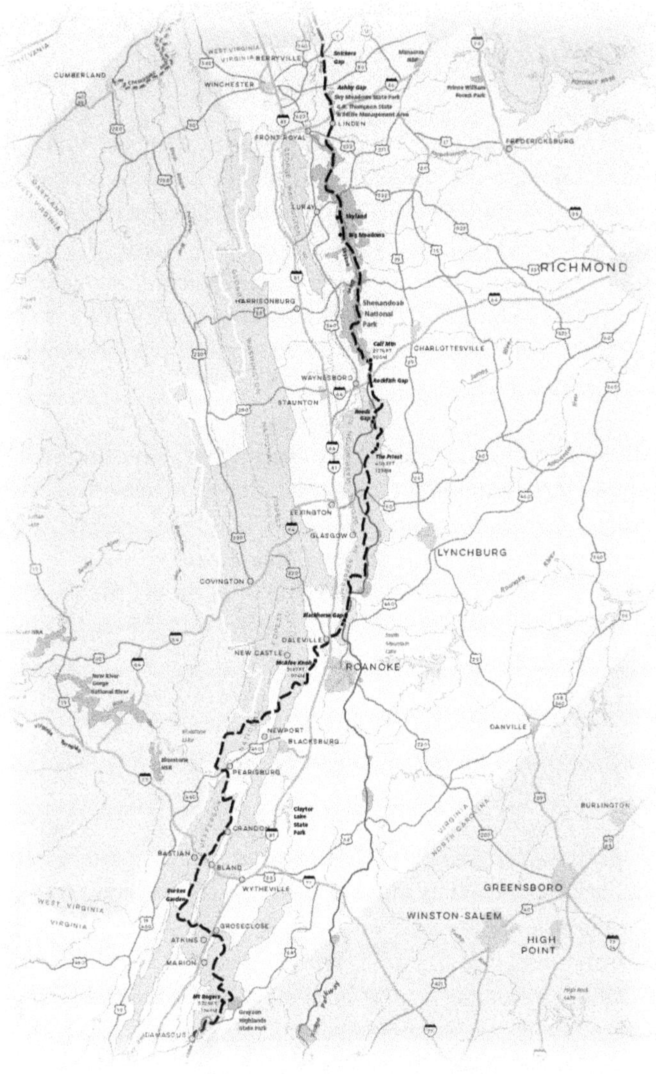

VIRGINIA

556.6 MILES

MONDAY, JUNE 14, 2021

Damascus, Virginia - 29.4 Miles

It rained last night.

Woke up early but didn't get out until 6:30 a.m. Made good time as always in the magic hour. Passed Matador and Tombstone camped a few miles up the trail, then met a trail angel named Marlene at 10:00 a.m., set up at a trailhead with a table and chairs the way Fresh Ground does it.

Pushed on through clearing weather. Ultra Burn didn't catch up until Abingdon Shelter, which was closed due to bear activity. We pushed on the 6.4 miles to the TN-VA line, where we took photos, then we dug in for the final 3.5 miles to Damascus.

I was making 3+ mph, reached Damascus by 7:35 p.m., but got southbound turned-around and hiked a mile out of town before I realized my mistake. Backtracked, found Ultra Burn, Matador, and Tombstone at 7 Trails Grill, where I had just enough time to get a burger and beer before they closed. Later, we threw down at Broken Fiddle Hostel.

Not quite 30 miles today—well I did thirty but those extra don't count.

TUESDAY, JUNE 15, 2021

Damascus, Virginia - Zero

Taking a guilt-free zero due to yesterday's big miles. Slept late and well, ran errands, resupply, and then—yes—I bought another backpack, a Gossamer Gear just like Ultra Burn's. It's that tent pocket, just too convenient.

Nothing much else to write except I ran into Gamer. Yeah, him. Egad! Also, K-Bar showed up late with Breezy. No sign of Midnight. Ultra Burn and Breezy went off across the yard to be alone. Weird. Called ahead to Dennis and also to Canyonman. We should have an interesting few days ahead.

—

Our last night in Tennessee brought light overnight showers, not a soaking rain but enough to wet our tents and dampen the ground around us. Because of the order in which I loaded my backpack, various items lay on the wet ground waiting their turn, each needing to be brushed of clingy wet leaf litter and soil before I stuffed them in. All buttoned up in his tent, Ultra Burn slept on nearby, as he would for at least another hour yet. Wiping my hands together and then finally on my kilt to get them reasonably clean, I jealously thought about Ultra Burn's backpack with its too-convenient tent pocket. He would have a much cleaner time breaking camp than I'd had.

The rain hadn't ruined the magic hour. The sun rose softly, casting delicate, tissue-thin rays between limbs and leaves. I walked charmed through this, taking snapshots with my mind. After four miles I reached the short side trail to the Nick Grindstaff Monument. I had passed this trail junction too many times at a sprint, never pausing to see what lay beyond. This time, though, the magic compelled me so I turned left on the side trail and went to see who Nick Grindstaff was and why there was a monument to his name.

It was only a short walk off trail to the monument, which proved to be of lichen-encrusted brick and stone, about the height of a man and resembling another of the several chimneys that appear incongruously along the Appalachian Trail, remnants of homes or cabins long since returned to nature. A cracked slate panel bore the inscription: *Uncle Nick Grindstaff, Born Dec. 26, 1851, Died July 22, 1923. He lived alone, suffered alone, and died alone.*

That epitaph was about as sad as one could possibly be. I then realized that this was not just a monument, it was the man's *grave*. I went around to the other side, and there I found Jeff's tent. A few feet away was Matt's tent. These were two guys in their twenties or thirties I'd met in a farm field the day before. They were taking in the shade beside the ladder we would need to climb to get over a barbwire fence. Close by, a herd of cows was also lolling in the shade.

"Do you think I could go up to them?" Matt asked me in passing as I stepped onto the ladder. I couldn't for the life of me understand why he would want to do that or why he might assume I would know the answer to his question.

Matt was dark complected, average build, with a smear of black beard. His expression was enthusiastic, even excited, as if he'd never seen a cow before. His friend, Jeff, was fair-haired with some gray. Jeff was tall, solid, tattooed, short on words, and had the air of a biker about him, if not a bar bouncer.

"I don't see a bull," I told Matt as I swung my leg over the top of the ladder. "Stay away from the calves and the others will probably let you come close." I dropped to the other side of the fence.

"So are those milk cows?" Matt asked me innocently through the wire.

I noted the plastic tags in the cows' ears, and shook my head. "Naw, they're not milk cows," I said. "They're hamburger."

Matt's eyes went round in horror. "Are you sure?"

"Yeah," I nodded. "Pretty sure."

I took off then. Looking over my shoulder, I could see Matt edging his way toward the cows, his palm out as if he were going to pet a dog.

And now here they were camping on what was evidently a grave, albeit reclaimed by the forest and unrecognizable as such if they'd arrived after dark. Jeff's tent was right against the monument, a headstone actually, or a tombstone.

"Who's out there?" he sounded from his tent.

"It's Solo. Sorry to wake you up. I didn't know you were here."

"That's cool," he said.

"I think you're camped against a tombstone, dude."

"Really? Is that what it is?"

"I think so."

"Huh."

"Well...see you all later."

"Yeah, see ya."

I pushed on. The magic hour melted away as the sun rose higher, but the day became prettier as it went. Being down here in the spring revealed a trail I hadn't experienced before, blooming with flame azaleas and mountain laurel, which dropped its petite white flowers onto the trail in what resembled nothing less than a petal-dappled bridal walk. There were even a few rhododendrons blooming at certain elevations, crimson sprays of startling color against the otherwise uninterrupted green. I made quick miles as I knew I would, arriving at Abingdon Gap Shelter after nineteen miles and feeling as if I could do nineteen more. The shelter was closed due to bear activity, which left ten miles to Damascus, miles I was committed to making whether Ultra Burn was or not.

He hadn't caught up to me yet. That was odd, but I had an idea why. At a trailhead ten or eleven miles back, I'd met a trail angel named Marlene who had tables set up with juice, fruit, cokes, and snacks of all kinds. This was something I'd only seen once before, on Hike 3 in Vermont when I'd met Fresh Ground. Fresh Ground was an enthusiast who followed the northbound bubble from Georgia all the way to Mt. K, pulling his van in at trailheads to set up his tables of food for the hikers. As a southbounder this was something I'd never encountered before. One quirk in my hike, an extra break, a stop to filter water, and I could have missed him completely. I stayed an hour to eat and visit with Fresh Ground, thanked him for his generosity then pushed on.

Months if not years later, early in the morning at Dickey Gap in Virginia, after being dropped off by a trail angel named Canyonman, I saw a guy in full bicycle attire off to the side fiddling with his bike. I went over to offer my help—I'm a bicycle mechanic among other things—and was surprised when the guy exclaimed in disbelief, "*Solo?*"

I looked him over, bicycle helmet, cycling glasses, hard to recognize detail, but his voice... "*Fresh Ground?* No effin way!"

It was! It was Fresh Ground, a face I'd never thought to see again, and a face from so long ago that it might have belonged to a previous century. This was a coincidence of such astounding proportions that my knees went weak.

Fresh Ground had finished his season and was now doing some recreational cycling along the Appalachian Trail corridor. His chain had come off, his rear derailleur wasn't shifting properly, and he had no idea what to do... and then along comes a thru-hiker whom he'd fed ages ago and who happened to be a bicycle mechanic. I adjusted his derailleur for him, got the bike shifting properly, and saw him off on his journey even as he saw me off on mine.

And now I met Marlene, doing the same thing Fresh Ground did. We visited for a while, I told her my story of Fresh Ground, and when I left I wondered if I would encounter her again in serendipitous circumstances (I did not). Ultra Burn would have pulled in after I left, would have lost track of time around all that food, and that's why he hadn't beaten me to Abingdon Gap Shelter.

He did show up not too long afterward, Matt and Jeff with him. I informed them that I was going for Damascus. Period. Ultra Burn readily agreed, but Matt and Jeff were less sure. Those would be the biggest miles they'd ever made and they weren't certain they could do it.

"There's an angry bear around here somewhere," I told them, "and no water until a mile before Damascus. Might as well do the whole thing."

They agreed reluctantly, and off we went.

I was pulling three-plus miles per hour in another race with the sun. Ultra Burn was out ahead, of course. Matt and Jeff were for a while but I passed them by and by. I reached Damascus with plenty of time before sunset, then, for the first time on this hike, fell victim to what I call *southbound turned-around.*

As many times as I've been to Damascus, by foot, car, and bicycle, that town has always confused me and I don't know why. This time I turned right instead of left, wound up on the Virginia Creeper Trail, and was a mile or more gone before I realized my mistake. Now the sun *was* getting low. My eyesight is poor at night, which is why I'm always in a race with the sun late in the day. I more or less jogged my way back to town, dark now, I couldn't make out a damned thing, my memory was betraying me at every turn, but somehow I took the correct one this time and made it to 7 Trails Grill shortly before they closed.

Ultra Burn, Matt, and Jeff were there, the leavings of their meals being cleared away as I came in. Ultra Burn—bless his true thru-hiker heart—had ordered food for me and it sat waiting.

"Where the hell have you been?" he asked not sarcastically.

"I got southbound turned-around," I answered in disgust. "I can't believe I did that sh—. I should have been here an hour ago. Are they still pouring beers?"

"For a few more minutes."

So I settled in with a cold beer and an enormous burger, couldn't help but hold that burger up to Matt and say with a grin, "Here's your cow, Matt."

"Aw, man. That sucks."

"Was yours good, though?"

"Yeah," he sighed. "It was."

"You need a trail name, Matt. Your trail name will now be Matador until someone comes up with something better. And you, Jeff, your trail name will now be Tombstone until someone comes up with something better."

These were the last two trail names I would give out on the hike. Tombstone only lasted a few more days on the trail. I had told him as I told everyone, that hiking the Appalachian Trail was a journey of discovery. If you found what you were looking for before the end, then so be it. Go home not in dejection but proud of what you'd learned about yourself. He'd taken this to heart more than I realized. Sometime during the next few days, he decided that he'd found what he was looking for, which was a greater appreciation of his life with his wife. He went home to her, told me later in a text that my words had helped him and that he was keeping the name Tombstone.

The last time I saw Matador was also a few days later, from a distance in the Grayson Highlands as he stalked the longhorn cattle that wander there. I never learned what his bovine fixation was about. Matador did complete the Appalachian Trail, and kept his trail name all the way.

There were now so many hostels in Damascus that choosing one took some thought. I left the decision to Ultra Burn, who thumbed his phone in serious contemplation before setting us up at The Broken Fiddle Hostel. I'd never stayed there, couldn't be sure the place had even existed last time, but it had laundry, showers...and a caretaker who worked at Sundog Outfitter.

To call my budget blown after only 470 miles would be not an understatement but a grievous one, nevertheless I wanted a backpack like Ultra Burn's, one I could load while inside a clean, dry tent, and so do away with these messy mornings. Sundog Outfitters, as I learned that evening, was suffering the same Covid-affected supply shortages as everyone else. They had one and only one Gossamer Gear backpack left in stock.

So I was there early the next morning, and I bought it.

Such a simple thing, an exterior tent pocket, but that single innovation changed my hike. From then on I would stealth more often than not, shrug off the rain, and pack up on bitter cold mornings with little discomfort.

My ULA was still a great backpack, trim and lean, and would see service again sooner or later. I mailed it home along with some other things, then Ultra Burn and I stepped out into the morning in search of food, my new backpack over my shoulder. We were taking a zero, what I call a *guilt-free zero*, because of our big miles the day before. As I explained to Ultra Burn, had we stopped to camp somewhere, even if after good miles, we'd still be making our way to Damascus right now. So taking our fourth zero was more like a paid vacation. He readily agreed.

We were proceeding on the sidewalk toward a cafe when I heard from a block back, "*Hey Solo!*"

I turned and screwed my eyes to focus, and...Good God it was Gamer! He was waving and plodding our way in his gargantuan shoes, which smacked the pavement loud enough that I could hear his progress even from that distance. Trapped, we were trapped! That morning in the woods on the way to Franklin and then that evening at Gooder Grove replayed in my mind, Sparky's maladroit malediction, and malcontent Gamer withal. I couldn't endure it, not again. I waved with a fake smile in his general direction, and then we took the first quick turn we came to.

Later that evening at The Broken Fiddle, we were all sitting out back drinking beers when Gamer banged through the gate. He eyed me with a penetrating look of hurt and betrayal, leaving me stranded bare under his gaze.

"Hey Gamer," I said with as much manufactured enthusiasm as I could muster.

"You hurt my feelings, Solo," he said right off. Every conversation paused, and now every eye was on me as if I'd committed some grave sacrilege.

"What do you mean?" I asked innocently.

"I waved at you and you ignored me."

"Oh?" I deflected with the skill of a stage actor. "That was *you*? Sorry Gamer, my eyes...I'm old, man. I don't see well anymore." I see well enough, but this excuse would spare me embarrassment more than once on the trail to come, when I would forget people's trail names and pass it off as an inability to focus on faces. Old men, I have learned, can get away with things.

"Oh, okay," he said, stowing his hurt and taking the seat next to me.

I drummed my fingers while the mass of him loomed on my blind side. "So," I asked queasily, "where's Sparky?"

"She went home. She was having trouble with her uterus. There was stuff coming out, you know? And her anus, too. That never did go away." Bile burned the back of my throat. I swallowed hard, which didn't help. Gamer went on: "I had to get away from her anyway. She was too violent. She hit me, man, and I won't let myself be abused that way. She's an abuser."

I couldn't shake off the incongruity of that image. "But I thought you two were, you know, pretty tight."

"Not anymore."

"So you're still hiking."

"Yeah. I've been yellow-blazing some, but I'm going all the way. Maybe you and me could hike together for a while."

"Uh...well—hey, I think my clothes are dry now. I'd better go get 'em so someone else can use the dryer. See you in the morning, yeah?"

"Yeah, Solo. See ya."

To my relief I never saw Gamer again.

WEDNESDAY, JUNE 16, 2021

Lost Mountain Shelter - 15.8 Miles

One full month on the trail.

Killed the morning until 9:00 a.m., when I went to Sundog Outfitters to buy a few more things, mainly a Gossamer Gear pouch to hold my phone on my pack strap, and a waterproof food bag that custom-fits into the pack.

Had breakfast with Ultra Burn and K-Bar, almost like old times if not for some undefinable tension. I don't get the sense that K-Bar is here to hike with us again. She was noncommittal when I asked.

Hiking by 10:00 a.m. I was alone all day on an easy section of trail, but lethargic from the zero so my pace was slow. Arrived this shelter at 5:00 p.m., the place crowded with tents. Tombstone is here, although Matador pushed on a few more miles. I think they've had some kind of falling out. Tombstone is tight-lipped, and seems preoccupied. Ultra Burn came in about 6:00, alone, and not talkative right now.

Set up the tent easily with the new backpack, geez what a revelation! Also saw a bear today. It came ambling onto the trail, looked up at me in surprise, I shouted, and it bolted into the woods as it's supposed to.

Nothing more. It's going to be a little cool tonight, I think.

THURSDAY, JUNE 17, 2021

Massie Gap - 17.4 Miles

For the first time in a while I did not sleep well. Woke up hour by hour after midnight, then finally just got up at 4:15 a.m. Coffee, breakfast, everything packed by 5:00, just waiting for the sun to rise. Started hiking at 6:00.

Alone all day. Saw herds of ponies, day hikers out petting them as if the ponies were tame and this was a petting zoo. We're not supposed to approach the ponies, let alone touch them. Sigh.

Made nobo climbs that were always downhill before, so worked up a sweat where I didn't expect it. Reached Massie Gap at 2:30 p.m., no cell reception so couldn't call Dennis, but I met a woman day hiker who drove up the road to a high point and called him for me.

In the meantime, I had no idea where Ultra Burn was, afraid he'd blown past the side trail and was on his way five miles farther to Wise Shelter. He did show up at 4:00 p.m., almost exactly as Dennis pulled up, so serendipity worked and Dennis shuttled us to his Grayson Highlands Inn, my third stay.

Not much else. We ate, drank beer, drank wine. Ultra Burn opened up a little more about his past, I think to deflect whatever went on between him and K-Bar, or him and Breezy, or him and whoever else. What I know at my age is that we make life more complicated than it needs to be. Maybe we just get bored, who knows?

Now I must sleep.

FRIDAY, JUNE 18, 2021

Dickey Gap - 17.4 Miles

Up early as always, had breakfast with Ultra Burn, then Dennis shuttled us to the trail at 10:00 a.m.

The trail was easy today, some rocks and light climbs but plenty of long flats where I could make 3 mph.

Reached Dickey Gap at 5:15 p.m. Canyonman was already there waiting, along with Ultra Burn, who'd blazed past me earlier. Canyonman drove us to a family restaurant, the same one he took me to last time, then to another restaurant where Alice was working. Alice was very busy, but took the time to see me and offer a warm hug. It was great to see her again.

Canyonman then drove us back the other way to the church hostel in Troutdale, where to our surprise K-Bar showed up an hour later. It was a reunion of sorts, but K-Bar is diverting to Marion tomorrow to meet up with her moms. I have a feeling of finality about all this. Damn, I like it when K-Bar is with us. I wish she and Ultra Burn had just been friends, nothing more, if my suspicions are accurate.

SATURDAY, JUNE 19, 2021

Chatfield Shelter - 20.9 Miles

Did not sleep too well, too much thinking about K-Bar and Ultra Burn. Up early, coffee, the usual.

Canyonman showed up at 8:00 a.m. We left K-Bar for her moms to come get, and were hiking by 8:30. It was a mostly fast day. Spoke with some trail maintainers who tossed me a beer as I was crossing a forest road, and a woman out for a test hike. She wants to thru-hike, but has all the wrong gear. I tried to tell her but she wouldn't listen, just argued with me so I pushed on.

Saw a bear, which ran off as it was supposed to. Reached Partnership Shelter at about 3:00 p.m. to find the water turned off. The visitors center was closed as well, so no cold drinks, but as we crossed the road we found K-Bar and her moms there doing trail magic. I thought I would tear up.

Drank lemonade and ate Little Debbies, shook hands with the moms, and pushed on for six miles that took three hours. The Glade Mountain climb was slow and rocky. I've always taken this going down so never noticed how rough it is.

Didn't arrive at shelter until 6:30 p.m. Tired now. Atkins tomorrow.

—

Our evening at The Broken Fiddle didn't end with Gamer's unexpected appearance. He wandered off at some point, whither I neither knew nor cared, so I was able to rejoin the group out back.

As dusk eased toward darkness, K-Bar came in with Breezy close behind. I lit up when I saw K-Bar, as if there were hope yet to preserve our tramily. She got herself situated in the bunk next to mine, then came back out to find Ultra Burn off in the far corner of the yard with Breezy. If this vexed her she didn't show it. In truth, I think she might have been relieved. We talked lightly for a while, any depth subsumed by her innate reserve. Ultra Burn would say something that would make Breezy laugh, then he would shoot a glance our way. I sighed at the universal adolescence of it but I had been there more than once myself in an earlier life so withheld judgment. Matters would eventually work themselves out, it was only that we might not all be there to witness it.

The next morning marked one full month on the trail for me. We had breakfast together, just the three of us, all expressions placid but there was still an indefinable tension at our table. I worked to re-conjure in my mind that elaborate breakfast we'd had at Fontana Resort, Hoosier Daddy there with us, everyone fresh and smiling, like an innocence, but I found it shadowy in my thoughts, hard to bring into focus. At ten o'clock I left the two of them to whatever they needed to work out, and started hiking.

That section of trail climbing from Damascus toward the Grayson Highlands was a beauty of wondrous hiking and equally wondrous views, but I felt lethargic, uninspired. I was alone for most of the day, reached Lost Mountain Shelter at five o'clock to find it crowded with families in tents and in the shelter as well. A baby was crying in there as its mother changed a diaper. Children argued and tussled. I spotted Tombstone stretched out on the shelter floor, seemingly oblivious of the commotion around him.

"Hey Tombstone."

"Hey Solo."

"Where's Matador?"

"He pushed on a few miles."

"Alone?"

"Yeah."

"Hmm."

Tombstone didn't want to talk, that was obvious. Now I know why. He was wrestling with a decision. Ultra Burn showed up by and by, alone and also not talkative. It was as if there'd been something in the water in Damascus. We pitched our tents and called it a night.

I didn't sleep much that night, too many thoughts circulating that I couldn't quell. At four fifteen I got up in frustration, shuffled out of my tent into a chill morning, and found Tombstone packed up and ready to hike.

"Hey Tombstone," I said quietly.

"Hey Solo."

"You're up early, dude."

"Yeah, I need to get going."

"Where to?"

"I'm not sure yet."

And with that he slipped into the dark, the last time I would ever see him.

Breaking camp was so easy with the new backpack that I was fed, full of caffeine, and ready to go by five o'clock, waiting only for the magic hour to rise. Climbing into the Grayson Highlands during the magic hour was an unrivaled reward. I cannot do justice with words to the beauty of it. Some places must be felt as well as seen, absorbed in their entirety. The only barriers to a perfect day were the swarms of day hikers out to see the wild ponies. The trail was wide enough to accommodate many people. This wasn't a reprise of Max Patch, that wasn't the issue, it was that people were crowding the ponies. The Grayson Highlands ponies are wild animals, perhaps gentle at first blush but still unpredictable in their behavior.

I pushed on through this under a remarkable sky that leant beauty to more than just the ponies, but the highlighted ridges and enriched greens were not where the phones were aimed, they were aimed at the ponies, where people blithely mingled and took their selfies. One woman posed with her arm around a foal while its dam stood puffing nervously nearby. If I had confronted any of these people I would have drawn explosions of belligerent indignation, which can't be defused without the authority of higher office. I've worked at national parks, I've seen this play out many times.

Once, while stalled in a bear jam on the park road at Denali, I observed a father holding his toddler out to a grizzly bear cub so that the child might pet the cute little fur ball. In circumstances like these, with tragic death but a paw swipe away, we act immediately whether we wear the uniform or not. I bounded out of my vehicle, hollered at the father to back away from the cub, nervously eyeing left and right for the sow. There were other people out of their cars as well, kneeling, grinning, their cameras tuned to the cub, their situational awareness narrowed through their apertures, and all in the potential path of a maddened bear mother.

The father turned on me in fury, meaning to reverse his foolishness to the many witnesses. Who was I to tell him what to do? He reddened, hurled insults. Spittle flecked from his lips. With his toddler tucked under his arm like a football, his back now to the cub and possibly an angry sow, he bunched a fist as if ready for blows; and as I hopelessly grappled for a way to calm the father down in a situation that had escalated in an instant, a patrol ranger stepped in and took the father in hand.

That blind belligerence evaporated as instantaneously as it had appeared. Here, now, was a man in uniform and with a gun on his hip, the authority of higher office. The toddler was taken bawling to its mother, and the father was taken meekly to the jail in Fairbanks.

So I left those posing people unchallenged, climbed the next ridge, and hoped no one, pony or human, would be hurt today.

Once beyond the ponies I had the trail to myself again. The day continued cool, the sun clean and bright, the sky a portrait of purity. Some of the climbs were strenuous enough to draw beads of sweat despite the refreshing breeze. These were climbs I had previously taken at a leisurely pace as a downward grade, now reversed and reminding me once again that my six thousand miles of southbound experience would not always translate accurately to this northbound venture.

I stopped for a break at Thomas Knob Shelter, a sturdy two-story structure where I weathered a weakening Hurricane Hannah during Hike 2, then went a few more miles to Massie Gap and the side trail that led down to a parking area. It was only two thirty. I could easily have pushed on another ten miles through that gorgeous day but I wanted to stop in and see Dennis Conroy, who owns Grayson Highlands Inn.

I met Dennis on Hike 3 when Wind Rider and I came through. The two of us had been aiming for Thomas Knob Shelter, which was closed at the time because of bear activity but, as I explained to Wind Rider (a flip-flopper of about my age), Thomas Knob Shelter had two stories with a ladder to the loft. The only other shelter on the Appalachian Trail that might be safer from bears was Chestnut Knob Shelter, a stone shelter with a heavy wooden door where we'd stayed three days earlier. I'd injured my left leg on the climb to Chestnut Knob, though, and by the time we reached Massie Gap that leg was so swollen that I had a difficult time putting my shoe on. At Massie Gap I decided not to risk pushing it farther, so we dropped down to the parking area, caught a ride, and spent two days with Dennis at Grayson Highlands Inn while my strained tibialis anterior healed.

Dennis, who was older than me but looked no worse for it, proved to be an interesting and attentive host, with a knack in the kitchen for producing some delicious and visually pleasing dishes, almost all of them organic. He had restored the old inn himself, and had surrounded it with gardens of grapes and herbs and flowers. A brisk stream lay across a smooth lawn behind the inn. It really was a pretty place, quiet and restful. I returned by car for Trail Days in 2019 and stayed another couple of days, feeling by then that I'd gotten to know Dennis pretty well, so I looked forward to seeing him again.

There was no cell service in the parking area. A day hiker I'd met just returning to her car promised to call Dennis for me when she reached a high point, so I settled in for the wait, praying that Ultra Burn didn't miss the side trail, which would not be hard to do since that area was crisscrossed with social trails.

An idle hour passed. For a thru-hiker, sitting idle for an hour in excellent weather translates into bemoaning regret, of the miles that could have been made, and the scenery gone unseen. At four o'clock I grew anxious. If Dennis arrived before Ultra Burn, and with no way to make a call, Dennis would either have to sit idle with me, wasting away a day that would have been crowded with repairs and other chores at his inn, or else I would have to send him back with an empty truck, which would have wasted his time on a considerable drive. Either way, I wouldn't leave without Ultra Burn. He would have no idea what had happened, would push on to Wise Shelter thinking that's what I'd done, and then we would be separated by enough miles to keep us separated. Our fellowship would end ignominiously.

It was with relief, then, that I spotted Ultra Burn bounding over the rise toward the parking area. At almost the same moment, Dennis came rattling up in his truck. Such coincidences occur continuously on the Appalachian Trail. It was as if Ultra Burn had planned it that way.

Dennis wore a black face mask and seemed uncharacteristically reserved. He didn't remember me at first, which caused a pang, but once I reminded him of Wind Rider and my injured leg, and then my stay during Trail Days, he came around, if not with the enthusiasm I had anticipated.

Because of Covid, we rode to the inn in the bed of his truck. Dennis got us settled then went about his business. The rooms at Grayson Highlands Inn are excellent if not inexpensive. I told Ultra Burn that I would be covering the cost. Ultra Burn was only there because I had come to see Dennis, otherwise we would already be at Wise Shelter if not beyond.

We went down for food and beers. Dennis continued to seem subdued, Covid perhaps. Who knew how his business might have suffered, what strains he might be under? I worked to draw him into conversation, reminded him of Rocky, the thru-hiker I'd met there during Trail Days. Rocky was a peripatetic woman of my age who suffered from a host of physical ailments but who swore she'd complete the trail. I'd shuttled her around during Trail Days, watched in awe as she successfully yogied gear from the vendors. Dennis and I had both seen her off when she continued her hike. I wondered if she made it. Dennis didn't know, didn't seem too invested one way or the other. When he shuttled Ultra Burn and me to the trailhead the next morning it was with little fanfare. I took to the trail hoping that whatever burdens were weighing him down would ease soon.

That day would see us to Dickey Gap and another reunion. On Hike 3, without a tent, I had reached Dickey Gap in the lowering light and stood futilely at the road with my thumb out for a hitch to the church hostel in Troutdale. As night fell further and no one would stop, I had retreated dejected to a split rail fence, where I sat and pondered what to do. In the last gray light, a red car swerved into the parking area. An aging, well-built man with a white goatee and a shock of white hair got out and hollered my way, "Do you need a ride?"

"Yes," I bounced up, saved.

This was Canyonman, a 2014 thru-hiker, and his wife Alice. The two drove me way off and gone to a family restaurant, where they left me to eat my fill, returning later to drive me way off and gone in the other direction to the church hostel in Troutdale. The next morning at eight o'clock they arrived to carry me back to the trailhead. In between, more appreciative than I could ever repay, I got to know them a little, and I liked them. So it went without question that I'd want to see them again when I went through Dickey Gap, and Ultra Burn was supportive all the way.

The 17.4 miles we made that day went quickly over a generous trail. Ultra Burn had gotten out ahead, and was there waiting with Canyonman when I arrived at five fifteen. Canyonman held out his hand for a firm handshake. He looked exactly the same except for perhaps a bit more beard. His dry jokes still made me laugh, and the family restaurant still served the same Southern comfort food. Canyonman stayed with us through the meal then drove us to a restaurant farther on where Alice was working. That restaurant was a higher-end affair, every reserved table taken. I spotted Alice right off, scooting from table to table, but she halted when she saw me and came in for a warm hug.

"Do you remember me?" she asked.

"Of course I do," I answered somewhat emotionally. I had been reunited with many people on the trail, but Canyonman and Alice were the only ones to extend me sincere recognition, reviving Hike 3 as if it were still ongoing.

Eventually Alice had to get back to work. Canyonman drove us to the church hostel in Troutdale, where Ultra Burn and I sipped our secreted beers and waited alone for night to fall. We were on the porch in the dulling light when a pick-up truck swung in. A long, lithe leg appeared beneath the passenger door, and out stepped K-Bar!

I was elated. Ultra Burn might have tensed somewhat. K-Bar bounced up with an astonished smile.

"Ohmygod!" she exclaimed.

"Did you know we were here?" I asked, dumbfounded.

"No-uh."

"What a freakin' coincidence."

But she hadn't caught up to rejoin the tramily. Her moms were in Marion, Virginia, one of them desperate to bring her home. They would be meeting up tomorrow.

This time I didn't leave the two alone but spent as much time bogarting K-Bar's attention as I could. Damn, it was good to see her again. She explained about her moms, how one of them supported her hike, albeit grudgingly, while the other remained completely unreconciled to the idea even though her daughter had already hiked five hundred miles without incident.

We said our goodbyes in the morning, another of those partings that felt permanent. I watched K-Bar waving from the porch as Canyonman drove us away.

That day also went quickly, livened by some trail maintainers who tossed me a cold beer as I crossed a Forest Service road. I stopped to speak with them and to thank them for the beer and their hard work. They're the ones who brought up the ATC after learning of my several thru-hikes.

"So do you think the ATC has changed since your fist hike?" one of them asked me. I cautiously nodded. "Yeah, I'm not too sure what's going on with them," he went on. "It's not the same anymore."

"How do you mean?" I asked.

"I don't know. It's like they think we work for them, that they can tell us what to do–like we're not volunteers–you know?–like we're employees or something."

"Well," I said, standing, "you all *are* volunteers and we can't thank you enough for what you do."

"We appreciate that," he said. I tipped my hat and returned to the trail.

Later, I came across a thirtyish woman in heavy hiking boots and with a backpack that would burden an elephant.

"Are you a thru-hiker?" she asked as I was going by.

"Yeah."

"But your pack is so small."

"Well, I'm not quite ultralite, but close enough."

"Do you have time to give me some advice?"

I pulled up short and turned. "Sure, if you want."

"I really want to thru-hike the A.T.," she said. "I came out today to practice, you know?" I nodded. "But I'm not sure if I've got the right gear. What do you think?"

I approached this hesitantly because of my earlier interactions with people who wanted advice, but she seemed assiduous enough.

"First," I said, "you need to lose those boots and wear a lighter shoe."

She immediately objected. "But I need the support. I have to wear boots."

"You can wear ankle braces if that's what you're worried about." I tapped my own ankle brace with a trekking pole tip.

"No, I don't want to do that. I'm gonna stick with boots."

This came out defensively, tinged with a bit of heat. I sighed, eyed her elephantine backpack, and chose to take this no further. "Well, good luck, then," I said, and resumed the trail. Why ask advice if you're not at least prepared to accept it?

Ultra Burn and I reached Partnership Shelter together at three o'clock. Partnership was a Hiker Hilton, multi-story with a shower on the side. I'd never stayed there, catching it early going south or north. On Hike 3 Wind Rider told me with disgust how weekenders had set their tents up inside, leaving no room for anyone else. "I pitched my tent out back that night," he grumbled. "Jesus."

Nevertheless, we were alone on that day and not planning to stay anyway. I thought a shower would be nice, though, and was disappointed to find that the water had been shut off. We pushed on the short distance to the Pat Jennings Visitors Center and the hope of a vending machine, but found the visitors center closed, practically derelict. That was a disappointment, so we downed tepid water from our bottles and pushed on another short distance to the highway, where we found K-Bar encamped with her moms and a car trunk full of trail magic!

Oh—my—word—I didn't know which to be most excited by, the sight of K-Bar or the prospect of food and cold drinks. We hustled over and dropped our packs, K-Bar made beaming introductions, and then we proceeded to stuff ourselves.

One of K-Bar's moms was about my age, while the other was somewhat younger. It was the younger mom who objected so vocally to her daughter's hike. The two were on the other side of the car in heated discussion as I jammed another Little Debbie into my mouth. Ultra Burn was sitting in the grass, inhaling a bag of chips while carrying on a conversation with the older mom.

"You need to come home," I overheard the younger mom firmly say.

I quickly washed that Little Debbie down with lemonade, then spoke up as if to no one in particular, "I wish more than anything that I'd hiked the Appalachian Trail between high school and college." Both moms paused in mid-sentence and focused on me, while K-Bar seemed to tip a little taller if that were even possible.

"Why?" the younger mom asked me, not perturbed but a little off balance.

"Because it's a character builder," I said. "I would have made better decisions."

"Like what?" she asked.

"Like I wouldn't have gotten married at nineteen, for one."

That took the wind out of any further argument. Conversation turned to more topical things, we finished our feast and helped load the leftovers back into the car, and then the younger mom came up to me and said with a beseeching look and a hand on my shoulder, "You look out for our little girl, now."

I replied: "I think your little girl is pretty good at looking out for herself." And then with a wink, "I'll keep an eye out, though."

That didn't satisfy but it did draw a begrudging smile. Now that it's done, I wonder what K-Bar's moms think about their little girl now?

The rest of that day slowed to a practical crawl for me as I made the climb up Glade Mountain, much more difficult going northbound than southbound. I still held out the possibility of making it to Atkins that day but when spatters of rain began to tap the bill of my hat as I descended the mountain, I knew we wouldn't quite make it. We dove into an empty Chatfield Shelter just as the rain came down in force, a disappointing 4.6 miles short of our goal but at least dry for the night. I was anxious to get to Atkins, which has stood as a milestone for me on every hike since Hike 1, but settled with consoling myself that it would still be there tomorrow.

SUNDAY, JUNE 20, 2021

Knot Maul Branch Shelter - 19.1 Miles

What a day! Up early and a fast hike to Atkins, resupply, beer, then an hour and a half wait for the restaurant to open. Used the time to dry out my tent, shoes, and socks.

Dave from The Station at 19E, the hostel up the road from Mountain Harbor, showed up at the restaurant doing trail magic. He paid for our meals, and for some other hikers as well.

Pushed on at 12:30 p.m. Passed a woman named Pink Panther and gave her one of my beers on Walker Mountain. Continuing on through hot farm fields, we found the Bear Garden Hiker Hostel where we had cold drinks and where Roberta (Bert) gave us cake and other food. She wanted us to stay, but we wanted to make that last climb to Knot Maul Branch Shelter and get it over with. Knot Maul was the last shelter I slept in on Hike 1. It was freezing cold then, I remember, and now it's burning hot.

All set up now. Time to sleep.

MONDAY, JUNE 21, 2021

Jenkins Shelter - 20.1 Miles

Hike Naked Day!

And yes, I did.

Slept well, out at 6:30 a.m. hiking naked for several hours until I encountered a group of (clothed) hikers at a stream with the bridge out. Hurriedly put on the kilt, forded the stream, and stayed in the kilt from then on, no witnesses to my first, only, and last exploration of naked hiking.

Pushed on, a hard climb up Chestnut Knob, much more difficult for nobos. Stayed till noon while my clothes dried from fording the stream and from a little rain. Ultra Burn showed up, then we pushed on for Jenkins Shelter, a slow, rocky trail with lots of ups and downs.

Alone in shelter with Ultra Burn. Maybe rain tomorrow. Thinking of an 11-mile nero to Robbie's place in Lickskillet Hollow. We'll see.

TUESDAY, JUNE 22, 2021

US 52 - 11.3 Miles

A spattering of rain overnight, then heavier in the morning. Gave up and stepped out into it at 7:00 a.m., thoroughly soaked in minutes. Made good time, though, and came out by the hamburger joint I've stopped at twice before.

Freezing cold and wet, enjoyed hot coffee and a burger while waiting on Robbie (Mongo) to pick us up.

Got to Lickskillet Hostel as the sky cleared. It was good to see Robbie again. He hasn't changed at all. Later, he drove us to Blacksburg so Ultra Burn could buy some equipment. Ate dinner there at a French bistro (ha!), then drove back to the hostel.

Damn it all, but my ziplock leaked and my diary got wet, making some of my entries smear. Robbie brought out a fan, so in a minute I'm going to prop this up in front of it and pray it dries out.

WEDNESDAY, JUNE 23, 2021

VA 606 - 18.4 Miles

Slept really well. Cold this morning, unseasonably so.

Robbie didn't get us to the trailhead until 8:30 a.m., but under clear and warming skies we made good time, racing through 18 miles by 3:00 p.m. and pulling up at Trent's Grocery for food and beer, which we had to go drink off the property.

Robbie brought us back to the hostel, where we learned that K-Bar is due in tonight.

Overall an enjoyable day. Also, this diary is finally drying out from yesterday's deluge. What a fiasco. I have lost some entries, but it could have been worse.

Lickskillet Hostel Me and Mongo

K-Bar isn't here yet. I'm tired so I'm turning in. Tomorrow we will try for Pearisburg.

THURSDAY, JUNE 24, 2021

Pearisburg - 25.9 Miles

Woke up early enough but couldn't get Ultra Burn moving until 7:00 a.m., which means we didn't start hiking until 7:30 or so.

K-Bar did come in last night with a couple of other hikers. I was already in the bag, so didn't speak with her much.

As soon as I said goodbye to Robbie at the trailhead, a red pick-up truck came speeding around the bend, forcing me to step back off the road, where I fell into a bar ditch full of poison ivy. I rinsed down at the first stream, changed shirts, and that was all I could do until Pearisburg, hoping I got it all off.

The hike started nice and flat and fast for 8 miles, then some climbs and rocks and overgrown trail. Still, I made good time. Finally, after 600 miles, I have my trail legs, woke up with them this morning. This always amazes me.

Racing all day with a focus. Ultra Burn got a call in to Doc, who reserved a room for us at Angels Rest. She remembered me, and gave us a discount on the room. I walked out of the woods at 4:30 p.m., amazing speed. Hot Tamale was driving by and picked me up, so I didn't have to walk the .7 to the hostel. As fast as I went, Ultra Burn was already here.

After a quick shower, Hot Tamale drove Ultra Burn and me to Doc's clinic, where both of us got chiropractic adjustments. After a full vegetarian meal at the Mexican restaurant, we came back to wash clothes. Now it's late and I'm very tired.

FRIDAY, JUNE 25, 2021

Mile 645.7 - 9.6 Miles

Wanted to sleep in today, but got up at 5:30 a.m. anyway. Our room was the same one I stayed in last time.

Lazed through the morning, hard to leave a place like Angels Rest. K-Bar did not come in. Once as little as 5 miles behind us, she apparently dithered at mile 611 and now she's 35 miles behind.

Had lunch at the Mexican restaurant, did resupply, then Hot Tamale drove us to the trailhead. Started hiking at 1:30 p.m., finally got to Rice Field Shelter at 4:30 p.m. What a long-ass climb! I did well, though, feeling my legs.

After a long break with disappointing views since the bald hasn't been mowed in a while, we pushed on an additional 1.5 miles to a campsite with water. We had hoped to push farther so we wouldn't have to call this a nero, but there's no water for the next 11 miles. Tomorrow we'll try 23.7 to War Spur, where I stayed with all those flip-floppers last time.

It's a breezy evening. Lots of deadfall around, not the safest place to camp but everywhere else is overgrown and full of poison ivy, so no choice.

SATURDAY, JUNE 26, 2021

War Spur Shelter - 23.7 Miles

Windy as hell all night, as if a storm were blowing in. Slept sparingly, expecting a branch to come down on my tent at any time.

Up at 4:45 a.m., broke camp and on the way by 6:00. The forest was foggy despite the wind, gloomy and eerie.

This was a tough hike. The trail was completely overgrown, so I have scratches and no few chigger bites. We might as well have just bushwhacked through on a straighter course and saved a few miles.

Reached shelter at 5:55 p.m., tired and filthy. Bathed in the stream, shared a pint of whiskey with Ultra Burn, and that's the end of this day.

SUNDAY, JUNE 27, 2021

VA 621 - 19.8 Miles

I slept incredibly well and woke to my first warm morning at 5:00 a.m.

Out of camp and hiking by 6:30 a.m. The first climb was tough, then came the second...

Still made good time overall, ahead of Ultra Burn until the last two miles, which was when a storm unleashed, soaking everything. This time I managed to get my diary and phone into the pack liner, but couldn't save the kilt, which is wet and heavy again.

Sprocket, a 6-time thru-hiker, picked us up and took us through the thunderous deluge to Four Pines Hostel, which is somewhat crowded this time. My fifth stay here. Almost lost my kilt going through the door, so heavy it was pulling off of my hips. That would have been awkward.

Showered and fed, I'm feeling well. I saw Joe, who still doesn't remember me and who looks as if he's not long for this world. I don't know what's happened to him. It's shocking to see him this way.

This place is full of stoners, and there's something off about Sprocket. Aimless Nameless is here, looking like Jesus and sharing bits of mystic wisdom. Tomorrow's hike will go over Audie Murphy and Dragons Tooth, a hard day ahead. I hope it doesn't rain.

MONDAY, JUNE 28, 2021

VA 624 - 21.3 Miles

I slept not too badly, woke up early but couldn't get shuttled to the trailhead until 8:30 a.m.

Set out with Ultra Burn in a warming morning for the long climb to Audie Murphy. This took a while and a lot of sweat.

Pushed on from there toward Dragons Tooth, a hellish hike of rocks and incessant climbs. I don't remember it being this bad. It's not a southbound/northbound thing, it all just feels different. I was cussing, pushing hard to reach Dragons Tooth, got there around 3:00 p.m., only 11 miles from Audie Murphy but it felt like 20.

So beat up afterward, and with a long, endless descent in the heat, we decided to bail out at the road to Four Pines Hostel. We'll make up the miles tomorrow, which is McAfee Knob day.

—

A clear sky greeted me the next morning at Chatfield Shelter. The magic hour had a wet sheen to it after the previous night's rains but there was no ponding on the trail. What soaked my shoes and socks within the first half hour was the tall grass on either side of the trail, grass that seemed determined to bend inward and meet in the middle of the trail rather than bend outward where its accumulated dew would not drench my feet.

Appalachian Trail thru-hikers encounter this peculiar grass off and on between Georgia and New England. It grows in preternaturally straight and narrow files along the trail edges as if it were sown by a farmer in a furrowed field. Bob Peoples believed that trekking poles caused this growth by punching holes at regular intervals and at the perfect depth for seeds picked up in passing. There's merit to his theory. In various sections of the trail, especially the climbs, the trail verges were churned into crumbling soil that ran as straight as the outer lane stripes on a roadway, this from the hundreds if not thousands of nobos who passed earlier in the big bubble, perfectly tilled for hitchhiking seeds.

The use of powered equipment isn't allowed in wilderness areas, so trail maintainers must rely on scythes to keep the trail cleared, implements that have no utility around rocks and roots. So the grass grows on, ever taller, leaning toward the middle, away from the wilder growth off trail, sometimes interweaving into a verdant quilt over the trail and soaking the shoes of those first to pass, such as early morning, magic hour hikers.

As a consequence, by the time I reached Atkins less than two hours later my feet were sloshing in my shoes.

The Atkins familiar to thru-hikers is not the town itself but rather an exit off Interstate 81. There is a truck stop, a pair of convenience stores, a motel, and a family restaurant. From Atkins, we walk along a road under the interstate, cross a farm field, and then reenter the woods, jarred in our passing by the heat off the pavement, by the roar of traffic, by a confused sense of dislocation.

On Hike 1 Atkins was salvation and sorrow. I had been freezing each night since Pearisburg, unable to sleep, unable to repatriate my cold-weather gear.

I lay shivering in a thin fleece bag liner each of those nights, heating water to hold in a bottle against my trembling core until my fuel eventually ran out, arising each frigid morning with stamina reduced in increments. When Kyle (a southbounder I'd been hiking with) and I reached Atkins, my demons were swirling so thickly they blotted out the sun. Kyle and I took a room at the motel, family owned then. Kyle paid for the both of us because I was practically broke. Once showered and fed, my disposition didn't improve. Kyle worked hard to wrench me out of that dark place. A few days off trail was all I needed, he said, a rest while my cold-weather gear came in the mail. I couldn't afford it, though. I didn't have enough money left to sit in a motel for a few days. The next morning, Kyle hiked on alone.

This was in the very front of my mind on Hike 2. I made it a point to stay at Knot Maul Branch Shelter, the last shelter I slept shivering in on Hike 1, then charged into Atkins in triumph the next day and took the same room I'd shared with Kyle seven years earlier. On Hike 3 I did the same, although by then the old motel had been sold and franchised, the quaint country aspect of it lost to history. Now, on Hike 4, those demons were exorcised in their entirety. I wanted nothing more than resupply and food, and then I wanted to push on and make miles.

I resupplied at the convenience store, always the best source for me. Convenience stores in the South have products that grocery stores do not, such as high-calorie energy bars for fifty cents, bags of peanuts two for a dollar, and plenty of beer on hand. I bought two extra beers and stowed them in my backpack for the energy boost I would need going up Walker Mountain soon to come.

The family restaurant was under new ownership and wouldn't open for two hours. I spread my gear out on the broad lawn to dry in the welcome sun, then sat back to await Ultra Burn, who came poking along about an hour later. We were the first in when the sign was flipped, followed by others in their Sunday clothes, fresh from sermons. As we ate, a man approached us.

"Are you two thru-hiking?" he asked.

"Yeah."

"Did you stay at The Station at 19E?"

"No," I said a little gruffly. "I always stay at Mountain Harbor."

"Well, that's okay. They're good people. I'm Dave from The Station and I'm buying your meals today. They're already paid for, so don't even worry about it."

I choked on a bite of biscuit, got it down, and thanked Dave profusely. As tradition-minded as I am, Dave's hostel had popped up as a competitor to Mountain Harbor on Hike 3, which is why my earlier tone was a little coarse. But it seemed I had misjudged him and his place. Passing through on the interstate, he knew Atkins was a waypoint for thru-hikers and had made it a point to exit and pass out some trail magic. You can never find the right words of gratitude in these situations.

We pushed on after noon into a day that was beginning to heat uncomfortably. Going up Walker Mountain, I passed a middle-aged woman named Pink Panther struggling on the climb. Did I think she could make it? she asked. Could she get all the way to Maine? I didn't think it likely, not if she was struggling down here. I didn't tell her that, of course.

"Sure you can do it," I said instead. "Look at the mountains you've already climbed. This is nothing compared to them. Tell ya what, I've got a beer for you when you get to the top. Just one step at a time and I'll see you up there."

I pushed on then, making the top soon after and pausing for a break with Ultra Burn. Our goal for the day was Knot Maul Branch Shelter, easy to reach now, so we lounged up there for a good long time. Pink Panther eventually drug in, sweating and spent. She sat back on a rock and fanned her face, her breath coming in gulps.

"See? You did it," I said with a grin. "Here, I've got that beer for you."

"What kind of beer?" she asked suspiciously.

"I don't know, PBR or Bud, something like that."

"*Budweiser?*" she muttered with epicurean distaste. "I've never had one of those."

"Well," I said, a little put off now. "It's liquid, it's got carbs—"

"And it's *warm*," she frowned as I handed her the can.

"Yeah, it is," I said testily.

She popped the top and slurped, revealing neither pleasure nor displeasure. Ultra Burn and I packed up then, said our goodbyes and carried on, expecting never to see or hear from Pink Panther again. In that trail eternity of months later while I was racing single-mindedly across the state of Maine, K-Bar texted me a photo of her and Pink Panther on Mt. Washington, where the two had crossed paths. Pink Panther had flipped somewhere south and was now on her way down the trail to complete her hike. She still remembered Solo, K-Bar wrote, and would always be grateful for the best beer she ever drank.

Knot Maul Branch Shelter came and went, and then it was June 21, Hike Naked Day. Hike Naked Day is an old tradition that I suspect dates back to the Hippies, but during three rounds of the summer solstice on the Appalachian Trail I had never actually seen anyone naked except a pair of nudists in Vermont on Hike 3. I had certainly never hiked naked myself, and debated whether or not I should do it this time. If this were to be my last thru-hike, though, it seemed vitally important that I incorporate as many traditions as I could; at the same time, a man my age prancing around naked also seemed puerile if not possibly creepy to any young women I might encounter.

It is perfectly legal to hike naked in national parks and other federal lands. That we don't encounter people hiking naked all the time is the oddity. My European friends are always amused by the native prudishness of Americans. Visit almost any beach on the European side of the Mediterranean and you'll get an eyeful. Hike in the Alps and you'll sometimes encounter completely unselfconscious free-hikers. As for my age, surely young woke people wouldn't descend into ageism. Older people might roll their eyes and think me ridiculously immature but I should at least be safe from any lecherous accusations by the younger ones.

So, with a kilt that could be whipped off and on in an instant, I went for it. I enjoyed a magic hour *au naturale*, and I have to say that this was thoroughly invigorating and came to feel so natural that I wondered why we wore clothes in temperate weather at all. This state lasted for exactly 3.7 miles. When I reached Lick Creek, where the bridge had been washed away, I spotted a crowd of campers on the far bank, some of them younger women. I was going to have to ford, and there was no way I could do that unnoticed. I dodged behind a bush, now more self-conscious than the dreamer standing naked in front of an audience. The kilt went back on and stayed on for the remainder of the hike, coming off again only at an empty Chestnut Knob Shelter where I laid everything out to dry. Ultra Burn walked up on me then, winced at the sight, and that ended my naked-hiking career.

Jenkins Shelter came and went, sending us into a morning of unceasing rain. No amount of waiting would dissuade it, so into it I hiked, soaked in seconds, my kilt again becoming a sodden burden around my hips. Worse yet, the rain became colder as the hours wore on. 11.3 miles later, at Brushy Mountain Outpost, my fingers were rigid, my trekking poles back in the crook between thumb and index finger. My lips were so numb I couldn't speak coherently.

Brushy Mountain Outpost has changed ownership several times over the years, but I have stopped there on each hike for welcome relief and whatever food was on offer during that particular time period. Since Hike 3, the place has kept the same ownership, pleasant people who see to thru-hikers' needs and with a menu that's manna on days like this. The trail comes out of the woods and onto a steep residential road that drops down toward U.S. Highway 52, a broad highway more like an interstate, which we pass under before climbing back into the woods on the other side. Coming down that steep road, northbounders will sight Brushy Mountain Outpost on their right.

Ultra Burn had made it in ahead of me. He was sitting in a booth inside when I stumbled in, able to sputter only nonsense because my lips wouldn't function. A man behind the counter brought me a cup of hot coffee, which I accepted gratefully and held between two ungraspable hands. I mouthed in the direction of my backpack outside, trying to let him know that I had money. He got the gist of what I was trying to tell him. "Don't worry about it," he said.

I sat with Ultra Burn, breathing in the warm vapor of that coffee until my lips loosened and I could speak again. Cold rain sheeted beyond our window.

"I've had enough of this," I said shakily. "Let's call Robbie."

Robbie, known as Mongo these days, ran a hostel in Lickskillet Hollow. I met Robbie on Hike 3 when he rescued me from similar weather albeit from Trent's Grocery farther north. If we called him he would come for us, I told Ultra Burn. Any further convincing wasn't necessary.

Robbie arrived within the hour, the rain by then a chilling sprinkle. He didn't remember me at first.

"Three years ago," I told him, "I drove with you to Pearisburg after dark to pick up a section hiker. On the way back we had a flat and were stuck beside the road till almost midnight. You didn't have a spare, and there was no cell reception, remember? A guy in a pick-up stopped, took your tire into Pearisburg, had it fixed, and brought it back to us. Otherwise we would have been camping beside the road that night."

"Oh, yeah, Solo!" he exclaimed with his broad smile. And with that it was like old times again.

Robbie was a younger man with the features of a haunted past. Hiking the Appalachian Trail himself one day, he crossed a state highway in Lickskillet Hollow and spotted an old derelict church. In a moment of inspiration he bought the church then went about restoring it, converting the interior into a soothing, roomy hostel. He knocked together a rustic shower house out back, and added a washing machine. For a few years now he'd been hosting hikers, shuttling them all over for resupply or repatriation with their vehicles. He didn't ask for money for any of this, but would accept donations if offered.

There were only the three of us there when we reached the hostel. Patches of cold blue were beginning to show above but didn't let enough sunlight through to warm the chill wind sweeping down from the hills beyond. I paused with a shiver to take in the old church. I have a fondness for old Victorian buildings (my own home being one of them). Robbie still had work ongoing, problems of rot and leakage to address by and by, but the church looked beautiful to me. Robbie had brought it a long way since my last visit.

After reinvigorating showers, we spread out our sodden clothes to dry, donning the loaner clothes Robbie kept in hangered rows up on the old pulpit. I discovered to my horror that the ziplock containing my diary had leaked and that page after page was smeared, like mascara running in tears down a heartbroken woman's face. In all my travels—all of them—this had never happened. Robbie brought out a fan. I propped my diary in front of it and prayed that this would be enough to dry it out. (It took two days but this did work; and with a magnifying glass and considerable patience I was eventually able to resurrect the smeared entries.) Afterward, Ultra Burn needed a new pair of trekking poles (the rocks had finally destroyed his first pair), the closest outfitter was in Blacksburg an hour or more away, so with Robbie we went.

The sky grew brighter as we proceeded, belying the misery we'd experienced earlier. Robbie described his travails, his daily struggle, a fall-off he'd had the previous year and his recovery from that.

"One day at a time," I told him from experience in my own family.

"Yeah," he repeated somberly, "one day at a time."

After the outfitter, we wound up at a fancy French bistro for a late lunch. I had to laugh at this. During my hikes across France I had subsisted on sacks of croissant and an occasional fast-food hamburger. A reviewer of my book *Hiking through History* had commented that I could have spared myself that if I'd just gone into one of France's plentiful bistros. The trouble was, after multiple trips and multiple hikes across France, I'd never found one of these ubiquitous bistros along my path. And here I was now, in a presumably authentic French bistro in Blacksburg, Virginia. The wait staff spoke English—thank God—and were completely unfamiliar with pastis, the other national alcoholic beverage of France. I educated them for the sake of authenticity and then we returned to the hostel.

The next day's hike saw us through 18.4 miles to Virginia Highway 606 and Trent's Grocery, where I'd huddled in freezing rain while awaiting Robbie last time. The weather had improved markedly, dry and warm, and we burned through those miles by three o'clock. With my diary and some of our clothes still drying at Robbie's place, we gave him a call for another stay, arriving to find that a couple of hikers had come in during the day and that K-Bar was due later that evening.

It was while lazing through the remainder of that day that Robbie began extolling the virtues of vegetarianism. He begged us to watch a video with him, a video that he'd watched countless times and yet he sat mesmerized throughout. He'd become a true believer. This was his lifestyle now, he said, and I should consider it myself. Many claims in the video were credible, others were nebulous about the science that backed them up, but because of my fondness for Robbie, and in support of this enthusiastic new drive in his life, I agreed to give vegetarianism a try. And I did try, but within a week, absolutely starving to death, I downed two pepperoni pizzas and broke the streak.

K-Bar hadn't arrived by nightfall. Weary, I turned in, awoken an hour or so later when K-Bar came in with two other hikers. I greeted her groggily then fell back asleep. If I had known that I wouldn't see her again from then until even now as I write this, I would have been more attentive.

I was up early the next morning, taking in the bracing air in the starlight. K-Bar was curled up tightly in her sleeping bag as I prodded Ultra Burn awake. She was still in that state when Robbie took us to the trailhead. We got the typical late start, the magic hour long past. The day was warming nicely, though, clear above, a promising day ahead.

We said our goodbyes, swore to keep in touch, and while Ultra Burn was still gathering his gear, I stepped out of the parking area to cross the road. Just then a red pick-up truck came barreling around the bend. I could see the redneck behind the wheel, I could see his Purina hat, I could see his eyes, and I swear he was aiming right for me. I took a step back off the road as hot exhaust wafted across my face, then tumbled into a deep bar ditch full of briars and—poison ivy! It was a scratchy scramble to get back out. Up on the road, the red pick-up had rounded another bend and was long gone.

"Son of a b—!"

I retreated in haste to Robbie's car.

"Oh, crap!" I yowled.

"What's wrong?" Ultra Burn asked, startled.

"A redneck just ran me into a ditch full of poison ivy. Robbie, do you have any wet wipes?"

"No, Solo, sorry."

A man in a car parked next to us got out. "Here," he said. "Use these."

He tossed me a carton of wet wipes and I went to work in a panic, wiping every inch of exposed skin and then wiping again. 12.6 miles later, at a stream near Jenny Knob Shelter, I doffed everything and dared any passerby to comment. I bathed, rinsed, soaked my kilt on purpose. I emptied my backpack, plunged it in the stream over and again until I was satisfied. I even doused my trekking poles. It was all I could do. Eventually I climbed back into my damp clothes and continued on. I did not come down with poison ivy, thankfully, but what awaited ahead was almost as bad.

We made 25.9 miles that day, but with a late start and what came later I have always wondered how we managed. The trail over Angels Rest was completely overgrown, and I don't mean some inconvenient grass along the verges but a bonafide bushwhack that left stripes on my shins and scratches on my arms—and later, I learned, more than thirty chigger bites running from thigh to belly. This was the worst I had ever seen a section of the Appalachian Trail. I remembered that section as being somewhat wild on Hike 3, which meant trail maintenance hadn't been done in more than three years!

I reached the road to Pearisburg at four thirty, amazing despite it all, sure in the knowledge (and with an inner smile) that my trail legs had finally arrived when I woke up that morning at Robbie's place. The hike would change now, but at the moment I was filthy, bleeding from uncountable scratches, and carrying who knew how many ticks. In addition, the previous days of cool weather had morphed into a broiling heat. I took the baked pavement toward Angels Rest Hiker's Haven and a reunion with Doc, but was spared when Doc's current caretaker, Hot Tamale, pulled up beside me.

"You going to Angels Rest?" she asked.

"Yeah."

"I'm Hot Tamale. Get in."

Hot Tamale was a youngish woman with a wild side, on her way to the trailhead to pick up some other hikers. Ultra Burn, she said, was already at the hostel. I described to her my previous visit to Angels Rest, and after that she treated me as if I were a returning hero. She passed me a beer, had me sit beside her up front where the air conditioning vents could blow cool on my face, and made sure the hikers we picked up knew I was working on eight thousand miles.

Back at the hostel, Hot Tamale got me set up with Ultra Burn in the same room I'd been in last time. Doc wasn't well, she told me, a possible bout of long Covid even though the tests had come back negative, as well as some personal losses that had hit her hard. I liked Doc a lot. She'd treated me as if I were an old friend on my last visit, and I was desperately sorry to hear about her misfortunes. I made arrangements to go to Doc's clinic later that day for a chiropractic adjustment, a good cover because I really just wanted to check in on her.

In the meantime we set to all the usual thru-hiker chores, laundry, resupply, checking for ticks, showering off any lingering poison ivy, and most importantly, food. Walking down the driveway between the various buildings, I spotted a guy in robes sitting cross-legged in the grass and ministering mystically to a man seated in front of him.

"What's going on over there?" I asked a hiker in passing.

"That's Aimless Nameless doing some kind of guru shit."

"Is he a hiker?"

"He says he only hikes at night. I haven't seen him with a pack or anything, so who knows."

"Huh."

Hot Tamale drove us to Doc's clinic at six o'clock. It was closing time but Doc squeezed us into her schedule. I lit up when I saw her, and to my relief she remembered me. "Anyone who'd hike thirty-two miles to get to my hostel is someone I'd pick up at any hour," she'd told me on Hike 3 as I'd stood in the darkness at the trailhead without the energy to hoof it across town to her place. I'd liked her immediately, the look of her confidence and positive energy. I was saddened by the way she looked now, tired, gaunt, empty. It wasn't my business to pry, but...

"Doc, are you well?"

"No." She shook her head. Her personal losses were beyond the bounds of propriety but this was more than that. "We thought it was Covid," she explained, "but the tests all came back negative so it's still undiagnosed."

"How long has this been going on?" I asked, concerned.

"About a year," she sighed.

She asked about my health. As good as last time, I told her. I confessed my trail vice, hand-rolled tobacco, which I always abandon as soon as I'm off the trail. "Uh, huh, I know how you thru-hikers are," she commented wryly.

She then went about popping my vertebrae back into position, making conversation the way a dentist does when your mouth is open and instruments are in there and you can't do anything but *ah* and *uh-huh* in response. In this case my face was pressed into the drop table. Doc told me she was planning to take her skills on the road, traveling from place to place in her RV. She wasn't going to close the hostel, she assured me, but she expected to be away for a while. This would be her journey of discovery, I realized, her own hike. I wished her well, invited her to Tennessee, and still hope to see her again.

We got a late start the next day. Angels Rest Hiker's Haven is a hard place to leave. Hot Tamale got us to the trail at one thirty and then it took three hours to climb up to Rice Field Shelter, where we stopped for a break. It was hot again, the grass dry and dusty. I remembered blowing by here in my race to Pearisburg on Hike 3. A flip-flopper named Milo had made it to the shelter ahead of me and was setting up for the night. I waved to his startled expression as I passed at speed, in such a hurry that late in the day that I couldn't spare even the time for a chat. I remember thinking what a beautiful night he would have, the gorgeous sunset even then adding soft, dusky color to the bald and the mountains of West Virginia in the distance.

This time there was no view. The grass of the bald had grown chest high, a tawny barrier between the shelter and the horizon. Twisted trees had dropped deadfall all around the shelter, the entire site tinder for a careless campfire. Discouraged and disappointed, we pushed on over a trail that resembled something less than a jungle track. After a mile and a half we stopped at the last water source for eleven miles and pitched our tents in the only camp clearing we could find, which was in no great shape and required us to move deadfall and rocks. The limbs above us looked less than solid but there really was nowhere else to go. We took our chances.

The wind howled all night, as if a sea storm were blowing ashore. I slept in fits, listening for splintering limbs and expecting one to crash through my tent at any time. Fortunately for us any weak limbs had already fallen, and we safely passed the night.

I was hiking the next morning by six o'clock. The wind gusted gale-force through creaking trees that were invisible in a fog so thick that I had to keep my eyes on my feet less I blunder off into the blanketed bush, which would have left me turned around and lost within a few steps. There might have been blazes, perhaps resolving at the very last moment, but with eyes down I never saw them. It was only the trail, or the trace, really, that kept me moving in the right direction, and this was problematic for the first few hours.

The trail was so overgrown that it wasn't recognizable as a trail, at least in that dense fog. I navigated by intuition and the barest clues—a scuff on a rock, a tenuous thread of passage between dangling vines, a broken stick in my path, a clump of flattened grass—always aware and even anxious that if I stepped off the trail at any point I would be lost in the gloom with no sense of direction. The trail could be three feet to my left and I wouldn't be able to see it. If that happened I would have to sit and wait for the fog to rise, however long that might take. To blunder on would only mean losing myself further, with no way to find the trail even if the fog did rise. A compass (which I haven't carried on the Appalachian Trail since Hike 1) wouldn't have helped, not the way the trail jinks and turns. In clearer air I would have no choice but to navigate by the sun and bushwhack my way off the mountain, and with all the hardships that would invite. *Stay on the trail*, I always advise. *Don't go into the woods.* These are not the woods of our pioneer forefathers or the Indians that preceded them. These woods have been forested over and over again. The former stately hardwoods are beyond memory, the understory congested with sun-greedy vines and saplings and invasive species, not to mention ticks, chiggers, and other biting bugs.

Not that I wasn't essentially bushwhacking now. My feet were soaked from the grass, wild raspberry vines tore at my arms, nettles stung my ankles, and chigger bites were popping up on my thighs and stomach like red pepper on pasta. Eleven miles later I dropped itching and scratching down that horrid mountain, the fog lifted, and the trail was once again a trail.

The next morning at War Spur Shelter dawned warm, the first truly warm morning of the hike so far, presaging the days and weeks to come. I could sense it ominously when I scuttled out of my tent at five o'clock, a kind of enveloping warmth that felt out of place at that hour. The unseasonably cool mornings that we had groused about, mornings we would soon berate ourselves for not appreciating—those mornings were gone. Summer had arrived. I would not experience cool temperatures again until Vermont.

That day would take us through a series of intensive climbs and through ever-increasing heat, past Keffer Oak, the largest or second largest tree on the Appalachian Trail depending upon whom you ask, past Sarver Hollow, the sad site of a once prosperous chestnut farm that was devastated by the blight and is now overgrown and gone back to nature, and over Sinking Creek Mountain toward Niday Shelter and Virginia Highway 621 beyond that. A storm boiled up after we passed Niday Shelter, which left us soaked and standing under the barest protection of a tree at the highway trailhead. We'd meant to push on across the highway and up Brush Mountain but that plan was running in rivulets along with the trail.

"Let's call Joe," I hollered at Ultra Burn over the drumming din. "He'll come pick us up."

Joe ran Four Pines Hostel, a place I'd stayed on each of my hikes and a cross-country bicycle ride as well. I had intended to stop in to see Joe anyway but that was to have been twenty-one miles farther on the next day, when I could walk to his hostel from the trailhead. With a storm lashing around us, I was prepared to pay for a shuttle if I had to, anything to get out of that weather.

A burly guy named Sprocket picked us up. We dove into his car, slammed the doors against the rain, then Sprocket jerked the shifter into drive and lurched onto the road, tires spinning on the slick pavement. The rain pounded a crescendo on the car, windshield smeared, visibility nothing. In that the kind of rain I would pull off the road and wait it out if I were driving my own car. Sprocket took it at speed, one hand on the wheel, twisting through bends and curves as if he had a close, personal relationship with friction. I was in the front, where I hurriedly buckled in. Ultra Burn was in the back anxiously jamming his fingers between the seat cushions in search of his own seat belt. Sprocket said he was a six-time thru-hiker, leaving me with the impression that after twelve thousand miles he still hadn't found what he was looking for unless the search itself was his journey.

Sprocket got us to the hostel intact, the rain tapering off but still steady. Ultra Burn and I exited the car with urgency and with deep sighs of relief, our gear bundled in our arms. A few hikers were loitering under a canvas canopy beside the door. None of them moved to open the door for us, so balancing my gear with one hand I reached for the door with the other, and this was when the weight of my sodden kilt chose to follow gravity toward my knees, exposing what shouldn't be exposed for the brief moment it took me to wedge myself in the door frame and retrieve my free hand for a hurried and embarrassed tug. So unique and practical at the beginning of the hike, my kilt was now becoming unwieldy. I questioned whether it would see me all the way to Mt. K after all.

Inside, every couch was crammed with diffident hikers in various stages of inebriation. I found a bottom bunk, dropped my gear, and then took a look around. The place hadn't changed since Hike 3 but it had changed dramatically since Hikes 1 and 2, as well as my 2012 Tour de Virginia. Joe had put a lot of work into the place. The set-up was nice, rows of double-decker bunks on one end, an open area of couches in the middle, a long table and refrigerator on the other end, and a counter along the back wall that held coffee makers and microwave. There was a single shower and toilet behind a corner door, first come, first served, and with that crowd agility counted.

The hostel was in a garage up the hill from the main house and formerly adjacent to Joe's chicken coop. Back when, we slept on canvas cots between the mowers and other equipment, leaving the garage doors open for air, and were awoken in the morning by a thunderous, strutting rooster. Nowadays the garage doors were kept closed, while the rooster and his harem had been moved elsewhere. This was my fifth stay, but among that group I felt foreign, out of place.

The rain trailed off late in the afternoon, and Joe trundled up in an ATV. I rushed out to greet him but then pulled up short in shock. Joe was unrecognizable, pale and withered. His speech was inarticulate, as if he'd suffered a stroke. I approached squeamishly, asked Joe if he remembered me and received an incoherent reply. He didn't remember me, he couldn't, any more than he could probably remember breakfast that morning.

I remembered Joe as a wily fellow in cowboy boots who was friendly enough but left you with the impression that he wouldn't put up with any foolishness. He claimed at each visit not to remember me, which became a running joke over the years; and yet whenever I asked for a ride to the store a few miles down the road, he would toss me the keys to his truck or his van and say have at it, as if we were the oldest of friends.

I reminded him of this in that fragile way we speak to the impaired. I laughed and reminded him of my 2012 visit, when I'd cycled in and found eight or nine northbounders in residence. I'd wanted to do some trail magic for them, was about to swing a leg over my bicycle for a ride to the store when Joe tossed me the keys to his truck. "Take my truck," he said. "You've probably been on that bike enough today." (I had, fifty-four miles through cold rain and over countless hills.) I drove to the store, loaded up pizzas and beer, and returned to spread the magic. "We're vegetarians," those hikers told me. "We don't eat pizza." My face fell. "We don't drink alcohol either," they added. Those pizzas sat on the table until they hardened into cardboard. I did the best I could on my own with the beers, wondering exactly what kind of hikers I'd gotten involved with.

Joe and I spoke at length on Hike 3, that is after I'd returned from the store with his truck. He'd gotten his demons under control, he'd confided to me, a couple of years now. His wife Donna was the angel of his salvation. Joe looked good then, vigorous. I felt happy for him, unexpectedly elated, but now...it seemed that Joe's demons had finally caught up with him.

The rest of the evening of my fifth stay was a test of endurance among a diverse group of hikers who'd left Springer Mountain in March or April and who seemed to possess no sense of trail culture at all. Aimless Nameless was there, confirming that he must indeed hike at night or else he'd yellow-blazed from Pearisburg. He was tall, lithe, and wearing robes that belonged in Arabia. A thin brown beard and goatee lent him an aura of Jesus, which I'm sure he'd purposefully adopted to suit his image of mystic wanderer. He pushed a broom around the place, pausing to pass out bits of doggerel as if he possessed the eternal wisdom of the ages. I scowled at that and kept a distance. I'd met people like him on every hike, their journeys so clouded beneath pretense that their true selves were as indiscernible as the center of a black hole. I had no patience for it.

Needing to shuttle back to the trailhead, we got a late start the next morning. The heat was already oppressive. Our goal was Catawba Mountain Shelter at 23.3 miles, with the Audie Murphy Monument and Dragons Tooth in between. I assured Ultra Burn we could do it. I remembered this section. There would be some climbs but it wouldn't be bad past Dragons Tooth.

The climb up Brush Mountain to the Audie Murphy Monument was short on miles but long on hardship in the heat. I stayed ahead of Ultra Burn all the way to the monument, dripping more sweat in those few miles than I had in all of the hike so far. I sat on a bench across from the monument to wait for Ultra Burn, leaving a wet butt print even through my kilt. I loved that kilt and still do, but on that day I finally accepted that our time together was limited. As much as the waterproofing had been washed off and the thing became saturated in the rain, I could always wring it out and carry on. Now sweat was soaking into it as heavily as a downpour, chafing a salt rash around my hips. Too many days like this and that kilt would begin to reek as well. It would soon be past time send it home.

Ultra Burn finally arrived, dropping sweat-drenched onto the bench beside me. There was no glitter in his eyes, and his smile was something I hadn't seen in a while. He puffed a few breaths and asked, "So who's Audie Murphy?"

In my childhood, when World War II was closer in years than 9-11 is now, Audie Murphy was the ultimate American hero. He was the most decorated combat soldier in that war, a good-looking kid from Texas who came out of the war with combat fatigue—or PTSD as we know it now—but kept all of that closely concealed until he could conceal it no longer, as was the stoic way in those times. He made movies in the fifties and sixties, starring as himself in one of them (which couldn't have helped his PTSD), and became nationally famous. Later he would open up about his PTSD, which had left him so chronically dependent on prescription drugs that at one point he locked himself in a room for a week in order to dry out. On May 28, 1971, he was killed in a plane crash on Brush Mountain in weather similar to what Ultra Burn and I had endured a couple of mornings ago, joining Buddy Holly, Ritchie Valens, The Big Bopper, Patsy Cline, and so many more with that tragic distinction. It's why Elvis only traveled by bus, after all.

"Well, I never heard of him," Ultra Burn said.

I sighed. His words were ashes on the tongues of heroes. *All glory is fleeting,* George S. Patton said, and he was sadly unmistaken.

The rest of that day was hellish in the heat, with exposed, rocky climbs one after another. Something was off. It was as if the very trail had changed, as if a relo had been put in to purposefully make the trail more difficult. I looked for clues to this but couldn't confirm anything. The blazes were fresh. That could be from regular trail maintenance, though. The rocks weren't scuffed as you would expect after decades of thru-hikers on the march, but then maybe I simply couldn't focus well enough in the blazing sun.

I didn't reach Dragons Tooth until three o'clock, ahead of Ultra Burn and several pounds lighter due to the loss of fluid. I waited for Ultra Burn, we took photos, cooled off in the shade, then continued on into a hellscape of exposed ridges and baking rocks.

"This isn't right," I hollered back to Ultra Burn. "This isn't how I remember it."

In my diary from Hike 3 I described that section as being tough. Not this tough, though. I specifically remembered making the southbound climb up to Dragons Tooth because I'd been joined that day by a trail maintainer named Bob Egbert from the Roanoke Appalachian Trail Club. We'd carried on a long and interesting conversation as we puffed up that climb, passing day hikers in twos and threes as we went, so I expected to descend from Dragons Tooth this time, swing away from the side trail the day hikers use, and then stroll down the mountain to Virginia Highway 624, the road to Four Pines, where we could hitch to a nearby store, drink a few beers, then push on to Catawba Mountain Shelter.

But that's not the way it went. We seemed forever in the rocks, climbing, descending, then climbing again, exposed to the sun throughout, no water, and never once meeting a day hiker. I became convinced that we were on a trail relocation that was decidedly more difficult than the trail it had replaced. I have never been able to confirm this, although that section through there is a couple of miles longer than it used to be. In the heat I began to spin conspiracy theories of a trail purposefully made more difficult in order to dissuade the ever-growing swarms of thru-hikers, pretty wild imaginings but that's what happens when your brain shrinks from dehydration.

By the time we reached the highway we were sun-burnished and had cracked lips, too spent to continue, so we headed back to Four Pines for relief. Once we were clean and fed, as always, the day's struggles didn't seem as bad. I wondered about that trail, though, and still do.

The hikers were the same we'd left that morning, and with not a mile under their shoes that day. A lot of zeros were taken at Four Pines Hostel, a lot of hikers who would probably leave the trail once they'd overstayed their welcome with Joe. I kept to myself while Ultra Burn joined the others in a game of beanbag toss. I watched as his smile reappeared, and as he easily mingled and joked with the other hikers.

By now enough weeks had passed on the trail to fill a book of experiences. I was fairly certain that K-Bar's chapter in our book had ended. That I wouldn't see her again wasn't evident yet but I knew we needed to rebuild our tramily otherwise we wouldn't be a tramily at all, just two guys hiking together, one of whom was growing faster than I could manage.

Ultra Burn was intensely loyal but it was only a matter of time before he would yearn for company of his own age. I had come to think of Ultra Burn as a son, and sons inevitably go out on their own. I'd tried to tell him—to tell all of them—hundreds of miles ago as they spun fantasies of climbing Baxter Peak together, of continuing on together into life afterward, saying I would welcome them if their journeys took them in that direction while knowing as the words left my mouth that it would never happen. The trail is too long, the elongation of time too pronounced to make such plans. I'd invested myself before, with The Dude on Hike 1 and with others during my journeys around the world, only to see those lofty ambitions collapse at a turning point along the way. For emotional self-preservation I no longer invested myself in those

I met during my travels, even if I was as fond of them as I was of Ultra Burn and K-Bar.

Still, I made an effort to prolong our journey together. I tried to recruit other hikers into a new tramily, with new blood and aspirations and the prospect of fresh conversation in shelter at night, but none of them could keep up with us. None of them wanted to keep up with us. I couldn't get my mind around it. On my first thru-hike I was the one who couldn't keep up as the others found their trail legs and took off on big, endorphin-filled miles, reveling in the joy of simply being able to do it, while I fell farther and farther behind, riddled with envy. That the hikers I approached now didn't have this same drive perplexed me. It didn't make sense, going for short miles when they were capable of more, refusing to push their boundaries, refusing to employ the stamina that the Appalachian Trail had given them. This wasn't generational, this was just–incomprehensible.

So Ultra Burn and I hiked on alone, his smile back where he kept it these days, work to do.

TUESDAY, JUNE 29, 2021

Daleville - 25.1 Miles

I slept reasonably well, had everything ready, and was out the door at 5:00 a.m.

The trail was serene in the magic hour. It felt good to get an early start again. After a couple of miles, I ran into Aimless Nameless walking south out of the morning mist. Geez, I thought he was still back at the hostel. I told him he was going the wrong way. He fell in behind me, then went off somewhere to sleep through the day. What a weird guy. Dressed in robes, he thinks he's some kind of mystic. What he is is very confused by life.

I made McAfee Knob by 10:00, met Steph and Claudia, day hikers who took my photo and gave me ice water. I waited 45 minutes for Ultra Burn, but gave up and pushed on for the Tinker Cliffs. Ultra Burn finally caught up and passed me. He made reservations at the Super 8. I preferred the HoJo because it's hiker friendly, has a full breakfast, and that's where I've always stayed, but he read something on Guthook, so Super 8 it is.

After much cussing and scraped knees, I finally got out at 6:00 p.m., bone-weary from all the ridge and rock work, which–I–simply–don't–remember–from–last–time.

We're going to zero tomorrow. It has suddenly gotten super hot, and we can use the rest.

WEDNESDAY, JUNE 30, 2021

Daleville - Zero

Zero number five. Not bad for 700+ miles, I guess.

I tried to sleep late, but was still up at 6:00 a.m. Much to do today.

Laundry, resupply, an expensive visit to the outfitter for a hiking shirt, shorts, and sock liners.

Took a long nap, then posted field notes and photos. Finished the day with an Uber drive to a nice restaurant, wine and good Scotch. Thunderstorms this evening. I hope they rain themselves out.

THURSDAY, JULY 1, 2021

Bobblets Gap Shelter - 18.5 Miles

Out the door by 5:30 a.m. I waited for the C-store to open at 6:00, had coffee and a biscuit, then started hiking at 6:15.

This was an easy section. I remembered it once I got going, and I made a fast pace, arriving here at 1:30 p.m. just as it began to rain hard. Ultra Burn showed up at 2:30, the rain intensified, so we stayed even though I really wanted to make 6 ½ more miles. I beat the rain here, though, so it's good to be dry.

A group of teenagers came in soaking wet and with no place to camp. We made a dry space for them in the shelter to sit and warm up, then they pushed on to tarp-camp elsewhere.

Tomorrow might be a rainy day too, hard to tell from the forecast. We aren't cramped in here so the night should be okay.

FRIDAY, JULY 2, 2021

Cornelius Creek Shelter - 18.4 Miles

Rain overnight. Slept well. On the way by 6:15 a.m.

Moved out sluggishly at first but then picked up speed. Made Cove Mountain Shelter by 8:30, wishing I had just pushed on here through the rain yesterday. Odd, there was a full backpack lying beside the trail today, no one around anywhere. No clue.

Never got rained on, but the wet grass soaked my shoes and pruned my feet.

The day went fast, that is until the climb started, which was a sustained climb for about 4. miles. I reached this shelter at 2:30 p.m. and could have pushed on but I was tired and starving. Ultra Burn showed up about 3:30, then a section hiker came in, then a flurry of thru-hikers, I can't remember them all.

Tenting out tonight, which is clear and cooler. Glasgow tomorrow. I'd planned to bypass Glasgow this time but Ultra Burn wants to go in.

SATURDAY, JULY 3, 2021

Glasgow, Virginia - 20.1 Miles

What a strange, convoluted day.

I didn't sleep well at all because of constant wind. Woke up at 4:30 a.m. and decided to just get going.

Made great miles, passing sleeping thru-hikers in their tents, others in Thunder Hill Shelter. Big miles by 9:00 a.m., so I expected to reach the road to Glasgow an hour earlier than planned. One of the thru-hikers from last night, Ant Farm or Ant Twerp or something like that, passed me on the climb up Highcock Knob and acting cockier than the knob itself, so I caught him on the way down, wore him out, then passed him and hiked hard all the way to the James River.

I got out at 12:45 p.m.—pretty amazing—met a woman thru-hiker named Mosey who was waiting for a shuttle into town, which arrived shortly, so I hopped in with her.

The shuttle driver rubbed me the wrong way from the beginning. By the time we reached the hostel in Glasgow I'd had enough. I walked out, fully intending to hitch back to the trail. I ate lunch at the restaurant, resupplied, then met some guys who were staying at the public shelter. I went there, had a shower, and packed away my resupply. The guys told me that two trail angels—Delaware and Cobra—were going to throw a Fourth of July party at the shelter, so I stayed and tented. Good thing, too. Lots of food, fireworks, whiskey, and good conversation. Ultra Burn showed up. He also walked out of the hostel.

Now it's very late, I drank too much, and I want to get out early tomorrow.

—

The next morning at Four Pines Hostel, I gathered my gear in the slumbering hours and slipped quietly outside. The faintest glow limned the eastern hills as I made coffee. The starshine seemed close and intimate. I'd tiptoed by Sprocket on the way out, sprawled on a couch with his mouth agape and with an outstretched hand bare inches from an empty whiskey bottle. There were demons in his journey that had clung tenaciously through all his miles. How many thru-hikes would he need to send them away for good?

Back into the magic hour, I felt as if I'd returned to an ancestral place, where earthy smells and awakening sounds became one with the quiet and solitude. I pushed on in that serene quiet, grateful to be alive, relishing my time, when out of the mist ahead appeared Aimless Nameless, padding toward me like a messiah from the wilderness. He seemed startled to see me, snapping out of a meditation or at least wanting to appear as if he had. I was startled, too, having claimed the magic hour as my own and thinking him abed back at the hostel.

"You're going the wrong way, Solo," he said.

"No, you're going the wrong way."

"I'm going north."

"No, you're going south."

"Are you sure?"

"Positive."

"Hmm...well that's why they call me Aimless."

Had he really been hiking in circles all night? If so he seemed unaffected, his journey even less scrutable to me now than when I'd first met him. A journey muddled in mystery seemed more like confusion to me. Life does that sometimes. But then maybe that was his journey, to walk in circles until he figured himself out. He fell into step behind me. Minutes later at a side trail, he slipped off quietly, perhaps to sleep through the day, perhaps waiting until I was out of view to resume a southward trek back to the hostel.

I made McAfee Knob at ten o'clock with an empty water bottle and in an early-rising heat that had long since vanquished the magic hour. McAfee Knob is perhaps the most recognized natural feature on the Appalachian Trail, a high shelf of rock that juts out over a wooded valley far below. The site is stunningly beautiful, overrun now with day hikers. Land managers are at a loss for a solution to the crowding but really there's nothing they can do, any more than they could relieve the crowding at the Coliseum in Rome. A man taking a selfie had inadvertently backed over this a while ago, fetching in a crag below where he lay broken and bleeding until he expired. It was some time before his body was found. I'm not sure if they found his phone.

None of this was on my mind as I dropped my backpack and walked out onto that high shelf, but rather that I was dying of thirst and greedily eyeing the rainwater that had collected in the dimpled depressions in the rock, water that would evaporate by noon in heat like this. I fetched a bandana to soak up this shallow water, and was about to squeeze the drops into my parched mouth when a pair of young women interjected, “We have ice water.”

It took my shrunken brain a moment to register this. *Ice water?*

Their names were Steph and Claudia, good friends from up north who were combining an Appalachian road trip with short excursions afoot here and there. And they did have ice water, which they’d frozen in liter bottles back at their hotel. Imagine the heat, the baking waves of it. I fell on that ice water as if I were back in the Mojave in 2002 and were as close to death now as I was then. I drained that bottle until only a plug of ice remained. We set the bottle in the sun, and minutes later I was able to finish it off.

Steph was the adventurous one, stepping near the edge with complete confidence while Claudia writhed in terror. Steph wanted to take Claudia’s photo near the edge but Claudia wouldn’t have it. “I’m not going near that,” Claudia said forcefully. “I’ll fall, I know I will.”

“Listen,” I said to Claudia. “You hiked all the way up here, so don’t miss out now.”

“But it scares me.”

“I know it does,” I said gently. “But look—I used to work near the Grand Canyon. I met people all the time who had come all that way but were afraid to go to the edge for the view. It’s a natural fear. Just do what I told them, lie on your stomach and push along a few inches at a time until you’re there. You won’t be afraid to fall if you’re on your stomach. And then when you’re out there, you can prop up on your elbows, Steph can take your picture, and you’ll look like you’re sunning yourself and having a great time.”

Claudia was dubious but she did it. When she scooched back to us her grin was wide in triumph, her photo made, and it did look impressive regardless the trepidation behind her smile. I suspect she’s framed that photo by now.

I waited forty-five minutes for Ultra Burn but gave up in the heat before he arrived, pushing on to the Tinker Cliffs. The Tinker Cliffs are fascinating geologic columns that seem to support the table rock in the heights above the valley as if they’d been emplaced by giant Greeks. They’re wooded on top, so in the shade I had some relief from the sun. I took my time through that section, one of my favorites on the Appalachian Trail. Ultra Burn caught up to me on the far end, then we pushed hard for Daleville.

The trail brought us out onto more exposed rocks and ridges, in conditions almost identical to those we’d endured coming off Dragons Tooth. It wasn’t long before we were scraped, scratched, bruised and contused, and with water bottles nearly empty. I was again jogged out of the moment. I remembered a southbound climb through the woods, skirting a short ridge, crossing a power line right-of-way, and then back into the shade of woods. This time we were exposed, weaving around sharp, baking rocks for an indeterminate amount of time. I again began to wonder if my memory had simply failed me or if the trail had been changed.

I didn't get off the mountain and into town until six o'clock, where I sighted Ultra Burn sitting in the shade against the wall of a convenience store.

"Damn, that was hard," he said as I came up. He was sunburned, with lines of sweat salt on his shirt.

"I swear it wasn't this bad before," I said with conviction.

"Was it a relo?" he asked.

"I'm not sure, but it felt like it."

Ultra Burn had used his phone to book us a room at the Super 8. I had been in favor of the Howard Johnson's but he'd read something on Guthook that turned him off, so to the Super 8 we went. The Super 8 had a hiker rate and was hiker friendly. I had no complaints at all, but there was a time in the past when only the Howard Johnson's would welcome thru-hikers, with a computer for us to use, a hiker box we could rummage through, and most important, a full breakfast in the morning. I looked longingly across the highway to the Howard Johnson's as we walked into the Super 8, all my memories there, another trail tradition foiled by phones.

I felt we needed to zero the next day, more out of concern for Ultra Burn. Was I pushing him too hard? He was so naturally athletic, so fast, but I couldn't get past the notion that our hikes were diverging, that he'd prefer to slow down, that he was too loyal to me to mention it. K-Bar was back there somewhere, and with each day we added to the miles between us. Perhaps that's all that troubled him. He wouldn't reveal his feelings, even when I asked him directly. He was the same reticent young man I'd met in Georgia, no more prone to express his feelings than a sequestered monk, so I had to rely on intuition.

I had finalized my decision during the previous sweat-soaked days, that it was time to give up on the kilt. We went to an outfitter, where Ultra Burn tried on shoes and I shopped for hiking shorts and a light, long-sleeved shirt to ward off sunburn. My arms were pink and tender. My dermatologist would be furious when I got home. I don't use sunscreen on the trail because this attracts more dirt, which clings uncomfortably and is hard to wipe off. At some point on every hike I've switched to long-sleeved shirts. On Hike 4, now was the time.

This outfitter was also low on inventory because of Covid. I looked again for a Z Lite, hoping to finally rid myself of my inflatable pad, but they hadn't had any of these in stock for a while, they said. I settled on some running shorts, not exactly what I wanted but all they had in stock, along with a light-colored OR shirt with a good UV rating. The prices were shocking, but

I'd already gone through the hiker box at the Super 8 and found nothing, so I paid up with a wince. I washed the kilt and kept it my backpack for use as a pillow or blanket, thinking I might wear it again farther up the trail when the weather cooled.

Ultra Burn summoned an Uber, which carried us across town to a nice restaurant for dinner. As much as I enjoyed the good food, and the best Scotch I'd sipped since Fontana Resort, I couldn't help but feel that my hike was becoming too pampered, too out of sync with the old-school experience I'd hoped to rekindle this time. I wondered if I should count our Uber as a paid shuttle, and how long it might be before Ultra Burn called up Ubers at trailheads to spare us from having to hitch. I wondered if our hikes were diverging as much from his perspective or mine.

He vented about K-Bar, spitting biting comments inflected by terse lips. He was in the anger stage now. Acceptance would come by and by, and then hopefully forgiveness. I had no words to console him, only another literary analogy. If K-Bar were a character I'd created for one of my novels, I told him, she'd be a young woman driven to find her own way but still insecure enough to want to keep a support system close by. As my character grew in confidence, she'd allow that distance to increase day by day until she finally felt secure on her own, independent and able to command her own destiny. That was a character we could be proud of, I said. My analogy did nothing to alleviate his anger. Instead, I think Ultra Burn was becoming weary of my literary analyses.

In all our talks, the reason for Ultra Burn's journey had never surfaced. He was probably still unaware of it himself. He was a character I couldn't write, a cypher who stuck with me day after day if not increasingly impatient in the passing. He was growing toward realization though, I could sense it in his hardening demeanor, which lent him an air of almost tragic denial because of what this would mean.

When I first met Ultra Burn—when I first met Jersey—when I first met Ron—he wore a smile that would light a midnight room. I hadn't seen that smile in so long that I had to work to tug it from memory. The trail was less for it. I thought I could glimpse his hike now, gauzily, in the wake of K-Bar and with wholly new possibilities on a long trail to come. These were marked days, I could sense that with certainty. The luster was losing its shine. My hard-driving style, once so admired by all of them, was now in the way.

The next days flowed into what had become a routine, with me up and gone before the sun, and with Ultra Burn catching up later. We passed northbounders now by the tens or more, the tail end of an elongated bubble that we were piercing deeper and deeper each day. While most of these nobos were good company in shelter each night, I no longer tried to recruit them for a tramily. They had mostly left Springer Mountain in April, sometimes five or six weeks before we had. They wouldn't want to keep up with us, there was no reason to even ask.

Through bouts of rain and heat, we fetched up at Cornelius Creek Shelter a couple of days after Daleville. The hike that day had been long and tough under skies that vacillated between baking sun and the threat of rain. The inevitable last climb before shelter had been a four-mile slog up and over Floyd Mountain, which delivered me to the shelter early enough in the day to add on the 5.3 miles to the next shelter, but too weary to top the three additional peaks it would take to get there.

Ultra Burn came in an hour later, a bit chagrined that he hadn't caught and passed me that day. Soon after, a passel of young northbounders arrived, a tramily of their own. They'd left Springer Mountain on April 5, they told us, and were in awe that Ultra Burn and I had departed in mid-May. They couldn't make those kinds of miles, they said, and wondered if they would ever be able to.

"Everybody told me that Virginia would be flat," one young woman said to me. There were so many of them that I couldn't keep up with their names even long enough to log them into my diary.

"Virginia was never flat," I told her with a grave smile. "But I don't remember it being as tough as this." She had a physique for hiking, lean and athletic. I suspected that she was being hindered by her tramily, and desperately wished that she might join with us. She would be a perfect companion for Ultra Burn. That wasn't going to happen, though. I knew better by then. I added, to boost her confidence, "You'll be out of Virginia before you know it, and then it'll be easier-going all the way to Vermont."

"But what about the Whites?" she asked in that deer-struck way I saw so often when the White Mountains came up in conversation. By now her entire tramily had gathered around to listen.

"Don't worry about the Whites," I told her. "You've already climbed higher mountains. I promise you—by the time you get to the Whites you'll say 'Meh, just another climb.'"

"Is that really true?" She had perked up prettily at that.

"Yeah, it really is."

A red-headed guy with the dumpling body of massive weight loss stepped up then. His name was Ant Farm, or maybe it was Ant Twerp, hard to remember. "How do you keep from getting fat when it's over," he asked.

"Yeah, the hiker hunger," I nodded knowingly. "That's hard to handle. Whatever you do, stop eating as soon as you reach Katahdin. Only eat whatever the calories are for your age and height. You can look this up online.

Don't go over that, no matter how hungry you are. It won't be easy, but after a few weeks everything will settle down and you'll be able to stay at a healthy weight from then on. It's one of the side benefits of the Appalachian Trail."

"Yeah, man, I got it all worked out. I'm gonna go on a diet when I finish, just chicken breasts and things like that."

I'm not a fan of diets. They always seem to lead to some kind of dependency, a neurotic focus on every chewed bite. "I think it's not so much diet," I told Ant-Farm-Twerp, "but total calories. Eat healthily, of course, and eat what you want, just don't go over your calories. A little extra exercise helps, too."

"Well, I'm going on a diet anyway," he rebutted as if we were in debate.

"Sure," I mentally shook my head, "whatever works for you."

I was out early the next morning, of course. I'd encouraged Ultra Burn to get an early start as well but he couldn't be persuaded. Twenty miles that day would get us to Glasgow, Virginia. There was a hostel in Glasgow. I'd originally intended to bypass Glasgow this time but Ultra Burn wanted to go in. "Then get there early," I told him. "Get the benefit."

This was another of my sayings. To *get the benefit* of a hostel or a motel, it was better to get there early. Then you could get all your frenetic chores done early as well and simply relax for the rest of the day, rather than getting in late, racing through those same chores, only to fall exhausted into your bunk afterward. Late arrivals at hostels often led to zeros the next day, and I'd used up my compliment of zeros for a while. None of this changed his mind—or any of the others—so the magic hour was once again mine.

I'd stayed in Glasgow on all of my hikes. On Hike 1 I was there with Phil and Devon—a pair of fine young southbounders—in search of a telephone so that we might go to New York City and volunteer our help. (When we eventually got through, we were told that they had more volunteers than they could handle, so please don't come.) On Hike 2 I hitched in to get out of the rain, staying at the old motel (which is now some kind of low-income housing), and on Hike 3 I went in with a flip-flopper I'd met named Idaho. There was a hostel in Glasgow by then, a sister hostel to the one in Waynesboro, Virginia. The caretaker had been a saucy gal from Texas named Texas Dreamer, who told me doe-eyed and unabashed that she was attracted to older men with well-tanned pates. I did not act on that, and kept my towel tightly clasped around my waist when I came out of the shower. I liked the hell out of Texas Dreamer, though. It was doubtful that she would still be there but it would be a pleasant reunion if she were.

I made my magic-hour way over the peaks beyond Cornelius Creek Shelter (the late sleepers simply had no idea what they were missing every morning), dropped down into Petites Gap, then dug in for the climb up Highcock Knob, still some ten miles or thereabouts from the trailhead near Glasgow. I'd been alone and expected to stay alone for at least another couple of hours until Ultra Burn caught and passed me. It came as a surprise, then, when someone bumped into me from behind, almost sending me off the trail.

"What the f—?"

It was Ant-Farm-Twerp, climbing with purpose and shouldering past me as if I were no more than a tree in his way.

"Hey, man, don't sneak up on people. Say something next time," I hollered at his back. He was already a few steps ahead.

"Sorry," he mumbled, never turning to look at me.

What a dick, I thought. I wanted nothing more than to catch up to him and give him the tongue lashing of his life, but he was a third my age and there was no way I could catch him on a climb. But my age really wasn't it, I'm just slow on climbs. Even on the Pacific Crest Trail I had dawdled on those elegantly manicured reaches. I have no explanation for this, just a quirk of my physiology.

He was out of sight once I topped Highcock Knob. From there the trail rounded a mountain in a long, twining descent to the James River, and then on a few tenths to Virginia Highway 130. Glasgow would be about six road miles west. The day was fully up now, hot. The woods were parched, with few water sources along the way. I picked up the pace once gravity was again on my side, nearing Ultra Burn's speed and without a single panted breath.

When I spotted Ant-Farm-Twerp going around a turn well ahead, I added an extra step to my stride. I leapt down the steeper declines, took the impacts in my knees and shrugged off the pain. On the level stretches I made a pace just short of a trot, my breaths regular and measured, my heart thumping a slow dance. I had entered *arete*, that gorgeous Classical Greek concept of balance and excellence, or what I call *hiking light*, when your body seems ephemeral and practically glides over the trail.

I drew closer to him every time he came into view. At one turn, he looked over his shoulder and spotted me. I watched him dig in with his poles, watched him kick a step faster. Moments later I was into that same turn and he was making the next turn ahead, darting into it as if he might get away unseen. Before another mile had passed we entered a level stretch. I could see him ahead, close enough to observe that he was floundering now. I laughed inwardly. He couldn't keep this up, I knew he wouldn't be able to. He didn't have the stamina for the long race. He didn't have *arete*, he wasn't hiking light. Soon thereafter I caught up to him. He turned as if startled and said breathily, "Solo—I didn't know you were back there."

Of course you didn't, I thought with a laugh. "Sorry," I said, blowing past him, and I never saw him again.

The race with Ant-Farm-Twerp had me across the James River and with twenty miles under my feet by twelve forty-five, an amazing feat for me—hell, an amazing feat for anyone. There was a price, though. My brain was shrunken to a nutshell, my skin was filmed with stinging salt, and I was mortally desperate for a cold beer. But the beer would come. I'd made it out early. I could now get the benefit.

I dropped my backpack in the full sun of the parking area, beside a woman thru-hiker whose name I learned was Mosey.

"Are you waiting for the shuttle?" I asked her hoarsely.

"Yeah. I called. They should be here soon."

"My friend Ultra Burn called from up on the mountain, but I don't know how far back he is."

There were day hikers out, cars coming and going. A white van pulled up and parked in front of us. "Do you think that's the shuttle?" I asked Mosey. She only shrugged, so I went to the driver's door to inquire. The window was up, the driver eyeing me as if I were a roadside panhandler. He was fiftyish, a little heavy, with a thin black mustache above a curling lip. That look lingered longer than necessary, then he grudgingly rolled the window down.

"Are you the shuttle to the hostel?" I asked him.

Again that look, as if a simple question were an impediment to his day.

"Yeah," he answered in a desultory way, that single syllable carrying an unmistakable Yankee accent, and I knew right then: *bad juju*.

Mosey moseyed over.

"Did you call?" he asked her.

"Yeah."

"You Mosey?"

"Yeah."

"Go ahead and get in."

"My friend Ultra Burn was supposed to call from the mountain," I said through the window. Mosey was loading her pack and poles into the back. "Did you hear from him?"

"Maybe." That came out as an insult, I'm not sure how.

"So can I catch a ride with you?"

"I don't know. *Can* you?" I blinked a blank reply at the non sequitur, unable in the hot sun of the moment to fit it into anything comprehensible. He exhaled and went on: "Look, I'm supposed to pick up some other hikers."

"Yeah," I wiped the salt off my forehead, "there's a lot of hikers coming, but still probably an hour or so back."

"How would you know that?" he asked, again stressed as an insult. I ground my teeth.

"Because I left out early and only passed one guy on the way here, and that was a while ago."

"So what's your name?" he asked.

"I'm Solo."

He looked me up and down with an insolence that begged for a punch in the nose. "Yeah," he said, "I can see why."

What? I'd just about had enough of his surly attitude. If not for Ultra Burn I would have walked away right then, but Ultra Burn would be along by and by so I swallowed my pride and rode it out.

"Okay, go ahead and get in," he said then.

I loaded my gear and climbed into a back seat. Mosey was up front. He waited fifteen minutes or so before he finally accepted what I had told him. My water bottles were empty, my throat so dry I could barely speak. I reassured myself that we would be in town soon, and that this guy, whom I will call The Tuna, would pull into the store on the way so that we could buy beers or other essential fluids. All I had to do was be patient.

We burned pavement toward Glasgow. I found enough spit to swallow so I could make conversation. I asked The Tuna if he knew Texas Dreamer and if she was still in the area, explaining that I had thru-hiked before and knew the hostel well. He seemed put off by that, turned his attention to Mosey and kept it there.

He slowed when we entered town, pointing out the various features of the place as if he were a tour guide. My heart fell when he drove past the store without stopping. We went up and down some neighborhood streets at a less than leisurely speed while my body and brain cried out for liquid, now *any* kind of liquid. At the hostel, he ordered us to drop our packs, remove our shoes, and then follow him inside for the tour.

"I already know the place," I informed him again.

He paused and looked at me with unmistakable disdain. "Well, we probably changed something," he muttered.

I was the last inside, stiffening and so weary now that I could only waddle along in that geriatric way we call the *hiker shuffle*. I found him with Mosey at the washing machine just inside the door. He was pedantically explaining the various features, commenting on every knob and dial, offering advice on the best cycles for various types of clothes. I thought I would pass out where I stood, began to tap my foot. The washing machine tutorial continued, feature after feature after damned feature, as if his whole purpose for being were contained in that single appliance.

The dryer was next, again the pedantic commentary. I couldn't bear it any longer.

"Look," I interrupted in desperation, "I don't mean to sound like a dick, but what a thru-hiker needs first thing is a cold beer."

He rounded on me about as aggravated as a bull in a ring with two or three swords already in its hump. "Well you are a dick, *Dick!*" he spat.

I blinked. My brain wasn't quite working. It took a moment, and then it registered.

"Oh the hell with this!" I bellowed in disgust.

I slammed back outside, muttering profanities all the way, got into my shoes, grabbed my pack and poles, and stalked out of there.

I charged directly to the restaurant, which has changed ownership and formats over the years and was currently serving Italian food. After a few beers, and two large bowls of pasta with olive oil and feta cheese, I felt completely recovered, ready to take to the trail and evaporate a few more miles. It was still early in the day, plenty of time.

I crossed the road to the store for resupply, pausing at the door to remember Texas Dreamer. She had stopped here first when she drove us in on Hike 3. Thru-hikers know what thru-hikers need. Having a non-hiker like The Tuna run a hiker hostel was only a bit less than a crime. I knew the owner of the hostel and I intended to give him a call.

Resupplied, packed away, and with a couple extra beers stowed for later, I went to the road and held out my thumb. Hitches in and out of Glasgow had never been difficult. What to do about Ultra Burn nagged at me. He'd be in sooner or later. Perhaps I'd cross paths with him at the trailhead. If not, Johns Hollow Shelter was less than two miles up the trail. I could leave a message for him in the trail register there then take it slow tomorrow. With his speed he'd catch up soon enough. While I was waiting with my thumb out, a couple of hikers crossed the road toward me.

"There's a party at the shelter tonight," one of them said.

"What shelter?" I asked.

"The public shelter. It's right over there."

He pointed back the way they had come. I could just make out a traditional A.T. shelter in a park-like area beyond the restaurant. The town of Glasgow, with assistance from the Boy Scouts, had set the shelter up, a shrewd move in a dusty town that was drying up ever more rapidly at each of my visits. Thru-hikers spent money, a realization that had taken too many previously hiker-unfriendly towns too many decades to figure out.

"It's got a shower, too," the hiker added. "And all kinds of food."

"Huh. Thanks."

I'd never noticed this shelter before, had no idea how long it had been there. I didn't need any food now, but a shower would be a welcome relief. I could get the sweat salt off me. And it was still early enough to get back to the trail, so I hoofed it on over.

There were a few hikers loitering in the shade around the shelter. I didn't know any of them. I showered, emerging fresh and energized and ready to make miles. I was just shouldering my backpack when Ultra Burn came ambling up.

"Hey U.B.," I said. "I didn't expect to see you."

"Yeah, man—so what did you do to The Tuna?"

"The Tuna? Man, that guy's a dick."

"I thought he was a nice guy."

I scowled. "Well you would, wouldn't you."

"What do you mean?"

Many Yankees—and by Yankees I mostly mean people from New York and New Jersey—have an abrasive wit that might seem natural and acceptable among themselves but which grates on Southern sensibilities. We find it difficult to endure these people. My youngest sister married one of them, which ruined every Thanksgiving afterward. It's how K-Bar got her trail name, after all, although her cutting wit was tempered by her sweeter personality. Ultra Burn and I had discussed this often, he believing I should be more abrupt with people while I preferred the more genteel if not passive-aggressive ways of the South. To counter his arguments I simply pointed out that he had always presented himself as well-mannered and respectful, otherwise we wouldn't be hiking together. His abrasive wit surfaced from time to time but he'd never directed it at me.

"So what are you doing here then if you like the guy so much?" I asked hotly.

"They had a crazy guy staying there. This guy threatened one of the women hikers, said he was going to kill her and shit. They called the police, and I got out of there. I'm not out here to be around violence like that."

"Huh." For a moment there I thought he'd walked out in support of me. It stung a little that he hadn't. "Well," I went on, "there's a crazy guy on every hike. It's another reason why we have trekking poles with sharp tips."

"So are you staying for the party?"

"Naw. This place has bad juju. I think I'm gonna make miles."

"No, Solo. Stay, man. Let's do something different for a change."

There it was, the divergence in our hikes, blown into the open by a crazy guy and an asshole named The Tuna. This wasn't the day, though. Not quite yet.

"Okay, man. I'll stay."

"Cool."

We pitched our tents on an open lawn. As the day settled, a couple of thirtyish guys pulled up in a gleaming pick-up loaded with groceries and beer and no few bottles of whiskey. They were Delaware and his pal Cobra. Delaware was a 2012 thru-hiker. He'd spent his Fourth of July in Glasgow on that hike, an event that had affected him deeply enough to want to come back and relive the magic with the latest crop of thru-hikers. I liked them both immediately.

Delaware and Cobra were in the military and had that look in the cut of their hair and the way they carried themselves. Their work had something to do with attack helicopters, or perhaps drones. Some of the details were secret so they couldn't share. They kindled a fire and brought out fat sausages and steaks, which would have ended my promise to Robbie right then if I hadn't already broken that promise a few days earlier.

A bottle of fine bourbon made the rounds. Some of us sat around the fire as the bottle was passed from hand to hand and lips to lips. One of the hikers asked me about the conditions ahead. Would Shenandoah National Park be as easy as people say?

"Thirty-three, thirty, twenty-six and out," I nonchalantly replied. This might have sounded like a boast but it wasn't. I meant every word, I'd done it three times before.

He pondered that and passed the bottle to Delaware, who went on between slugs of bourbon to describe his time on the Appalachian Trail. As he spoke, he had that faraway gaze I knew so well, his experience of nine years earlier still vivid in his mind. He'd never been able to let go. Neither had I.

Later in the darkness, Delaware and Cobra's fireworks competed with some sparkling flashes beyond a hill on the other side of town. I stumbled woozily to my tent in the still of night as the fire crackled behind me, a few silhouetted figures continuing to pass the bottle.

SUNDAY, JULY 4, 2021

Mile 804.8 - 17.5 Miles

Didn't sleep well at all, humid and sticky, and no breeze so the tent was wet inside and out from condensation. I stayed late to eat breakfast with everyone, taking advantage of the time to dry my tent in the early sun. No coffee first thing because damn if somebody didn't steal my lighter last night.

Delaware and Cobra drove us to the trailhead at 9:30 a.m., another late start but worth it for the food and good company. I offered the usual thanks that are never enough.

The climb up Big Rocky took almost three hours, then some flat on top, then Bluff Mountain, then Punchbowl Mountain, then Rice Mountain—geez!

Had a talk with Ultra Burn to make sure we're still in agreement on the hike plan. He says he's on board but weary of big days. It's the heat and terrain getting to him, I think. He would also like more side activities.

We met Mosey slackpacking southbound to avoid the hard climb up Big Rocky. Her hike, her business, but such gimmicks don't appeal to me.

With our late start we couldn't make our full 20 miles, so threw down here to camp by a stream. I beat Ultra Burn in once again. A local guy named Gary is here, my age, nice guy. He gave us some food.

I bathed in the stream, ate, and now to sleep.

MONDAY, JULY 5, 2021

Mile 828.8 - 24 Miles

Slept quite well this time, and was up at 4:30 a.m., packed and ready when Gary got up at 5:00. We visited and had coffee together, then I set out at 6:00.

Made a good pace despite the long climb up Bald Knob, 13 ½ miles by noon and I never saw Ultra Burn. I waved and laughed when I went by the side trail to Cow Camp Shelter. Not this time, you wretched mice!

I arrived at our designated camping spot at 2:00 p.m., then waited two hours for Ultra Burn to arrive. I was a little frustrated because I could easily have topped The Priest and gone down the other side if I had pushed on.

When Ultra Burn finally arrived, we decided to push on five more miles to this site. After arriving, a family drove up the Forest Service road to camp across the way. We were afraid they were rednecks and would ruin our night, but these people were nice. They gave us cold cokes and some bottled water.

Ultra Burn wants to go over later and see if he can yogi some food as well. I'll be asleep by then.

TUESDAY, JULY 6, 2021

Mile 851 - 22.2 Miles

This was the day I knew would come.

It began at the usual time, on the trail by 6:00 a.m. Some climbs and a quick descent of The Priest, across the road and then the climb up Three Ridges

Mountain, which took hours and wore me out, I mean really wore me out. It was freakin' hot, the trail was overgrown in places, and the nettles stung like hell.

Still, I was in Reeds Gap by 2:00 p.m. Ultra Burn showed up soon after and we caught a quick hitch to Devils Backbone Brewpub 5 ½ miles away, where there are showers, free camping, and of course BEER.

The first hiccup was when we went into the brewpub. I wanted to stay for a beer, but Ultra Burn wanted to shower and pitch his tent first. So we split up.

I had a burger and salad and a few beers, struck up a conversation with some old folks, and they bought my beers. Ultra Burn came in looking clean and suave, began working the old folks and got them to buy his food.

We started talking, an ominous discussion, pretty much the culmination of a lot of frustrations on his part and mine. He'd never been abrupt with me before, reminded me of a son who's had enough of Dad.

So it was finally time, at a brewpub in the middle of nowhere, and after more than 800 miles together.

I hitched back to the trail, where I was unable to find a campsite. I wound up hiking about 6 miles over rocks until near dark, found a stealth site and pitched a dry camp.

Tomorrow I'll get into Waynesboro early and take a motel room because I'm not going to stay at that hostel, not with the bad juju in Glasgow. I need to email Shawna and Chad and Vicki, see if we're still on to meet in Front Royal.

I will miss Ultra Burn. I was fonder of him than he knows, but I now know that it's past time that he got to hike for himself. As for me? I guess I'll hike alone from here on.

WEDNESDAY, JULY 7, 2021

Waynesboro, Virginia - 13.1 Miles

Slept well enough despite a brisk wind all night. Awoke at 4:45 a.m. feeling grungy, on the way by 6:00.

Started out slow but picked up speed after I topped Humpback Mountain. It got hot, sweat drizzling off my elbows. Reached Waynesboro at 11:00 a.m.

I caught a hitch to the Quality Inn, which is the refurbished and rebranded old Ramada Inn we always stayed at before hostels started popping up all along the trail. Ultra Burn hasn't replied to the text I sent him yesterday.

Very tired, but did laundry and ate at the Chinese buffet. While showering I found an attached tick in my groin area and wondered how it got there. I washed out the backpack and other things, they were getting rank.

Walked to the library to post field notes, mailed some stuff home, and met a multiple thru-hiker named Trouble who was great to speak with since he understood all I have been through. I'd love to hike with him, but he's taking some time off here in Waynesboro. Now I'm resting. I've lost too much weight too early in the hike, so I'm going to zero tomorrow and eat a lot of Chinese buffet.

THURSDAY, JULY 8, 2021

Waynesboro, Virginia - Zero

Zero number 6, and I needed it.

I slept luxuriously late (6:30 a.m.), had breakfast, a shower, then lunch and a trip to the store.

Now I'm back in the room. It's not yet 2:00 p.m., I have food, beer, and I don't intend to leave this room again until 6:00 a.m. tomorrow.

Shawna has been in touch, so it looks as if Front Royal will be our rendezvous. Also, an employee here says he'll drive me to the trailhead in the morning, says he has to get up that early anyway. Groovy.

Delaware and Cobra drove us to the trailhead the morning after the party in Glasgow. I stuttered to find words of thanks.

"Don't worry about it," Delaware said. "I was there too—on the trail, I mean. I know how it is. All of this—" he swept an arm toward the bed of his truck, still loaded to the side rails with food and beer for the party that would continue that night, "—all of this still isn't enough to make up for all the people that helped me on my hike."

We fist-bumped on that, and then Ultra Burn and I turned for the trail, Ultra Burn turning left to cross the highway, and I turning right.

When hiking southbound I had always stopped at the highway for a hitch into town. When I returned to the trail I would be dropped in the parking area, where a spur trail would lead me to the bridge over the James River. What I discovered on this hike was that there was a short section of the Appalachian Trail from the bridge to the highway that bypassed the parking area. I had never noticed this little section before, which was a triviality really, but that was the actual trail, a section that I had *never hiked*. I intended to hike it this time. Ultra Burn thought this was silly when he could look across the highway and see the trailhead on the other side. What did it matter to do a little section of trail only to come out at the same place? Well, it mattered to me.

When I caught up to him some minutes later, he asked with mirth, "So, was it worth it?"

"Yeah, there were three blazes in there."

"Three whole blazes, huh."

"You know my deal, U.B., pass every white blaze, right?"

"Whatever, Solo."

There's a vital point to be made here, which is that everyone's hike is their own. We make our own rules and follow them if we will. Some hikers will do things I find vexing. They'll take shortcuts and engage in all manner of gimmicks that conflict with my notions of what thru-hiking actually means. I might criticize them in my mind but I've never criticized them vocally or led gossip in shelter. They aren't hiking by my rules, they're hiking by their own rules. That I might disagree with their rules is irrelevant. What I present to the reader is only for the purposes of comparison. The reader can decide for him or herself whether these hikers represent the spirit of the trail or not. Ultra Burn didn't want to take the time to hike that little section. It wasn't important to him. That's okay, that was his hike. This one was mine.

The climb up Big Rocky out of the Glasgow hole was tough and took a while. Ultra Burn pulled well ahead but then stopped for a break on top where a rocky outcrop opened into a panoramic view. The sun was bright and blazing. He had his stove out and was boiling noodles as I went by. This was one of the essential differences in our styles, a difference that had remained consistent from the day I passed Ultra Burn and K-Bar heating noodles in the rain that time in the Smokies. I only used my stove twice a day, morning and night, subsisting on energy bars and peanuts in between, most often chewed and swallowed as I was hiking. To stop and cook would mean pulling everything out of my backpack and then having to wash up afterward, an investment of time in which I could have gone two, possibly three more miles. When I sat for breaks of ten or fifteen minutes, I couldn't help but think that I'd be a half mile or so farther on if I'd just kept moving. This seemed beyond peculiar—even eccentric—to Ultra Burn, but this was the rigor I'd honed in the course of my three thru-hikes, and now this one. I didn't possess Ultra Burn's blazing speed. If not for my early starts and self-discipline I would never reach Mt. Katahdin in time.

And then there was the matter of fuel. I carried a single can, which could last me a long, long time (I never actually emptied one). Ultra Burn carried two and yet he was always running out. I passed my own fuel can to him more than once, more than twice, more than I can remember. At his pace he was burning calories unsustainably to cover the same distance I was. He *had* to stop and heat those high-calorie and high-priced camp meals he carried, otherwise he would waste away and pass out on the trail. I encouraged him over and again to slow down a step, fearing that he was burning himself out. He would agree with me but then blaze off at that same pace anyway. I eventually accepted that he'd found his *arete*, his joy of physical excellence. I hiked on with the nagging–and soon to be proved prescient–notion that he was bound to burn himself out too soon. In the meantime I had started carrying an extra can of fuel to give him when he inevitably ran out.

After I passed Ultra Burn I entered those mostly level few miles between Big Rocky and Bluff Mountain. A hiker approached me from ahead, and as she resolved I saw that it was Mosey. We offered greetings in passing but no commentary. None was needed. She was slackpacking in reverse to avoid the big climb. The Tuna would have dropped her off at the trailhead at Mile 798.5, and be there to pick her up at Virginia Highway 130 for another stay at the hostel after 11.2 easy miles. This was a practice we seldom saw on the Appalachian Trail prior to the advent of phones, but which had now become endemic. I'd met flip-floppers on Hike 3 who did this kind of thing every day, shuttling out each morning, hiking sections in whichever was the easiest direction, then shuttling back to the hostel for the night. Their hikes, their business, but I could never understand what their hikes were about, what they were getting from the experience, or what they thought they were achieving. I still don't understand.

On Bluff Mountain I stopped for a break at the Ottie Cline Powell Monument. There were good sitting rocks there, and cool shade. Not too far ahead the trail would break out of the woods to cross a wide powerline right-of-way in the full heat of the sun, so a break was warranted and this was the place.

I always stopped here anyway, to pay homage amid the sadness of tragedy. Few sites on the Appalachian Trail carry as much emotional weight. Ottie Cline Powell was a little boy a month shy of his fifth birthday when, in November 1890, he wandered away from his school. A frantic search ensued in ever-widening circles around the school but the child couldn't be found. On April 5 of the following year some hunters discovered the little boy's body melting out of a snow drift where the monument now rests, more than *seven miles* up the mountain from the school. The child had climbed and climbed and climbed through the howling wilderness until the cold of autumn had killed him, perhaps lying here to sleep, lost, alone, terrified, drowsy from hypothermia and with pitiful cries for his parents. Damn that's sad.

Ultra Burn came up as I finished off a protein bar. He dropped pack and took a seat, wiping sweat off his brow and flicking it into the bush.

"So who's Ottie Cline Powell?" he asked. I told him. "Damn," he said.

I tossed him a protein bar. "Put this in," I said. "You need the calories."

"Thanks, man."

He sat contemplatively while he chewed. "You know, Solo," he offered between bites, "I think the days of me catching up to you are over."

"What do you mean?"

"I mean–you've gotten fast, man."

"I'm not fast," I objected as always. "I just get earlier starts."

"Not today you didn't. You've got your trail legs, man. I don't think I can keep up with you."

"You can hike circles around me, U.B., but you don't need to. You can slow down a little and we can still make our miles."

Our agreement after Damascus was to try for at least twenty miles per day, this to keep me on track for my goals on this hike but also to get us to New Jersey in time for a family reunion that was important to Ultra Burn. He'd invited me to come. I looked forward to meeting his family, or at least the half of his family he talked about, but this meant that we had to make our miles.

"I don't know if I can keep this up," he said.

"Sure you can," I cajoled him but with a note of concern. "Look at me, I'm doing it."

"But you're different. You're Solo, man! You've done this before, I haven't. These relos you talk about? I don't know them. If you didn't tell me I wouldn't know the difference."

"I understand," I said. I still wasn't sure if parts of the trail had been relocated or not, but I groused about it enough that it had become a major conversation topic. "So what do you want to do?" I asked then.

"Let's slow down a little and get off trail every once in a while. We don't have to be hiking so hard all the time."

The vision that jumped into my mind was of Mountain Goat and his tramily, who'd gone to Asheboro from Hot Springs to pub crawl. We'd never seen or heard from them again. Before phones, the trail towns were where we took our rest and relaxation, usually in the form of pizza parties with plenty of beer. The idea of leaving the trail to shuttle or Uber to a far-off town for these kinds of activities was foreign to me, antithetical to the kind of Appalachian Trail experience I'd drummed into Ultra Burn and the others early on. They'd accepted that vision at the time but now the miles were beginning to weigh. Ultra Burn was sensing his hike now, as K-Bar had already. The day was drawing nearer, I felt it with remorse, but that day still wasn't here, not just yet.

"Okay, U.B. I'm good with that," I said in resignation.

We agreed to pull up short that day and camp at Mile 804.8. I left Ultra Burn to catch up later, and hiked out into the sun.

We camped by a brisk stream that night after 17.5 miles. We agreed to go 19.4 miles the next day and pitch camp at Rock Spring. The terrain was not bad, I told him, just the one long climb up Bald Knob. After that it would be an easy day. He would rather have held it to twelve or fifteen miles, but with my assurances he agreed to go the 19.4.

I climbed Bald Knob in the magic hour amid earthy smells and blessed quiet. Once over the top I paused at the side trail to Cow Camp Shelter, where I'd stayed and fought mice on Hikes 2 and 3. There was a rumor that someone had been killed in that shelter. I followed up later, and yes, a man had been murdered in 2011, not in the shelter but on a side trail to the shelter. The murder remains unsolved. I didn't know this when I stayed there, don't know that it would have dissuaded me, but other hikers avoided the place now. My only thoughts about Cow Camp Shelter were how far off the trail it was (six tenths of a mile), and how overrun with mice it was. They had been a nuisance on Hike 2, chewing into my food bag where it hung from the rafters, and I awoke to find them *on* me on Hike 3. Not this time, I laughed, and took a moment to scratch into the soil: *Not This Time, Ha!*

I made thirteen and a half miles by noon that day, arriving at our agreed upon campsite at two o'clock. I sat on a log and waited for Ultra Burn as the minutes and then hours passed in slow agony. I didn't pitch my tent because it was just too damned early. I paced through the leaf litter, sat, paced some more, growling under my breath that I could have cleared The Priest by now if I'd just pushed on. Ultra Burn came in at four o'clock and confirmed that yes, that section had been pretty easy. We agreed to push on five more miles to a campsite that he'd found on Guthook, a campsite that AWOL didn't list. We made those miles in quick time, turning down a rutted dirt road at the base of the last climb to the top of The Priest.

We walked a long way down before we reached a clearing beside a stream, worrying as we went—and as the day descended—that Guthook might be wrong. But we came to the clearing by and by, and found it rutted by ATVs and with broken beer bottles all over. We went across the road instead and scraped out a place in the woods to pitch our tents. Not long afterward a pick-up truck and a minivan pulled up. This is the downside of camping near roads, places rednecks can reach and party wild all night. I would pack up and hike out in the dark before I'd camp near raging rednecks. Fortunately I didn't have to.

They were a family on a camping trip, some young children in the mix so there wouldn't be any late-night mayhem. We approached them and introduced ourselves, and found them to be nice people who were fascinated by us. They gave us cold drinks, I gave Ultra Burn another can of fuel to heat his meal, and then we turned in for what was to be a pleasant night, the last that Ultra Burn and I would share together.

I took The Priest in the magic hour the next morning. Rock outcrops provided views of misty layered mountains and the Blue Ridge Parkway far below. I caught this in gentle light and under a clean sky reminiscent of Hike 1, when I'd sat right here through the sunrise as I learned over my radio about the 9-11 attacks. I'd scattered some of Freewind's ashes on The Priest on Hike 3 so I stopped at that site to pay my respects to him as well. I was in Reeds Gap by two o'clock after 16.4 miles and a brutal climb over Three Ridges Mountain on an overgrown trail that had left my legs striped with angry welts. I sat in the shade to await Ultra Burn, hot, filthy, and spent.

We had agreed to meet in Reeds Gap. This would be one of the side excursions he wanted. He'd found on Guthook that there was a brewpub five miles or so up the road, a place that offered showers and free camping in addition to the brewpub and restaurant inside, the kind of place that could lure a thru-hiker into multiple zeros. The beers were what I wanted, what I desperately needed after that last hellish section. To my relief, Ultra Burn arrived soon after. We caught a hitch in minutes.

I shuffled into that brewpub as if I'd just emerged from the desert, dirty, desiccated, and desperately dehydrated. Three Ridges Mountain hadn't affected Ultra Burn. He said he felt fine and wanted to go shower and pitch his tent first. I wanted a beer first. Period. He gave me a look I hadn't seen from him before, of determination and defiance. This was it, then. This was the day. I thought it would come in town, probably Waynesboro, another day away. I'd been anticipating this but that didn't make it any easier.

The knowledge had been percolating in me for days if not weeks, that I had taken Ultra Burn as far as I could. His loyalty to me was what had held this off for so long. I could have made it plain at any time since about Four Pines, but Ultra Burn had to be the one to break away. It was the only way his hike would be his and not something thrust upon him. I'd been waiting for him to say the words. *Just say it, U.B.*, I'd been thinking for a while now. Make your stand and exorcize your demons. I wish it wasn't I who had to play the role but if that's what you need to find your hike *then just say it!*

I could see it now. If Ultra Burn were a character I'd created for one of my novels, he would be a young man in search of something he'd never had and couldn't define, a search through heartache and want and emptiness; and when he found what he was searching for he would need it to send him on into the rest of his journey, sure in the knowledge that he had earned it, that he was ready to be the man he was meant to be.

I sat alone at the bar and drank my beer in morose contemplation. Some older folks at a nearby table struck up a conversation, startled to find that I was their age and actually hiking the Appalachian Trail, something they swore they couldn't do if their very lives were at stake. They paid for my beer and bought another round.

Ultra Burn returned, clean and collected. He maneuvered his way into the running conversation I had going with the old folks.

"Is this your son?" they asked with delighted smiles.

"No," I answered sadly. Would it were otherwise.

Ultra Burn yogied a full meal out of them then took the seat beside me.

"See how that's done?" he gloated, a bit of that native abrasiveness directed at me for the first time. "You just gotta be direct with people. Man, I got this."

"Yes you do, U.B." I said in a small voice. "You've got this now."

Swirling in my beer glass was a question, the answer of which seemed so obvious that I'd never asked the question of myself: Why was *I* hiking? The freedom, of course, the clarity of mind to bring new words to paper. But that wasn't all of it. There was something else, something unresolvable, like a fading dream, or snatches of vision without the whole. It had always been with me, haunting the back of my mind, waiting until the time was right, like Ultra Burn's own journey.

And then it came in a flash of insight. Hiking northbound was wholly new to me, as my first southbound hike had been then. But that hike had not gone well. My following hikes had redeemed that first effort but they'd been over familiar terrain. Going northbound this time, it was as if I'd never hiked the Appalachian Trail before, as if this were a fresh start on a new trail, a way to get it right from the beginning, to exceed myself as never before, to stave off senescence that little bit longer—to make this last thru-hike the triumph of them all!

I pushed back from the bar. Ultra Burn was digging into his food.

"I'll see you out there, Ultra Burn," I said.

"Yeah, see ya, Solo."

With that I walked out to the road and hitched a ride back to the trail.

Revived though I was from the food and the beers, I was still so filthy that I couldn't bear the feel of my own skin. I was also a little wobbly on my feet from my excess at the brewpub. My plan had been to camp near the trailhead, sleep this off, then push on for Waynesboro early enough in the morning to get there and get the benefit before the big climb into Shenandoah National Park.

The only campsite I found near the trailhead was overrun with teenagers who were setting up for a tailgate party. Worse still, there were no water sources in the area. I had foolishly failed to refill my water bottles at the brewpub, which left me no choice but to hike on unsteadily a couple of miles to the next stream. When I got there the site was overcrowded with campers. I searched in futility for a place to stealth but there was nothing in that terrain not already taken that would accommodate even the small footprint of my tent. I filled my water bottles, gazed longingly at the stream, where I could have bathed myself clean if not for all the people everywhere, then sighed and pushed on.

There was supposed to be a pair of springs another couple of miles farther on, a chance to get clean, and surely a place to stealth camp nearby. So I set that as my goal in a day getting long, my stomach not quite settled, my head a bit wooly. When I reached the springs, both were dry.

Twilight was on me now, the woods becoming quiet, sinister in my imagination. I pushed on in search of a stealth site, urgency in my stride now. I have a policy of never making camp after dark. This comes from Hike 1 when, after lingering much too long at Gyp's Tavern in Culvers Gap, New Jersey, I stumbled out in the dark and unwittingly pitched my tent in a patch of poison ivy. I knew I was doomed when I realized this the next morning, and was still dealing with the itchy, oozy aftermath in central Virginia a month later.

I finally sighted a spot at the leafy base of a rock formation, setting up camp in the last diffuse light. I washed down with a bandana and water from my bottle, shinnied into my light Capilene long johns so that I wouldn't feel as sticky through the night as I actually was, sent a text to Ultra Burn to explain the situation, then fell asleep as fatigue and regret weighed on my mind.

I awoke early the next morning, feeling as if I'd slept in a garbage pail. I was hiking by six o'clock, no magic in that magic hour because of my mood. The woods and rock formations were pretty but I was unable to appreciate them, feeling only a need to put distance between me and yesterday. The day grew stifling, breaths hot in my throat and with sweat drizzling from my elbows. Even my shoes filled with sweat. I made it into Rockfish Gap at eleven o'clock after 13.1 sweat-slogging miles, Waynesboro beyond a confusing spaghetti of roads. I caught a quick hitch and had them drop me at Waynesboro's Quality Inn.

The Quality Inn had once been the Ramada Inn, where I had stayed on Hikes 1 and 2 in the days before hostels were everywhere. I remembered Hike 1 with a laugh, when seven of us had crammed into a small room, sacking out on every inch of exposed floor. Sweatbucket had gotten in first so rightly claimed the bed. The rest of us were just happy to be showered and in out of the bugs.

It felt right to be there again, reconnecting with those earlier times. Ultra Burn wouldn't have understood. Earlier in the hike he would have humored me but by now he would have gone to the hostel on his own, which is why I thought our parting would occur here. I wasn't going to the hostel, not after the bad juju in Glasgow. I'd tried to get a call in to the hostel's owner but hadn't been able to reach him. The people at the hostel had been so derisive of him on the phone that I was stunned. There was bad juju at the Waynesboro hostel too, it would seem.

The people at the Quality Inn were hiker friendly, treating me much better than I looked. It was early, I could get the benefit, so I got to it.

A shower first—oh, how glorious! The simplest pleasures are exponentially magnified on the Appalachian Trail. Food at the Chinese buffet—I do love that place. Laundry. Resupply. Rinse out my rank equipment. A walk to the post office to mail some things home, and then to the library to post field notes. While I was at the library I met a man named Trouble who was on his third thru-hike. He was fortyish perhaps, dark hair and beard, smiling white teeth, and with the gracile physique that would have announced him as a thru-hiker even from a distance. The Waynesboro library had set up a hiker area, with seating, separate computers, hiker boxes, and plastic tubs of free toiletries and supplies. This was a hell of a gesture from a town that hadn't always been this accommodating. Trouble and I settled in to talk.

"So have you noticed anything different this time?" he asked me.

"What do you mean?"

"I mean the trail. It's changed, hasn't it?"

"I think so, but I'm not sure."

"Well I am," he said defiantly. "They've done this on purpose, man. I promise you they have."

"Who has?" I asked.

"Who else?" he shrugged. "I've gotten to where I can't stand those people."

"I wish I knew for sure. I haven't been able to find anything online. That Dragons Tooth section was different though, I'm pretty sure about that."

"That Dragons Tooth section sucked."

"I wrote in my notes last time that that was a tough section. Maybe we're just not remembering it right."

"I'm pretty sure we are."

"Oh, well—"

"Hey, I heard what you did in Glasgow. Good goin', man. That guy's a dick. Somebody has to stand up to these people. The young hikers don't know any better, so it's up to us."

"Yeah, I wish they knew it, though."

"I hear ya, brother."

I felt much better after talking with Trouble, less alone and trapped in tradition. I practically begged him to hike with me but he was taking time off in Waynesboro to see to some personal business. I regret that I never saw him again.

I knew before I opened my eyes the next morning that I was going to zero, which would be an unplanned zero number six, but I weighed in at 148 pounds that morning, too much weight loss and I wasn't even half way to Mt. Katahdin yet. I needed to eat, I needed to eat a lot, so I did, stuffing myself until my belly was as taut as a weight lifter's and my stomach felt as if there were a bowling ball in my belly. I lay down for a nap, let that digest, then went out to eat some more, carrying a grocery sack of food and beer back to the room with me. It was by then about two o'clock. A hotel employee had offered to drive me back to Rockfish Gap at six o'clock the next morning. Between then and now I was determined to lie in that soft bed, eat and drink indulgently, and not leave the room again for the duration.

I felt free if not melancholy. Everyone had gone off on their own hikes. Now I could go off on mine.

FRIDAY, JULY 9, 2021

Pinefield Hut - 33.7 Miles

A huge day, and not just in miles.

That hotel employee drove me to the trailhead before 6:00 a.m. as promised, so I got an early start.

Cool weather, a nice morning. I made good time, with the goal of Pinefield Hut to match my last hike. All was going well. I made Blackrock Hut by 2:00 p.m., and was then certain that I could make my miles for the day. Things got interesting when I made it to Loft Mountain Store at 4:30 p.m. They close at 5:00 p.m., so I rushed in for beer and food, soon followed by a second serving of the same.

The store closed at 5:00, so I decided to take a shower—$1.75—and felt great. I took my OR shirt and camp towel out to a picnic area to dry, then returned for my shoes. When I came back out minutes later, the shirt and towel were gone!

I searched everywhere, then thought maybe a custodian had taken them during clean-up. I spotted what looked like an NPS maintenance building through some trees below, so went to inquire. Rounding the corner, I saw a plump white girl talking through a screen door to a demure black girl, the same girl who'd waited on me in the store. I asked the white girl if there was a custodian, but before I could finish she began barking that I was trespassing and had to leave immediately. I said I was sorry, but my question was not unreasonable. She continued to bark, wouldn't let me speak, threatened to have me arrested, to which I finally lost patience and told her to fucking do it then.

Realizing I would get no answer from the girl, I gave up and left, and also gave up on my clothes. I grabbed my gear, got on the trail, and made miles. After an hour, I saw a park ranger ahead who took me aside to ask if I had threatened the girls. Of course not, I said, then told my side of the story. His name was Kevin, early fifties, and very professional.

We hiked a mile to his truck, where he took my identification and explained the full situation. I had to write out a statement, and then after 1 ½ hours he let me go. Getting late, I made it to Pinefield Hut at 8:30 p.m. to find a 74-year-old thru-hiker named Bruiser already in the shelter. Too tired to do anything but go to sleep, that's what I did. Didn't even have the energy to write these notes until the next morning.

SATURDAY, JULY 10, 2021

Big Meadows Campground - 29 Miles

Slept poorly but got up at 5:00 a.m. as usual.

Spent too much time talking to Bruiser, who was a religious guy, so didn't start hiking until 6:30 a.m. I was slow today, with a lot of small climbs that slowed me further, but I had decided on Big Meadows so I pushed it.

No waysides today. The hours passed and I was quite sore. At one point, a rattlesnake lay across the trail and refused to budge, a peculiar velvety black snake with six rattles. I spent 15 minutes throwing rocks and sticks before he moved, then I pounded on to Big Meadows. I was so tired during that last mile to the campground, where I met Pat, who let me camp next to her van. Her husband Steve gave me beer and bourbon, and Pat gave me food. I really needed this. I'm lucky I met them.

This all went on until about 10:00 p.m., so now I'm in the tent and ready to collapse.

SUNDAY, JULY 11, 2021

Mile 952.9 - 25.8 Miles

Got to sleep late so slept late till 6:00 a.m. Didn't get moving until 7:00, Pat and Steve still asleep in their van. I left them a thank-you note.

The day started well, but I faded by noon in the rocks. So much worse than it used to be. Did stop in for sandwiches and cold drinks at Skyland, where I met some hikers whose names I have forgotten.

Pushed on for Elkwallow, where I arrived a little after 7:00 p.m. The store was closed, of course, so I had cold drinks from the vending machine. The custodian running around was kind of a dick. I waited until dark, then beat it to the picnic area to stealth camp near a water fountain.

If I get going early enough in the morning, I should have no problem getting out by 2:00 p.m., not quite 20 miles.

MONDAY, JULY 12, 2021

Front Royal, Virginia - 19.1 Miles

Slept not my best but enough to make the aches go away.

Up at 4:00 a.m., had everything packed and ready to go by 5:00. Turned around in the dark, I couldn't figure out which way to go so didn't start hiking for real until 6:00, off to a pretty quick start. Passed eight nobos whose names elude me. Didn't speak with them much anyway, they weren't very outgoing.

Moving fast, but the climbs hurt and took a long time. Out of the park at last (thank God!), but still some rocky, buggy miles to go. I do not believe the mileages in this section are accurate. It sure took a long time to do 4 miles.

Out on the road at 1:30 p.m. but couldn't get a hitch. Started walking after 30 minutes of waiting, and then got a hitch.

I'm in the Super 8, ate a big lunch across the street, hand-washed some clothes, and spoke with Shawna on the phone. We will meet tomorrow night.

I'm tired, I ache. I pushed it too hard but I'm glad to be out of that damned park.

TUESDAY, JULY 13, 2021

Front Royal, Virginia - Zero

Zero number 7, not bad I guess but I'd better keep an eye on this. Slept deep and well, of course, and got busy pretty early.

Posted field notes then took off to an outfitter. Bought my first replacement pair of shoes and a new OR shirt. Then I walked around to gather resupply, then I returned to the room and slept.

Shawna and Chad rolled in at 5:00 p.m. So great to see them again, scarcely changed except for Chad's tattooed arms.

Also met Vicki Valentine, who designs my books. Very friendly, very outgoing. It was great to finally meet her.

We ate and had beers for two hours, then said our goodbyes. All of them are now driving the hour to their homes in the D.C. area. I could probably use a trip to Wal-Mart, but I don't absolutely have to. I have enough supplies to reach Harpers Ferry. I hope I can get an early hitch out of here.

Me with Shawna and Chad in Front Royal

—

The climb out of Rockfish Gap was not too hard but it was long, a pretty much continuous upgrade all the way to Calf Mountain, seven and a half miles. I had taken this as a downgrade on my southbound hikes, tearing through those miles in order to reach Waynesboro early so that I could get the benefit. Going northbound this time, I was having to work a bit harder.

The magic hour made it enjoyable, though. That hotel employee delivered me to the trailhead by six o'clock as promised. It was rare to get such an early start after a day in town so I made the most of it, stabbing with my poles, pulling with my arms as well as pushing with my legs, making a quick pace while breathing easily despite the incline. The weather was perfect, still the cool of morning.

I set my goal as no less than Pinefield Hut at 33.7 miles, a goal I knew I could achieve because I'd done it before, albeit without the long climb at first light. Ultra Burn would never have agreed to push it that far, but we were on separate hikes now. This was *my* hike. I reiterated that to myself as the miles fled under my feet. I could do as many miles as the trail and my body would allow, and as often as I wanted. If any compromises needed to be made, they would be made only with myself.

I paused at the side trail to Calf Mountain Shelter to remember that time on Hike 2 when I'd trudged in past ten o'clock at night to find Rocklayer and his family already in residence. That had been a day. I'd pulled big miles to reach Blackrock Hut near sunset, only to find it overrun with Boy Scouts who were led by a pair of incompetent and indifferent scout masters who'd spread their gear over the entire lower deck and then refused to move it. Boy Scouts lined the upper deck like pigeons on an eave, propped on their elbows and looking down at us with bored expressions. There were some tense moments, some heated words. Weary though I was, I'd pushed on to escape the bad juju, thirteen more miles through the dark of night to Calf Mountain Shelter, singing country songs along the way to notify any foraging bears of my presence.

All but catatonic when I arrived, I found the shelter occupied by Rocklayer and his family. Rocklayer was a young southbounder of blazing speed from eastern Kentucky whom I'd last seen at the monastery in New York and whom I'd never expected to see again. He'd slowed down to hike Shenandoah National Park with his family, otherwise I actually wouldn't have ever seen him again. It was an exciting reunion, so rare was it to encounter a quick southbounder twice. His family were good, friendly people. They invited me into the shelter the way true thru-hikers would, never complaining about the crowding or the late hour. That day and night became one of my more memorable experiences of that hike.

After that pause to reminisce, I continued on with a fleetness I hadn't yet exhibited, *arete* surging through my blood and brain, hiking light in the way that usually doesn't come to me until the Smokies when going southbound. I felt indefatigable, the miles as nothing. For more than twenty-five miles I never saw another human being, or a bear for that matter, and that was odd. I reached Loft Mountain Store under an inspiring sky at four thirty after 27.8 miles. This was a triumph because the store closed at five o'clock. I'd made it in time. Food and beers awaited, the reward for determination.

I entered the store with a gratified grin and engaging gabble. An older woman behind the counter was unaffected by my conviviality. She seemed tired, uninspired, and unimpressed by my Southern humor. I let that glide off my rarified spirits, and went to the cooler in the back to claim beers and burgers. There was a face-masked woman back there stocking the coolers. I will call her Demure Young Black Woman. I greeted her and received no reply, no acknowledgment whatsoever. I refused to let that dour my mood, reached past her to retrieve what I needed, paid the tired old lady (who neither laughed nor even faintly smiled when I made a humorous show of synchronizing watches with her so that I might get back for a second helping before they closed), then went outside to consume this largess under the sun.

With ten minutes to spare, I dodged back in for seconds. This time Demure Young Black Woman was behind the counter, still masked and anonymous. She diffidently took my money in silence, deflecting all my attempts at conversation as if she were little more than a mannequin with a motorized arm to work the cash register. I sighed and went back outside, my arms laden with food, my beer precariously balanced. After that next restorative beer I thought no more of those two women or whatever it was that ailed them.

The store closed quietly at five o'clock, the staff scuttling off to wherever they went at the ends of their shifts. In minutes the site was bereft of activity except for me, which left me with that peculiar sense of having been abandoned at some remote place far from the comforts of civilization. I then remembered that there were coin showers at Loft Mountain Store. I still had about six miles to go, but in the cool breeze of that elevation I could make those miles without loosing a drop of sweat. I could spend the night completely clean, and how much better would I sleep then? So I went for the shower, counting as my quarters clanked in the change box and praying that the water would come on after I'd made that irretrievable investment. It did, so I enjoyed another of those trail-magnified pleasures. I rinsed out my new (since Daleville) OR shirt, walked outside naked to spread my shirt and towel on a picnic table to dry in the sun, then returned for my shoes and shorts, backpack and poles. When I came back out those few minutes later, my shirt and towel were gone!

It had to be the wind. What else could it be? I searched the bushes, following the wind where my things might have blown, and found nothing. Next I checked every trash can on the site in case a custodian had come through thinking my things had been abandoned, and again found nothing. Looking around bewildered, I sighted a cinderblock building beyond some trees downslope from the store, painted in Park Service brown and resembling nothing more than a maintenance shed. If there were a custodian, that's where he would be, so now dressed in shorts and a spare T-shirt, clean and groomed, I went down there to inquire.

I rounded a corner, and twenty feet or so ahead I sighted a woman—whom I will call Plump Young White Woman—speaking through a screen door to Demure Young Black Woman, who now had her face mask off to reveal a fetching face.

"Hi there," I said with a smile and a wave. Plump Young White Woman was dressed all in black. She turned on me with a glare of outrage that would give a ruthless dictator pause. "Uh," I stuttered at the sight of that, "is there a custodian—?"

"*Get out of here!*" Plump Young White Woman all but screamed. Demure Young Black Woman took on the eyes of a mesmerized deer.

"Uh, uh—"

"I said *leave!*" she screamed again.

"But, uh, I just need to know if there's a custo—"

"*I said leave now!* You're trespassing! You can't come here!"

The air was so clean and cool, the sky a watercolor masterpiece. None of this fit; none of this made sense. Revived though I was from the food and beer, I'd still hiked over twenty-seven miles in ten and a half hours. My brain wasn't quick enough to keep up with this, whatever this was.

"Uh, uh—it's not an unreasonable question." This was the first sentence I'd managed to complete, delivered in dumbfounded syllables.

Demure Young Black Woman took a step back from the door while Plump Young White Woman imperiously charged toward me, hands on her hips and with a face of fury. I looked toward Demure Young Black Woman, met her widened eyes with my own beseeching gaze. She'd seen me twice in the store, surely some familiarity could calm this crazy scene; surely she would speak up and restore sanity to whatever this was.

Plump Young White Woman was in my face now. I could smell a perfume on her that made me gag for breath.

"*I said leave!*" she screamed again. "Leave right now or I'll have you arrested!"

This was belligerence beyond reckoning. I could as well have been in a melee with the rednecks back home. No sanity could pierce this, no reasoned argument, even if sentences were allowed to be completed. Have you ever tried to debate someone who will not accept the fact of climate change, or someone who refuses to be vaccinated, or someone who supports the former occupant of our White House? Nothing could control this but the authority of higher office, and perhaps that might not be enough. This kind of behavior was beyond pitiable, it was outright disgraceful. My patience snapped.

"Then fucking arrest me!" I growled back at her. "But first tell me if you have a custodian."

"Well listen to you," she haughtily smirked. Demure Young Black Woman slunk another step back.

It was futile, just futile. A simple question with no answer forthcoming. Plump Young White Woman would expend a year's worth of stress hormone before she'd deign to answer. I looked at her in disgust, spun on my heels and tramped back toward the store.

"Yeah—good riddance white trash," she hollered at my back.

I chuckled darkly. *White trash?* Did she not have a mirror?

I grabbed my backpack and poles, and returned to the trail feeling as if I could use another shower to rinse away the filth of that encounter.

It seemed ironic now, how gorgeous the day was. The trail through there was easy to hike, the woods healthy and full of life, parting here and there for glimpses of a pristine sky. As my mind calmed I realized that the cinderblock building was not a maintenance shed, but seasonal housing. The two women weren't Park Service personnel, but employees of the park's concessionaire. They would therefore be barely competent to do their jobs, having received the minimum training necessary to get them in the field to maximize profits off the visiting public. I've worked at national parks, I know how this goes. If there had been any signage to warn me off I would have abided by it, but there were no signs, nothing to indicate anything other than what I thought that building was.

This did not excuse Plump Young White Woman's behavior, though, or Demure Young Black Woman's reticence. Over the years, thousands upon thousands of thru-hikers have passed through Loft Mountain Store, probably thousands that year already. You couldn't not know how to properly engage with thru-hikers unless you simply paid no attention to the world around you, like the father who held his toddler out to the grizzly bear cub, or the guy who backed off McAfee Knob while taking a selfie. We are by-damned stuck with these people. What else can we do with them?

An hour later, maybe a little more, on a gentle albeit rocky upgrade and in softening light, I sighted a park ranger ahead high-stepping and picking his way toward me. This could have been anything, but I had that national park itch now, it was crawling up my neck. I paused and waited for him to come to me.

"Hi," he said. "Can I speak with you for a minute?"

"Of course," I said.

"My name's Kevin."

"I'm Solo."

Kevin was in his early fifties, fit, with reddish hair laced with gray and a trim beard to match. His posture was professional, his manner unthreatening. His uniform fit him as if it had been tailored. The gun on his hip identified him as a patrol ranger, Park Service police if you will. I have never known a patrol ranger (and I have known many) who wasn't a portrait of professionalism. Local jurisdictions could improve much by sending their officers for the same training that patrol rangers receive. Despite this authority of higher office, I wasn't self-conscious in the least. I had done nothing to be self-conscious of.

"Do you know why I want to talk to you?" he asked.

"I have an idea," I answered in disgust. When Plump Young White Woman had hollered *white trash* at my back, I knew right then that she'd be vindictive enough to concoct something for revenge. Women like her enjoy being able to dominate older men, I've run into it before. Perhaps they have father issues, who knows?

"There's a stealth site right up there," Kevin pointed. "Will you walk with me?"

"Of course."

Kevin slipped in behind me as naturally as if we were hiking partners, revealing no indication of his wariness. We entered a nice little campsite with a sitting log.

"May I drop my pack?" I asked Keven.

"Sure," he said. "But first, do you have any weapons on you?"

I chinned to my backpack strap, where a can of bear spray and a small utility knife were clipped.

"May I take those for a minute?" he asked.

"Sure," I said.

"Do you have any other weapons?"

"No."

I dropped pack and sat on the log.

"So," he said then. "Did you threaten a couple of women up at Loft Mountain Store?"

"No, I did not." Sweat was popping out on my forehead, not from uneasiness but because the breeze had died off. "May I get a bandana to wipe my face?" I asked him.

"Yeah, go ahead."

I retrieved a bandana from my backpack and wiped my face. When you're in strange company with a man who has a gun, you never make sudden moves. This was something we learned as kids in south Texas.

"So why don't you tell me your side of the story, then."

I did. In detail. Calmly. Kevin sighed.

"So it's their word against yours."

"Yeah," I said, "except they're lying and I'm not."

"They were locked in their room afraid to come out when we got there," Kevin said.

"If she was so afraid of me why would she insult me as I walked away? Wouldn't that have risked me coming back to get even? By the way, may I reach over for my water bottle?"

"Sure, go ahead. I appreciate how careful you are with our concerns. And you do make a good point. I mean, they told us we were looking for a threatening, overweight guy with a thick ponytail."

I coughed up some water. "I'm a hundred forty-eight pound old man. I'm not a threat to anyone, and I don't have enough hair for a thick ponytail."

"Yeah, when I first saw you I thought you couldn't be the one."

"So what's next?"

"I need to check your I.D. and run you for outstandings. Is that okay?"

"Sure. May I reach into my backpack for my I.D.?"

"Go ahead."

Kevin squawked on his radio, feeding the information on my I.D. We sat in silence for a little bit, then: "So you're really sixty-three years old?"

"I really am."

"Man, you're in good shape."

"Thanks."

"And you've worked at national parks?"

"I have."

"And this is your fourth thru-hike?"

"It is."

"Amazing."

Dispatch finally got back to him, no wants, no warrants. "I haven't even had a traffic ticket since the eighties," I told him.

"Yeah, you're clean. And I'm inclined to believe you, but since you've worked at national parks then you know the drill." I nodded. "I have to fill out a report because they've made an accusation. I can't do anything about that."

"Kevin," I said, slowly standing and with a tight smile. The light was beginning to get low now and I wasn't looking forward to having to hike in the dark. "You can take me to jail if I can get a coke and a pizza out of it. I wouldn't mind sleeping indoors. I've pulled big miles today already. You all can always bring me back in the morning." Kevin took this as a joke but I was serious.

"No, it's not going to come to that. There's a parking area another mile up. That's where my truck is. Let's hike up there and I'll have you fill out a statement. Write exactly what you've told me, and then you can keep going."

That drew a defeated sigh. So I would be hiking in the dark after all.

I shouldered pack and took off, Kevin behind me and pushing it to keep up. "You don't have to hike so fast," he said.

"This is my normal pace," I responded to that, which it was, but yes, I *did* have to hike fast. I was still three miles or so from Pinefield Hut and the day was not going to last that long. I would be in bear country at night with the smell of chocolate bars all over me. After my adventure in New Jersey on Hike 3, when the bear had stalked me in the dark of night, I had become wary of night-hiking.

We reached his truck in the soft sunset, parked in an overlook of scenic beauty that was lost in my rush to get my statement written out so that I could get on the trail again. There were several other patrol rangers there. I tried unsuccessfully to yogi a coke out of them but they did give me a bottle of water. When I finished my statement, Kevin returned my bear spray and knife.

"Happy trails, Solo," he said then.

"Yeah, you too," I said with an edge of resentment.

The sun had just slipped below the layered horizon. I sped through the dusky woods, grinding disgust between my teeth. After all of this I still didn't have an answer: Did they have a damned custodian or not?

I reached Pinefield Hut as the very last gossamer shadows merged into night. There was one hiker inside, mummied in his sleeping bag. He propped up on an elbow when I shouldered out of my backpack and set it on the floor. It was too dark to see his face.

"Hey," I said quietly. "Sorry if I woke you."

"It's okay," he said. "I don't sleep so well anyway."

I had expected to pitch my tent, but now that it was dark, and with only one guy in the shelter, I climbed in and began to lay out my things. I was too tired to make conversation with the guy, too tired to cook, too tired to write in my diary. It was physical fatigue compounded by the emotional strain of the past few hours. If I had found my shirt and towel where I'd left them to dry I would not have encountered Plump Young White Woman. I would not have encountered Kevin. My mood would still be soaring and I would have reached this shelter at least two hours ago, early enough to enjoy the evening and make conversation. As it was, I shinnied into my bag and prayed for sleep.

The night passed horribly. My inflatable mattress scrunched and crunched on that hard floor, making me "that guy," and I couldn't bear it. I let the air out, turned on my side and tucked my knees. I prefer a hard surface anyway. Sleep was just coming on with its heavy hand when a crackling sound of plastic from the other side of the shelter snapped me back awake. The guy was shuffling over there, doing something. He settled down by and by, sleep began to come again, but then I had to get up to pee, which brought me fully awake as I stumbled in the dark for my shoes and then outside to let vent.

Back in the shelter I turned on my side and tucked my knees, was about to drift off again when that crackling sound of plastic intruded once more. This went on throughout the night, timed, it seemed, for that moment when I was about to slip under. At five o'clock, hiker sunrise, I was fully awake and had been for a while. The only reason I'd stayed in my sleeping bag was so as not to disturb the guy sleeping across the shelter from me. By hiker sunrise, though, I'd observed etiquette to the very minute. If he woke up now...well, he should be up anyway.

I made coffee, had a breakfast of protein bars, then began quietly packing up, using my red headlight and observing as much decorum as possible. When his own headlight snapped on, I switched to white light and stopped worrying about the noise.

"I'm Bruiser," the guy said in a gravelly, aged voice.

"Hey, I'm Solo."

"Are you a thru-hiker?"

"Yeah."

"Me, too.

Bruiser was seventy-four years old and on his third thru-hike. To meet a multiple thru-hiker his age would normally have left me excited, but I had no spirit that morning, no desire other than to get away.

"You should get one of these," he said, holding something up that I couldn't really make out in the dark.

"What is it?"

"It's something that keeps me from having to get up and pee in the night the way you did."

He made a motion with his hand that produced the crackling plastic sound that had tormented me all night. I understood then that he had some kind of pee bottle over there, and did not comment that the night would have gone better if he'd just gotten up to go instead of squeezing that thing like a silicone breast. It was like Ultra Burn with his bidet, it seemed everyone had their own specialty device nowadays, a device that could as easily have been replaced by a sports bottle.

"Good to know," I said as if I cared.

"Do you read the Bible?" he asked out of nowhere.

"Uh, yeah, I've read it a few times."

"But did you *really* read it?"

"You a preacher or something?"

"We're all witnesses to God's glory. Every time I read the Bible I'm more convinced that it was written by his own divine hand."

There's a religious guy on every hike, nothing wrong with that but they do tend to prattle on, seeming to want to make their religion your religion. The New Testament was written by the apostles and the Old Testament was written by the ancient Israelites. I don't think there's much to dispute that but I was not going to be drawn into a debate.

"Well, uh, that's great," I said, then I hopped out of the shelter into the pre-dawn and started hiking.

I pushed myself over a trail that had once been a soft pad through the woods but was now a rocky trip hazard due to the erosion of countless feet. There were no waysides right off the trail in that section, no oases of largess along the way. Considering my mood I might not have gone into one anyway for fear of encountering another Plump Young White Woman, or worse yet, the actual bitch herself. My neck itched and no amount of scratching would soothe it. Disgust pounded trail with every step. I wanted out of Shenandoah National Park, and would have hiked straight through if my body could have endured it.

It was in this section that I'd spotted the mountain lion on Hike 2. I had come around a turn off Hightop Mountain and there it was, crouched across the trail and intently focused on something in the bush. I remember the tawny coat, the muscular abdomen and long tail. It was ironic that after all of my years in the west, the first mountain lion I would ever see was in the east. I quietly retrieved my disposable camera but alerted the lion when I ratcheted to the next frame. The lion snapped up and gazed at me, held that look for some moments, more puzzled than threatening. With a carbon-tipped spear in each hand, I wasn't afraid for my safety. Some internal decision crossed its eyes, then it leapt into the bush and was gone. I was so excited I couldn't contain myself. I hiked out at the next crossing of Skyline Drive to report the sighting to park rangers, and was told that I was mistaken, that there weren't any mountain lions in the east. I must have seen a bobcat, they said, brushing me off as if I were an eager amateur. Since I hadn't been able to snap a photograph of the lion, I returned dejected to the trail.

My only wildlife encounter in Shenandoah National Park this time was a species of rattlesnake that I'd never seen before, in the wild or in books. It was long enough to lie across the trail, the richest velvety black with bright yellow highlights. I counted six rattles, and the darned thing refused to move. I pulled up with a start when I recognized what it was, at first thinking it was a fallen limb. I skipped rocks at it then advanced to sticks, larger and larger sticks as the snake seemed unconcerned and equally unwilling to move. I finally aggravated it enough to draw the cautioning rattle. The snake then coiled off the side of the trail, its pitted head following my movements with menace, and from that attack position it would move no farther. I hopped onto a stump, and then onto another, balancing above what I hoped was its reach until I was able to leap far enough across for safety. It didn't occur to me until later that I should have taken a photo, but at the time I was more focused on immediate matters. The snake was probably a black timber rattlesnake with a unique phenotype, or perhaps in seasonal or breeding colors. Regardless, that snake was beautiful.

Twenty-nine miles got me to Big Meadows Campground at about six o'clock. I hiked up to the store, assuming it was closed but with hope in my heart. The store was indeed closed, the campground full of families. I sighed. There were a couple of hours of daylight left so I could easily make it to Rock Spring Hut for another thirty-plus-mile day. I was turning back for the trail when a red-headed woman came out of one of the restrooms.

"Hi," she said as if she knew me. "Are you a thru-hiker?"

"Yeah," I said.

"Are you camping here?"

"Naw. I was just checking out the store. The place looks full anyway."

"We're in our van over there. We're not tenting so you can use our tent space if you want it."

My first impression was to say thanks anyway and move on, but the emotional weight of Loft Mountain Store still weighed on me, making me more tired than I would have been. Suddenly, throwing down at twenty-nine miles felt like a pretty good day.

"Sure," I said. "Thanks."

Her name was Pat and her husband's name was Steve. Pat was the hiker in their family, Steve the husband who indulged her through section after section as she stitched together what she hoped would eventually become a complete Appalachian Trail hike. They were nice people who went a long way toward suppressing the misanthropic thoughts I'd been gestating all day. Steve made a fire, brought out beers and then a bottle of bourbon. Pat heated some food on a propane stove, and then we settled in for conversation. I felt renewed but with a dark edge I couldn't drive off.

Night fell and the conversation continued. I told them what had happened at Loft Mountain Store and they were shocked.

"Why would she behave that way?" Pat incredulously asked.

"I have no idea," I answered in truth.

"And why would anybody want to take your clothes?" Steve asked. "Even a custodian would probably have known that somebody was in the shower."

That was true. I have no idea where my clothes went, and don't to this day.

I wasn't up until six o'clock the next morning, a little muzzy from mixing beer and bourbon. Pat and Steve were in their van sleeping. I left a note of thanks on their windshield then took to the trail at seven o'clock.

I felt all day as if the energy had been drained from me, like a spent battery. This was also a more taxing section of rocks and climbs, and in a heat that I hadn't dealt with in a while. The trail around Skyland was being rerouted, which caused me some confusion but I eventually found the place and was able to stop in for food and beers. There were quite a few thru-hikers at Skyland. I was passing them now in droves, pushing ever deeper into the northbound bubble. My miles startled them, perhaps intimidated them, placing me outside their experiences. Conversations were awkward and brief.

Pushing on, I reached the Elkwallow Wayside at seven o'clock after 25.8 miles, well after closing hours so I settled for cokes out of a vending machine. There was a custodian running around who eyed me with suspicion, as if he could read in my mind what I was going to do, which was to stealth camp in the picnic area. He kept returning on his rounds, pausing at each pass to ask why I was still there.

"I'm waiting for a ride," I told him each time, while what I was really waiting for was him to go home so I could pitch my tent.

I last saw him just before nightfall, then went onto the smooth lawn of the picnic area and set up in the dark. I was alone, as I had expected. No one would be picnicking after dark. I'd chosen that site because of the water fountain, where I'd filled my bottles on all of my previous thru-hikes. Ample clean water meant that I would be able to bathe, that I wouldn't have to filter anything, that I would be able to leave with clean full bottles in the morning. As a bonus I would be able to sleep through the night without interruption and could stash my food bag in the restroom, safe from marauding bears. I had only this one more night and then I would be out of the park, the itch soothed at last, all the bad juju behind me.

It was dark when I broke camp the next morning. I set out into the darkness to get a head start on the day, nineteen miles to Front Royal and if I moved fast enough I'd be able to get the benefit. I got turned around on the side trails, though, so wound up having to wait until first light anyway.

Afterward I made a good pace. The trail on that end of the park alternates between long flat stretches and rocky climbs. The heat came up, and with it came mosquitoes. I passed thru-hikers wholesale, entire tramilys that had managed to stay together since Springer Mountain. They were insular and unapproachable. I pushed on and left them behind. Finally, in some sticky and level woods, I came to the self-registration box. I paused with a grin of triumph and relief, took my next step and laughed. Shenandoah National Park was behind me now, I'd done it, not quite what I'd said in Glasgow but close enough: thirty-three, twenty-nine, twenty-six and out. The itch was gone.

There were still some buggy miles to make, but downhill miles. I made it to U.S. Highway 522 at one thirty, Front Royal three and a half miles west. After thirty minutes in the sun with my thumb out, I hadn't been able to get a hitch. In thirty minutes I could have easily gone a mile and a half, I thought with rising impatience, so I started hiking. In bare minutes, someone stopped to pick me up.

Front Royal has come a long way since my earlier thru-hikes, when people would view us with suspicion if not outright loathing. I never actually spent a night in the town until Hike 3. There were brewpubs now, a hiker hostel or two, and a nice outfitter. I had my ride drop me at the Super 8 so that I could be alone. I wasn't yet ready to mix with people again.

Even though I arrived early enough to get the benefit, the next day would still be a zero for me, zero number seven but this one was planned. My friends Chad and Shawna lived in the Washington D.C. area these days. It had been a few years since I'd seen either of them. Chad and Shawna had once been teenaged employees of mine in Alaska. Chad's military career had seen them stationed all over the world, where they hosted me during my international travels. Without their assistance, many of those travels would not have been possible, and none of them would have been as authentic. They were adults now approaching middle age and with two all-but-grown children. We'd made plans to meet in Front Royal for dinner tomorrow.

Also planning to attend was Vicki Valentine, who was responsible for the beautiful cover art and design of my last several books. Vicki lived in the Washington D.C. area as well. Book design is all done digitally these days, so Vicki and I had never met. I looked forward to seeing her and finally being able to thank her in person for her outstanding work on my behalf.

So it would be an exciting zero day, to connect with old friends and colleagues certainly, but more than that. Through all of my hikes, no one had ever visited me along the way. I'd watched with envy over the years as other hikers met up with family and friends, such as Tollbooth Willy's girlfriend on Hike 1, or Ultra Burn's forthcoming family reunion on this hike. Trail time distends relationships into eternities apart, which develops into a creeping sense of aloneness, not so much loneliness as a sense of being adrift and left to wander. Perhaps Technicians are able to deflect this with their gadgets, with their video calls and so on, but those of us going old-school didn't have that ability, nor any of us prior to phones. To see friends while inside the experience would be emotionally restorative the way a cold beer is physically restorative. So no, I would not begrudge this zero.

I began that zero day with a trip to an outfitter for shoes. I had discovered the Salomon XA Pro 3D in Damascus, Virginia on my last hike. That pair of shoes took me all the way to Springer Mountain, 470 miles, and were in good enough condition when I finished that I still wear them at home today. Prior to the Salomon shoes, I wore the other popular brand on the Appalachian Trail and was unimpressed. I went through five pairs of shoes on Hike 3. Contrast that with two pairs on Hike 2, and a single pair on Hike 1. Quality has obviously suffered over the years. The XA Pro was rugged, though, with a stitched toe bumper that didn't peel off in the rocks. (I'm disappointed to report that the toe bumper is no longer stitched on this model.) I thought I might be able to do Hike 4 on two pairs of shoes. It ultimately took three pairs, but close enough.

In the meantime, my current pair of shoes had lasted 972 miles, not bad considering that other thru-hikers were already on their second or third pairs. I also bought another OR shirt, wincing at the price. Of Z Lite sleeping pads, that outfitter had also been out of stock for a while.

Chad and Shawna pulled up at five o'clock, seeing me as they'd never seen me before, in shorts and my new OR shirt, stringy ponytail, and thin to the point of vapor. It was a sight they wouldn't be able to reconcile with their bespoke-suited and slightly overweight employer from the 1990s. Damn it was good to see them! They drove me to a restaurant, where Vicki Valentine was already enjoying a beer. Vicki and I hugged warmly, as if we had been close friends for years. I made introductions and then we ate, and I continued to eat, and too soon the evening came to an end. I said my goodbyes as one might before boarding an ocean-going ship in earlier times, at once sad but excited by adventures to come. Being able to meet up with them slew the demons of Shenandoah National Park, snatched me out of my head and grounded me in the present. Harpers Ferry was but a couple of days away, the midpoint in Pennsylvania soon thereafter.

It felt as if I were embarking on a new hike.

WEDNESDAY, JULY 14, 2021

Mile 998.9 - 26.9 Miles

Time is flying, I mean flying. Ten days ago I was in Glasgow. It feels as if I should be in Massachusetts by now.

Woke up feeling very relaxed. Packed up and back to the trail by about 8:00 a.m. Went at an easy pace on a forgiving trail, all alone all day until I reached Rod Hollow Shelter at 4:30 p.m., my goal for the day but it was too early to stop, and the two section hikers in the shelter didn't have enough personality between them to form an imaginative thought.

I got rained on before the shelter, but then the sky cleared so I pushed on into the Roller Coaster. Stopped here at 6:45 p.m. Met some nobos along the way who all pushed on. I expect to pass them in the morning. Man, it's hot and sticky! Love the new shoes.

THURSDAY, JULY 15, 2021

Harpers Ferry, West Virginia - 27.1 Miles

Wow, what a day!

Slept okay, up at 4:00 a.m., broke camp and hiking by 5:45.

The Roller Coaster kicked my butt, much harder for nobos. Pushed on hard and fast, went past the tents of all the people I met yesterday. Met only one new nobo today, a young guy who gets up and hikes early the way I do, but he pulled out at David Lesser Memorial Shelter with only 10 miles to go until Harpers Ferry. Well, it was damned hot. I thought for a while there that I might have found a new hiking partner. No such luck.

I pushed on in the heat hoping to reach Harpers Ferry before the ATC office closed. I got in—wiped out—at 5:40 p.m. The office was already closed, and shock!—there are no hostels in Harpers Ferry anymore, including the Teahorse Hostel where I stayed last time. I guess Covid is the culprit. I'd really hoped to stop in and see Ben at the Teahorse, but oh well...

I asked a guy passing by on a bicycle to make my photograph in front of the ATC office in case something happened between then and tomorrow, then I hitched to the Clarion Inn, formerly the Quality Inn, where I stayed on Hike 2. This is a hiker friendly place with a hiker rate and supportive staff.

Too tired to write more.

—

I left out of Front Royal with a renewed spirit and a pair of shiny new shoes, a little late for the magic hour but the day made up for that. I was alone for most of it, hiking a trail that demanded no blood price. It was a joy to just *hike*, not to scramble, not to climb incessantly, but to be able to go along at a good pace, eyes off the trail for a change and into the forest for a glimpse of a sheltered orchid, or a wary striped garter snake, or an indignant squirrel. I breathed easy and deep of the rich smells, of loam and fungi and the honey mix of flowers. This was how it should be every day, I thought with a pang.

An afternoon shower caught me as I neared Rod Hollow Shelter at 23.6 miles, which had been my goal for the day anyway. There were a couple of younger hikers already in the shelter when I arrived. I tried in vain to strike up conversations with them, found them too oddly aloof for my elevated mood, so when the sky miraculously cleared within the hour I took off with no goal in mind, only to make that perfect day last as long as possible.

I fetched up at Morgan Mill Stream as the woods went dusky, 26.9 unweary miles beneath my new shoes, a soft, leaf-littered clearing for my tent, and a natural bathing pool beside a boulder below. There was a collection of other hikers there, all watering up and pushing on. Soon I was alone with the woods and the stream and the night to come.

The next morning began for me in the dark of four o'clock after a quiet and restful night. I stepped into the magic hour at five forty-five, reveling in the mist and the solitude and the awakening woods, passing the tents of yesterday's water gatherers one after another after another. The Roller Coaster came on as a minor inconvenience in the cool of the morning, but as a slurry of heat and humidity rose around me, the Roller Coaster became a trial.

The Roller Coaster, blazed in 1989 and purposefully made difficult, is described by AWOL as "thirteen and a half miles of tightly packed ascents and descents." Taking this three times as a southbounder, I've said (and meant) that I barely noticed the thing. Going northbound, though, the grades are different, more strenuous. Sweat drizzled out of me, leaving puddles on the trail whenever I paused. I had to put my phone in a ziplock to keep it dry. When I reached the end of this, a few miles past Bears Den Rocks and after stepping into and out of West Virginia a few times, I sighed in relief and kicked up a step.

The heat punished me but I kept up the pace. I came up on a young thru-hiker as he was taking a break, so took advantage of the shade and the plentiful sitting rocks to join him. He was a good-natured guy going solo. Like me, he arose early every morning to take in the cool and solitude. He knew exactly what I meant by *magic hour*, and was gratified to hear it described that way. No one, he said, understood why he preferred to hike so early—no one, that is, until he met me. My heart sped up noticeably. I thought peradventure I'd found a perfect hiking companion. He was dubious about my miles, though, and when he pulled up short at David Lesser Memorial Shelter, spent in the withering heat, I swallowed a knot of disappointment and pushed on, ten more miles to Harpers Ferry, which I'd vowed to make come what may.

Those last miles into Harpers Ferry tested my resolve. Poor blazing and sections of overgrown trail competed with the heat to reduce me to a two-mile pace. The character of the trail was too different from the southbound experience, with climb after climb until that last final climb up the steps

The ATC Office in Harpers Ferry

from the trail to the town, which I took one at a time on wooden legs. But I'd made Harpers Ferry, 27.1 miles that day, over the Roller Coaster and through the devil's own heat. I shuffled bent and aching up to the ATC office at five forty. The place was closed but that didn't matter now. I'd done it!

I flagged a guy passing by on a bicycle to take my photograph, proof that I'd made it on that day in case some misadventure occurred to prevent me from returning tomorrow. All the hostels in Harpers Ferry had closed, including the Teahorse Hostel where I stayed on Hike 3, so, sunburned, dehydrated, and gritty from sweat salt, I hitched to a hotel just outside of town, bringing a comfortable end to a satisfying if not difficult day.

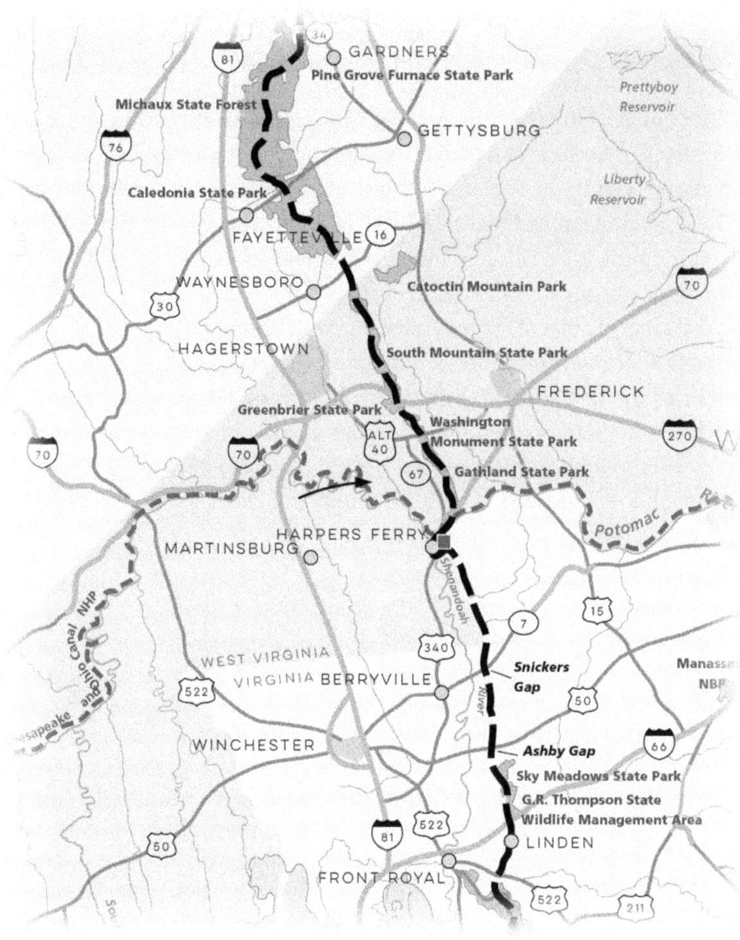

WEST VIRGINIA/ MARYLAND

43.3 MILES

FRIDAY, JULY 16, 2021

Dahlgren State Park, Maryland - 17.5 Miles

Another one of those really great days. I thought I would be too wiped out to hike today, but I awoke at 6:00 a.m. feeling quite well. Coffee first, then downstairs doing laundry by 6:10. Everything was sweaty, sweaty, sticky and sweaty.

Got it all done, plus breakfast, by 10:00. A hotel employee named Joe gave me a ride to the ATC office. There I met a few other nobos, and one young Adonis-looking guy completing his Triple Crown. We had our photos made, then the others took off for breakfast in town. I hung around the office until about 11:00 doing interpretation for some visitors, then took off for what I thought would be a short 10 miles or so, but set a goal along the way to reach Dahlgren State Park at 17.5 miles instead so I could get a (free) shower and then go up to Old South Mountain Inn for food and beers.

All of this worked out. Afterward, sated and clean, I hiked back to Dahlgren (only ¼ mile) and pitched my tent.

What a great day!

SATURDAY, JULY 17, 2021

Pen Mar County Park - 23.1 Miles

I should have slept well but didn't because a guy hung his hammock right next to my tent and made various noises all night. There was also a brief shower, so I had to close my tent flaps, which led to condensation in the tent.

I woke up for good at 4:00 a.m., packed and ready to go by 4:45. Took another shower (why not?) and was on the trail by 6:00.

Hiked not fast despite the initial flat trail. Eventually, beyond Potomac Appalachian Trail Club country, the trail went into rocks and climbs that I didn't remember. I passed a portly and well-dressed ATC guy leading a young woman, possibly a ridgerunner trainee, and told him that I didn't remember the Maryland trail as being so rocky. He didn't stop to talk, just walked on and smugly said as he went, "It gets worse, ha, ha." Also met a pair of PATC trail volunteers who had a lot of gripes about the ATC. Something must really be going on with that organization.

I sweated through the day, met a guy named Gollum, a 2019 thru-hiker out doing the Maryland section. He offered me a ride to Waynesboro, PA so I took it.

We made it out by 4:00 p.m., he drove me to the Cobblestone Hotel—same place I stayed last time. They were out of rooms, but after I whined and looked pitiful they found one for me. Ate a big meal at Applebees, also same as last time, took a shower when I got back, and found a tick on my back. Damn the ticks on this hike!

Now it's storming furiously outside, and I'm glad I'm in here.

—

When I awoke in Harpers Ferry the next morning, I felt so well that I was startled. Dragging into the hotel the previous night, I was by then so weary and withered that I'd talked myself into taking a zero—and I didn't feel too guilty about the decision. But now I felt incredibly, magically vigorous. I did laundry, ate breakfast, then caught a ride with a hotel employee back to the ATC office.

There were a few thru-hikers out front when I arrived, one of them a shirtless and physically perfect Triple Crowner named Cougar who'd completed the Pacific Crest Trail in May, and who'd started his Appalachian Trail thru-hike the first week of June.

"Any of you guys had your photo taken yet?" I asked.

"Naw," one of them answered. "They've been too busy."

"Hmm."

I went inside the venerable building only to find it antiseptic and unrecognizable. There was no merchandise on display, and worse than that, the entrance to the hiker lounge had been boarded over.

"What's going on?" I disquietly asked one of the staff, a dowdy man whom I will call Dough Boy.

"We're remodeling." The phone rang and he went for it.

"So is the hiker lounge closed?"

He held out a finger, nodded at something said over the phone, then hung up. "Yeah," he told me then.

"Darn, I wanted to show the guys out front the photos from my other thru-hikes."

"Do you want me to go get them?" he asked in a way that meant he hoped I'd say no. Retrieving the photo albums might be time consuming. If the hiker lounge hadn't been closed we could have all been in there and out from underfoot, perusing the collection of books and flipping through the photo albums at leisure. Of course Covid might be the reason the lounge was closed, which would not be an unreasonable concern. Itching the back of my neck, though, was a premonition that the hiker lounge might be closed forever.

"No, that's cool," I said with a sigh. "It was just a thought. So are you all still taking photos?"

"Yeah, it's just that we've been a little busy this morning."

A domineering, middle-aged woman whom I will call Aikido walked up then. "Are you all ready out there?"

"For photos, you mean?"

"Yeah."

"Yeah, I guess so."

The others had come in while this went on, including Cougar, who was still shirtless and looked as if he should be carved in Roman marble. Aikido eyed him with distaste.

"You need to put a shirt on if you're going to come in here," she said the way she might correct the behavior of a child. Cougar threw her a defiant look then turned and left. The rest filed after him.

"Can I register my hike here?" I asked Aikido.

I'd never registered any of my hikes. On my earliest hikes, many of us had been too counter-culturally inclined to submit to something like that. The new ATC office in Monson, Maine had been closed when I came through on Hike 3, so that hike wasn't registered either. No one from the ATC had been at Amicalola Falls State Park when I began this hike, but now that I was here I thought that I might finally have a chance to make one of my thru-hikes official, at least by their reckoning.

"You can do that on your phone," she said dismissively, as if my question had been an inconvenient intrusion.

"My phone is old-school, it won't work for that. And I thought you all would help me with it." I eyed a computer that was sitting right there.

"You can go to the library, then," she bluntly told me, and that was going to be her last word on the matter.

I blinked a few times trying to puzzle it out. Every time I'd come into the ATC office in years prior I'd always been met by an engaging and eager staff person, all former thru-hikers themselves and none who would dismiss a fellow thru-hiker that way. I soberly turned and went back outside to join the others.

We made conversation while we waited. Cougar was beside himself about the trail.

"Man, I can't believe this trail," he said. "It's kicking my ass. The CDT and the PCT weren't anything like this."

"I know," I said, recalling my lash on the PCT almost twenty years earlier. "Sometimes you forget what it's like to just hike, you know? You can go from sea level to eleven thousand feet on the PCT and never get beat up like this."

"Yeah, man, I hear ya. And you've done this shit *four times?*"

"I'm working on the fourth."

"Well, once will be enough for me. I've even thought about quitting this shit a few times."

"You can't do that, Cougar," I hastily countered. "You need your Triple Crown, dude."

"I know," he said with a shake of his head. "I won't quit but I sure do miss the PCT, man."

Aikido came out then, acidly eyed the shirtless Cougar then turned her attention to one of the other guys. "So are you all looking to get your tags?" she asked.

"Yeah," we said in unison.

The tags were something I saw for the first time on Hike 3, plastic A.T. logos, color-coded each year, that you fastened onto your backpack as proof that you'd registered your hike. They were blue for 2021. I'd never had one but I wanted one this time.

"Okay," she went on. "But I need you to answer some questions first." She singled out a tall guy with a scrappy beard. "So, how deep do you bury your poop?"

"Uh—" This was a guy who obviously did not bury his poop. "—a couple of feet?"

Aikido rolled her eyes. "That would be good" she said, "but six to eight inches would be enough. Are you carrying a trowel for this?" she asked him.

"Uh, sure," he said.

She turned to me. "And are you?"

"Oh, yeah," I lied. "I've got it right there in my pack."

"Good." She turned to another guy. "So how high do you hang your food bag?"

The guy grinned. "I use my food bag for a pillow."

She rolled her eyes again and turned to another hiker. "And you?"

"Uh, eight feet, right?"

"At least eight feet high and six from the tree," she corrected him. "Okay," she sighed then. "Let's take your pictures."

We posed one by one for the snaps, Cougar lasciviously bouncing his hairless Adonis pecs at Aikido as he stood waiting. I laughed and slapped him on the back. I really liked that guy's irreverent style. Resist much, obey little, that's what Ed Abbey said.

Afterward, Aikido gave us our tags, reluctantly it seemed. But I had mine in hand and that was all I wanted. I never registered my hike. I did try later on but I couldn't figure out the complicated website. Someone at the ATC office could have helped with that if they'd been willing to take the time. So it goes.

The others took off for breakfast down the street. I went back inside, hoping that maybe some of the former enthusiasm of the place would surface. Aikido was off somewhere, leaving Dough Boy to hold down the fort. A pair of visitors came in, a youngish couple. They approached Dough Boy, who held out his finger when the phone started ringing. I stepped up to them then.

"I can show you around if you'd like," I offered.

"Are you hiking the trail?" the man asked.

"Yeah."

"That's awesome!"

I walked them around the place, and the few exhibits on display. There was the relief map of the A.T., the photo of Earl Shaffer, and the sign from Baxter Peak, either a facsimile or perhaps a weathered original. If there'd been merchandise in the place I could have sold those two anything and everything. I enjoyed guiding them. It had been years since I'd worked at a national park and had been able to do that kind of interpretation. Visitors are always thrilled by authenticity and sincerity. Their appreciation bolsters your delivery and enthusiasm, the same way a live audience enhances a performance on a stage. After about half an hour they thanked me and left. Dough Boy was on the phone, Aikido wasn't around, so I left as well.

The 43.3-mile section between the Virginia-West Virginia line and the Maryland-Pennsylvania line is known as the Four State Challenge. Intrepid hikers will take this on in one hike, starting out in the early hours and then pushing hard into the night. I have never been tempted by this myself, even though the southbound challenge is significantly less punishing. Looking back now, I wish I had given it a go if only to round out my Appalachian Trail experience.

This was not on my mind on that day. I left out of Harpers Ferry before noon, across the bridge and up the long tow path, content to do ten miles. The heat was up by then, wilting even in the shade of the tow path. Once I climbed back into the woods, into a cooling breeze and along a trail that allowed a quick pace, I reset my goal and decided to go for Dahlgren State Park at 17.5 miles.

Maryland's Dahlgren State Park is a nice patch of woods and level campsites not far from the road to Boonsboro. There are free hot showers just off the trail. A quarter mile or so beyond is Old South Mountain Inn, an upscale place with a well-stocked bar and a fine menu. I had a great evening there on Hike 3, excellent food, plenty of beer, and an attractive bartender who knew how to tickle an old guy's ego. Afterward I'd pushed on a short two miles to Rocky Run Shelter, a nice double-decker with skylights.

A storm blew in after I reached the shelter. Alone, still buzzing from good beer and clean from the shower I took along the way, I spent an enchanting night as the sky raged above, simple satisfaction as only being dry and clean on the Appalachian Trail can provide. I looked forward to rekindling some of that this time.

I made Dahlgren State Park well before dusk, showered, changed into a clean shirt, then trotted on up to Old South Mountain Inn, where I was welcomed warmly and took a seat at the bar. The inn has had some negative comments online from hikers but this is only because the people at the inn ask that we shower before we come in. Those who refused might have been turned away, churlishly retaliating with their online comments. While I fully embrace the Bohemian thru-hiker attitude, I cannot sympathize in this circumstance, not when a free shower is a quarter-mile car race away. Regardless the online comments, I had a good time. The bartender was friendly and chatty, the food was epicurean, and the beer was sublime. I returned to Dahlgren to pitch my tent, fully content in the softening light. A dozen thru-hikers had shown up by then, keeping to themselves across the way. A few raindrops splattered on my tent as I drifted off, dry, clean, and cozy in my sleeping bag. The sky could now roar for all I cared, which would be a serendipitous reprise of my experience last time.

Would the night have gone as well as before. Well past dusk, as rain pattered outside, a guy strung his hammock right next to my tent then proceeded to snort, snore, fuss and fart all night. I had to close my tent flaps when the rain started coming down harder, which led to condensation inside. One bump of a tent wall would then loose a shower on me. I awoke early the next morning, feeling funky and not well rested. Once I had everything packed, sparing no noise for the guy in the hammock, I went in for a hot morning shower and emerged feeling much better.

I was lethargic through the magic hour, though, as the trail wound through and over wet rock piles that had no place in my memory. Could this be a trail relocation, I wondered, or just different from the southbound grade? I simply couldn't tell.

I met a pair of Potomac Appalachian Trail Club volunteers, and older man and his wife, who were removing rocks from the trail with a pickaxe and an iron bar, heavy work for people their age. I stopped and offered to help but the man declined my offer with a friendly smile.

"We've been doing this for years," he told me. "We're used to it."

We found stumps to sit on, and then his wife joined us.

"They don't like us doing this," his wife said, "but what good's a trail if you can't walk on it?"

"You mean they don't *want* you to take the rocks out?" I asked in incredulity.

"No, they don't. It's not natural, they say, but we get hundreds of day hikers through here, going up to the monument, you know?" She meant the Washington Monument not too far ahead, the first monument erected to our first president. "People twist their ankles and complain, so what are we supposed to do?"

I described to them how I'd watched a Georgia Appalachian Trail Club volunteer who must have been eighty going after a big root across the trail using a pickaxe that I couldn't have wielded but for a few strikes. That man, too, had declined my help, taking pride in the improvements he put into a trail that had probably come to seem his own.

"So I don't understand," I said after that. "Keeping the trail clear—that's what you all volunteered for, right?"

"You wouldn't think so the way they treat us," the wife replied with an edge of bitterness. "You'd think they were paying us the way they go on. They even told my husband once that they didn't want him working on this trail anymore."

"Fat chance," the husband spoke up then. "I've been working this trail too long to be run off by the likes of them. What are they going to do, anyway? Arrest me?" He laughed. "Well, tell them to come do it."

That conversation left me shaken. Something unsettling was going on in the Appalachian Trail world, something I'd never sensed before let alone seen. "Well, I want you to know that we all appreciate your hard work," I told them as I stood to continue on.

"And we thank you for noticing," they said to that.

In the later morning, well beyond the Washington Monument (which is a moving site and well worth a visit by all) and into a renewed section of rock scrambles, a chubby man dressed in khaki slacks and a blue button-down shirt approached from ahead. He was leading a young woman who was more appropriately dressed for the outdoors. As they came closer I recognized the ATC logo on his shirt. Perhaps the young woman was receiving training to be a ridgerunner or volunteer. Regardless, she seemed to know more about what she was doing than he did.

"I don't remember the Maryland trail as being this rocky," I commented as they passed.

The two never broke stride, shouldering by me as if I occupied no space on the trail at all. "It'll get worse," the man said with a smug chuckle as the two turned around a bend.

Somewhat later at a water source, I met a youngish guy named Gollum, a 2019 thru-hiker who was out doing the Maryland section as a way to extend his experience of two years before. We hit it off right away, making easy conversation as we continued on together. If he'd been thru-hiking this time, we would have made good hiking partners. Our paces were nearly identical and his love of the trail was as deep as mine. His car was parked at Pen Mar County Park. He offered me a ride out if I wanted it. In the sticky heat, and worn out from all the frustrating rock scrambles, I took him up on his offer.

In a hollow not too far from Pen Mar, we came upon an older man sitting beside the trail and sipping a beer. "Do you want one?" the man asked as we approached.

Gollum and I were by then dripping sweat and as filthy as a barroom floor.

"Hell yeah," I said.

We sat, cracked beers, and then familiarity came to me in a blast of recognition.

"Hey man!" I exclaimed. "You're Oggie, aren't you?"

"Yeah, that's my name. How'd you know?"

"I met you, dude!" I was giddy with delight. "It was at Pen Mar three years ago. I was resting in the shade by the museum and you came up and gave me a beer. Damn, I needed that beer. We talked for a long time. You told me to keep my beer hidden because we weren't supposed to have them in the park. I can't *believe* I've run into you like this."

"Well, I can't say that I remember you exactly, but the story sounds familiar, so it's good to see you again, too."

We discussed serendipity on the Appalachian Trail, how we never experienced it with such frequency anywhere else. After that restorative break we gave Oggie our thanks and pushed on, reaching Pen Mar County Park at four o'clock. Gollum drove me into Waynesboro, Pennsylvania to the Cobblestone Hotel, where I stayed on Hike 3. We bumped fists, wished each other well, and then I went on in.

The place, as it turned out, was fully booked. There's always an extra room, though, you just have to push the right buttons. I informed them of my previous stay, what a great night I'd had, how pleasant everyone had been. I made myself look as pitiful as possible, like their own grandfather lying in the mud beside a road. It worked. I scored a room at a discounted rate and was soon showered and gorging myself at the Applebees up the road. The sky became angry as I walked back to the hotel, roiling black clouds and malevolent streaks of lightening, the potential of a funnel cloud in the making.

I had just cleared the front doors when the heavens opened with hurricane fury, trees bending toward their roots and a riot of rain that could have left bruises in its intensity, but I was inside, dry, and thankful for it.

Although I was sleeping in Pennsylvania, on the trail I was still officially in Maryland, a few tenths shy of the state line. I would correct that first thing in the morning.

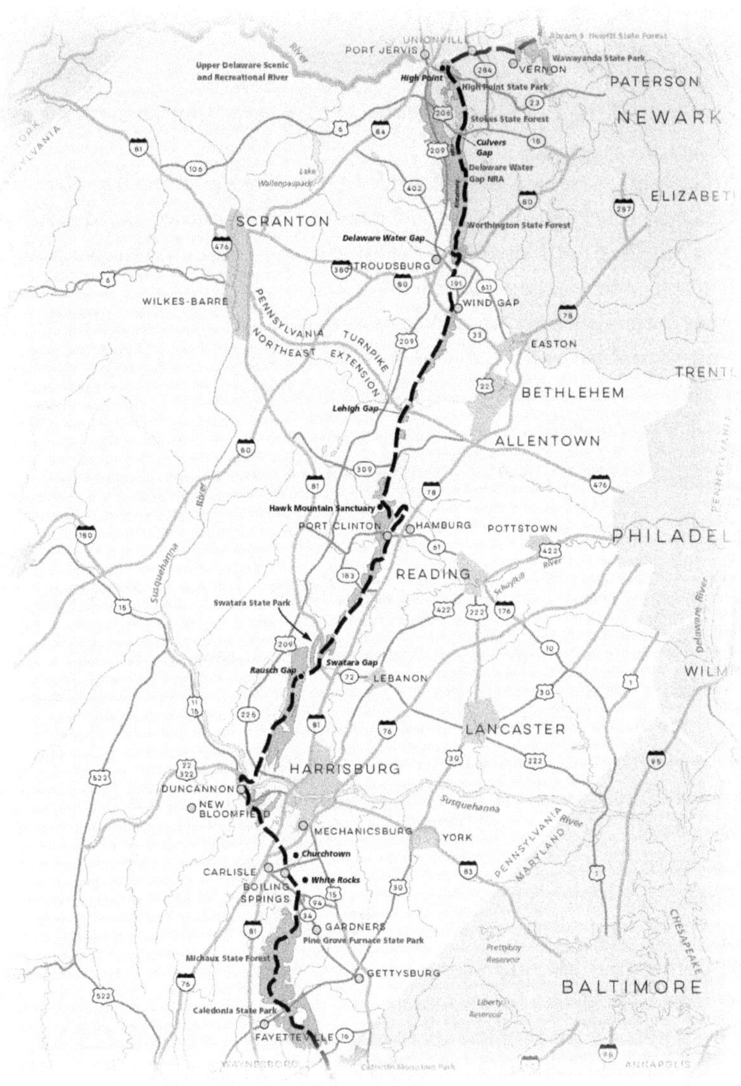

PENNSYLVANIA

229.5 MILES

SUNDAY, JULY 18, 2021

Mile 1084.8 - 18.2 Miles

Hitched out of the Cobblestone Hotel at 10:00 a.m. after resupplying at the Wal-Mart.

Today's hike was easy and fast under a cloudy sky and much cooler weather. I reached U.S. Highway 30 at 3:30 p.m. and decided to go ahead and throw down at the Trail of Hope Hostel. This is a multi-denominational ministry, with ample food and so on for thru-hikers.

They have a nice set-up here. I'm surprised no other thru-hikers came in, but no problem with that, I'll take the solitude and the soft bunk—and what's this? Hey, I think I'll even watch a movie tonight.

Half way tomorrow!

MONDAY, JULY 19, 202

Pine Grove Furnace State Park - 19.8 Miles

Slept really well last night. Up at 5:00 a.m. and out the door at 6:00.

Passed several hikers in their tents, and met Specs, a super-distance thru-hiker from New York. Stopped for photos at both midpoints, 2021 at Mile 1096.5, and the traditional midpoint a little farther on—the 2018 midpoint sign is still up, I scattered some of Freewind's ashes there last time; no sign for the 2021 midpoint, though, just some rocks arranged aside the trail.

Hiked into Pine Grove Furnace State Park at 2:30 p.m. with Specs. We both did the Half-gallon Challenge, first time for me since the store has always been closed when I've come through before. My time was 27.07, and I froze the inside of my cheeks. Ouch!

Specs pushed on with his super speed and endurance, while I went over to the A.T. Museum, which was closed and has always been closed on my hikes so I've still never been able to see inside. I guess I'll just have to drive up here someday.

I decided to throw down at the Mansion for tradition's sake. There wasn't a caretaker this time—something about Covid—so everything was on the honor system. I saw wads of bills left in plain sight on the desk, left by people who didn't read the posted directions, I guess. I thought to hide them, but then thought I'd better not touch them. Hopefully anyone else coming in will be honest.

A couple of older section hikers are in the downstairs bunkroom, plus a mysterious woman in a private room upstairs. Otherwise I was alone until dark, when a horde of insular and arrogant young thru-hikers swarmed in, so annoying that I wished I had pushed on instead of staying. They spread out, took over everything, and wouldn't respond if I spoke directly to them. What is it with these people? Thankfully, they all piled into the bunkroom upstairs, leaving me alone with the section hikers, who were decent people. The night should be okay down here.

TUESDAY, JULY 20, 2021

Carlisle, Pennsylvania - 27.3 Miles

I was so disgusted with those young nobos that I couldn't get away from them fast enough.

Up at 4:00 a.m., hiking in the dark by 5:00, I had 16 miles behind me by noon. Those nobos caught me from behind, so my hope is that they will blow on ahead and I won't have to see them again.

In the meantime, today was mostly level and fast except for a couple of rock mazes. The A.T.C. office in Boiling Springs was closed, fourth time in four thru-hikes. I wonder why that place is even there. I got here to the Quality Inn at 3:00 p.m. Would have gotten here sooner if I hadn't gone down to Interstate 76 thinking it was U.S. Highway 11. Southbound turned-around once again. Fortunately I discovered my error before I went too far.

I could have pushed on for 5, maybe even 10 more miles, but I wanted to give that nobo horde plenty of a head start on tomorrow.

I have stayed here before, and had a restful night that I clearly recall. They even still had my cell number in their system, which scored me a discounted rate.

So now I will relax, and put on more big miles tomorrow.

WEDNESDAY, JULY 21, 2021

Peters Mountain Shelter - 28.6 Miles

This day started out wonderfully.

Out of bed at 4:45 a.m. feeling well-rested, out for breakfast at 5:15. The breakfast area wasn't open yet, but the desk manager (nice young lady) gave me three breakfast biscuits with egg and sausage, and four granola bars. This fueled me to Duncannon.

Made good time through the farm fields, slowed in some rocky climbs and scrambles, but still made the 17 miles to Duncannon by 12:30 p.m. Two beers and a burger with fries at The Doyle filled me up and refreshed me. It was still not 2:00 p.m., so I pushed on under threatening skies, but only spatters of rain.

The climb out of the Duncannon hole was tough, tough, tough, with major rock scrambles up top that took a lot of time. This was yet another section that felt different. Relo?

Full water-up at Clarks Ferry Shelter because this is a dry section, then pushed on an interminable 6 miles to this shelter, arriving at 6:45 p.m. Got rained on along the way, but only briefly.

There were four people in the shelter, so I tented out.

THURSDAY, JULY 22, 2021

Mile 1184.6 - 24.1 Miles

Did not sleep well because some small varmints kept visiting my tent during the night.

Hiking by 5:45 a.m., I took it easy at first but then picked up speed even though I felt fatigued. There was a definite relo in this section, sending me scrambling into some rock piles. I dolefully waved at the old A.T. as I passed by.

16 miles by noon despite the rocks and climbs, but these beat me up so much that I bailed at Swatara Gap and went into Licksdale to get a hotel room. I need food, and I need good sleep. You can make good time over the rocks, but they hurt and they wear you down.

K-Bar completed her Four State Challenge today, quite an achievement, and quite a change from who she was when I first met her. She'll probably catch up to me soon (I look forward to that). Ultra Burn has probably gotten off the trail for his family reunion. I haven't heard from him. I hope he gets back on the trail when he's done with his family, and doesn't decide to call it quits in New Jersey.

FRIDAY, JULY 23, 2021

Mile 1216 - 17 Miles

Today really was a great day. I slept luxuriously late for me (6:00 a.m.), took my time getting up, went for resupply, then back to the hotel for breakfast and ate a lot.

I didn't leave until 9:15, couldn't get a hitch so hiked the 2 ½ miles back to the A.T. on a side trail I learned about. Reached the A.T. at a little after 10:00, then hiked a fast and easy 9 miles, then a harder and possibly reloed 2 miles to 501 Shelter, where I met some thru-hikers and stopped for a break. One of the guys gave me a slice of his pizza and one of his cokes.

I hung around for an hour, then took off at 3:30 p.m., got off on a side trail, retraced my steps, and started again at 4:00 p.m.

The next 5.6 miles were a boulder-ballet, pitifully slow and with the constant risk of a twisted ankle. Threw down at a campsite on a spit of ground between a forked stream, nice site. Some other thru-hikers came in, but pushed on at dusk. There's a father-daughter section-hiking team here. He is TMI, she is a young girl named Squid who is inquisitive, curious, and respectful. The father is testing his skills and asked questions one after another, never arguing with my answers. I was pleased to give him all the information he asked for. I do envy these father-daughter teams, an experience I'll never know.

SATURDAY, JULY 24, 2021

Port Clinton, Pennsylvania - 18.3 Miles

I can't help but notice that I'm slowing down. It's all these rock scrambles, many of which I do not remember from last time.

Up at 4:45 a.m., hiking by 5:45. I made good time over a brutal trail and through some monotonous woods. I had intended to hike through Port Clinton, stopping only for food and beer, but long before I reached town I decided to stay at Port Clinton Hotel for the third time in a row.

Arrived in Port Clinton at 1:30 p.m. only to find that the hotel was closed and that there were no other services available in town, no food, no nada. I was hot, thirsty, and starving, so I hitched into Hamburg for food and such, and then it got so late I just stayed, throwing down at a hotel. The desk manager, a nice woman named Amanda, gave me a cold beer, which kept me going until the pub opened, and then I ate a lot of spaghetti and drank a few mugs of Guinness.

My weight worries me. I have no body fat left at all, and the veins are standing out on my thighs as if I were cycling the Tour de France. What will this mean when I get into the really tough terrain farther north?

SUNDAY, JULY 25, 2021

Mile 1240 - 20.1 Miles

Today was a good day. I tried to sleep late but couldn't, so at 6:00 a.m. I went for resupply then back to the hotel for breakfast.

I caught the Cabela's shuttle to Port Clinton at 10:00 a.m., and was hiking by 10:30. Bought a new pair of insoles at Cabela's, heading off an incipient blister on my right heel. The new insoles seem to have solved the problem.

There were a couple of long climbs, some boulder-ballet along the ridges, but I still made good time.

Stopped in at Eckville Shelter (where I've stayed three times) at 3:30 p.m., took a break, watered up, then pushed on.

I'm not sure where I am exactly, just a good way past Dan's Pulpit but not as far as Allentown Shelter. I'm stealthing here. I saw no thru-hikers today. No one was at Eckville Shelter, so who knows where everyone is?

Lehigh Gap tomorrow, I'm looking forward to seeing Mechanical Man again.

Rocky Pennsylvania doesn't start out that way. There are gentle rises and pastoral fields early on, satisfying hikes that are closer akin to the idealized, bucolic walks that many would-be thru-hikers envisioned. For a time there is a satisfying sense of rightness, of a trail bordered by cows and corn over land that has been farmed this way for a couple of centuries now.

I took this at a relaxed pace for 18.2 miles after an unhurried start from the Cobblestone Hotel. The previous night's storm had left a wet varnish on everything. The sky was overcast, although unthreatening. I wended through woods still dripping, mucking my way up a few inclines that had flash-flooded overnight like cataract streams, dislodged rocks and dams of sticks and leaves left behind as evidence of water's cumulative power. It was impossible to reconcile that tranquil, breathing morning with the violence that had rushed through there only hours before.

Alone all day, I reached U.S. Highway 30 at three thirty. Up the road a way was the Trail of Hope Hostel, while two and a half miles ahead were the Quarry Gap Shelters, a pair of conjoined shelters lovingly maintained, complete with rocking chairs and fresh flowers. I weighed my two options, assumed that the shelters would be full of hikers, so chose the hostel as my destination for the night.

This wound up being a good choice. Trail of Hope Hostel is a multi-denominational ministry that welcomes thru-hikers without impressing any religious dogma. They have a food bank, which is so abundantly stocked that they offer much of it to thru-hikers at no cost. I gorged myself on everything from corn chips to fresh ravioli with pesto, then retired to the bunkroom for the evening. I was alone, no other hikers in the place. I read from Luke for a while, dozed in luxurious comfort, got up, ate some more, then watched a DVD all the way through and without interruption, another of those simple pleasures magnified to pure bliss on the Appalachian Trail.

I passed Quarry Gap Shelters during the magic hour the next morning, found that they were indeed full of sleeping hikers, and congratulated myself for yesterday's decision. With less than ten miles ahead to the midpoint of the journey, over mostly level terrain, there was an urgency in my steps. The midpoint was a milestone, a psychological as well as physical mark of achievement. All of what was behind would transition to all of what was to come. I'd crossed the Mason-Dixon Line the day before yesterday, left my familiar South at a stone marker in the woods. There would be new landscapes soon, new ecologies, accents and attitudes, culminating in those final grueling miles through New Hampshire and Maine. At the midpoint you can glimpse the end, even though that end is still as far away as the beginning.

The midpoint changes most every year because of trail relocations. It was at Mile 1084.6 on Hike 1, Mile 1088.1 on Hike 2, Mile 1094.9 on Hike 3, and Mile 1096.5 this time. Nearer to Pine Grove Furnace State Park, there is an elaborate, traditional midpoint marker that has stood since the eighties. It was rendered obsolete almost immediately after it was erected but still serves as a memorable, photogenic landmark.

I flew through a warming day and under a clearing sky. The breath caught in my throat when I sighted the midpoint sign ahead. When I reached the sign, I found to my simultaneous dismay and delight that it was the 2018 midpoint sign, still standing. I'd scattered some of Freewind's ashes there on Hike 3 and had expected to hike past the site unknown. That it still marked a place where Freewind lay was emotionally reassuring, although why the sign still stood was a mystery. No sign had been erected for 2021, it seemed, only some stones arranged beside the trail.

On the way to the traditional midpoint marker I came upon a young and exceptionally fit thru-hiker named Specs, who would customarily hike thirty to forty miles per day and was bewildered by the absent 2021 sign. I explained the situation to him and informed him of the traditional marker ahead. There would yet be an opportunity for a memorable photo. As we struck up a conversation, I learned that he knew K-Bar and that through her he knew who I was. This was a rare treat for me, not only news of K-Bar, whom I still missed even after all that time, but also that my name was propagating up the trail. This was a small thing but felt large because in previous hikes there'd been no one ahead to propagate my name *to*. This gave me a sense of being part of something larger rather than a solitary pursuit.

I liked Specs. He was from New York, as was K-Bar. There might have been something amorous going on between the two, but I decorously did not pry. We hiked together into Pine Grove Furnace State Park, and both sat for the Half-gallon Challenge, a first for me. The Pine Grove General Store had been closed on each of my previous hikes, with nothing but stories from others of what it was like to eat a half gallon of ice cream in one sitting. Some hikers brushed the experience aside as if it were a minor event while others talked of going green and nauseous. Some couldn't finish, some went back for more. Some returned their half gallons to the bushes out back. I wasn't sure what to expect.

I don't crave ice cream on the trail as many thru-hikers do, but I found the taste of my half gallon of vanilla so divine that I relished every bite. I finished my portion in 27:07, a minute or two after Specs and with no ill effects except that the insides of my cheeks were frozen, and painfully so. Specs got up to push on, while after 19.8 miles that day I was content to stay put and throw down at Ironmasters Mansion Hostel across the way. We said our goodbyes and then Specs was gone at a sinuous sprint. He would set a speed record while crossing the state of New York, and he and K-Bar would meet up after their hikes, although the nature of their relationship is still unknown to me.

Lazy now from all the ice cream, I ambled over to the A.T. Museum and found to my disappointment that it was closed that day, as it had been on each of my previous hikes. This was a compounded disappointment because the Earl Shaffer Shelter had been reconstructed and was on display inside. I stayed in that shelter on Hike 1, and on Hike 2 I helped carry parts of it off Peters Mountain, which were then transported here. My connection to the Earl Shaffer Shelter was not insignificant, nevertheless destiny arranged that I wouldn't see it again unless I drove up to Pennsylvania in my car.

The afternoon was getting long, time to throw down for the night. The Ironmasters Mansion Hostel was just up a grassy rise from the store, a grand old red-brick building with a wide, white veranda, built in 1815. I stayed there on Hikes 2 and 3, alone with only the caretaker in a building that could have housed nobility. There was no caretaker this time, just a note taped to the glass describing where the towels were located, the blankets and sheets, what food could be taken from the kitchen. Money was to be slipped into a slot in a locked door. Covid had caused staffing problems. A nice letter begged us to take care, that the Mansion could have been closed but had been trustingly left open so that hikers would have a place to stay. There were wads of bills on the desk, out in the open and easily pocketed. I was about to push that money into the slot but drew back my hand before I touched it. I didn't know why that money was there. It might have been left out on purpose for a gardener or other worker, how could I know? I could only hope that anyone else coming in would leave it there as well.

I selected a bunk downstairs. There were only two section hikers in the bunkroom, a pleasant, older couple from the South. We hit it off with our accents. A younger, well-dressed woman glided down the stairs from a private room above, mysteriously smiled our way then went back up. As best I could tell, we were the only ones in the place.

After a shower, I raided the kitchen, all that ice cream quickly metabolizing. There was plenty of food in the refrigerator, with notes of what could be taken and what was private. I took my fill of what I could then went out onto the veranda to watch the sun set.

It had become a lazy evening, perhaps all that ice cream working its way through. I could have fallen asleep where I sat, with the softening sun on my face. As the stars began to twinkle, a pack of irreverent young hikers came pounding up the steps, one woman, the rest men, or rather boys considering their behavior. Some were shirtless, others dressed in preppy, designer labels. They were loud, raucous, and went by me as if I weren't present. I didn't know any of them but I knew what they were. They were what I call a *mobile frat party*, the hikers who do the most harm to the trail and to trail life. In a post-apocalyptic movie, they would be the slovenly-armored fiends in the over-powered cars chasing the good guys against all rational reason. They are the scourge of every thru-hiking year, although as a southbounder I'd always been able to avoid them. Not this time.

The pack spread out inside, roughly falling back on the couches, scraping chairs across the floor, fiddling with things and then tossing them back, thumbing at the TV and carelessly rummaging through the DVDs. They swarmed the kitchen, brought out food and beverages and then plunked onto the couches, feet propped on tables and food falling on cushions. It was disgusting behavior, which threatened to introduce them to the ice cream in my system.

I made an attempt to engage them in conversation, thinking I might redirect them from their disrespectful activities, but standing right there, looking them straight in their faces, I received no acknowledgment whatsoever. The lone woman was behaving like a tart, lap-dancing from one guy to the next. My gorge did rise then. I retreated wary to the downstairs bunkroom, where the two elder section hikers wore widened eyes. I shrugged and we waited. As darkness deepened around us, the mob banged upstairs to that bunkroom. Only then did we allow ourselves to drift off, our trekking poles close at hand.

By four o'clock the next morning I'd slept long enough to get an early start on the mob. I quietly gathered my things then slipped out of the bunkroom, using my red headlight to navigate the serpentine rooms and hallways. Crossing the common area toward the door, I high-stepped over guys passed out comatose on the floor, one dirty-blond guy sprawled on the couch with his mouth agape and his johnson exposed. In their state I could have done anything to them, any indecent prank that came to mind. Perhaps I did, who knows but me?

I took that long, flat run out of Pine Grove Furnace State Park in the dark. The magic hour rose around me, vanquishing for a time any thoughts of the barbarian horde. It was just woods again, chittering birds and croaking toads and soft morning mist, a far horizon from human chaos. Nearing noon, after sixteen miles and as the sun blazed full in a puffy sky, I stepped out of the woods into the cornfields, hiking the dusty tracks where tractors roamed. Soon I entered the town of Boiling Springs.

Boiling Springs is an enigma of trail towns. It's a pretty place but offers almost nothing to thru-hikers beyond a bit of limited resupply. On Hike 1 there'd been a woman in town named Mother Goose who had a disabled young son. She would secret thru-hikers into her home as if it were a way station along the Underground Railroad, relying on our donations to help ends meet. I inquired about her on Hike 2 and received a disdained reply. She was there no more, I was told with something between relief and satisfaction. There is no other lodging in Boiling Springs, no hiker-friendly pub, no reason but to kick heels and keep moving. There is an ATC office in the town. It has never been open on any of my hikes. I wonder to this day what that office is for, and how much money from membership dues is spent to maintain it.

I tore through there. The next eight miles were a flat run to U.S. Highway 11 and the town of Carlyle, which was my goal for the day. Interstate 76 comes a mile short of that when you're going northbound, virtually unnoticeable going southbound, so when I reached I-76 I got southbound-turned around, climbed over the rusty chain-link fence, hopped down the steep grassy embankment, and took off west on a busy interstate shoulder for the half-mile walk to Carlyle. I hadn't gone that far when I realized my error, so turned around in frustration, clumsily climbed that steep embankment while drivers gawked, scrambled back over the fence, then continued on the mile to the correct highway.

While I'd been making my turned-around detour, the mobile frat party had gone by. I could make them out well ahead, and with dread, so slowed my step until I was sure they'd crossed the bridge over U.S. Highway 11. Once confirmed, I dropped down onto the highway and walked the half mile to the Quality Inn, hoping the horde would push on far enough that I could never catch up to them. (And I never did, thank God.)

I stayed at the same Quality Inn on Hike 3. The place caters mostly to truckers so is deserted during the day, no problem getting a room. To accommodate their usual clientele, they put on a full breakfast in the morning. That feature alone made the place attractive to me. My phone number was still in their system from last time, which earned me a discounted rate, another bonus. I turned in for what I knew would be a restful night after a twenty-seven-mile day, the horde hurrying ahead.

The observant reader will notice how I was now staying in hotels or hostels almost every night, and might wonder why. A relief map of southeastern Pennsylvania reveals clues to the reason. The Blue Mountains of Pennsylvania appear as unique diagonal striations across that region, resembling a uniform mountain wall from a distance. Once atop these, we hike for miles over a mostly level surface, albeit on the infamous rocks, which I call *glacier gravel*. These are dry tops with few running springs, especially in the summer, cleaved here and there by water gaps where rivers cut through. There are shelters and groomed campsites along the way, well-spaced for short miles but for long miles they come mostly too early or too late, often leaving you with no option but to stealth camp without water on the jagged glacier gravel. Hotels, on the other hand, are spaced more or less evenly at the road crossings through that section, so after long, tedious miles on glacier gravel, and with the attendant throbbing or twisted ankles, you have to ask yourself: Do I want to pitch a dry camp on rocks or just hike on down to that hotel right over there? The decision is not difficult to make.

I spent the magic hour in farm fields the next morning, hiking between impenetrable walls of tall corn, the ears tufted with silk and almost ready for harvest. The air smelled of turned soil and Triple 10, familiar smells from home. A faint mist lingered on the footpath.

The climbs would begin soon, into even rockier terrain. I took these stoically, navigated the obligatory rock scrambles, then made the steep descent into Duncannon at twelve thirty after seventeen miles.

The Doyle is in Duncannon, a venerable old hotel that probably saw its best days before Roosevelt was elected the first time. Since then, the decades have eroded the edges and peeled the paint. You have to stand back and imagine the place as it once was, the ornate balustrades and crown moldings, the crystal fixtures and rich wainscoting. Having restored my century-old home, perhaps I viewed The Doyle with practiced eyes. The tired surroundings looked beautiful to me, the urge to roll up my sleeves and get to work difficult to suppress. Even though The Doyle has been a thru-hiker tradition for decades, the only time I ever stayed there was on Hike 3. The austere room I took was the height of luxury after the thirty-plus miles I did that day, but most important was the pub downstairs, the cold beer and generous portions. That's where I was heading now.

Vickey Kelly greeted me at the door with her wry and often dry humor. She couldn't possibly remember me but she carried on as if she did. I settled in for a couple of beers and a really large (and really good) burger. Covid had hurt them, Vickey said. Her husband Pat had been ill for a time. Their future was uncertain. I wondered with foreboding what would happen to the old place without Vickey and Pat there, and wished I was young enough to take the place on myself. Oh my, what a grand, grand place it could be again with some investment and enough energy to see it through. That wasn't in my destiny, though, as much as I wished I could divide myself into multiple versions and permanently reside at every special place I've visited during my travels. A single life is simply not long enough for all the great works there are out in the world.

Vickey and Pat did sell The Doyle later. It's undergoing restoration now so perhaps it will rise to opulence once again.

Rain began to spatter as I crossed the bridge over the Juniata River, growing in intensity as I made the climb out of the Duncannon hole. The rain trailed off and stopped before I made the top, but the rocks were now wet and slick. There were some rock scrambles up there, or rather, not rock scrambles but what I call *boulder ballet.* There are rock scrambles aplenty in states below, but it isn't until this part of Pennsylvania that we first encounter the obtruding mounds of boulders that we have to hop from one to another, which can be treacherous when the boulders are wet. One slip could mean a broken leg or worse. (And indeed, later on in New York a thru-hiker did slip while doing the boulder ballet in the rain. She broke her leg and thus ended her hike.)

I've never understood why the trail planners laid the trail out this way, not when there were numerous alternate routes and even sedate sections of the old A.T. that wound off forlorn and lost into the woods, a previous path that thru-hikers (including myself) once trod. As a day hiker I might enjoy a rocky excursion, especially when the comforts of home awaited in the evening, but as a thru-hiker I had to negotiate this and keep on going, my pace slowed to lip-biting tedium. Off and on, and with more frequency of late, I could identify the old A.T. as it branched away from the trail I was following, its former white blazes painted over in black or brown. I often felt the urge to follow the old trail. The problem was that there was no way to tell how far I could go before the woods finally overwhelmed the unmaintained old A.T., or where I would be if I lost the blazes. At that point I would be all but lost in the woods, with no means of determining where the new A.T. was save backtracking to the last white blaze.

And then of course there's this: We follow the white blazes. Regardless the historicity of a section of the old A.T., the white blazes show the way now. We'd follow those blazes down the middle of a busy interstate highway if that's where they led. Why would we do that, someone asked me once. Because it's the damn Appalachian Trail, that's why. No matter the changes of leadership and philosophy at the ATC, the white blazes are the trail so that's the way we go. I do wish though, with mournful memories of the past, that the old A.T. were at least blue-blazed so that those miles we all once trod would not be lost to time.

I pulled in at Clarks Ferry Shelter to water up before I pushed on. There were no water sources for eight more miles to Peters Mountain Shelter, my destination for the day, and the water source there was a desultory spring some three hundred rock steps down the mountain. I'd never gone down there and had no intention of going down there this time, so the water I took from the piped spring at Clarks Ferry Shelter would have to serve me into tomorrow.

I don't filter water that comes straight out of the ground, a practice that has caused varying degrees of consternation in others. Ultra Burn filtered all his water, even tap water, not trusting the purity of local utility districts. I do filter water that has flowed over the ground for any length—bears do caca in the woods, after all, which has already been discussed—but water coming directly out of the ground has already been filtered by stone and time. It's nature's gift to the surface, frosty cold even in the warmest climates, and with a clean, crisp taste no plastic bottle of water can emulate regardless the claimed source. In any event, I've never become ill from water on the Appalachian Trail.

Peters Mountain Shelter was a Hiker Hilton, built in the nineties near the aging Earl Shaffer Shelter. When I crawled into the Earl Shaffer Shelter on Hike 1 I wasn't aware that a luxurious Hiker Hilton was sited close by. There were four thru-hikers and one section hiker in Peters Mountain Shelter when I arrived at six forty-five, one spirited younger woman declaiming that there were not three hundred steps down to the spring, but three hundred and two. The spring was running fine, she informed me. I should go on down. I declined with a thin smile. My water bottles were full and I'd put in 28.6 miles that day. I didn't need any more climbs. Instead I went off to pitch my tent.

The twenty-four miles I made the next day were pro forma over a trail that did not change in character. There were rock scrambles, boulder ballets, and glacier gravel. From time to time I would sight the old A.T. twining off into obscurity and I would wave longingly as I went by.

Varmints had pestered my campsite all night so I was weary that day, short on sleep. When I descended into Swatara Gap in the later afternoon I decided that I'd gone far enough so hitched into Lickdale to get a room.

When I climbed out of Swatara Gap the next morning I felt fully refreshed. The trail was in better condition than last time. The section north of Swatara Gap had been overgrown with poison ivy on Hike 3, dangling vines of the evil stuff. I'd had no choice but to push through them as if I were machete-chopping in the deepest jungle. When I reached the gap not long afterward, I discovered that runoff from heavy rains the previous day was still cascading over the edges of various high points. I urgently stripped naked and stood under this overflow while drivers flying by on Interstate 81 looked over agape. I must have gotten all the poison ivy oil off because I didn't come down with any rashes later.

But the trail was clear this time so I made a good pace to 501 Shelter, where I stopped for a break. 501 Shelter is a cabin with a caretaker. I've slept in it three times. I was there with Crispy, Kyle, Motion, and The Dude on Hike 1; on Hike 2 with an amiable British guy whose visa was about to expire; and on Hike 3 with Mr. Hiker, a fellow sobo whom I'd been hiking with on and off since Gorham, New Hampshire. He got out ahead the next day, and stayed ahead all the way to Springer Mountain.

This time I wasn't staying, just taking a break. 501 Shelter shares a distinction with RPH Shelter in New York. Both are cabins and both are sited near roads where pizza delivery is available. Some hikers had already ordered their pizzas. I wasn't going to stay around long enough for that, but one of the hikers kindly gave me a slice, as well as some of his coke. We talked for a while and then I pushed on.

The area around 501 Shelter was tramped up with local trails and social trails. I lost the blazes at a confusing junction then spent half an hour retracing my steps. With this delay, and my late start from the hotel that morning (I couldn't get a hitch so had to walk two and a half miles back to the trail), that day was held to only seventeen miles. I camped in a pretty clearing between two forks of a stream, sharing the site with a father and daughter who were out hiking for a few days.

The father's name was TMI, his young daughter's name was Squid, and the two were delightful company. Squid was twelve, perhaps, and rattled through questions with a sense of wonder that only a child could conjure. TMI hoped to thru-hike the Appalachian Trail with his daughter someday, so peppered me with his own questions, never debating me, grateful for the information. Was his food bag hung properly, he asked. Which was the best water filter? Did he really need to worry about bears, and if he did encounter one, what should he do? As night came on he asked Squid to quieten down because there was a thru-hiker over there who would need his sleep. Squid complied without complaint, and I thought again how rewarding it must be to hike with your child, what a bonding experience, what a character builder.

The trail became even more punishing the next day. I left TMI and Squid sleeping in their tent at five forty-five and enjoyed a splendid magic hour, but then the boulder ballet began and continued on for much of the day. The trail profile through there showed a deceptively flat grade, an opportunity to make quick miles, but over the rocks I simply couldn't do it.

I gave a nod to Eagles Nest Shelter as I went by. I never stayed at Eagles Nest Shelter but I knew the place because I helped Elk get there on Hike 1. Elk was an older southbounder who was suffering from some kind of degenerative disease. When I first met him in New Jersey I thought he was addled, but it turned out that his mind was perfectly clear, he simply struggled to form words. He hiked hunched over and with a kind of sideways gait, off balance it appeared, but he'd made his miles from Mt. K without incident. The Pennsylvania rocks were his undoing.

I passed him that morning, which was warm and growing hot. "Hey Elk," I said going by, receiving a garbled return but I knew by then that he meant this as a friendly greeting. Less than twenty steps later I heard a grunt and a crash from behind. Elk had tripped on a rock and had gone down, face first.

I rushed to him, took him by the shoulders and lifted his head from the rocks. "Elk, are you okay?" I asked in alarm.

His slushy response was of a man furious for having fallen. He tried to lift himself, but with his heavy backpack and weakened knees he couldn't do it. I guided him into a sitting position and then I saw it—his forehead was flayed open from the outside of one eyebrow to the other, and down to his skull. I'd never seen a living skull. It was a creamy yellow color. I wasn't squeamish, so betrayed nothing. There was no blood. I thought that odd but was grateful because if Elk knew the extent of his injury he might go into shock.

"H-h-how i-i-is it?" he managed to stutter.

"Oh, it's fine," I said as reassuringly as I could. "Just a scratch. Here, let me wrap it up for you."

With my teeth I tore open the ziplock that contained the bandana that I always kept clean for just this reason. I tied it around his head then got him to his feet. "Why don't I walk with you for a while," I said then. "Just to make sure you're okay on these rocks."

He nodded his assent so we resumed the trail, taking it at Elk's sidling gait. This went on for a few miles. Because of Elk's degenerative disease I couldn't tell if he was going at what would be a normal pace for him, or if he was struggling, or whether he might be concussed. Those miles were slow and difficult. I kept up a light banter all the way, trying to keep him engaged and moving forward. I didn't think I could carry him if it came to that.

When we reached Eagles Nest Shelter I released a breath that I felt as if I'd been holding the entire time. I got Elk inside and lying down then went outside to figure out what to do. There were side trails nearby that led to roads, but hiking out for help would take time. Elk had to be feeling his wound by now. How long before he took out a mirror and saw what I had seen? How could he not go into shock at the sight? And what if he had a concussion? By the time I could return with help he might be dead.

This dilemma was resolved when a pair of day hikers came up. I explained the situation to them. One of them had a flip phone so we were able to call the paramedics, who were up there within the hour. There was a road not too far away, so their hike had not been a long one. Carrying a stretcher, they went in to tend to Elk, who did not want to be taken off the trail. Elk fought them. I felt bad but none of us could know if Elk were concussed, whether his next breath would be his last. I followed them all out, down a side trail to the road, where an ambulance was idling, a fire truck as well. One of the paramedics offered me a coke while Elk was being fitfully loaded into the ambulance. "He's lucky you were there," the paramedic told me. "Good thing you didn't tell him how bad it was. He might not have made it."

I don't know what happened to Elk. I still think about him from time to time.

I dropped down to Port Clinton at one thirty, early enough to push on for more miles but only after a tough climb out of the hole on the other side. I'd already made the decision to throw down at the Port Clinton Hotel anyway, where I stayed on Hikes 2 and 3. It was still early enough in the day that I could get the benefit. There was also a nice pub-style restaurant at the hotel, with fare similar to The Doyle. My stomach growled as I followed the blazes across the hot railroad tracks, the concrete apron beyond, and then into town. I wasn't just tired and starved, I was also aching in knees and ankles, so it was a blow to the belly when I discovered that the Port Clinton Hotel was closed.

When you build up an idea in your mind mile after rugged mile, disappointment steals your resolve. There were no other services in Port Clinton, no restaurants, no bars, no place to recover. I didn't have to stay. A burger and a beer would have revived me. I could then have made the climb out of that hole, possibly put on ten more miles that day, but as it was I was hot, starving, and too lightheaded to contemplate the coming climb. The town of Hamburg was a couple of miles up the road. I'd been there only once, on Hike

3, to buy some replacement gear from the Cabela's located there. Cabela's ran a free shuttle back and forth, although I'd already missed it for that day. So I stuck out my thumb and caught a lucky hitch.

I gorged on Southern comfort food at the Cracker Barrel, biscuits and gravy and chicken fried steak, fatty dishes I never ate at home so that I could keep my weight down and my arteries clear. But the Appalachian Trail allowed me to shrug off those concerns. If I drank a cup of bacon fat I would burn it off before it found its way into my arteries, another reason to love the Appalachian Trail.

Stuffed and sated in a day now going long, it was too easy to just stay and take a room, which I did. The friendly desk manager gave me a much-appreciated beer (the Cracker Barrel did not serve alcohol), and I learned something new. It turns out that guests will often leave beer in their mini-fridges, which the housekeepers will remove when the rooms are cleaned. These beers will then accumulate in the manager's office until someone can figure out what to do with them. Armed with this knowledge, I quizzed desk managers about this from then on, and successfully yogied free beers thereafter.

I hiked to Cabela's the next morning and bought some new insoles. The ones I'd been using since Three Eagles Outfitters were worn through and had been pounded flat, rubbing the beginnings of a blister on my right heel. The thought of getting a blister after all of my sage advice was anathema. The new insoles solved the problem, and I was able to continue on blister-free for the remainder of my journey. I was also able to take the Cabela's shuttle back to Port Clinton, although it left later than I'd hoped. I wasn't able to begin my climb out of the Port Clinton hole until ten thirty.

The initial climb went faster than I expected, leading into more drops and climbs and enough boulder ballet to impress the Bolshoi. I reached Eckville Shelter at three thirty, where I pulled in to water up. Eckville Shelter is another cabin with a caretaker, who was absent when I arrived. No other hikers were there. I've stayed in that shelter three times, and if there were a good group of hikers present I might have stayed for a fourth out of tradition if nothing else, but instead I pushed on another five miles into the lengthening day, found a stealth site somewhere past Dan's Pulpit, and pitched camp for the night.

It had been a satisfying if rigorous twenty-mile day, a fair night ahead, and Lehigh Gap after twenty miles tomorrow. I would be able to call John (The Mechanical Man) from Lehigh Gap, and on a day that had become serendipitously significant. I looked forward to seeing him again, and I knew he would be as excited to see me.

MONDAY, JULY 26, 2021

Lehigh Gap - 20.3 Miles

Slept well enough, up at 4:30 a.m. but wanted to sleep longer for a change. Broke camp and hiking by 5:45.

Today went fast except for the inevitable rock scrambles. Saw no thru-hikers until near the end. Called John to pull me out at Lehigh Gap. Did not want to make that rock climb on the other side in the heat, plus today I finally crossed my 2018 thru-hike, and it happened here! Three years ago today I was in Lehigh Gap with John!

Sadly, John didn't roll out the red carpet for me. His wife Linda didn't remember my name, and John[3] didn't care at all. More than disappointing.

I don't want to stay here, but I've shuttled off the trail and can't get back on my own. How can my history with John and his family mean so little to them? I romanticized them in my mind, I guess. I'm out of here tomorrow one way or the other, and I'm not coming back.

***Tuesday, July 27, 2021 – Wind Gap – 20.3 Miles

Slept okay, but not John. He had a meltdown overnight and blew up my phone with texts, then refused to drive me back to Lehigh Gap. Linda felt bad so gave me a ride to Palmerton, where a kind woman named Tara drove me to the trailhead.

Started climbing at around 9:00 a.m., not as bad going up as coming down. Push, push, push over a scalloped, relocated trail and piles of rocks. Saw a lot of hikers, including a girl I'd seen at Cabela's. She was slackpacking southbound to avoid the big climb. Geez.

Reached Smith Gap hoping John would be waiting contrite and with cold beers, but no, so I pushed to Wind Gap, arriving footsore at 5:00 p.m. I took a room at the nastiest fleabag I've ever encountered anywhere in the world, bugs everywhere and not even a TV. Still, I'm showered now, ordered Chinese delivery, and I'll be out of Pennsylvania tomorrow. Thank God!

On Hike 1, after 23.7 desiccating miles over radiating rocks and under a sadistic sun, out of water, the poison ivy I'd picked up in Culvers Gap, New Jersey now breaking out all over my body, I stumbled out of the woods and onto Smith Gap Road in Pennsylvania. The spring behind me had been dry and there was no water ahead for at least twelve miles, most of those miles through the infamous Palmerton Superfund Site, where not a tree survived to provide shade. I'd wondered how that day would go when I left out of Delaware Water

Gap during the magic hour. Now, with that magic hour a far memory of much earlier times, I had my answer: I couldn't go on. I wouldn't make it.

My Wingfoot *Thru-Hiker's Handbook* glowingly described a pair of trail angels who lived in a domed house a mile down the road, The Mechanical Man and Crayon Lady. According to Wingfoot they had a water faucet, an outdoor shower, and would allow thru-hikers to camp in their yard. There was really no decision to make, I turned right and began the road walk, scratching at my poison ivy and about as miserable as I could be.

When I reached the house, barely coherent, I met John The Mechanical Man, who was enthusiastic and friendly, about my height and age, and wore a toothy white smile. He ushered me inside at once, directed me to their bathroom shower, and had me drop my gear in a spare bedroom across the hall. His wife Linda, the Crayon Lady, got home a little later with their son, who was perhaps two or so. The boy's name was John III. He was a cute kid. I thought of him almost immediately as John *Cubed*, or more like this, *John*^{3}.

After a shower and a change of clothes (long sleeves and pant legs to hide my poison ivy outbreak), they invited me to dinner at their table. Even though I was a stranger to those people, and of uncertain mental acuity after my dehydrating hike that day, I was treated warmly. I felt relaxed, comfortable. John told me story after story of the Appalachian Trail, of Earl Shaffer and Ed Garvey and many others. The man was surely destined to become a trail legend himself one day, the way Keith Shaw was up in Maine. I felt honored to have made his acquaintance.

After the dinner dishes were cleared, John invited me to go to a circus with them that evening. In truth, what I really wanted to do was go lie down. I was exhausted, used up for the day, lethargic after that big meal. At the same time, I had—incongruously—never been to a circus in my life. Not only did I not want to decline and possibly give offense after their generosity, but the more I thought about it I really did want to see a circus. This had to be one of those gifts the Appalachian Trail gives, to be exposed to and experience new things. I *couldn't* decline, even though I could barely keep my eyes open.

This was the Clyde Beatty-Cole Bros. Circus, not quite Ringling Brothers but what difference could that make to me? I had a great time. We posed for a photo out front of the big tent before we went in, Linda, myself, and John^3, with the elder John behind the camera. John even ungrudgingly paid for my ticket when I realized I had no cash left at all.

I slept deeply and well that night, and when I hiked on the next morning I felt as if I'd made new friends.

I knew the way on Hike 2 so didn't pause when I stepped onto the road, just turned right and kept on going. Even after seven years, John and Linda welcomed me as an old friend. I ate at their table, dropped my gear in their spare bedroom, and later that afternoon, was invited to join them at their son's BMX race. John^3 was now tenish and handled his bicycle with the agility of a rodeo wrangler. We ate hot dogs and drank beers as John^3 dominated the race track. I could see the pride in the elder John's eyes, and felt some of that pride myself.

Things were a little different on Hike 3 ten years later. John was bald now, heavy in the middle, his smile not quite as forthcoming. He had set up a hostel in his garage, where he directed me to drop my gear. There were three other thru-hikers there, nobos whom I thought would probably not make it although I never revealed that, just encouraged them on and hoped they would find the inner strength to see it through.

John drove us all to a restaurant in Kunkletown, where we were offered free beers with our food orders, this because the place didn't have a liquor license. We took advantage, of course, although we also ate a lot of food so perhaps it all evened out. Back at John and Linda's Blue Mountain Dome, I kept expecting John to invite me upstairs for the night, but he didn't. That stung, I have to say, but it *had* been ten years since I'd last seen them, a galactic eternity in trail time. And John had put in the effort to convert his garage into a hostel, had probably gotten used to that as the default option, so I stowed my feelings and went with it, spent a comfortable night, then hiked out the next morning.

There was this, though, what had become a tradition to John and me: John ^{3} was now a fine looking young man who had turned his interests toward music. He played guitar in a rock band and had a gig in Allentown the next night. It would be a shame to miss that after our long history together, so I arranged for John to pick me up in Lehigh Gap. This would hold me to a short twelve-mile day but I thought it would be worth it to keep the tradition alive, to see John^3 at this point in his life.

I made those miles in quick time despite the disappointingly relocated trail. I'd come to enjoy hiking through that otherworldly Palmerton Superfund Site—where a century of zinc smelting had denuded the mountain and all but turned the soil into regolith—to witness its recovery between each hike, but the trail had been rerouted off the ridge, tediously scalloping along the flanks where there was no view of the progress above. To have followed the old A.T. would have led to the conundrums I have already described. That recovering mountaintop, therefore, has gone unobserved by thru-hikers ever since.

John was there waiting for me in the hot early afternoon. He drove me to his house for a shower, then to Kunkletown for food and beers. The other hikers had pulled out, so I was alone in the garage, still expecting John to invite me upstairs, which never happened. Something had changed and I didn't know what it was. Linda wasn't around, and John's behavior was often sullen. Rumors were circulating up and down the trail of a man in Pennsylvania who was scaring thru-hikers with fits of temper and acts that seemed out of character for John. I didn't pry. His personal life was not my business unless he made it so. He kept whatever was eating at him to himself, while I hoped he could work out whatever was going on. To the thru-hikers who voiced their concerns to me I said only that I'd known John for years, that I trusted him, that any errant actions of his had probably been misunderstood, and that he seemed to be going through something that he would work out by and by. In the meantime, thru-hikers had nothing to fear from The Mechanical Man.

A storm boiled up as we drove to Allentown that night, sheeting rain and lightning that battered against the widows of the venue as we watched John[3] perform. Linda sat across the way, as if she were in separate company. We all congratulated John[3] at the end of the performance. His little band was talented and I told him so. Who knew how far he'd be able to take this, where he might be in his life when I made my next thru-hike.

John drove me back to Lehigh Gap the following morning, fidgeting for a way to ask money from me for the ride. I'd pulled out some bills anyway, as we do in the South. The expectation among friends is that the offer will be politely declined, but I wasn't in the South and John accepted the money.

Now on Hike 4 I was coming from the other direction. It was mid-afternoon in Lehigh Gap and I had twelve miles of that tedious, scalloped trail between me and Smith Gap, not to mention a long rock climb over exposed, blistering rocks. The Jailhouse Hostel in Palmerton had been closed (due to the behavior of a mobile frat party depending upon whom you ask), so my intention had been to throw down at George W. Outerbridge Shelter just short Lehigh Gap and then hike into Smith Gap tomorrow. At my stealth camp the previous night, though, I discovered from reading my diary that I would be hiking into Lehigh Gap on the exact same day that I had hiked out of it last time!

I don't know how to calculate the odds, that over a length of two thousand miles I would cross my previous thru-hike in the exact same place on the exact same day. A northbound hike is so different from a southbound hike that I had no reason to expect that this would happen at all. It felt like serendipity to me, and something the Appalachian Trail has taught me is that when serendipity happens, pay attention.

So I hiked on into Lehigh Gap and called John, who seemed less excited to hear my voice than I his. I waited in the hot sun. After an hour I called again. He'd forgotten, he said. He would be along shortly.

When he did arrive he expressed none of the excitement I expected. He was perfunctory, harried, as if I had inconvenienced him. The restaurant in Kunkletown was out of business (did anyone see that coming?), so I settled for a six-pack and a submarine sandwich, and then John drove me to his house and deposited me in his garage. The significance of the day left him unimpressed.

John^{3} had switched from guitar to drums and was now playing in a new band. Their performance that night had been cancelled at the last minute, so for the first time I would not see the young man in action. I showered upstairs, across the hallway from John^{3}'s room. When I came out, his door was open to a dusky interior. He was pulling on a T-shirt. I couldn't make him out well, backlit as he was.

"Is that you, John^{3}?" I asked.

"Yeah."

"Hey man, it's Solo."

"Who?"

"It's Solo, man. Don't you remember me?"

"I don't remember the hikers," he answered flatly, and then he stepped forward and closed the door in my face.

I was heartbroken. It wasn't that John^{3} didn't remember me. He was a young man with a lot on his mind, from girlfriends to gigs and everything else that a young man must ponder. What broke my heart was that there was no family lore, no stories of the thru-hiker who appeared every few years and had watched a kid grow into a man, as if the circus, the BMX race, the gig he'd played three years ago to the day—as if none of it were worth remembering.

I despondently went up the stairs to say hello to Linda, whom I could hear rattling around in the kitchen. Mouth-watering smells came down, of marinara and basil and oregano. Despite my submarine sandwich earlier, my stomach growled. Linda would invite me up to dinner, I knew she would. That was the kind of person she was and I had a long history with her family, after all.

I stopped at a gate at the top of the stairs, originally meant to keep their dogs in but which had evolved into a border between the private rooms above and the common rooms below. I didn't want to move it without permission, so peeked over the landing. I couldn't see the kitchen from there so I announced my presence. "Hey Linda."

She walked over and looked down, where I stood a few steps below the landing. "Hello?" she said.

"Hey Linda, it's Solo."

"Who?"

I winced. "It's Solo. I've been here three times before. We went to the circus and to the BMX races, and to John^3's gig in Allentown."

"Oh, yeah, Solo."

"So how have you been?" I brightened.

"We're doing okay. But look, I've got pots on the stove, so..." She trailed off, revealing just enough annoyance to ensure that the message was understood.

I felt dismissed, as if I were just another ratty thru-hiker, worthy of decorum up to a point but nothing beyond that. I'd dipped food from those very pots. I'd sat at her table, now gated off, and I'd slept in the room John^3 now occupied. How could all of that not have drawn a sincere expression of surprise and pleasure? I took this hard in the gut.

"I'm sorry I bothered you," I said, downcast.

"No problem. Maybe we'll see you later."

With that she returned to the kitchen and I went down to sit alone in the garage.

Later, I was on the porch out back sipping a beer when John came out. My mood was descending into depression faster than the night falling on the woods beyond the house.

"Hey John."

"Hey man." He sat and said nothing.

Don't pry, I advised myself, but something was very wrong. The rumors up and down the trail were worse this time than last. John had been removed from the AWOL guide. Guthook was exploding with negative comments. There were stories that John had poured out the water that had been left at the trailhead by trail angels, that he had actually done this in front of desperate thru-hikers who couldn't close the distance to that water in time. Hikers were being warned about him as far south as North Carolina. None of it made sense, not from the John I knew, or thought I knew.

"So John," I ventured carefully. "What's been going on?"

He rounded on me. "You read Guthook, didn't you?"

"I don't have Guthook, John."

"Well, you read something."

"I haven't read anything, but I've heard things. I tell people it can't be true but you know how it is on the trail."

"Fuck the trail!" he exploded. "Fuck the ATC and fuck AWOL and fuck Guthook!"

I reeled as if a tornado had just plunged out of the sky.

"Holy shit, John!"

"It's all bullshit," he flared, his color rising and leaving me looking for something defensive to hold in my hand. "I didn't pour out that dammed water. A guy's been leaving those jugs by the trailhead, and he never cleans up the empties. They were all over the place. Litter, that's all they were. Just litter. I was only cleaning them up. I said something to the Forest Service and they told him to stop but he keeps doing it. I never poured any water out. I left the full bottles."

This was not an unreasonable defense. John had always been testy about trail magic, not the idea of it but because people often didn't return later to clean up the trash. I appreciate trail magic as much as the next thru-hiker but I don't want it at the expense of trash by the trailhead. I agreed with John on that one.

"I figured it was something like that," I said, hoping to reassure him. "I told people."

"I don't give a shit about thru-hikers anymore," he growled.

"I don't believe that, John."

"Well, why should I? I mean, I've had Earl Shaffer here, and Ed Garvey. Nimblewill Nomad was here just last week. I found that spring, and that wasn't easy. It's a good spring but nobody will use it. I don't get credit for shit."

I knew about John's spring and I knew he was proud of it, but it was six tenths of a mile down the mountain. No one was ever going to hike all the way down then climb all the way back, not when they could push on a few more miles to Leroy A. Smith Shelter and get water there—or at John's house, for that matter. I didn't tell him any of that, though.

"You know, John," I said instead. "I'm going to stop in at your spring when I hike through tomorrow. It's about time that I got to see it."

I thought this would calm him but it didn't.

"So fuck 'em," he said. "If they want water they can go down to my spring."

He got up then and harried off, leaving me in the twilight with a warm beer and a queasy stomach.

I felt as welcome as I would be in Pyongyang, and as foreign, too. I wanted to flee, to grab my gear and go, but that wasn't practical. I'd unwittingly allowed myself to be shuttled twelve trail miles north of Lehigh Gap, on a serpentine road with little traffic. Always forward, never backward, and there was no way I would get a hitch. I was stuck. I had to see this through.

John came out with Linda about an hour later. Linda didn't talk much but I tried to engage her if only to deflect John's rancor. I described my hike, how much different it was going northbound than southbound. I described the old-school rules I was using this time. When I mentioned avoiding paid shuttles, Linda looked up with a start. She said nothing, though. John seemed to seethe.

"You know," he said, teeth clenched, "I've had Earl Shaffer here, and Ed Garvey, and Nimblewill–"

"And you've had Solo," I reminded him with a bit of my own pique. He made no comment to that. "So look," I stood, "I'm going to turn in now. When can you get me back to the trail in the morning?"

"I don't get up before eight," he said hotly.

"That's fine. I'll see you then. Goodnight, you all."

I left them on the porch, guiltily glad to get away. Whatever was going on was beyond my ability to influence. The plan had been for John to return me to Lehigh Gap the next morning, where I would then hike the twelve miles back to his place. That wasn't going to happen, though. Once I got away I wasn't coming back.

I slept poorly, was up early as usual, then spent a few hours on the porch waiting for John to get out of bed. My phone had blown up with texts from John overnight, text after text after text descending into profanity and madness. The impression I had was that John had stayed up all night prowling Facebook and Guthook, internalizing each negative comment like another blade in his kidney. Don't read the negative comments, I'd told him the previous evening. I'm a writer, I reminded him. If I worried about every negative review, I'd never write again. But his pride had been too sorely assailed. He thought of himself as a trail legend deserving respect. He should be worshipped the way Earl Shaffer was, not debased. Fuck them all.

John didn't come out at eight o'clock. He didn't come out at eight thirty. Eventually, Linda came sheepishly out.

"He's still in bed," she hesitantly told me. "He says he won't take you. You can go up the hill and hike out."

"*What?*" I was on my feet now, my mind reeling. Always forward, never backward. I'd never get a hitch out of that place. I wasn't even sure which roads to take back to Lehigh Gap. *Why?*" I added as if it mattered.

"You said you wouldn't pay for shuttles," she said. "That got him upset."

"I said I *avoided* paid shuttles," I quickly countered, "not that I wouldn't pay him if that's what he wants."

"Well," she shrugged, "it's too late now. He's not getting up."

If John felt disrespected, now I felt that way too. "I'm *Solo*, Linda," I hurled at her. "I'm freakin' *Solo!* I am *not* some common thru-hiker you can leave stranded. *Do you hear me?*"

Linda blanched at my outburst. "Okay, look," she said, her eyes on her hands. "I can drive you to Palmerton but no farther than that."

"Okay, then." I grabbed my backpack and poles. "Let's go."

Minutes later we were in Palmerton, not a long drive but with several left and right turns. I wouldn't have been able to hitch it, too complicated. Linda dropped me at a convenience store. There was a look in her eyes, something of regret. I passed her some money, which she accepted.

"Thanks," I said brusquely, then I took off without a look back.

I scored an easy hitch into Lehigh Gap, and within half an hour I was making the rock climb and feeling as if the previous events belonged to someone else. John's texts were on my phone, though, a sorry reminder that all of it did happen. I negotiated the new A.T., passed the side trail to John's spring with no thought of going down, then stepped out onto Smith Gap Road, looking to the left this time. I'd held out a last hope that John might redeem himself by being there waiting with some cold beers in hand. He wasn't, so I crossed the road and kept on.

I made Wind Gap by five o'clock, twenty miles under my feet, and threw down at a motel that was nastier than the nastiest shelter I have ever slept in, including Cow Camp Shelter, and that says a lot. I was too hungry to care, more disgusted by John's behavior than by the bugs crawling on the walls.

I left early the next morning and pulled 27.6 miles, not nearly enough distance from Smith Gap but at least I was in New Jersey now.

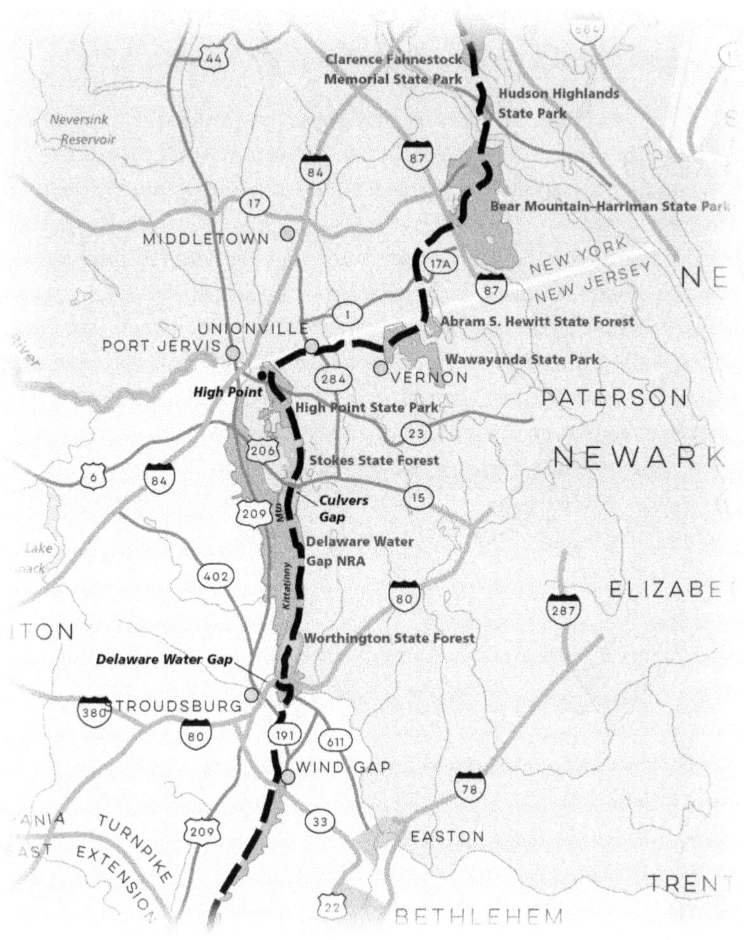

NEW JERSEY

72.3 MILES

WEDNESDAY, JULY 28, 2021

Mohican Outdoor Center - 21.6 Miles

That motel was about as nasty as they come, but at least it had hot water. Slept poorly, a drug deal going on in one adjacent room, prostitution in the other, and then a storm overnight that sounded as if it would lift the roof off the decrepit place.

Got out of there at 5:30 a.m. Made quick time through PA, met a ridgerunner named Smat who thru-hiked in 2003 and also stayed with John. We shared stories for a while, then I pushed on and reached Delaware Water Gap by noon, 16 miles. Walked into the first restaurant I saw and had food and beer, then to a C-store for some resupply, then back to the trail at 2:00 p.m.

I only meant to go 20 miles, but I blew past the campground without realizing it so pushed on to Mohican Outdoor Center, where a cool 2020 thru-hiker named Jello gave me a beer. The dorms were closed due to Covid, so tented out after a shower. I'm very tired, but I feel okay.

THURSDAY, JULY 29, 202

Gren Anderson Shelter - 19.5 Miles

Up early, broke camp in the dark, had another shower (why not?), then got moving by 6:00 a.m.

Took it slow at first, just going along. Met my first traditional sobo, Magic Mike, who left Mt. K on June 3. I gave him the wristband for free laundry at Angels Rest, as I promised Hot Tamale I would all those years ago, then we talked for a while.

Passed several nobos today without trying. Picked up the pace once the sky began to cloud up. Made 14 miles by noon, and Gyp's in Culvers Gap by 1:00 p.m.

Had food and beers, still not raining by 2:30 p.m., so took off for this shelter. Didn't quite make it in time. Got soaked, and of course the shelter was full. Set up the tent in the pouring rain, got in, dried out, everything fine except the tent has started leaking! It's going to be a long, wet night.

FRIDAY, JULY 30, 2021

Unionville, New York - 20.1 Miles

Ridgerunner – Skirt
Sobos – Thumper (m), Locomotive (f)
Secret Shelter owner - Jim

The trail goes in and out of New York through here.

Wet, but slept surprisingly well, down by 6:00 p.m., up at 4:00 a.m., packed the soggy mess up and was hiking by 6:00.

Started out slow just because. Enjoyed the cool, breezy morning, no bugs, and rays slanting through the trees. Arrived High Point State Park Headquarters at 11:00 a.m., spread everything out to dry in the sun, and had cokes and snacks while I waited. Many nobos arrived. My stuff dried quickly, so by a little after noon I was off again.

Met a pair of sobos, then a ridgerunner named Skirt who hiked with me for a couple of miles and led me to the Secret Shelter, which was nothing as I remembered it from Hike 1, or think I remembered it. Need to check my 2001 diary when I get home. Met the owner, Jim, who thru-hiked in 1989, and the spoiled donkey that had been abandoned on the property.

Now I'm in Unionville, New York. Had a beer, pizza slices, and met a nobo named Dips. She's a writer, too. I'm jealous of her ultralite keyboard, and must find one for myself. I set my tent up in the park, and now I'm drinking wine in the notorious tavern from Hike 2. Unionville has really changed. Sad to learn that The Mayor has died.

SATURDAY, JULY 31, 2021

Warwick Drive-in Theater - 17.3 Miles

Slept really well, and it was quite cool in the morning. Up at 5:00 a.m., at Horler's Store at 6:00 for some resupply, coffee, and two egg sandwiches.

Started out fast and stayed fast. This was the day of the long boardwalk, but also the Stairway to Heaven. Met a trail angel, Time Out, who thru-hiked in 2018, which means we crossed paths at some point. He gave me a cold coke and his phone number. Met nobos Rocky and Switz, and had pizza with them later.

Met trail angel Miss Janet, who drove us to Warwick Drive-in, where I am now camped in a true nobo tent city. I made reservations at Tuxedo Motel for tomorrow, just have to figure out how to get back to the trail in the morning.

Just met a nobo named Care Bear! Like the character in my novel, *Timewall Speaks*. He was unexcited to be immortalized in print.

—

Good God, that motel in Wind Gap, Pennsylvania was awful. The business end of a busy privy would have been more sanitary. The walls were too thin to apply any appropriate analogy, crawling with millipedes or centipedes or some similar many-legged bug. I curled deeply inside my sleeping bag with it tucked over my head against the bugs, and would have gone outside to sleep on the ground if a storm hadn't unexpectedly blown up. A romp of commercial amorousness was going on beyond one window-film of a wall, pounding and grunting and moaning, but that didn't last too long, nothing to brag about there. Through the other paper-shell pecan of a wall, a drug deal went ongoing, no part of the transaction that I couldn't follow in detail. Sleep is not what I did but at least the shower worked and the water was hot.

I got out first thing, hurriedly leaving miles of Pennsylvania behind me under a mottled sky and in weather that was cooler than it had been. I had to pause at Kirkridge Shelter to remember Tollbooth Willy and his girlfriend that time. I wondered if the two were still together after all of these years. There was a city water faucet above the shelter, but in that cool morning I didn't need water. I kept on going.

Heading down into Delaware Water Gap, I met a fortyish ridgerunner named Smat who was going the other way. We stopped briefly to chat then found ourselves dropping packs and sitting on logs to discuss weightier matters.

Smat was a 2003 thru-hiker who'd weathered the eighteen years since then very well. He was fit and looked much younger than his age (I had guessed late twenties or early thirties at most). The same has been said of me off and on, probably through flattery but perchance in sincerity. It's difficult for us to truly see ourselves, so if I do appear younger than the years I've lived then the Appalachian Trail is why.

Nevertheless, Smat had parlayed his 2003 journey into a sustained outdoor lifestyle that had done him no harm. We discussed the differences in the trail of our earlier experiences and the trail as it was now, in both geography and culture. As a ridgerunner he had grounds for comparison. We both agreed that the Appalachian Trail of the early 2000s was a more rewarding experience than today, immersed in an authenticity that had become as rare as the ivory-billed woodpecker.

"When we were thru-hiking back then," I said, "we had no idea that we were closing out an era."

"How do you mean?"

"I mean phones."

He nodded solemnly. "Yeah, you're right. I hadn't thought about it that way. Phones *have* changed the trail, I mean completely changed it."

"We're not as free now because of them." I went on. "Back then we never knew what was coming. Everything was spontaneous. We were *alive*, man. Sure, there were days when I would have given anything to be able to call someone to come get me, but I couldn't so I had to deal with it. And the hostels were all famous places run by people who loved the trail. Even some of the motels. And they were cheap, remember?" He nodded at that with a pained chuckle. "Today a lot of that is gone, and too many of the new hostels are all about money, even the ones run by thru-hikers. Thirty dollars for a bunk, forty dollars for a shuttle, reservations paid in advance..."

"Yeah, I hear ya. Even The Mechanical Man's all about money these days."

I yanked to attention. "You know John?"

"Yeah," he said, trailing off into disquiet. "I stayed with him on my hike and I've seen him a few times since. He's not the same. It's pretty bad."

"What the hell happened?"

Smat told me what he knew, which descended into gossip. How much of it was true and how much of it the invention of thru-hikers, I couldn't judge. What was clear, though, was that Smat had once been as fond of John as I had been, and deeply regretted the way things were now.

I described my thru-hikes, my history with John and his family. "Still," I said, "I just don't have patience for adults who can't get their shit together. I have plenty of my own problems. You have to deal with that stuff, not take it out on everyone else."

"Yeah," he sighed.

"You know, John could end all of this today if he'd just go stand by the trailhead with a cooler of beers and greet every thru-hiker that came through. People would love him. They'd write good comments on Guthook, and in no time all the bad comments would be too far down the list to matter."

"Man, you are absolutely right! That's all he has to do. Easy."

I pondered our discussion as I continued on to Delaware Water Gap, and made up my mind to reach out to John one last time. I sent him a text of Smat's and my solution to his problem, how easy it would be to do, and how quickly it would rehabilitate his reputation.

John texted back: *Fuck 'em.*

Afterward I deleted his number and mentally closed out our history.

Delaware Water Gap is a nice, hilly town that seems to belong to neither Pennsylvania nor New Jersey, as if it were an independent duchy with its own rules and norms. I had a run-in there with a redneck at an outdoor shop on Hike 2, when I'd been about to drop more than a hundred dollars on a pair of shoes but was treated so shabbily that I walked out. Otherwise the people have been pleasant and I've never had another issue. There are bakeries, eateries, and places to enjoy a beer. There's a hostel, Church of the Mountain, where I stayed two days on Hike 1 as my New Jersey poison ivy began popping out all over.

I was in Delaware Water Gap by noon after sixteen miles. The trail goes through town, the blazes on telephone poles and trees. I dove into the first restaurant I saw, ate until I was sated, drank until I was tipsy, went for resupply at a convenience store, and then pushed on at about two o'clock. Crossing the I-80 bridge over the Delaware River, I paused to take a photo of the line painted on the pedestrian walk about halfway across the bridge. I savored the moment, took my next step, and I was in New Jersey. I'd crushed Pennsylvania, I was out of the worst of the rocks for a while, and now it was time to make miles that didn't leave cuts and bruises.

I had decided to throw down at a campsite about four miles on but the signage was so poor going through those woods that I unwittingly blazed on past. I didn't realize my error until about a mile later at Sunfish Pond. By then I decided to just go on another six miles to Mohican Outdoor Center, where I stayed on Hikes 2 and 3. It was getting late in the day. Because I would probably arrive after closing time, I called ahead and reached the hut master, a 2020 thru-hiker named Jello.

I was in awe, and held Jello on the phone for a while. The 2020 thru-hikers are the heroes, I told him. Those guys had hiked an Appalachian Trail that had been all but abandoned due to Covid. Most hostels were closed, there were limited services, and the Appalachian Trail Conservancy refused to recognize their hikes. It was, indeed, the closest anyone would come to thru-hiking the A.T. as it had been in the old days. I envied Jello, regretted not being able to get out in 2020 myself. My effusion embarrassed him. "We were just thru-hikers," he said; then added, "It was tough, though."

At any rate, there would be plenty of campsites available when I got there. The dorms were closed due to Covid but the showers were available. Since I'd be getting in late he would leave a registration form in the common room for me. I could settle up in the morning. That was great. I thanked him and then jokingly asked him if he would leave a beer out for me. To my delighted astonishment he said he would.

I reached the place as night fell, found my registration paperwork and a map to where Jello had secreted a beer for me. I sipped that beer thinking that it was probably the best beer I'd ever had, then went out into the dark to pitch my tent.

I flew through the next day, so relieved to be out of Pennsylvania that I seemed to float over the trail. I took a section in the magic hour that I'd night-hiked last time. The promontories and woods were dreamy in the soft light, with none of the sinister intent they'd had that night on my last thru-hike when the bear had come crashing out of the woods behind me, approaching close enough for me to tag it on the nose with my trekking pole.

That bear would not break off, no matter how loud I yelled or how many rocks I threw. It trailed after me, would go up into the woods and parallel me, its eyes shining malevolently in my headlight. This went on and on. I would take three steps, turn and look back, take three more steps and do the same. When the trail turned onto a ridge, a rock face to my right and a drop-off to my left, the bear came out as if it had me trapped. I shouted, threw rocks, backing around the ridge and into the woods, where I slipped on a wet, bowling ball-sized rock and went down. Knowing bear behavior, I assumed that was the end of me. I scrambled to my feet. The bear was so close I could smell it, that sour reek of wet dog. I was grasping my poles down their shafts as if they were long knives, prepared for desperate hand-to-hand combat. The funnel of my headlight revealed only darkness with a bear in the middle of it. This is where it ends, I thought. Unless I made a lucky plunge with a trekking pole into one of the bear's eyes, it was over. I doubted my poles would pierce its hide deeply enough to stop it.

That bowling ball of a rock was at my feet, I was stumbling around it trying find a strong stance for myself. The bear was even closer now, much too close. Somehow, instinctively, it occurred to me to lift that rock. I bent and wrapped my arms around it, could barely get it off the ground. With an enormous grunt I lobbed it at the bear.

That heavy rock thudded with an impact I could feel through my feet. It came nowhere near striking the bear but the sheer mass of it got its attention. The bear spun and bolted the other way, and with muscles aching in my arms I continued on to Mohican Outdoor Center, looking over my shoulder every few steps. My hands were shaking when I got there, all of that adrenaline. I downed a little bottle of tequila in one gulp, went inside and locked the door. That was not a night I intended to camp outside.

I walked out onto that same ridge this time, could identify exactly where I'd lifted the rock and made my stand. The view was nice in the daylight, a carpet of trees with a few buildings in the distance. I had no fear of the bear now, not in the light of day.

After some moments of reflection I pushed on into the section that Tri-Pad and I had hiked together on Hike 3. Tri-Pad was a limber young nobo with a fondness for tequila who was doing that section in reverse. At some point he would meet his nobo buddies going northbound, toss them the keys to his van as they went by, and they would then drive back to pick him up. It seemed a convoluted way to hike the trail but I wouldn't have met Tri-Pad otherwise. He was wicked fast, sidestepping obstacles as if they weren't present.

I went twenty-six miles with him that day, leaving him at his van at sunset and continuing on toward my bear misadventure. During those miles I observed him, the fluid way he moved, the way he held his poles up and out for balance rather than poking the ground at each step. I began to emulate his style, picking up speed as a consequence. That's the way I hike now, poles up, scanning ahead, contemplating each step in advance.

Continuing on after those memories, I met my first traditional southbounder, an affable guy named Magic Mike who'd left Mt. K on June 3 and who'd earned his name by carrying trail magic into the shelters, sharing with all. I'd wondered how I would feel when I met my first sobo. Corn Nut, whom I'd met in Tennessee, was a winter sobo, not of the traditional crowd. Magic Mike would know the same state of Maine I knew, the same White Mountains in New Hampshire. That was what we had in common and what I would have in common with every sobo I met from then on. I also knew what it was like for a sobo to crash into the northbounder bubble, the crowding, the flippant and insular attitudes. Now I was a part of that and quickly appended that I'd done three southbound thru-hikes. Guilty, that's how I felt.

Magic Mike was in awe of my multiple thru-hikes, not discomfited in the least that I was going northbound this time. He asked about trail conditions ahead and if what he'd heard about The Mechanical Man was true.

"Yeah, it is," I informed him with a sigh.

"Too bad," he said.

Way back in Virginia in a previous life, Hot Tamale at Angels Rest had given me a wristband that would earn the wearer free laundry. She'd made me promise to give it to the first southbounder I met, so that was of course Magic Mike. He accepted the gift with a bit of uncertainty. From his perspective, Virginia was so far in the future that he could barely contemplate it, nevertheless he slipped the wristband on with gratitude and promised to make use of it. I also informed him that Greasy Creek Friendly in North Carolina would be open when he got there. Those duties discharged, I continued on.

I made fourteen miles by noon, and then Culvers Gap at one o'clock. I went into Gyp's Tavern for the fourth time and under a sky that was threatening to unload at any moment. I congratulated myself. It could rain now all it wanted, I was inside with food and beer and could wait it out.

An hour and a half later, full of food and feeling impatient with the weather, I stepped out under the still-threatening sky and put on my quickest pace for Gren Anderson Shelter just three miles on. Maybe I could make it. Maybe I would have made it if I hadn't stayed so long at Gyp's. The sky broke in a torrent just as I reached the side trail to the shelter. By the time I made it to the shelter proper I was sloshing wet.

The shelter was jammed full of bedraggled thru-hikers who looked out at me with the hollow eyes of refugees. I couldn't cram myself in, they'd already done that. Those were thru-hikers who would be spooning that night, I knew from experience. So I went on past the shelter, found a flat spot of mud, reached under the garbage bag that covered my backpack, and pitched my tent as the rain roared in my ears. While I had been rained on aplenty, that was the first time I'd had to pitch my tent in a driving downpour—and it went not badly. The selection of that Gossamer Gear backpack way back in Damascus had proved prescient. I got the tent up and everything inside, remarkably dry except for the clothes I was wearing. After changing into dry things I even felt cozy.

My tent began to seep around the bottom seams, though, which formed a puddle. I had pitched on a slight incline so all of this water pooled along that edge of the tent. Rain crashed against the fabric outside, not a drumbeat but a concussion. I made a mental note to pick up some seam sealer at my next resupply, then shinnied into my sleeping bag for what would become an unexpectedly restful night, nineteen and a half miles farther into New Jersey.

The storm broke overnight, revealing a cool, misty morning. I woke up damp throughout but not in the least miserable. We human beings can endure much more than we realize. I scooped all of my wet things into my nifty backpack then took the trail at six o'clock. By the time I reached High Point State Park Headquarters at eleven o'clock, the sun was shining brightly, all hints of last night's storm re-gathering into the cotton clouds above.

I spread out my gear on the broad lawn to dry then went inside for snacks and cokes. Once upon a time the High Point State Park people would give a free coke to any thru-hiker who came in. That tradition had sadly ended but I didn't complain. I paid for a coke and sipped it with gratitude. I felt just wonderful and wished I knew why. If I could can that I could keep it and apply it as needed.

Thru-hikers began to arrive en masse, many of those who had been sardined into Gren Anderson Shelter. I gathered my things, which were now dry as new, and pushed on. A mile later I met a ridgerunner named Skirt, a young man of engaging conversation. Skirt led me to the Secret Shelter, where I'd stayed on Hike 1 but hadn't been able to find subsequently. The landscape had changed. I warred with my memory on Hikes 2 and 3 but couldn't find the place. Skirt walked us directly to it, nothing as I remembered.

The Secret Shelter is a cabin owned by a 1989 thru-hiker named Jim. I met him on Hike 1 but after twenty years could not have recognized him. Thru-hikers sat on the porch enraptured as Jim and I recounted old times. There was a donkey now that someone had abandoned on the property, a donkey that made its living my nuzzling candy bars out of thru-hikers, to which I yielded as well. I looped my arm under and around its neck and held it close, the way you would with a horse, and I made a friend. The candy bar I fed it didn't hurt either.

The Secret Shelter was Jim's way of giving back to the trail. It sat on private property so was unsanctioned. It might have appeared on Guthook (I wouldn't know) but not in AWOL or the official ATC books. Jim intends to donate the shelter and property when his day finally comes, so someday that shelter will be secret no more.

I said my goodbyes to Jim and Skirt and the donkey, then pushed on for Unionville, New York through that undulating stretch where the trail winds in and out of New Jersey. I met another pair of sobos who were as affable as Magic Mike had been. I made Unionville early enough to push on, but after twenty miles and a mellow day I decided to stay.

Unionville has not always been a thru-hiker destination. It's not exactly on the trail, but rather a walk down either of two roads that cross the trail. I knew nothing of the town on Hike 1. It was late in the day in a steady downpour on Hike 2 that I learned of Unionville and a man called The Mayor.

The Mayor had been the mayor of Unionville, a small hamlet of little outside appeal that was gradually wasting away as so many little towns were. The Mayor had a vision of turning his town into a proper trail town, luring in the money that hiked past unspent year after year. His constituents were not pleased with this notion, so on his own he converted his house into a hiker hostel, hoping that over time the good people of Unionville would eventually come to accept the idea. I'd heard rumors of this on the trail so I trudged in sopping wet that evening on Hike 2 to inquire of The Mayor.

There wasn't much to the town. The only life I saw as I wiped the rain out of my eyes were people coming and going from Wit's End Tavern. Where The Mayor lived was a mystery, so I went to the tavern for directions only to be rebuffed by a man whom I assumed to be the owner, who steadfastly refused to give me directions or even let me in out of the rain. I stood there holding the door open, rejected and dejected, rain drizzling off the bill of my cap. Some people at the bar threw mocking comments my way.

It was now full night, and although it had been a hot day, I shivered with a chill. I let the door spring itself closed then turned into the downpour with no idea what I should do. Perhaps there would be a gas station, or an awning I could sit under. Either way it was going to be a long, miserable night. As I took the steps down to the street, a woman with the look of a barmaid came out of the tavern, a newspaper over her head to ward off the rain.

"Look," she told me. "I'm sorry about all that. The Mayor's house is up that street and to the right. You can't miss it." She paused before she turned back. "And I'm really sorry about what they said in there."

I thanked her, followed her directions, and minutes later I met The Mayor, an older man with a savvy disposition who had a full house of thru-hikers. He fed me Hot Pockets then found me a place to sleep on the floor. The bunkroom he'd built in his basement was full, as was every couch in view. I was grateful nonetheless and spent a comfortable evening in out of the wet.

I didn't stop in Unionville on Hike 3. I caught those road crossings early in the day so kept on going, pushing hard for a hostel near Port Jervis. Now on Hike 4, though, I'd heard that there had been a renaissance in Unionville, that it had become the ultimate trail town, so I went on in, still early enough in the day to get some benefit, and found that what I'd heard was true. The townspeople had set up an area in their city park where thru-hikers could camp. The local store, Horler's, carried hot food and ample resupply. There was a pizza parlor now, cold beers aplenty, and Wit's End Tavern was now a hiker-friendly oasis of a good time.

It felt surreal, sitting in that crowded tavern, a glass of wine at my hand, free Wi-Fi, and with food on the way. The Mayor had long-since died and was buried in the city cemetery. I mourned his memory even as I celebrated his achievement. He'd brought his town around through hard feelings and all the rest. Unionville was a nice town now, vibrant, and it showed.

The trail chatter in Unionville had been all about the Warwick Drive-in Theater, which was two and a half miles west on the Warwick Turnpike, which crossed the Appalachian Trail about seventeen miles ahead. The owner, Ernest Wilson, allowed thru-hikers to camp for free on a grassy rise above the three movie screens, and went so far as to offer free access to the audio. There would also be the concession stand, hot dogs and popcorn and soft drinks. With free camping, free movies, and plenty of food, thru-hikers were flocking there as if the place were Woodstock.

It sounded to me as if it might be fun to go, but seventeen miles was a short day and the trail crossed into New York once and for all just a few miles farther on. I had set New York as my goal so doubted I would be joining the others at the Warwick Drive-in Theater.

I left early out of Unionville and took the Wallkill Reserve in the magic hour. And magic it was, two and a half miles around the perimeter of that wetland reserve, dewy cattails bobbing in the misty breeze, egrets standing patiently erect, their stiltish legs in the water and with their bills poised like spears to strike at unwary frogs or fish. Signs warned of the Jamestown Canyon virus, which was transmitted by mosquitoes. I'd never heard of that virus, another in a lengthening list of viral concerns on the Appalachian Trail. Fortunately for me there were no mosquitoes aloft in the cool of the magic hour. Those thru-hikers asleep in Unionville might be less fortunate when they came through in the heat of the day.

I made miles. I went over Pochuck Mountain with little strain then dropped down to the long boardwalk over Pochuck Creek Swamp, another preserved wetland but one that has been overwhelmed by invasive bamboo. Someone had once unwisely planted that bamboo in their yard as an ornamental and now it was here taking over, crowding out native species. Getting rid of the stuff would be next to impossible.

I stopped at New Jersey Highway 94 to buy some food at the hot dog stand. The sun was high now, quite hot, but a few hot dogs and a couple of cold cokes revived me. Down that highway was the town of Vernon. There used to be a church hostel there, where I stayed on Hike 1, and there was the Appalachian Motel, a nice, hiker-friendly place where I stayed on Hike 3. This time I kept on going.

The Stairway to Heaven up Wawayanda Mountain was next. This was a steep climb but only about nine hundred feet over a mile and a half, so I took this one also without strain. Dropping down the other side I came upon a trail angel named Time Out, who was doing trail magic at the Barrett Road trailhead.

Time Out was a young man of infectious enthusiasm who'd thru-hiked in 2018. I was still sated from the hot dogs earlier but I had to stop. Time Out's northbound thru-hike in 2018 meant that we had crossed paths at some point. We puzzled over this for quite a while, comparing places and experiences, desperate to determine if we had met. The consensus was that we had not but that we were crossing paths now so that's all that mattered. Time Out lived about an hour away, and like so many of us, had not been able to let go of his Appalachian Trail experience. He was there doing trail magic as his own way of holding on and giving back. I envied him, living close enough to do some good. I live too far from the A.T. corridor to capture an experience like that for myself.

While we were talking, a pair of young nobos came up, Rocky and Switz. Rocky was a beaming guy with round eyeglasses and a wooly black beard, while Switz wore an hispanic influence and an alluring smile. She had gotten her trail name because she had lived in Switzerland for a time. We compared hikes in the Alps with fond recollection. I learned that she was from Texas, which explained why she was able to talk properly. While they were both Technicians, still they were hiking with as much old-school ethos as they could, never slackpacking, always northbound, passing every white blaze. (Much later in the state of Maine, they would ford the Kennebec River rather than going across in the canoe. Rocky described the experience as *gnarly*. Now *that's* old-school thru-hiking.)

I liked them both immediately.

I pushed on, and after a few more miles came to the Warwick Turnpike. It was still plenty early enough to push on into New York but I had to stop and recollect. It was right there on Hike 1 that I'd met Dave and Nadine.

New York and New Jersey had been mercilessly hot on Hike 1. Water sources had been dry across both states. At one point in New York I'd had to sop water out of a depression in the rock with my bandana. When I crossed into New Jersey it was late and my water bottles were empty. I collapsed alone at Wawayanda Shelter (which I call *Waywayyonder* Shelter) without water, spent a fitful night, then arose dangerously dehydrated the next morning and went the wrong way. (It's for this reason that I scratch arrows into the soil whenever I take a side trail to shelter or elsewhere.)

A half mile later, stumbling over a trail I'd already hiked, I blundered out onto the Warwick Turnpike, dizzy and disoriented. A black SUV screeched to a halt across the way and a man's voice sounded.

"Are you okay?" he asked.

I blubbered a reply, and then a woman got out and came to me.

"Are you all right?" she asked with genuine concern.

I mumbled something about water, or not having water. Whatever came out was surely too garbled to understand. The woman ushered me to their car and the two drove me to their home. They were, I learned, Dave and Nadine.

Dave did computer work and Nadine did something for the state. They filled me full of fluids, shoved me into their shower, and while I was in there, Nadine threw my clothes in her washer. I emerged to a cold beer, a plate of food, and relieved smiles. As always, I recovered quickly. I couldn't thank them enough. Soon I was wearing clean clothes, feeling fit, and ready to resume the trail.

"Why don't you stay for the night?" Dave asked. "We're going to a drive-in movie tonight. You're invited if you'd like to come."

That startled me out of any lingering torpor. When was the last time I'd been to a drive-in movie? I knew exactly when it was, 1981 in Sugar Land, Texas. My first son was barely two years old and we'd gone to the drive-in so we wouldn't disturb other people if he got fussy. We saw *Raiders of the Lost Ark* that night. Twenty years later I wasn't aware that drive-in theaters still existed. This was a novelty that I couldn't pass up, while Dave and Nadine were so sincerely welcoming that I felt not in the least self-conscious. So we went, saw one of the *Planet of the Apes* movies, and the theater we went to was the Warwick Drive-in.

I kept in touch with Dave and Nadine for a few years, tried to find them on Hike 2 but they'd moved away. Now, another twenty years later, I was sensing a serendipitous harmonic of twenty-year intervals. Pay attention, I told myself, so I stood beside the road and stuck out my thumb.

Rocky and Switz came up soon thereafter. We stood together as cars rushed past, had about resigned ourselves to the long road walk when Miss Janet pulled up in her colorful van. As a southbounder I'd never met Miss Janet but I knew of her. She was a trail treasure, one of those endearing personalities on the Appalachian Trail that leave us less for having not met them. If Dave and Nadine hadn't stopped to help me on Hike 1 I wouldn't be meeting Miss Janet now. Serendipity indeed.

Miss Janet was lusty with life, and possessed a wit and bearing that reminded me of the late Texas humorist Molly Ivins. She carted us to the theater then combed the cluttered cave in the back of her van for a tube of seam sealer while I pitched my tent. After what seemed a futile search she emerged in triumph with a partly dried bottle of seam sealer, which was enough to solve my leakage problem from there all the way to Mt. K.

Tents were popping up all over as thru-hikers arrived in twos and threes, streaming in as if to a concert. Tent cities are accumulations southbounders seldom experience unless they break from the trail for Trail Days, which no southbounder I'd ever known had. I thought I would feel crowded and claustrophobic but I didn't. I was enjoying myself, thru-hikers coming and going, all the different personalities on display, some exotic, like a crossroads in antiquity. I couldn't take notes fast enough to capture it all. I was dozing away the remaining afternoon in my tent when I heard someone call, *"Hey Care Bear, come over here."*

I popped my head through my tent flaps in an instant.

"Care Bear? Where's Care Bear?" I asked anyone listening. A diffident, fair-haired kid gave me a feeble wave. "Hey dude," I said, full of excitement. "I'm a novelist, and a character in one of my books was named Care Bear. How cool is that?"

Care Bear was nonplussed by this knowledge. He shrugged and walked off while my jaw hung. Well, *my* Care Bear, an important influence in the life of the protagonist of my novel *Timewall Speaks*, was a cool thru-hiker. This Care Bear was a dick.

The sun finally set and the movies began. The rowdiness that had been going on all day simmered to quiet. I couldn't run the app on my phone that would let me hear the sound, but I didn't mind. The night was perfectly pleasant, the air cool, carrying the nostalgic aroma of popcorn. I watched from my tent, propped on my elbows until I fell asleep, awaking early the next morning to continue my journey.

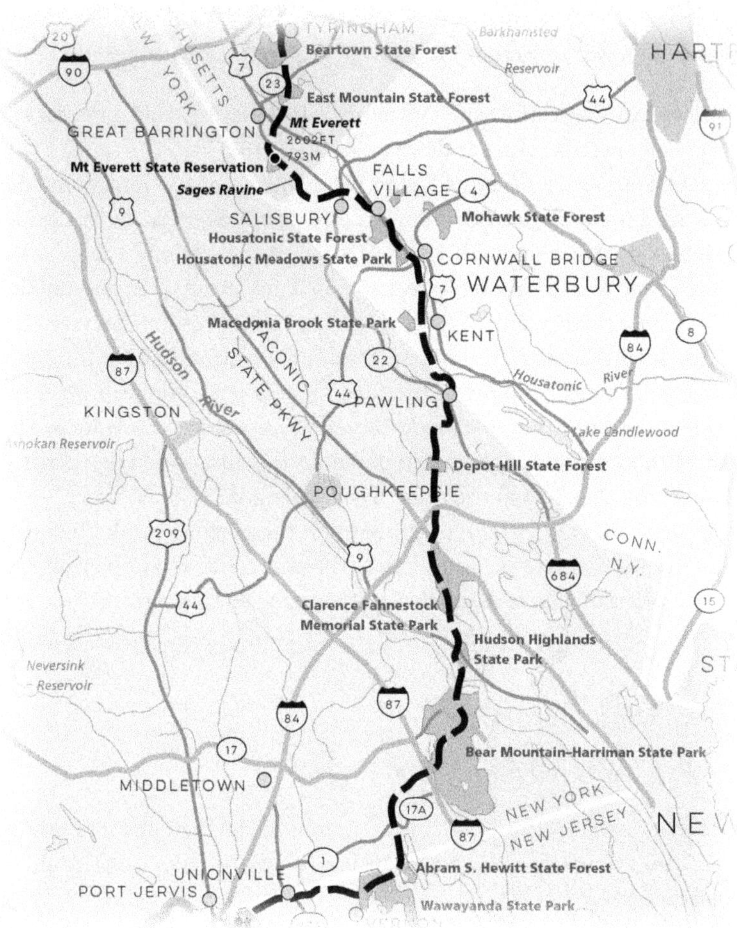

NEW YORK

90 MILES

SUNDAY, AUGUST 1, 2021

Tuxedo Motel, New York - 21.6 Miles (+2)

Fell asleep last night while the movies were still playing. Had a restful night, the whole tent city as quiet as dawn.

Up at 4:30 a.m., out front trying for a hitch at 5:45. Rocky and Switz joined me. I was surprised that anyone else would be up so early. I really do like those two! We caught a hitch at 6:30—everyone else still asleep or sleeping it off—and started hiking fo real at 6:50. I got ahead of Rocky and Switz, and didn't see them again.

Rock scrambles that I didn't remember had me cussing a lot and not making great time. Still, made the road by 3:00 p.m., couldn't get a hitch, so walked the two miles to Tuxedo Motel, where I stayed on Hike 3. This is probably the last reasonably-priced motel for the duration (well, there's that one in Dalton, Mass), and their rate hasn't changed since last time.

I just beat the rain, which is howling out there now. I think I'll take zero number eight tomorrow. I need a trip to the post office and library, and some resupply. None of that is close, so will use up the day anyway.

MONDAY, AUGUST 2, 2021

Tuxedo Motel, New York - Zero

Gorgeous weather today, what a change, and in the high 40s this morning. I hope I don't regret taking a zero today. In weather like this I could have gone far.

Slept till 6:00 a.m., then set about to make a productive zero out of the day. Did laundry, hiked to a C-store for breakfast biscuits and some resupply, then had to call a taxi to take me to the post office and library, there was no other way. The driver was a good guy, though, and his fare was cheap. Filled up at an IHOP, lots of pancakes, posted field notes, and mailed some stuff home. I went looking for a pair of lightweight hiking pants but couldn't find any. I was going to mail the kilt home if I found some pants, but I guess I'll be hanging onto it for a little longer. Cut the feet off some compression socks to MacGyver some leggings that might help keep the ticks off. Looks as if they're going to work out. Also gave myself a haircut, I was starting to look like a Duck Dynasty guy.

Now I'm drinking beer and resting, and I'm hungry again.

TUESDAY, AUGUST 3, 2021

Bear Mountain Bridge, New York - 198 Miles (+2)

Woke early, got out early, and felt great. Made the two-mile road walk to the trailhead before 6:00 a.m., then set out, hiking fast.

Met a nobo named Birdie at the Lemon Squeezer, made a video of it for her, then pushed on. Met Ike, Nectar, and Jack-O'-Lantern and hiked with them a while, then got out ahead and stayed ahead. I wanted to make the zoo before it closed, so I pushed myself hard and fast over the rocks. Reached the zoo at 3:00 p.m., where I met Purple, Grateful, and Ginseng, who were staying at the Bear Mountain Inn (not cheap) and were browsing the zoo. Met a nobo named Stash and walked with him to the bridge. I called Grandpa at Bear Mountain Bridge Motel from there.

Glad to be here for the fourth time. Grandpa remembered me, and I signed the register right under Nimblewill Nomad's entry. He flipped from here just yesterday, so the only way I'll meet him now is if we pass as he goes south.

I pushed too hard today, but I feel okay. The new MacGyvered leggings worked very well.

WEDNESDAY, AUGUST 4, 2021

RPH Shelter - 25.4 Miles

An overall good day, although the section above Clarence Fahnestock State Park was long and annoying. There used to be a pavilion we camped at, but I never saw it. Relo maybe?

Woke up at 5:30 a.m., walked to the deli for breakfast, then packed up and was ready to go at 7:00. Grandpa drove me back to the bridge and we said our goodbyes. I really like that old guy. Hiking by 7:30.

Hiked happily alone for a while, then caught up with Ike, who fell in behind. Made quick miles to the Appalachian Deli, where I ate muffins and drank a few energy drinks.

Pushed on across Graymoor, met up with Cannonball, who stayed with me for a while. Good conversation, then caught up with Ike again.

Arrived at RPH Shelter at about 5:30 p.m. Two sobos here, plus beaucoup nobos. The sobos were dicks, telling stories of the Whites to scare the nobos. I contradicted most of what they said, which earned me appreciation from the nobos and scowls from the sobos.

Ordered pizza and cokes. Ate well. It's late and time to sleep, so now it's off to the tent.

THURSDAY, AUGUST 5, 2021

Wiley Shelter - 25.6 Miles

Woke up at 4:30 a.m., hiking by 5:30. Cannonball, Ike, and the others? Still sleeping. I doubt I'll see them again.

Started out leisurely then picked up the pace. Met a husband-wife nobo team who kept up with me for a while. I enjoyed the talk, but eventually pulled away. I made 16 miles by noon, a damp morning, 20 miles by 1:30 p.m. Took a refreshing shower at the Garden Center on NY22, then hiked the ½ mile to Tony's Deli, where I had a big burger and a beer.

Back on the trail at 3:00 p.m. Wanted CT today (it's not even 2 miles away) but I was dragging from the beer and big burger. Pitched tent here at 5:00 p.m. Connecticut will still be there tomorrow.

—

The Appalachian Trail in New Jersey might come as a surprise to the first-time thru-hiker, who probably visualized the Garden State as a bleak urban rumble akin to *The Sopranos*, and with no notion whatsoever of the pleasant wooded contours in the west of that state. The trail corridor in the state of New York, however, lies closer to the mark.

The Appalachian Trail spends ninety miles in New York, threading a crooked needle between areas of dense habitation and coming near thirty miles of the big city itself. It's only through wooded illusion, boulder ballet, and numerous rock scrambles that a sense of wilderness perseveres. To have routed the trail away from this at the onset would have deflected the trail from its original mission, which was to provide convenient outdoor activity for those very urban dwellers close by.

I awoke at Warwick Drive-in Theater in the dark of morning, amid tents packed as tightly as the favelas of Rio de Janeiro. There was a penetrating stillness to the theater now, the empty screens, a few odd cars parked below as if their drivers had fallen asleep during the movie, here and there the spent detritus of last night's beers and bowls. An empty plastic cup tapped a lonely tempo against a darkened lamppost, then skittered free on a sigh of breeze. Somewhere in a tent close by, a dog huffed and was groggily scolded by its owner.

To spare the sleeping thru-hikers, I pulled my tent stakes and drug the whole thing across the dewy grass, downslope to where cars had been parked when the movies were playing. There I made coffee, ate my protein bars, then packed everything away. I was standing out front for a hitch at five forty-five. Headlights approached and retreated in succession, the early local rush hour. No one stopped.

Rocky and Switz unexpectedly emerged from the morning to stand thumbs-out at my side.

"Hey guys," I said. "I'm not used to seeing other hikers this early."

"We like to get an early start," Rocky said.

"And I like the quiet," Switz added.

Once again I entertained a glimmer of hope. Perhaps we had here the makings of a new tramily. Our hiker ethics were certainly aligned and their personalities rose well above the usual insular nobo insolence. We made easy conversation as we waited, and waited. The sleepy dawn rose. From the tent city behind us, not a stir. A man stopped to pick us up at six thirty. We scrambled into his car amid effusive thanks and were soon deposited at the trailhead, hiking by ten minutes to seven. The light was well up by then, the magic hour holding on by fingertips. I got out ahead of Rocky and Switz, kept expecting, with their youth, that they would catch up at any time but I never saw them again that day.

The first miles went quickly. I soon crossed into New York, topped Prospect Rock, and then on to Mombasha High Point with its boulder ballet. This was where I'd sopped water with my bandana in the heat of Hike 1. I went through there in the rain on Hikes 2 and 3, terrified at each next slippery step. Hike 4 provided a cool breeze and dry rocks, a first of that experience for me, so I bounded through in good spirits. In agreeable weather, I learned, you could walk those tops with thrilling agility.

The sky grew crowded as I negotiated a rocky ridge that I didn't remember, up and down, up and down while an old Forest Service road ran derelict below. My pace slowed but I pushed myself because the air carried the musty smell of rain now. I came out at New York Highway 17 at three o'clock, twenty-one and a half miles under throbbing feet, and depleted from all the rock work. I stuck out my thumb for a hitch as a light mist began to fall, gave up on that and started walking, two miles to Tuxedo Motel where I stayed on Hike 3. I pulled open the office door just as the sky unleashed in earnest.

Tuxedo Motel is an artifact from earlier times, with a fifties Route 66 feel. It rests well up a hill from the road, giving glimpses of an era when city families on vacation would emigrate here in their station wagons, take in the wooded sights from their lounges beside the pool, perhaps with martinis in hand, and shoo their kids off to play elsewhere. There's a dated sense about the place now, although it remains clean and well maintained. The rates hadn't changed since Hike 3, rates that are unusually low for New York and in line with many hostels. I was glad to be back.

With the exception of RPH Shelter to the north, I don't use the shelters in New York, nor do I camp. I distrust groundwater sources that are in close proximity to major urban areas, and the shelters are all situated near roads, which makes them accessible to riff raff, underscored on Hike 1 when some raggedy drunks tumbled into Fingerboard Shelter with me, so obstreperous that I left them in that hotbox and went off to cowboy camp.

I settled into my room while the sudden storm loosed slanting curtains of rain, the wind blustering through the woods beyond the parking area. The downside of Tuxedo Motel is that there are no services nearby save a convenience store down the hill. I'd stocked up on beer and food there before I'd made the climb up the hill so wasn't wanting for any of that. I needed to do things, though, mail some things home, visit a library to post long overdue field notes. I would have to hire a taxi for that, no other choice, and this would consume a good part of a day.

So I decided to take zero number eight, and awoke to a most spectacular morning. The sky was as blue as lapis, the temperature in the crisp high forties, and here it was August 2! Out on the trail, the weather alone would have carried me thirty miles, but I'd made my decision so kept to it.

I made the most of that day, eating, visiting the post office, eating, then on to the library. I went looking for a pair of lightweight hiking pants, something to dissuade the ticks that were finding their way onto me as never before during my thru-hikes. That search proved futile. I bought a pair of compression socks instead, cut off the feet, cauterized the loose threads, and jimmied myself a pair of leggings, which went on to work out very well. I had no more problems with ticks, and as a bonus I could thereafter crawl into my tent without muddy calves.

The next day took me through the Lemon Squeezer and on toward Bear Mountain Bridge. The Lemon Squeezer, a narrow cleft between some large rock formations, is always a fun obstacle to negotiate. With my trim backpack, I got through almost too easily.

I met thru-hikers throughout the day, hiked with some of them for a time but always got out ahead. I took a short break on Black Mountain to take in the view of the New York City skyline (and where I'd last seen the World Trade Center on Hike 1), then pushed on, leaving a crowd of thru-hikers behind.

I was pushing hard miles for Bear Mountain and the Trailside Museum & Zoo on the other side. The zoo is a novelty on the Appalachian Trail. The blazes pass through the zoo, past cages of rescued animals and a sad black bear. There's a concession area just before that, with pizza and beer (albeit not inexpensive). The only problem is that the place closes at four thirty, no one allowed in after four o'clock. A blue-blazed route circumnavigates the zoo but I'd never had to take it and didn't want to this time either, which meant I had to push, and push, and push up Bear Mountain, and then down the other side through jams of day hikers.

I moved with urgency as the day went long but did arrive by three o'clock. My urgency unwound like a tight spring, and I went through the zoo at a relaxed gait, taking in the exhibits with ample time. When I came out the other side, a couple of cold cokes in me by then as well as a hot slice of pizza, I felt relaxed, the tension of the day an abstract memory. I hiked on to Bear Mountain Bridge, where I called Grandpa at Bear Mountain Bridge Motel for my fourth stay in twenty years. To my delight, Grandpa remembered me. He was along to pick me up within half an hour.

Bear Mountain Bridge Motel is a quaint but tasteful old place with only six or so rooms. It changed hands sometime after Hike 2, purchased then by Grandpa's family. I first met Grandpa on Hike 3 and found him folksy and welcoming, with a hiker-friendliness that leapt well beyond the previous owner. He directed me to his trail register first thing, where I wrote my entry directly below Nimblewill Nomad's.

Nimblewill Nomad is an old fellow from Alabama who has hiked all over the place and has been doing it for decades. He did the Triple Crown the year I made Hike 2, and was now out to set the record for the oldest person to complete the Appalachian Trail, which he did achieve at the age of eighty-three, tacking on the Pinhoti and Benton MacKaye Trails withal. Along with Earl Shaffer and myself, Nimblewill Nomad lamented that so many sections of the trail had been routed away from towns and villages and up into the rocks, diverting thru-hikers from the many cultural encounters they'd once enjoyed. I wanted to meet him, thought surely I must be getting close by then (he had stayed with The Mechanical Man the week before I walked into all that drama), but was devastated to learn from Grandpa that the old thru-hiker had flipped to the state of Maine just the previous day.

So serendipity would not find me this time, and I would (as of this writing) never meet Nimblewill Nomad. I berated myself that if not for zero number eight we would both have been at Bear Mountain Bridge Motel on the same day.

Twenty-five and a half miles the next day brought me to RPH Shelter, the cabin with the old iron water pump, all situated near a road where pizzas could be delivered. I crossed the grounds of the Graymoor Spiritual Life Center along the way, which is a Franciscan retreat that occupies acres of pretty woodlands. I stayed there in the heat of Hike 1, lingering under the cold outdoor shower to the consternation of the other thru-hikers. In those days the friars would invite us in to eat dinner with them, potatoes and fat sausages. One friar led me on a tour of the grounds after our meal, alone since none of the other thru-hikers were interested.

We made easy conversation as we went, eventually sitting on benches atop the hill and below the statue of Jesus and Mary. I thanked him for all the amenities they offered, from the meal to the shower to the baseball field where we were allowed to camp. I asked him how it had all gotten started.

"A long time ago," he said, "we were gathered one evening when a stringy hiker came stumbling in. He looked emaciated and in poor health so we fed him and nursed him, and he eventually moved on.

"After that, more hikers started showing up, just one here and one there. We brought them in and fed them, and soon learned that what they really wanted was to shower, so we set up the shower out by the ball field and it has all come from that."

I chuckled at that story, I understood it too well. Faced with a choice between food and a shower, most of us would choose the shower first, especially in hot and dry New York.

I left a donation afterward which, apparently, few others did. Thru-hikers aren't invited in for meals anymore–I'm sure it simply got too expensive for the friars–but the ball field and shower remain. I scattered some of Freewind's ashes near the statue of Jesus and Mary on Hike 3, there to rest peacefully and with views of the New York City skyline on clear days.

From Graymoor I pushed on toward Clarence Fahnestock State Park on a trail that twisted through suffocating woods well above the park. It used to be an easy drop down to the park, where we would stop for hot dogs and cokes, then out the other side to a pavilion, where we weren't supposed to camp but did so anyway. This time I recognized none of it so I was pretty sure that the trail had been relocated since Hike 3, perhaps because a tornado had come through that year, flattening large swathes of the woods.

As a pleasant surprise, I caught up to Rocky and Switz, who'd gotten ahead while I was taking the zero at Tuxedo Motel. Great, I thought. Here we were on the way to RPH Shelter, a good night ahead and perhaps some serious hiking partners yet, but Rocky wasn't feeling well. The two pulled out mid-day to stealth camp and give Rocky a chance to rest. I said goodbye until tomorrow, when we would surely link up and carry on. While we did communicate regularly afterward, I never saw either of them again, still hoping as late as New Hampshire that they might yet catch up.

I reached RPH Shelter at five thirty and found it populated by a squad of nobos who were listening in horror as a pair of sobos spun yarns about the White Mountains ahead, how difficult those mountains were, how absolutely excruciating.

"You nobos are going to have a hard time," said one sobo, a middle-aged guy with a scratchy gray beard, a permanent scowl, and an air of superiority that was intolerable. "I bet most of you quit right there."

I stepped into that, barely restrained. Sure the White Mountains were tough, but those nobos had journeyed 1430 miles so far, while the sobos had barely cleared 760. And yet here was a sobo talking down to the nobos as if they were amateurs on his trail.

"The Whites are tough," I said to all gathered around, cutting off the sobo in mid-sentence, "but they aren't anything you guys haven't already done." A few of them seemed to regard me then as a savior, while the sobo turned hardened eyes my way. "Always remember, guys," I went on, "you've hiked fourteen hundred miles to get here. You've climbed all the stuff these guys don't even know about yet, so don't worry about the Whites. You'll crush 'em, I promise."

"What makes you an expert?" the sobo threw at me with face-slapping sarcasm.

"Three southbound thru-hikes," I answered in flat syllables, and then I went off to pitch my tent.

I ordered pizza with some of the nobos, then found to my dismay that the iron water pump had been locked. There was too much coliform in the water, a posted sign claimed. I would encounter this at every iron pump from there through Connecticut. Too bad. I really appreciated those pumps. They were a refreshing way to wash down after a hot day, but alas no more.

I rounded Nuclear Lake the next day, the site of a laboratory explosion in 1972 that scattered plutonium dust throughout the area, supposedly clean now but one still had to wonder. Nevertheless it's a pretty lake, running with fish and wildlife. If not for its well-published history and bleak name, none of us would have been the wiser.

Soon afterward came the boardwalk over Pawling's Great Swamp, then the railroad tracks and the A.T. Railroad Station, which is not a station but a train stop, a novelty I'd never enjoyed because stops were only made on the weekends and I'd never been through there on a weekend. At New York Highway 22 just beyond, I went into Native Landscapes & Garden Center for a quick outdoor shower, then the half mile up the road to Tony's Deli.

Delis are probably the most celebrated feature of the trail in New York. With proper planning you can eat at a deli just about every day, aligning them the same way you might the waysides in Shenandoah National Park.

On Hike 1 I hoofed the half mile to Tony's Deli with a rumbling stomach only to discover that they didn't accept debit cards. With no cash left, and no ATMs even remotely close, I had to turn my back on all that food and return to the trail, my stomach then rumbling even louder. Technology has caught up with Tony's Deli now, though, so I was able to enjoy a big juicy burger and a cold beer, which made the mile round-trip well worth the effort.

I pushed on for Connecticut then, but found after that big meal that I was just listlessly plodding along, so I threw down at Wiley Shelter, another twenty-five and a half miles behind me and less than two miles to the state line. I pitched my tent and settled in for my last night in New York.

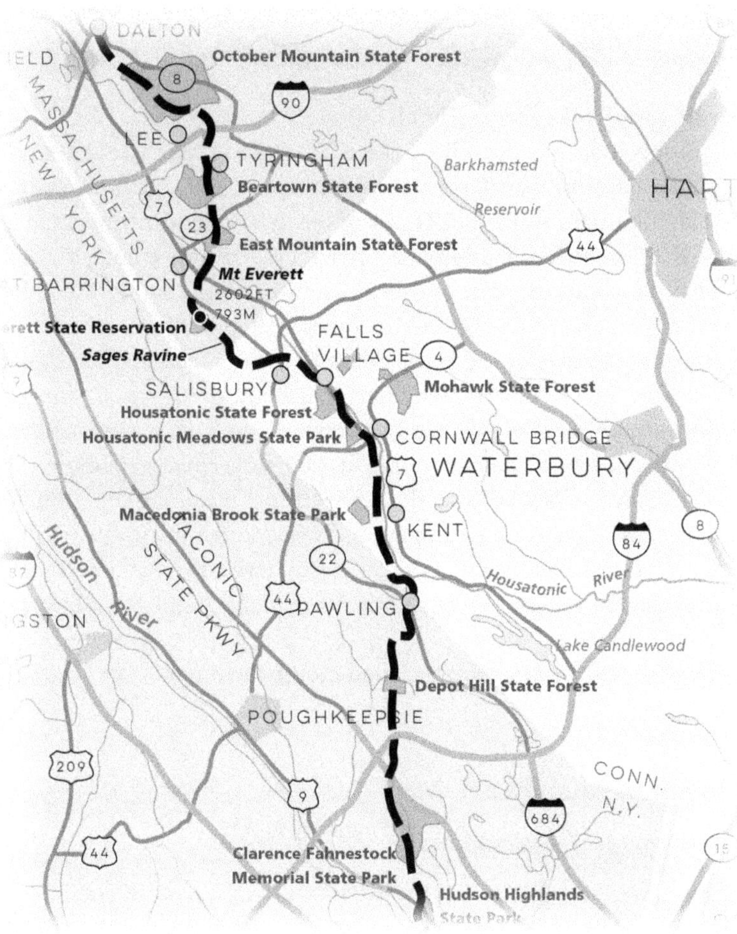

CONNECTICUT

50.1 MILES

FRIDAY, AUGUST 6, 2021

Silver Hill Campsite, Connecticut - 23 Miles

Woke up early, broke camp early, hiking by 5:45 a.m.

Cool this morning, but a little damp. Made good time and glad to reach CT at 6:30 a.m., but then Ten Mile Hill was a pain, and the climb over Schaghticoke Mountain really took it out of me. It was suddenly hot, suddenly buggy, the trail rockier than I remembered. I met a trail volunteer who was vocally bitter about the state of things. Through all of that, I wasn't able to cover the 13 miles to Kent, Connecticut until 1:30 p.m.

Hiked into Kent, stopped at the Fife & Drum for beers and food, then to the Welcome Center for a shower, then I hiked out.

Met some nobos at the trailhead who gave me a locally brewed beer, which was very good, then rejoined the trail at 3:00 p.m. There were more climbs up to St. Johns Ledges, but also that long flat section along the Housatonic River. The last climb to the campground was a long one, steeper than I remember but probably because I caught it late in the day this time. I met nobos Fourth Quarter and Gourmet, who were middle-aged. We talked about trail condition for a while.

The campground is full, but a good group. Tired now.

SATURDAY, AUGUST 7, 2021

Salisbury, Connecticut - 22 Miles

A hard day. Up at 4:45 a.m., hiking by 5:30, going slow on an absolutely unrecognizable trail.

Didn't see any hikers for most of the day, then met Big Spoon at the shower in Falls Village.

Kept hiking and climbing, my energy so low that I downed a 5-Hour Energy just to keep going. God, it's hot, hot, hot, and mosquitoes in clouds. Reached Salisbury at 5:00 p.m. and threw down at Maria's place. She doesn't remember me, and seems more than three years older than last time (she's 92 now). Big Spoon decided to stay as well, so we shared laundry, dinner, and now a bedroom.

Maria's grandson Ed is somewhat pedantic. I don't think he approves of hikers. Still, he drove us for food and laundry, and we appreciated that. Maria's friend Tim is quite strange, something odd going on there.

I'll get a late start tomorrow—need to resupply—but I'll make Massachusetts regardless.

—

Connecticut arrived in a milky magic hour, the Gateway to New England. The sky was a gray blanket lying heavily across the treetops. Humidity clung to every leaf and limb, while the air, although damply cool, betrayed a hint of worse to come.

I topped Ten Mile Hill soon after, expending as much energy sucking in the humid air as I did fighting gravity. Next was Schaghticoke Mountain, which proved disturbingly indifferent to my memory. The heat rose with alarming intensity, and with it clouds of mosquitoes desperate to feed. I swatted, climbed, tripped; swatted, climbed, tripped. The air seemed too thick to breathe, as if it belonged to New Iberia and not New England.

Near the top, I met a trail volunteer whom I will call Algernon. He was an erect man of later age, with a neat gray moustache and leathery skin from years in the outdoors. I found him sitting on a rock swatting at mosquitoes, a bottle of water at his knee.

"Hello," he greeted me heartily as I walked up. "These mosquitoes are terrible, are they not?"

"My God," I said, grunting and swatting as I sat. "Where'd they come from?"

"It is this weather. You can never know anymore when it will be cold or when it will be hot. The mosquitoes will live on so they come out when they must."

Algernon offered me some mosquito repellent, which I declined. I don't use repellent because it makes my skin oily, attracts dirt, melts plastic, and can permeate a sleeping bag with a sickening chemical smell. It will also sweat into my eyes, or else get there when I unthinkingly run the back of my hand across my forehead to wipe away the sweat. The last time I'd used the stuff was on Hike 1 and I'd managed to get through all the thousands of miles since without it.

I told Algernon about my earlier thru-hikes. "Has this trail been changed though here?" I asked him.

"Yes," he said, averting his eyes as if guiltily.

"So what's the deal?" I asked then.

"They tell us what we have to do, so we have to do it."

"Who tells you what you have to do?"

"Those people in Harpers Ferry."

"But you're a volunteer," I objected. "They can't *tell* you to do anything."

"That is not the way they think. I know a man who maintained his section for many, many years. He knew three years they were going to change it, so he quit maintaining. Why should he bother with it if the trail was going to move? Right?"

"Yeah, that makes sense."

"So now they won't talk to him. They brought in people to do his section, and now nobody thinks about him except me, and maybe soon they'll forget about me too."

"Man, can't you all do anything about that?"

He shrugged. "What can we do? They make all the rules for us."

This weighed heavily on Algernon. I could tell that he loved the trail the way a Ukrainian might love Kyiv, stoic to the end but bombs were falling on the suburbs and there was nothing that would stop them. His favorite shelter, he told me, was Ten Mile River Shelter.

"Did you see the water pump was locked?" he asked.

I didn't go into that shelter on this hike but I knew the pump. Considering that the pump at RPH Shelter had been locked, it followed that more of them might be locked as well. Come to think of it, the only pump I knew of in New Jersey had also been locked.

"Yeah," I nodded. "The water's contaminated isn't it?"

"No," he shook his head sharply, "that water is good. It is only that some government people say we must test the water three times a week. We cannot do that. We do not have enough people and enough money to do that, and the government will not help us so we have no choice, we have to lock the pumps."

My ire rose at that. Those old iron water pumps, from RPH Shelter in New York and on through Connecticut, were a unique trail feature we took for granted but which provided blessed relief, especially on hot days. We would all line up, taking turns at the handle as we built up the pressure, sometimes cranking thirty or forty times before a trickle would start, and then the cold gush and we'd all cheer, an exercise in commonality on the Appalachian Trail that breached generations. The way Algernon talked, those pumps might never be unlocked again. It would be groundwater only from then on, as if the pumps stood in the way of someone's vision of an all-encompassing Appalachian Trail wilderness, which would always be an illusion no matter where they routed the trail, there were simply too many towns and cities near the corridor.

I rose with a sigh. "Well, I'm sorry about all of that. Just know that we thru-hikers appreciate everything you do."

"Thank you. It is nice to know some people care that we are here."

I continued on to the town of Kent, making a slow pace in the debilitating humidity. Kent was only thirteen miles from that morning's magic hour but I didn't get there until one thirty. The town is eight tenths of a mile off the trail, along an open highway in the brunt of the sun. The pavement was hot through the soles of my shoes.

I hiked into town, sweating and salt-streaked. Kent is another peculiar trail town. There are ample hiker services—eateries, crafts, and a great bookshop, even a Welcome Center where we can shower—but there's no lodging except the Fife & Drum Restaurant and Inn, which is an upscale place a bit too expensive for most thru-hikers. There's a motel and a B&B outside of town, but neither are too convenient. It's as if Kent were saying, "Come in, shop, have a good time, but be gone by sunset." Despite that notion, I've met my share of trail angels in Kent over the years, people who offered rides, food, and sometimes even money. So Kent is a hiker-friendly town, if not a town where you might spend the night.

I went into the Fife & Drum for food and beers, then across the road to the Welcome Center for a shower. I hiked out immediately afterward and met some nobos at the trailhead who were carting locally brewed beers up the hill to Mt Algo Shelter where they were setting up for a get-together that night. It was three o'clock, late enough in the day that I might have joined them, but Mt Algo Shelter was behind me now. I yogied one of their beers, sucked it down, then continued across the farm fields toward the saw-toothed St. Johns Ledges, where Mr. Hiker went down hard on Hike 3. St. Johns Ledges could be easily yellow-blazed along an adjacent road but I'd never been tempted. Despite their rugged contour, and some hand-over-hand climbing, I always enjoyed St. Johns Ledges. There was something about the grain of the trail, the lay of the rocks, familiar to me no matter which direction I went. But then I'd never had to go over them in the rain. That might have changed my outlook.

I navigated St. Johns Ledges without difficulty then dropped down to that four-mile flat walk along the Housatonic River, beginning to feel the miles now but keeping up a good pace. The climb to Silver Hill Campsite came in the barely-lingering light, a steep, final ascent for the day. It was still light when I got there, tents dotted all over but with people of good company. The iron pump was locked, as Algernon had said it would be. I'd filled up at a stream below, and had not spoiled my shower in Kent, so I was fine with what I had. I pitched my tent and lay back, twenty-three miles that day, looking forward to Salisbury tomorrow, and Maria, hoping she was well.

They were all still asleep when I left out at five thirty the next morning. The magic hour brought little relief, the air tepid even at that hour, the bugs rising with the sun. I made listless progress, drained in the heat over an alligator-jaw of a trail, and with mosquitoes probing my eyes and ears in continuous torment. Ten miles on, atop Sharon Mountain, I paused for the novel view down to the raceway at Lime Rock Park. The cars weren't running this time, although on previous hikes I'd been able to sit on that perfect sitting rock and watch the car races underway far below, the rumbles of powerful engines thundering up the mountain.

I had never crossed Connecticut in such heat, struggling on a trail that I had never taken at anything less than an exuberant step. It was with relief that I dropped down finally onto the flat, two-mile road walk toward Falls Village. Along the way was the hydroelectric plant on the Housatonic, ivy-covered red brick, the infrastructure of an earlier era. There was a manicured lawn, a broad shade tree, and an outdoor shower that had provided welcome relief to thru-hikers for generations. I collapsed onto the shaded grass and wiped the sweat out of my face. A shirtless nobo lay napping a few feet away. Southbound turned-around, I went to the wrong building in search of the shower.

"It's over there," the nobo pointed, rousing on an elbow.

I turned, took in the site as if I were going southbound, and of course there it was.

"Thanks."

That spray of cold water was a gift I could never repay. I stripped to my shorts, rinsed everything, and wondered if I could get away with stripping out of my shorts as well. Probably not a good idea, I decided. When this had gone on long enough that I couldn't justify wasting any more water, I spread my things in the sun to dry then went to join the nobo, whose name was Big Spoon.

Big Spoon was a youngish guy but in no way aloof.

"God, it's hot," he said. "I feel like I want to sleep right here all night."

"I hear ya, man. Glad this place is here, aren't you?"

"Yeah. I was fucked, man. I can't hike in this shit."

I was gratified to learn that I wasn't the only one who suffered in these conditions. I lay back on my elbows and looked around. The place hadn't changed in twenty years, except maybe a park had been put in a field over yonder. The hydro plant and shower had come as an unexpected and welcome relief on Hike 1, an example of how being able to come down off the ridges from time to time actually enhances the Appalachian Trail experience. I wondered if the trail would someday be relocated away from this as well. What a loss that would be.

My clothes were already dry, even my backpack straps, which were crusty white with dried sweat. I rose and gathered my things.

"Well I'm pushing on, man," I said. "Good meeting you."

"Where you headed?"

"Salisbury. Maria's place."

"Oh, man—that's like what? Eight or nine miles?"

"Yeah."

"So who's Maria?"

"An old lady who lets us stay in her house. It's the only cheap place to stay for a long time, and there's a pizza place in town, and beer, and a grocery store. She's only a half mile off the trail, and she shuttled me all over last time."

"Well, good luck, dude. I can't make that shit, not today."

"Well, if you change your mind maybe I'll see you there."

I took off in the sun, crossed the iron bridge, and began my climb up Mt. Prospect, wilting before I made my second mile. When you have your trail legs, eight or nine miles come as easily as a park stroll, and Mt. Prospect is not a difficult climb, but in that heat a few miles came as an eternity. I plodded on, and on, lifelessly, no longer certain that I could make Salisbury; no longer certain that I could plant my next step.

I walked in a heat haze, losing all track of time. When at last I stepped out onto the baking road across from the cemetery, I got southbound turned-around and went the wrong way, which compounded my fatigue and added desperate minutes to my struggle. I turned and retraced my steps, just shuffling now. Back to the cemetery, I made a right, and then a left, and then I was there.

Maria was secluded in her room when I stumbled in. A man named Tim was looking after things for her. Tim was an odd but friendly guy, middle-aged or more, hairy, disheveled, and remarkably out of place in that proper Victorian setting. He got me settled upstairs, where I showered barely able to stay on my feet. Back downstairs, Maria was still in her room.

"I was hoping to see Maria," I told Tim. "I wanted to see if she remembered me from last time."

"She's resting right now. Maybe she'll be out later." He said this with a proprietary air that signaled without doubt that he was her gatekeeper and that no one would get past him.

"Is there anyone who can drive me into town for food?" I asked.

"Ed will be here in a little while. He can take you."

It was well after five o'clock, and twenty-two miles through the heat. I wasn't sure I would last a little while.

"So who's Ed?"

"He's her grandson."

"Okay," I said, and fell into a chair. After a few minutes, and as my eyes were closing from fatigue, the door rattled and Big Spoon came in, looking worse than I had when I arrived.

"Big Spoon!" I said, surprised. "You went for it."

"Yeah, man. I got to Limestone Spring Shelter and it was so hot I just said fuck it and went for it. Man, I'm fuckin' hungry."

Tim took Big Spoon upstairs to the room I was in. After a shower, Big Spoon came downstairs looking much better. Ed arrived then.

Ed was fiftyish, maybe less, well-dressed and with an imperious attitude. "Is an hour enough time for you to do what you need?" he asked us in an impatient tone.

Big Spoon and I shrugged. We needed food and to do laundry, resupply could wait until the morning.

"Sure," I said.

"Sure," Big Spoon said.

"Okay," Ed said.

Big Spoon and I hopped into the back seat of Ed's car, our laundry in our laps, and took off for the two-mile drive to Mizza's Pizza, a short drive in which Ed was able to introduce a lifetime of commentary.

"Are you vaccinated?" he asked both of us.

"Yeah," we answered in unison.

"Good, because my grandmother's very old. We don't want Covid in that house. I don't know why she still takes you people in but she won't listen to me."

"Is she doing okay?" I asked.

"Well, she *is* ninety-two, you know."

"She was a young eighty-nine the last time I saw her," I said with fond recollection.

"And she probably told you all about her childhood in Italy and the Nazis and all the rest, right?"

"Yeah. I thought it was fascinating."

"Yeah, well, she tells those stories to everybody."

"They're still fascinating. I'm quite fond of her."

Something about that piqued him. "She *is* my grandmother, you know."

"Sure. Yeah."

A can of something had been opened. If Ed were a character I'd created for one of my novels, he'd be a man who yearned for his grandmother's attention but had to share that attention with a continuous parade of strangers. The day would inevitably come, and I suspected Ed would be right there when the papers were read, looking for the portion he finally wouldn't have to share.

I met Maria on Hike 3 in much better weather, unexpectedly staying for the night. I'd been hearing about her on the trail, so when I hiked into town to resupply, and walked past her house, I stopped in to meet her. She'd been taking in thru-hikers for decades but I'd somehow gotten through on Hikes 1 and 2 without learning of her. I found her to be refreshingly authentic, spry at eight-nine years old, and with a wealth of stories that held me transfixed. I wound up staying the night just to hear her talk.

She'd been born and raised in the Dolomite Alps of Italy at a time when Austria still controlled the region. The Nazis arrived when she was in grade school, using the children for distasteful propaganda purposes.

"We had to write letters to the German soldiers," she told me. "They made us do it. We didn't want to but we had no choice. These were Nazis, you know?" She spat *Nazi* with a loathing only people of her generation can truly understand. "We even had to send pictures of ourselves," she went on, "so some German soldier probably had my picture in his pocket when he was fighting and killing." She paused with a look of remorse or perhaps disgust. She continued:

"So after the war the Americans came and I married one and he brought me here. And then he died and I married again, and then he died, too. So now it's just me in this old house, so I let the hikers come in."

I looked around. The walls were lined with books and mementoes, a trove of history. Later that day, Maria drove me into town for food and resupply, stopping in at Mizzi's Pizza to crack wise with the staff while I shoveled food into my mouth A petite woman who had obviously been stunningly beautiful in her youth, she sat dwarfed in her not-so-large car, barreling around corners and bouncing into parking lots. Age had made her wise, even shrewd, but it hadn't claimed her spirit. I described her on the trail afterward as perhaps the most interesting woman I'd ever met.

Back at Maria's house, Ed took his leave with a sidelong scowl at Tim, some undercurrent there. Maria didn't make an appearance, so in vague disappointment I went upstairs to turn in for the night.

I was up early the next morning, Big Spoon still fast asleep. I slipped quietly down to the kitchen for coffee. Maria's breakfast service was set up on the table with Emily Post propriety, every dish, fork, spoon and knife perfectly placed in advance. It was six o'clock, still an hour or more before anyone would be up, so I set out for town to do resupply and perhaps find something to eat.

This was a Sunday, and Salisbury dozed late that morning. Nothing was open. I kicked heels at the grocery store until it did open, then burst in on a mission, filling a shopping basket with all the lightweight, processed trail food that I'd never consider eating at home. I gave it a thought, grimaced, then went in search of mosquito repellent. The store was out of stock, which solved that conundrum for me.

I passed Big Spoon on the way back.

"Did you go to the coffee shop?" he asked.

"Naw, it was closed."

"It should be open now. Why don't you come with?"

"Naw, I don't think so." The morning was rising, and with the light I could only think of making miles.

"Okay, then. See ya later," he said with a wave.

I never saw Big Spoon again.

Maria was at her table when I got back. I gulped at the sight of her. Still petite, still evidencing the beauty of her youth, she nevertheless had obviously aged. Her carriage was not quite as erect, her countenance not quite as forthcoming. She didn't remember me. That didn't hurt. At her age I would have been surprised if she had. What was missing was that mischievous gleam she'd had three years ago, the sprite-like way she'd conducted herself then. We spoke about not much and then I paid her for my stay. She folded the bills and tucked them away as if they might be molested otherwise.

"So you put me in your book, did you?" she asked frankly.

I'd given her a cameo in *More Notes from the Field*, not a lengthy description but a flattering one.

"Yeah, I did," I said.

"Then you need to send me a copy. Don't forget to do that."

I did not comply with her request, instead left a note of the title to show her local bookseller. Writers get these requests all the time and with little forethought, as if what we produce is not work but the free exercise of a hobby. No one offered me free lodging, so why would I be expected to offer a free book?

I said my goodbyes with a note of sadness, knowing that it was unlikely I would ever see Maria again, then turned toward Massachusetts, just six miles away.

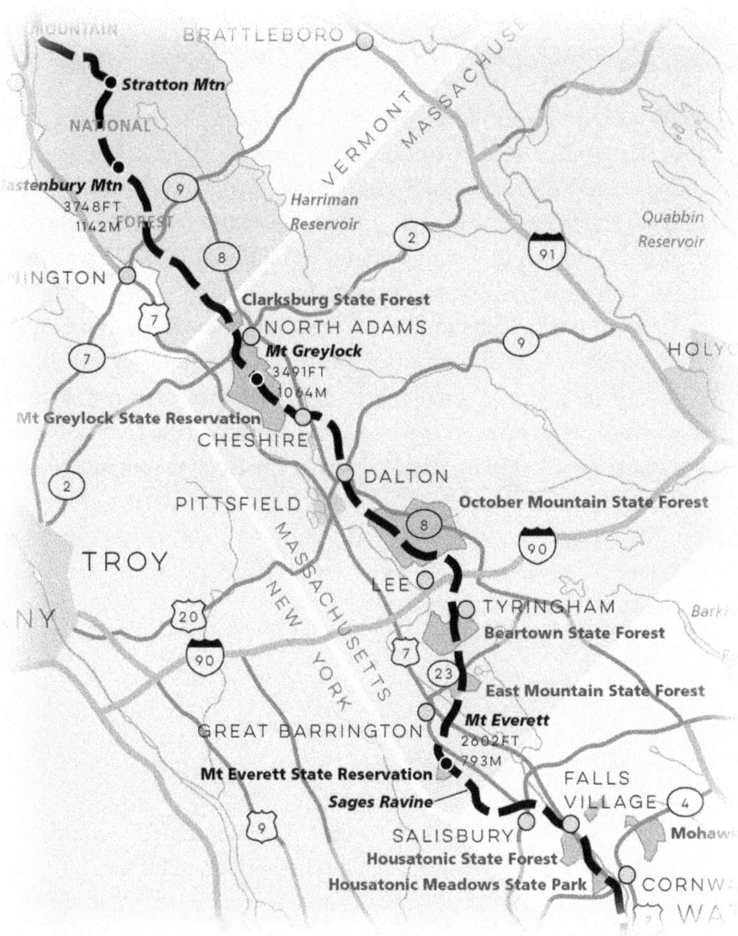

MASSACHUSETTS

90.8 MILES

SUNDAY, AUGUST 8, 2021

Great Barrington, Massachusetts - 21.4 Miles

Up at 6:00 a.m. and walking to get food and resupply. Everything closed, waited for the grocery store to open at 7:00. Back to Maria's, Big Spoon was hiking into town. Never saw him again.

Didn't get started until 9:00 a.m., many climbs and rock scrambles—slow. Met nobo Ball Sack, an interesting young woman with a wince-worthy trail name, then Cornbread, whom I met yesterday.

Pushed hard over hellish climbs and through ungodly mosquitoes. Went down hard on a bog log while swatting a mosquito, scrapes on my left leg.

Got out at 6:00 p.m. but couldn't get a hitch so walked to a restaurant that had just closed. They gave me ice water—a lot of it—and I yogied a ride into town. No room at the Travelodge, so I threw down at the Holiday Inn, way expensive. Ate at a brewpub, saw Ball Sack and Cornbread, who were sharing a room at the Days Inn. Wish they'd said something earlier, we could have split it three ways.

I feel weak and worn out. I don't know what to do tomorrow, zero or push on later in the morning.

MONDAY, AUGUST 9, 2021

Mile 1531.4 - 7.5 Miles

Had a good sleep, but still tired down deep. Up early. Ran a few errands to buy needed things, ate a big breakfast, then hitched out at 10:00 a.m.

Fully intended to hike 10 or 12 miles and camp, but the trail was so bad that I hitched back to Great Barrington and the Holiday Inn (doubly expensive). Glad I did, I need the rest. Beer, food, and now I feel much better.

TUESDAY, AUGUST 10, 2021

Upper Goose Pond - 20.2 Miles

Up early after a deep sleep, had breakfast, then couldn't get back to the trail until 9:00 a.m., hard to get a hitch.

Met Bare Paw along the way and hiked with him for a while. Stopped in at the "A.T. Stand" for a cold coke, reached Upper Goose Pond at 5:45 p.m.

Spoke with Liz the caretaker, nice young woman, then some surly nobos and indifferent sobos. Talked with Mighty Mouse about books and so on,

Me at the A.T. Trail Stand in Massachusetts

swam in the pond and feel quite clean now. Pitched my tent down by the pond. A good, breezy night ahead, I think.

WEDNESDAY, AUGUST 11, 2021

Dalton, Massachusetts - 20.6 Miles

Did not sleep well after all, and then what a god-awful day.

Up early, helped Liz make pancakes and coffee, hiking by 6:30 a.m. The trail was horrible. I felt as if I were trapped in hell, or more like the Mekong Delta, everything wet, sticky, muddy, the mosquitoes like a biblical plague. Stopped for a breather at the new Cookie Lady's place, then back to hell.

I mean hell.

Can't believe this is Massachusetts and not Vietnam. What the hell has happened here? The trail is like nothing I remember, and does not match the trail profile in AWOL. I think this is a relo, but why would they do that here?

Reached Dalton at 4:30p.m. and took a room at the Shamrock Village Inn. I'm too tired to even go out for food. The manager here, John, makes us wear masks in the office and laundry room, and hovers over everything, more suffocating than the humidity.

Tomorrow is supposed to be hot, hot, hot. It might be as bad as today. I never had a hard time through tomorrow's section before, but then I never had a hard time through any of this. I just don't trust the Massachusetts trail anymore.

Bare Paw pushed on to Cheshire. Tough kid. I was wobbling when I got here.

THURSDAY, AUGUST 12, 2021

North Adams, Massachusetts - 23.3 Miles

Today was a much better day. Up early as always, hiking by 6:00 a.m.

It was all old A.T. north of Dalton, so I flew into Cheshire early, rested, and pushed on over Mt. Greylock without too much trouble. Ran into Cornbread again, who must be yellow blazing.

All was well but got caught in a hard rain coming down Mt. Greylock. Stood out of the rain at the covered A.T. sign, ample trail magic in a cooler. Met a tough old gal named Mighty Mo. Now I'm at the Willows Motel. Nice place. I stayed here last time.

—

I have always appreciated the state of Massachusetts. Philadelphia gets credit for our Founding documents but Massachusettsmen led the action. Without them we wouldn't be the nation we are now, of that I am certain. The Appalachian Trail goes nowhere near any of the Revolutionary history of the coastal east, of Boston and Concord and Bunker Hill. Instead it cuts an almost straight line through the westernmost part of the state, through the rising terrain of the Berkshires, which form a gradual stairway toward the big show in New Hampshire.

My affinity for history aside, I have also appreciated Massachusetts for its Appalachian Trail, which climbs to serene pastoral views without inflicting wounds for the effort, and passes through small towns as a welcome diversion. Along the way are farms and fields, pretty hardwood forests, deep, still ponds, and decades of tradition. For the southbound thru-hiker, Massachusetts is the well-earned reward after grueling weeks in New Hampshire and Vermont. For the northbound thru-hiker, Massachusetts is a last state of grace.

Or was.

The two days I spent in Connecticut could have been weeks in my perception, considering the heat and humidity and marauding mosquitoes. I left out of Salisbury at nine o'clock in the morning, looking forward to better conditions ahead. Massachusetts was barely six miles away, Bear Mountain my last obstacle before the cool depths of Sages Ravine and the state line. I would take this as nothing, I assumed.

I assumed wrong.

The mosquitoes did not relent, nor the humidity, so the climb up Bear Mountain, which peaks less than 2500 feet, was disproportionately difficult. I dropped into Sages Ravine in sweltering heat, sweat drizzling from my elbows. Mosquitoes assaulted me through my clothes, became trapped in the tight weave of my leggings like fish in a gill net. Those six miles could as well have been sixty. Then came Mt. Race and Mt. Everett, two mountains that had never given me a moment's pause but this time demanded my deepest resolve. By the time I cleared them and began my descent toward Great Barrington, I was barely holding myself together.

I was wavering when I reached the Shays Rebellion Monument, with less than two miles to U.S. Highway 7 and relief in Great Barrington, but those two miles seemed insurmountable. I dropped pack in the shade of a tree near the monument, lay back to rest but was so overwhelmed by mosquitoes that I had to force myself up and keep moving. This was doubly debilitating. A quick pace would keep me mostly ahead of the mosquito cloud, but a quick pace in that heat consumed more energy than I had to spare. I reached the highway at six o'clock, twenty-one miserable miles behind me and feeling as if I'd just emerged from an equatorial jungle.

This was a Massachusetts I had never experienced, had never conceived. I held out an unsteady thumb for a hitch into Great Barrington, three miles to the west. The futility of this was soon apparent. I was a filthy, sopping mess. No one would ever stop to pick up someone who looked the way I did then, someone who would soak sweat into their seats and probably smelled worse than the rancid bottom of a grease pit. With barely the energy to swat the evening's mosquitoes, I turned and shuffled toward Great Barrington.

Not too far along I came to a restaurant on my right and went to it as if salvation had descended from heaven, only to find when I got to the door that the place had just closed! It was as if I could sight a cool, life-saving desert oasis just ahead but an impenetrable barrier stood in the way. I wasn't sure I had the strength to turn back for the road. While I was standing dizzy and indecisive, the door opened as if miraculously and a woman let me in.

I trudged in under the gaze of sympathetic eyes, managed to croak, "Water?" and was answered with a tall glass of ice water that could have been the best beer in the world the way I gulped it down. The woman gravely informed me that the kitchen was already closed, but she kept the ice water coming and soon I was restored enough to have a look around. Her last two customers, a middle-aged man and woman, were paying their bill and about to leave. I would soon have to follow them out the door, and with Great Barrington still three miles away, so in desperation I put on my best performance and successfully yogied a ride into town.

When I was in Salisbury, Big Spoon told me that he'd reserved a room at the Travelodge in Great Barrington, paid and nonrefundable, and that he doubted he would make it. It was there for me if I wanted it, so I tried. The desk manager, however, didn't share Big Spoon's generosity.

"What his name?" the guy asked me.

"Big Spoon," I answered wearily.

"No. What his real name?"

"His real trail name is Big Spoon. I don't know what his off-trail name is."

This nomenclature of mine often led to confusion with non-hikers, and often enough led to rolled eyes with thru-hikers. The Appalachian Trail is not a casual endeavor or, as I have already noted, easily forgotten. Trail names can imprint, creating a personality as authentic if not more so than the personality that began the hike. To me, a trail name is as real as a birth name, which is why I believe they should be accepted with sobriety. I'd met an interesting young woman that day whose trail name was Ball Sack, which drew a wince even though she went on to explain that her trail name did not refer to the prurient obvious. Later in the hike I would meet a young woman named Dick Nipple, which drew a double wince. To those two, their names might be perfectly fine, accepted in humor and perhaps left aside when they left the trail. Or perhaps not. And perhaps I'm too prudish about this but trail names can stick, the same way mistakes of youth can stick to unknown futures, surfacing at embarrassing moments. Perhaps those two would go on to brandish their trail names proudly, or perhaps they might go on to wish their trail names had been more representative of their journeys. Regardless, I didn't consider names as *trail* and *real*, but rather as *trail* and *off-trail*, each as legitimate to me as the other.

This did not impress the desk manager. I had foolishly failed to get Big Spoon's phone number, so I encouraged that desk manager to give Big Spoon a call. How could he possibly know which guest Big Spoon was, he flippantly asked, to which I wearily responded: "There can't be too many single guys registered for today who haven't checked in yet." It was now around seven o'clock.

"No." He shook his head. "Too many."

No, he just didn't want to put in the effort.

The Travelodge was also fully booked, or so he said, so I went dejected across the street to the Holiday Inn, not an inexpensive place to stay but when you feel as beaten down as I did you'll take anything without complaint. The Holiday Inn did have rooms—yes, pricey—and the staff were so gushingly hiker-friendly that I would have paid twice the price just to experience the novelty of it. Later, after a shower and food at a brewpub across the way, I felt much better, although with a weariness down deep, something slumbering in my bones. I'd pushed it too hard. One night of good sleep might not be enough.

I spent another of those nights that are rare for my age, rousing not once. I should have felt fully restored after such a deep sleep, but the weariness was still there the next morning, an intangible sense of sluggishness undeterred by multiple cups of coffee and a large breakfast. I was going to get a late start so perhaps this might pass. I needed some resupply and, despite years of avoidance, I needed mosquito repellent. I would endure the slimy, icky feel of it on my skin if it would give me any relief at all from those ungodly, pestilent clouds.

The resupply was easy, the mosquito repellent was not. Every store was out of stock. I finally settled on the very last bottle on the shelf at one store, not DEET but some lemon oil compound that claimed to work. I bought it in desperation, sprayed it on with a grimace, then sent a text to Ultra Burn, K-Bar, Rocky and Switz: *The mosquitoes are sick in MA. Bring DEET. Believe me!*

I caught a hitch out and was on the trail by ten o'clock. That lemon oil stuff actually worked, or at least worked well enough, although it left me feeling as greasy as the leavings in a frying pan. The mosquitoes were less of a menace but the humidity hadn't lapsed in the least, or the heat. That lingering weariness now seemed to infuse every bone. After seven and a half miles, at Lake Buell Road, I gave up in exhaustion and stuck out my thumb. I was picked up in minutes by a guy in a bright red Tesla who seemed not to spend a second thought on my oily, dripping condition. He drove me back to Great Barrington, where I was greeted by the same effusive staff at the Holiday Inn. I went to my room, showered, and fell right to sleep.

That was the first nero I'd taken in longer than I could remember. Rocky would say that a nero done properly was a beautiful thing, but to me it felt like a capitulation. It was what I needed, though, and it worked. I couldn't get a hitch out until nine o'clock the next morning, but when I finally did get back to the trail I took off with a renewed step, bound for Upper Goose Pond Cabin come what may, and damn the heat and mosquitoes.

Along the way I stopped in at the A.T. Stand, a cute red kiosk on a farm road near Tyringham that I understood to be the project of a couple of young girls who lived in a house up the hill, although their parents certainly had a hand in it. I discovered it for the first time on Hike 3 when I came through with Mr. Hiker, who was flabbergasted by the sight, even more flabbergasted when he found that he could charge his phone there. I was more impressed with the little refrigerator and the cold cokes. Everything was on the honor system, cokes, snacks, and all sorts of goodies. I left a little extra money for the girls in case a less scrupulous thru-hiker came through.

Afterward it was push, push, push, on a trail memorable in contour if not in heat. I reached Upper Goose Pond Cabin at five forty-five after twenty miles, sorely tired but no longer bone weary. The caretaker was a pleasant young woman named Liz, who'd brought out hot dogs and buns for everyone. The place was packed with thru-hikers going both ways, some of them too surly to endure. There was a thru-hiking family—there's always a family—mom, dad, a kid or two, and a toddler who rode in a frame the dad wore like a backpack. I spoke with them a while, about the challenges they faced, the courage it must take, the indelible memories their kids would surely retain throughout their lives, and what interesting lives those might become. Then I went to pitch my tent and swim in the pond.

Upper Goose Pond Cabin crowns a craggy and heavily wooded 112-acre pond. The site was purchased by the National Park Service in 1984 specifically for the Appalachian Trail. A provision of the sale was that the cabin and pond would remain free for use by hikers. The Appalachian Mountain Club manages the site, employing volunteer caretakers who, over the years, established the tradition of cooking pancakes every morning for the hikers.

The only person stirring when I broke camp the next morning was caretaker Liz, who was in the kitchen rattling pans in the light of her headlight, the stove warming in preparation for that morning's pancakes. I went in to assist, showing her how to light the old-fashioned propane lamps so she wouldn't have to work in the dark. There were no hikers staying in the cabin because of Covid precautions, so Liz and I were able to speak at a normal volume. I learned that she was the daughter of the new Cookie Lady, whom I would be visiting later that day. The original Cookie Lady had lived on a blueberry farm just off the trail nine miles or so farther on. She gave cookies to thru-hikers, another Appalachian Trail tradition that went back decades. I met her on Hike 1. She was ill on Hike 2, and on Hike 3 I blew through so I wasn't aware that she had passed away. Liz told me that her own family had been chosen to take over the blueberry farm, and that they intended to keep the cookie tradition alive.

Dawn rose as we ferried pancakes out to the picnic table. I ate my fill, said goodbye to Liz, then took off at six thirty with a bounce in my step. I knew the next section well. It would be an almost flat run for 20.6 miles to and through the town of Dalton, a chance to pick up the pace and recoup some energy. After Dalton I would push on the nine more miles to the town of Cheshire, where I'd be able to stuff myself at a hot dog stand on the trail route and then camp in a trail angel's yard, an easy twenty-nine miles behind me and Vermont coming the day after. I'd done it before, albeit going the other way, so I knew I could do it again.

But that's not the way it went.

I crossed the footbridge over the Massachusetts Turnpike less than half an hour later, paused to wave at the traffic passing below, and drew a few acknowledging honks in return. I felt buoyant, just the single climb up Beckett Mountain on the other side of the turnpike and then an easy day of big miles afterward. I could already visualize Vermont. Vermont! The Long Trail, the Green Mountains, the beautiful maple woods, lakes, and cold rushing springs. Vermont was my favorite state on the Appalachian Trail, and it was so close now. So close.

Beckett Mountain went well. The heat rose as I made the climb but at least the mosquitoes had dissipated, presaging the trail to come, or so I thought. I lulled myself into a sense of heady optimism, came cheerily down Beckett Mountain, and hiked into hell.

The trail was muddy, boggy, humid and sticky. The mosquitoes returned in frenzied clouds, so thick that I inhaled them, gagged on them, went into convulsions of coughing to get them out of my throat. The trail became what I call *picayune*, tediously crisscrossed with slippery roots, poor footing, jinking this way and that, and rocky little climbs one after another that took their toll on my reserves of energy early on. My pace slowed. The mosquitoes dove in, oblivious now to my lemon oil repellent, diving in with even greater frenzy when I slowed on those innumerable little climbs. By the time I reached the Cookie Lady after barely nine miles, I was bitten, slimy, soaking in sweat, and completely exhausted.

I sat on the porch out of the sun and munched on cookies. The Cookie Lady gave me a glass of cold lemonade, which I downed in a single gulp. I eyed the woods beyond the fields of blueberries as if they held a malign motive. The trail was different, not the trail I remembered. The heat was part of it, the mosquitoes certainly, but I had never, *never*, struggled through there, even in the rain. I couldn't reconcile it in my mind.

I reluctantly left the refuge of the Cookie Lady's porch and continued on, less secure in my step. The picayune trail grew worse. I went down on a slippery root. The mosquitoes descended like hyenas to a kill. I lifted myself, scraped and mud-streaked. I pushed on for suffocating hours, plashing through puddles, fighting mosquitoes, making little climb after little climb, on and on endless. This was not Massachusetts, this was the Mekong. The only things missing to solidify the image were poisonous snakes and stealthy Viet Cong. I had never been more miserable on a section of trail, notwithstanding the Hundred-Mile Wilderness on Hikes 1 and 3. I'd never experienced anything like it.

My mind sought an explanation, no, demanded one. This must be a trail relocation, I thought. There was no other explanation. But why would they do that? Why here? In that daze I again conjured conspiracy theories, of a trail deliberately rerouted in order to make it harder. That section of Massachusetts had been too easy so they'd stepped in to correct that oversight. I went down again, got up with a muddy throbbing bruise on the side of my right knee. I pushed on. I cursed. There was no reprieve, no good water, no place to take an untainted breath. There was that last climb before Dalton. I barely made it without having to crawl. When I hobbled into Dalton at four thirty it was as a haggard survivor of jungle warfare. There was no way I could push on to Cheshire as planned. I took a room at the Shamrock Village Inn and collapsed.

Later, after showering off the mud and the slime, eating two pizzas and drinking two beers, I felt better physically but emotionally I was furious. I fired off an ill-advised email to the Appalachian Trail Conservancy, accusing them of failing in their duty to maintain the integrity of the trail. That email was admittedly acerbic, although not profane. I regretted sending it the moment I tapped the button. Still, I wasn't the only thru-hiker who'd ever had a bad day on the Appalachian Trail. Surely they'd heard worse. In truth, I didn't know for certain if that section of trail had been relocated or not, or for what reason if it were. I made calls at the end of the hike, checking in with trail maintainers and others, none of whom knew anything one way or the other. The ATC could have disabused me of any misapprehension if they would have replied to my email but that was not a practice of what I had come to regard as the *New* ATC. I never heard from them, and still haven't.

I left out of Dalton the next morning in the same sultry air. Mosquitoes pricked my arms and ears as I walked through town, but fewer and fewer until I came to a sudden halt at the edge of a farm field and realized that the mosquitoes were gone!

The trail returned to the comforting familiar, no part of it outside of my memory, which made me even more skeptical about the trail of the previous day. I made quick time into Cheshire, too quick as it turned out because the hot dog stand wouldn't open for an hour and a half, longer than I was willing to wait. I pushed on, hot but unbitten, and began my climb of Mt. Greylock.

This was a long climb up the tallest mountain in Massachusetts. I took it at an easy step despite the heat, and made the nine or so miles to the peak in less time than I'd made those nine presumably flat miles through the jungle yesterday. I stopped for a break and a cold coke on top, took in the Veterans War Memorial Tower, Bascom Lodge, and a panoramic view that from some angles might look no different from what Thoreau had seen in his time. It was still stickily hot but that didn't seem to matter. A bank of dark clouds crowded the horizon, flowing toward the mountain like oil, so I cut my break short and started down the six miles to North Adams.

The sky went from blue to black before I got there, fat rain letting loose just as I reached Phelps Avenue in town. I took this for the half mile and found shelter under the awning of the Appalachian Trail information sign. There was a cooler of trail magic under the awning that had just been replenished, full of cokes and snacks and granola bars. I looked across the street to see an older woman with an oversized orange backpack making stoic progress through the rain. She seemed startled when I gestured her over for some of the trail magic. Her name was Mighty Mo. How old she was I could not tell, but she was definitely older than me. She had wizened features and a military bearing, as if she'd been a drill sergeant once. We spoke a few words, she selected one and only one granola bar, then resumed her trek through the rain.

Tough gal, I thought. Vermont was barely four miles away but the climb to the state line would be rocky and steep. It was getting late in the day and the rain would make that climb treacherous, so with twenty-three more miles behind me I called my friends at the Willow Motel in Williamstown and saved Vermont for tomorrow.

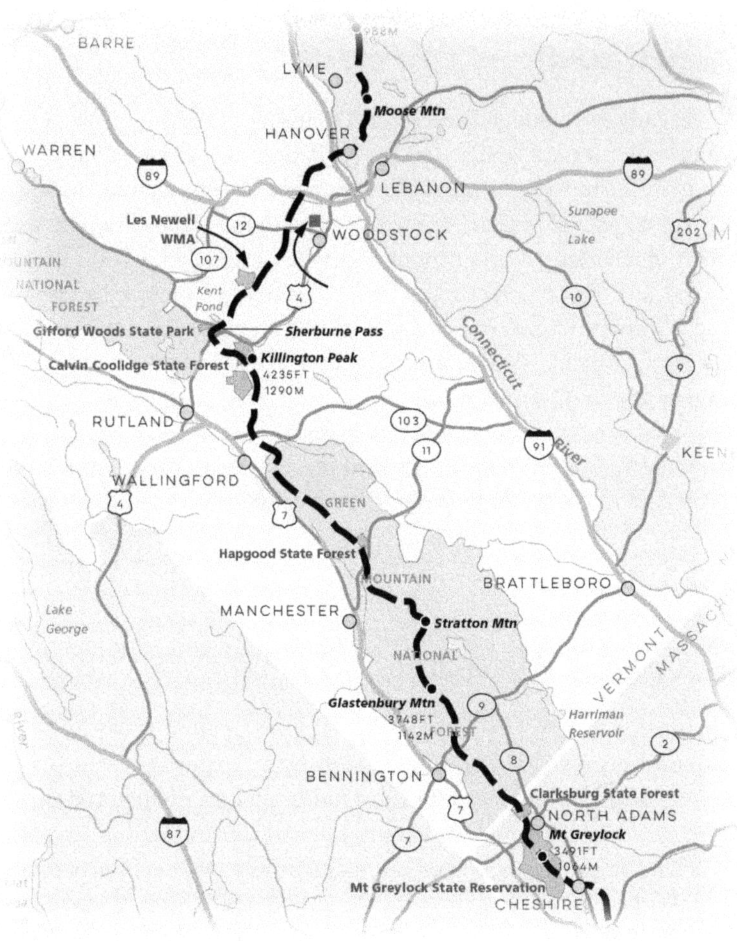

VERMONT

150.8 MILES

FRIDAY, AUGUST 13, 2021

Congdon Shelter - 14.1 Miles

Woke up early even though I tried to sleep late. Out of bed at 5:30 a.m. Breakfast wasn't served until 7:30, so I didn't get back to the trail until 9:00.

Long rock climb out of Massachusetts, poor blazing, humid, much sweat and I had no energy. Way off the trail, I saw Mighty Mo picking her way up through the bushes. At first I thought maybe she'd fallen, but she was moving along, and didn't answer when I hollered after her. I met a young woman on top who knew Mighty Mo and said that the lady was hard of hearing, and not to worry. Mighty Mo had probably lost the blazes, but would make it to the top by and by. Okeydokey.

The trail was a muddy mess. Threw down early because the climb over Consultation Peak in the heat just took it out of me. The shelter is full of thru-hikers and Long Trail hikers, so I'm tenting.

SATURDAY, AUGUST 14, 2021

Bennington, Vermont - 4.3 Miles

Another nero.

It rained most of the night, but I stayed dry inside the tent. Up at 4:30 a.m., hiking by 5:45, and not liking it. Muddy, muddy, muddy, and the mosquitoes were back. Hitched to Bennington and took a bunk at Catamount Motel. They've converted one of the rooms into a hostel. There's only one other hiker here.

Met and spoke with a group of sobos who were all crammed into one room. Can't remember their names, but they were good people. I made sure they knew that Greasy Creek Friendly would be open by the time they got there. They still have a long way to go, but maybe they'll remember.

The bunkroom filled up with thru-hikers this evening, but they all seem to be good guys. I hope I feel stronger in the morning.

SUNDAY, AUGUST 15, 2021

Mile 1635.6 - 21.1 Miles

I'm supposed to finish the trail in a month, but that seems unlikely.

Slept incredibly well despite all the latecomers. Stayed in my bunk until 5:45 a.m., then walked to the store for food and coffee.

Didn't get back to the trail until 9:00. It was cool, blessedly so, and no bugs! Had a glorious day of hiking, didn't even sweat. Met a few sobos, Long Trail hikers, and Mighty Mo once more. That old lady is really tough.

Stealthing here at 7:00 p.m. The best sites were taken, but I found a good spot to myself.

Good night.

MONDAY, AUGUST 16, 2021

Mile 1654 - 18.4 Miles

Cold this morning, fingers and toes numb. Really? Really?

Hiking by 6:00 a.m., up and over Stratton Mountain in the cool, then the trail conditions became poor and the next 14 miles were awful. I meant to push on past Manchester Center, but the trail wore me out. I threw down at an inn ½ mile off the trail. Some tourists took me out for pizza. That was nice.

Met a trail angel named Dandelion today, nice gal. She had beers and food, yum. I'm out early tomorrow and hope for better trail.

TUESDAY, AUGUST 17, 2021

Mile 1674 - 20 Miles

I now feel quite foolish.

The day started early, hiking at 6:00 a.m., over Bromley, which wasn't hard. Heavy sky but no rain. The trail was rocky in places, but I made good time. Passed Deja Vu, and caught up to Old School. We hiked to mile 1671.6 and caught a lucky ride to and from the store 3+ miles away. Resupplied and had a burger. Meanwhile it began to rain. Hiked 2 miles in the rain to Little Rock Pond Shelter, which was full, so hiked another ½ mile and stealthed at 4:00 p.m.—and then the rain stopped and the sun came out and I could have hiked 5 more miles! I didn't want to pack everything away wet, though, so I stayed.

WEDNESDAY, AUGUST 18, 2021

Mile 1700.3 - 26.3 Miles

Finally got some big miles, but this was not the plan and it nearly killed me to do it.

Slept soundly, up at 4:30 a.m., hiking in the dark at 5:30. Did 12 miles by noon, and never saw any of the people from yesterday. I thought I'd go 20 and camp, but it was too early at Governor Clement Shelter–and I don't like that area anyway–so I pushed on over Killington Peak in the damp and misty rain.

The nobo climb wiped me out. It took 2 ½ hours to get to the top. I was wobbling for lack of food when I got to Cooper Lodge Shelter on the peak. The shelter was nasty and it was cold up there, so I figured I would head down and find a place to stealth.

No such luck. 2 ½ hard miles later, getting dark, cold and wet, I found a little flat spot next to the Pico Camp sign and quickly pitched my tent. Cleaned up as well as I could, but I feel slimy. The tent is still wet from this morning, but I'm too tired and hungry to care.

I think I'm actually sticking out onto the trail a little, but no one's going to be through here this late, and I'll be gone early in the morning.

THURSDAY, AUGUST 19, 2021

Mile 1704.1 - 3.8 Miles

Yet another nero.

Slept surprisingly well, always do in the rain. Up at 6:00 a.m., proud of what I did yesterday. I endured, pushed through discomfort, and did okay. But I'm really tired. Killington Peak took everything I had.

Hiking by 6:30 in the rain, trail all mud. At U.S. Hwy 4, I realized that I didn't have to make the next climb to get to the side trail to the Inn at Long Trail, but could road walk less than ½ mile. So I did, and the inn was fully booked!

Okey, it turns out, is not the owner after all, but only helps on the weekends so he's not here this time. The lady who actually owns the place–didn't get her name–was unimpressed with my history at the inn, but she did find me a room at Killington Motel, where the owner Steven was quite nice and respectful. I did eat a big breakfast at the Inn at Long Trail, so got here, took a shower, then collapsed for several hours.

Now I'm washing clothes in the sink. Bought sandwiches and beer next door. I'm going to zero here tomorrow instead of Norwich. That tiredness is back and I need the rest.

FRIDAY, AUGUST 20, 2021

Mile 1704.1 - Zero

Zero number 9.

Took a zero here instead of Norwich because that's how things worked out and it's cheaper here anyway.

Took the bus into Rutland for resupply. Met all goals. The tent is drying in the sun even now, and I will lie around and do nothing for the rest of the day.

Nice people here at Killington Motel.

SATURDAY, AUGUST 21, 2021

Mile 1728.7 - 24.6 Miles

K-Bar's nineteenth birthday!

I figured out that my camp the other night was actually on the blue blaze to Inn at Long Trail! So I could have saved some muddy miles. Oh well, southbound turned-around again.

Out of the room by 5:30 a.m., then walked the mile and a half or so back to the trailhead. There were a lot of steep climbs today, slow, slow, slow. At 4:30 p.m., on the steep climb up Dana Hill, it began to rain heavily. I pitched the tent in a hurry—everything wet again—got in and set up, and then after 5:00 the rain stopped and the sun came out!

Decided not to push on. Why? Because 24.6 miles is enough for today, and I'll reach Norwich tomorrow regardless. I only have ½ liter of water, so no cooking. I hope to have a good night.

SUNDAY, AUGUST 22, 2021

Norwich, Vermont - 20.8 Miles

Slept well with the odd spatter of rain from the trees. Up really early—no coffee because no water—so hiking in the dark by 5:00 a.m.

Pushed on into a day that was wet for a moment, then sunny, then cloudy, then wet again. There were a lot of muddy climbs today. Norwich often seemed farther away than 20 or less.

Stopped in to see the trail angels in West Hartford, the same as last time, gave me the energy for a final push. Arrived at Norwich Inn at 3:30 p.m. The inn is almost empty because Hurricane Henri is on the way, lots of cancellations. They offered me a nice discount, so I'm going to settle in for a couple of days to wait out the storm.

MONDAY, AUGUST 23, 2021

Norwich, Vermont - Zero

Zero number 10, and I do need it. Things ache and need to heal.

Up at 5:00 a.m. of course, killed time until breakfast was put on. Walked into Hanover for some supplies, then back to the Norwich post office for my mail drop, which contained my cold weather gear and my third and—better be—last pair of shoes. Went ahead and mailed the kilt home. Carrying my cold weather gear now, I needed to save some weight. That kilt made a nice pillow and a warm blanket. I'm going to miss it.

That little bit of exercise wore me out. I am really bone tired.

TUESDAY, AUGUST 24, 2021

Norwich, Vermont - Zero

Zero number 11.

Get this: Hurricane Henri was a no show, everybody all worked up for nothing. The weather was actually great today, so this was an unnecessary zero. Oh well...

Up early to post field notes. Dried the tent in the sun that wasn't supposed to shine today. Resupplied and loaded the backpack. Now I'm just resting and waiting for the pub to open.

New Hampshire tomorrow. Time to get it on.

—

The Appalachian Trail is routed concurrently with Vermont's Long Trail for the hundred-odd miles between the Massachusetts state line and Sherburne Pass, where the Long Trail then branches off to the west toward Canada while the Appalachian Trail turns east toward New Hampshire. Three tribes of hikers share the trail during this interval: northbounders, southbounders, and Long Trail hikers.

I enjoyed meeting the Long Trail hikers. Their trail is about 273 miles long, much of it in terrain that's as grueling—if not more so—than the seventy-nine miles of the Appalachian Trail through the White Mountains of New Hampshire. Most of the Long Trail hikers I met were hardy souls with unique perspectives, who undertook their rugged hikes without the benefit of trail legs or tramilies. Most were also decidedly more approachable than many an aloof A.T. thru-hiker, pausing to talk without betraying any gesture of impatience or intrusion.

They often expressed their admiration for A.T. thru-hikers, the sheer enormity of the undertaking, ceding an almost shy deference, which I undertook to ameliorate with the same alacrity I'd shown section hikers farther south. Today we were both hiking the Appalachian Trail, I would tell them, and we were both hiking the Long Trail. I would go on to describe how every time I reached Maine Junction near Sherburne Pass, where the trails diverge (or converge for southbounders), I gave serious thought to making a hard right on the Long Trail and heading for Canada. Going northbound this time, that turn if taken would be a hard left into an undiscovered country. I envied them and their trail and hoped to join their ranks one day. In the meantime, though, we had one hundred miles in common regardless where we began our hikes.

My comments were usually well received, although not all Long Trail hikers were as sanguine. Some of them groused about the crowding, about the cavalcade of A.T. thru-hikers who swarmed the trail, swamped the shelters, and exuded intolerable airs of entitlement. At the same time I'd heard no few A.T. thru-hikers complain with equal vehemence, begrudging any inch of shelter space occupied by what they considered a lightweight Long Trail hiker. I would point out in these situations that the Long Trail was by no means a lightweight adventure, and predated the Appalachian Trail by a decade or more. In other words, we were guests in their house and should mind our manners.

I still had four miles of Massachusetts to complete before I could join the Long Trail, though, a couple of those up a steep boulder field, rising to a thousand feet or thereabouts above the North Adams hole.

The Willow Motel put on a unique organic breakfast that morning, which was so prettily displayed that I felt as if I were a vandal every time I replenished my plate, which was often enough to have done a vandal's work. The morning had dawned clear but sultry, the humidity cloying even in the early hours. I was returned to the trail at nine o'clock, took the footbridge over the Hoosic River, crossed Massachusetts Avenue, passed through the fenced alley between the houses, and began my climb.

The boulder field resembled a rockslide on a titanic scale. In level terrain it would have been a boulder ballet. In that steep terrain it was hand-over-hand in places. As a southbounder I'd skipped down that boulder field to North Adams and called it a good day. Now as a northbounder I had to work for every foot of elevation. In the full sun, the rocks were stovetop hot. Waves of heat rose as if from Alabama asphalt. The humidity was asphyxiating. I made steady progress just the same, pausing here and there to wring sweat out of my gloves. The blazing was poor, sometimes steering me far to the left or right to blaze my own way. On either side of the boulder field, which was perhaps a hundred or more feet wide, tangled bushes sprouted from between the rocks. Beyond these were the woods, cool shade but any bushwhack to reach that shade would be akin to navigating through prickly barbwire.

I wedged against a large boulder to catch a sultry breath, and spotted an orange figure scrabbling up through the bushes. That was odd. The figure was unmistakably Mighty Mo, who had either fallen from the ledge above or else had lost the blazes and gone bush.

"Hey," I hollered. "Are you all right? The trail's over here."

Mighty Mo continued her painstaking progress, never looking my way, so I shrugged and continued on, reaching the top a few minutes later.

There was a pretty view up top, some shade and sitting rocks. If memory served, Thoreau had made this climb, writing of the reward that comes from spirited exertion. I wondered if he'd made his climb on a broiling day like this one. Doubtful. I met a young woman up there taking in the shade. Her backpack identified her as a thru-hiker.

"There's a woman down there in the bushes," I said. "I hope she's all right."

"Yeah, that's Mighty Mo. I know her. She'll be okay."

"I hollered at her but she ignored me. I thought maybe she'd fallen or something."

"Naw, her hearing's not good. And those blazes sucked. She probably got lost is all. She's a tough lady. I've seen her get up in the morning and bust out a hundred push-ups."

"Really?" Geez, I couldn't do that even if I wanted to.

"Yeah. So don't worry, she'll make it."

"Okay, then."

I pushed on, joining the Long Trail a little over a mile later. The trail became muddy, squelching around my shoes. The nobos had always referred to Vermont as *Vermud*, which had been a mystery to me because I'd never encountered conditions on a southbound thru-hike that were any different from anywhere else. Now I knew what they meant, because while there were many strenuous climbs in Vermont there were also long saddles that acted like catch basins, as well as some lower-lying sections of trail that would not drain. I also noticed for the first time that there were no water diverters carved into the trail, not at all like the diligent water management on the trail down south. Therefore after a period of sustained rain, Vermont became, well, Vermud.

The climb up and over Consultation Peak, another thousand feet and on a trail of mud, wore me down in the heat. I pulled in at Congdon Shelter after only fourteen miles, pitched my tent and crawled wearily in, my leggings caked with muck.

It rained overnight, turning the trail into a sloppy, running mess. I was out early, sloshing through mud and slapping at mosquitoes, which had returned as if from nowhere and were in no way deterred by my lemon oil repellent. After only 4.3 sluggish miles, I reached Vermont Highway 9 and stuck out my thumb for a hitch into Bennington.

I had them drop me at Catamount Motel, where I stayed on Hike 3 and spent most of an evening describing mile-by-mile trail conditions in the White Mountains to a hyperactive nobo named Epic. The motel was fully booked this time but they'd converted one room into a hostel, which had plenty of bunks, so I took one, showered off the gritty lemon oil and the mud, then lay down with a nagging worry. This was another nero, prompted by the same weariness that had overtaken me in Massachusetts, and probably due to the heat but what if it went deeper than that? With my body fat long since burned away, what if I were doing damage to my heart muscle? My only remedy was to eat and eat and hope for the best. Surely after a good rest I'd get my strength back. I had to because the only other option was to quit, and that wasn't going to happen.

The bunkroom filled up as evening came on, but with amiable thru-hikers who understood the ethic. I slept surprisingly well, and woke up the next morning feeling refreshed and eager to make miles. From one day to the next the weather went from tropical to terrific. The air was cool and clean, not a biting bug aloft. I made the climb out of the Bennington hole without investing of a drop of sweat. Now *this* was my Vermont. The woods were a gorgeous green, the trail muddy but not picayune.

I stopped in at the Melville Nauheim Shelter, which was still crowded with hikers, one of whom was Mighty Mo. I shared a chuckle with her about her bush climb, then pushed on over the corrugated ridges, reveling in the day. I hiked until seven o'clock that evening, almost twenty-two miles beyond Bennington, and pitched my tent at the base of Stratton Mountain. I felt well, and came to the conclusion that it had only been the heat that had worn me down. It was now August 15. My goal had been to complete my hike on September 15. Looking ahead, that date was still possible although improbable. It all depended on New Hampshire and Maine. Vermont wouldn't stand in my way, of course it wouldn't.

When I awoke early the next morning, mere days from the tropical hell of Massachusetts, it was so cold that my fingers were too numb to operate my stove! I broke camp, my breaths lingering in the air, and began my climb up Stratton Mountain, which was a long although not difficult climb. The wind on top was ominously chill. I stopped for water at the caretaker's cabin, eschewed the lookout tower (because I was damn cold), then started down the mountain. From then on the trail went to hell, Vermud earning its reputation with a vengeance. Puddles in the middle of the trail became pools, became ponds. Skirting these led to trail widening, eventually creating oval muddy sloughs from one side of the trail to the other. The Green Mountain Club had posted signs entreating hikers not to widen the trail but to splash on through the puddles. Guiltily, I could not comply. To splash through would lead to saturated shoes, which would then lead to pruned feet, which would then lead to toe cramps and blisters. I hopped as many puddles as I could, stayed on rocks when I could, but too often I added my own damage to those who had come before me. I felt bad about that but helpless at the same time.

The entire day proceeded this way, constantly dodging puddles, hopping from one rotten bog log to another. In places, the trail maintainers had gotten away from bog logs, which had to be replaced every few years, and had substituted stepping stones as a more durable way to preserve their trail. Perhaps after years of hard work they might eventually lay stones along the entire trail in Vermont, which would be their only long-term solution short of cutting water diverters and relocating some lower sections.

A little over eighteen sloppy miles brought me to Vermont Highway 11, with Manchester Center some five odd miles west. I'd stayed in Manchester Center before but was reluctant to go there this time because, after late starts from Bennington and North Adams, I didn't want to spend another night so far from the trail. In the trailhead parking area I met a trail angel named Dandelion who was ferrying hikers back and forth. She offered me a ride but I declined. I did not, however, decline the beer she offered, or the snacks. Late in the day now, and with the climb over Bromley Mountain beginning right there, I hiked a half mile up the highway to Pinnacle Lodge, saving Bromley Mountain for the magic hour tomorrow.

Pinnacle Lodge catered mostly to winter sportsmen and was eerily deserted. The only other guests were a middle-aged husband-wife duo who were out on a New England road trip. The husband took a fascinated interest in me, then invited me out with them to a pizza place a few miles up the road, where they sat even more fascinated as I downed enough pizza to feed a lawn party they might throw back home. Afterward I yogied a side trip from them for resupply, then we returned to Pinnacle Lodge for the night.

I did take Bromley Mountain in the magic hour, which provided sensual rewards aplenty despite an occluded sky. I met thru-hikers who'd camped on the grassy, rounded top, only then stirring in the gray dawn as I powered by, the melon-glow of the misty sun casting the summit in a delicate peach hue. The trail was rocky in places, muddy in others, but I kept a good pace. The mud was tedious and messy but Vermont remained my favorite state anyway, with its splendid views and rich forests. In times past, pipes ran down the mountains from maple tree taps, delivering the sap that would become the famous syrup. I hadn't seen these since Hike 1, and wondered if the trail had been relocated or if those taps had been removed. Stepping over the pipes back then, which had eroded out of the trail in places, had never seemed an inconvenience or an intrusion to me, but instead served as evidence that the trail and local industry could exists side by side.

The sky became heavier as I continued on, the air cool and bugless. In the early afternoon I caught up to a young thru-hiker named Old School, whom I'd met a few days earlier. Old School wore a lock of purple hair and had earned his trail name because he, unique for his generation, still sent handwritten letters to people. I liked him from our first meeting. His avant-garde persona might have deterred other people of my generation but I found it charmingly genuine. Earlier in the hike I might have asked him to partner with me. By now, though, I accepted that I would be finishing alone. Ultra Burn and K-Bar were so far back that they'd never catch me, while Rocky and Switz remained variously five to seven days behind. I was pushing deeper and deeper into pockets of northbounders who'd left Springer Mountain a month or more before I had, thru-hikers I would meet once and never again. Old School and a couple of others were the exception. Beyond them, I had become a southbounder on a northbound trail, with the same attitude, the same solitude, and the same dearth of community.

Old School and I stayed together for a few miles, my pace often too much for him but then he would get out ahead for a time. We were together when we reached the trailhead at Danby-Landgrove Road. A family in a camper van offered us a ride three miles down the mountain to a general store, which left me leery because a hitch back to that remote trailhead would be difficult if not impossible. To our surprise, the father of the expedition offered to wait on us down there and then bring us back. With that assurance we jumped into his van without reservation, meandering down the winding road to Danby, a crossroads of little traffic. The rain unleashed in a chilling deluge just as we arrived.

A lady ran the store with her younger daughter. Both were exceptionally polite and attentive, although their shelves had been picked over as if from a public panic. The lady apologized and explained that they'd been having a hard time getting merchandise because of Covid. They had a kitchen, though, and cooked us some fat hamburgers. Afterward I selected a few sugary things to add to my food bag and then we returned to the trail.

Old School and I hiked together the two miles to Little Rock Pond Shelter, bundled against the chilling rain. The shelter was full of dripping thru-hikers so we pushed on. A half mile later, at about four o'clock, I stepped into a stealth site and tugged out my tent. Old School pushed on through the rain, his purple lock pasted against his face. Once set up, in and dry, the rain stopped at once and the sun came out, bright and warm. I couldn't believe it–I couldn't believe it! If only I'd stayed with Old School...it was early enough that I could have hiked five more miles! And I debated doing just that, which would mean rolling up a wet and muddy tent only to repeat the process in a couple of hours. So with twenty miles done for the day, I stayed, tapping my foot against the tent wall through what became a long evening.

I was hiking by five thirty the following morning, twelve miles by noon and meeting no thru-hiker whom I'd ever met before. The day was routine and fast: Greenwall Shelter, Minerva Hinchey Shelter, Clarendon Shelter. I stopped in at a store near North Clarendon and bought a couple of breakfast biscuits for later. Soon I reached Governor Clement Shelter, almost twenty miles for the day but still too early to throw down for the night. Governor Clement Shelter is an interesting and historic stone building with a fireplace, but it lies too near a gravel road and is often visited by Vermont's version of rednecks. I'd never stayed there but would have if it had been located in a more remote area. As it was, the climb up Killington Peak began right about there, only 4.3 miles to the top, easily doable. I had, after all, done it three times before. There was also a stone shelter on top and a wonderful piped spring. It was a good goal, a good place to spend the night. What a magnificent sunrise lay ahead, what a magic hour to follow, and with relief soon after at the Inn at Long Trail in Sherburne Pass. The decision wasn't difficult. I went for it.

There had been patchy sun throughout the day, interspersed with layered clouds that thickened toward the end of the day. I left Governor Clement

Shelter in a patch of that warming sun, which drove off the chill I'd arrived with and set me in good spirits for the climb. I hadn't gone far when the sun slipped once again behind the clouds, this time to stay. The rain began soon after, more of a cold, permeating mist than anything with a purpose. I hunched into it and kept on going, then came around some rocks to the base of my climb and looked up in horror.

I'd only ever come down this, and early in the day on each hike. The sky had been a picture of blue last time, the air warm but not hot. The rocks had been dry, the footing secure, the descent so unmemorable going southbound that I'd never paid it much notice. This time I did notice, yanking myself into the present tense and writing in my field notes later:

> Imagine a damp, boulder-clotted gorge about a half mile long. The boulders are stained granite-dark in the dripping wet of a chill, overcast afternoon. Some are sharp wedges, others are rounded. Some are small enough to lever with heavy iron bars while others are the size of stalled cars. All are furry with moss, slick at their tops, and beading water like the pates of sweating football players. Now tilt that gorge to near vertical, just below the angle of repose in which the boulders could begin to tumble out, and you have the opening climb for a northbounder going over Killington Peak in Vermont.
>
> As a southbounder I've gone over this mountain three times. There's a shelter up top, an old cabin less its windows. There's a gushing piped spring and a bit of a view. The surrounding forest is dense with spruce, the very air is scented with it. It's a lovely place, one simply has to climb up to it.
>
> Climb.
>
> The southbound climb is no passive endeavor, but it's nothing like this. In the past, I have only gone down this waterfall of boulders, which presents its own challenges and opportunities for hike-ending injuries but at least gravity was working with me then. Now gravity will work against me for at least the next couple of hours.
>
> Climb.
>
> Shorten up on the poles, grasp them by their shafts. Catch a tip in a crack and pull, high-step, right foot slipping into a wedge that squeezes toes into a painful point. High-step again, swing the hips around, change direction, slip to a knee, a little blood, not enough for further notice. Push up, step over, throw a leg as if over a saddle. Green crud coats an inner thigh now. Do it again, step over there. Risk jumping from one boulder to the next. A fall would be calamitous. Keep going, working with stolid determination.

Clear the boulders at last and onto a steep, narrow rock-studded track laced like a Medusa with tendrils of slippery roots. Skate off a root, spread-eagled now and tipping backward, throw out a pole to arrest the fall. The tip catches between two roots and won't come loose. The stance is precarious. Groin tendons are pulling. Another centimeter and something will rupture. Take a breath, yank, the tip comes loose. Hop in place, reposition the feet. Push hard with the poles to take another stutter-step up. A mosquito at the back of a knee, stings, can't free a hand to slap it.

Climb.

Two and a half hours under almost constant strain, here and there a muddy slough to squelch through in two steps, but at least gravity eases for those brief moments, one section so steep I crab up it sideways stabbing hard with the poles. Without trekking poles I couldn't climb this. Some hikers do but I don't know how they manage.

The climb itself is not the issue. After almost 1700 miles, I'm in full thru-hiker form. I'm lean, I have my hiker legs. My heart does not race, but stays well below 100 beats per minute. I'm breathing deeply through my nose, not panting. My quads do not burn. I have no fat left between my muscle fibers. There's nothing there *to* burn. No, the issue is that climbs are slow, climbs are boring, and they burn calories at an unsustainable rate. I swear I can feel my stomach empty as I go, the two breakfast biscuits with egg, sausage, and cheese I put in earlier metabolizing and going into this effort. Were I to eat two of those at home they would metabolize into the fat of my butt. I have no butt now to bother with, and no more breakfast biscuits in my belly. My stomach gurgles and complains. Wedged against the incline, I pull out an energy bar, gobble it down. I'll fall if I reach back for my water bottle. My throat is dry, my lips sticky with chocolate, bits of peanut between my teeth.

Climb.

I pass a thru-hiker I've met before, he going down the incline rather than up. He's slackpacking in reverse, a gimmick to avoid the hard climb. My respect for him drops a measure. His hike is not subject to judgment by me, but we don't have this in common now. Our hikes have diverged. At camp or shelter we won't be able to share this experience any more than if we were hiking different trails. Still, his hike, not mine.

It begins to rain in earnest.

I make the summit at six thirty, shivering in the splattering rain and cold wind. The cabin shelter less its windows offers little protection from the wind. The floor is cold rock, the bunks filthy from the sweat of countless hikers past. Wearily, I decide to go down the mountain, find a place to stealth camp. The days are much shorter now, it's dusky, a shade pulled on the day, but at least another hour's worth of languid light. I'll find someplace to stealth down below in the trees, which will block the cold wind and provide a better night's sleep. There'll be something, there must, maybe around the next turn, a bit of forest floor just flat enough for my small tent...

Down.

Slipping in the mud, a root catches a toe and I fall. Pain stabs into my right knee. I lever myself up and continue on, the forest at a sharp slope on either side of the trail. I scramble up into the woods at one point, thinking I eye a flat spot up there, but it's an illusion. Down, sliding a few feet here and there, big toe numb from kicking into rocks. Down, down, darkness falling, trees sentinels in the mist and dripping steadily like their own canopy of cloud.

Down.

Two and a half miles in the gloom with nowhere to camp until I come to the blue-blazed trail to Pico Camp with a spot next to the signpost just large enough and flat enough to accommodate my tent. I pitch my tent right next to the trail as night finally falls, get inside muddy and wet and am suddenly so desperate for food that I don't care about the mud smears where I'll soon sleep or how wet and grimy I am. I get my stove going outside the tent flap, boil water, urgently rip open a pack of noodles with my teeth. The water doesn't seem to boil fast enough. I turn up the heat. If I empty the canister I don't care, I just need food with a desperation that's primal.

I pour boiling water into the foil pouch of noodles, burn my fingers but that's a secondary concern. Crease the pouch and wait for the noodles to soften. This is taking too long. Probe with my spork, stir the noodles. They're still a bit crunchy, but soft enough to digest. I put 600 hot calories in my stomach in less than a minute, follow that with a 480-calorie protein bar, 300 calories of peanuts and then 300 more. 1680 calories stills my stomach but comes nowhere near what I consumed on that climb. I burned some muscle going over Killington Peak, and wonder distantly which muscle it was.

I wipe myself down with a bandana and water from my bottle, wriggle into my sleeping bag and am unconscious in an instant. This was one climb among many, slow, calories dripping into the mud, no rest, no respite, and yet we go on, we follow every white blaze. Why? Because it's the damn Appalachian Trail, that's why.

I slept the sleep of total exhaustion, rousing not once in the night, and awoke at my usual time feeling more functional than I had expected. It was a murky morning, damply cold but at least my fingers weren't numb. Mist ticked against the tent walls like an excited collision of atoms. I set coffee to boil and then marveled at my accomplishment while I sipped, 26.3 miles culminating in a physical strain I'd never borne before. I'd climbed above 8000 feet on the PCT with less effort!

But I didn't begrudge the climb. It was, after all, what MacKaye had envisioned from the outset, a way to test one's self in a reality far beyond any urban existence. If I'd caught Killington Peak in good weather it would have been the exultant finale to an exceptional day. I might even have pushed on to Sherburne Pass for my first thirty-miler since Shenandoah. As it was with the rain and the muck and the slippery roots, each next step an effort of will, twenty-six miles was a triumph, something to take pride in, something to boast about, especially at my age.

I felt weary down deep though, no doubt about it. That climb had consumed the very last joule circulating in my body, searching it out wherever it resided and then greedily burning it, fueling those last miles by cannibalizing any hapless muscle available. My stomach knotted in hunger, painful spasms that belied the calories I'd put in last night. I ate my last bag of peanuts, boiled my last two pouches of noodles, then broke my muddy camp and pushed on into the gloom for a short 3.8 miles that felt like forever.

My mind was not quite clear when I reached U.S. Highway 4 and Sherburne Pass. I stood in a light drizzle as cars swished by, tried to organize the landscape into something comprehensible but found this almost as trying as yesterday's climb. There was a blue blaze somewhere to the Inn at Long Trail, a trail fixture since long before my time, and a place I'd stayed three times before. On Hike 1 The Dude and I had followed the white blazes down to the inn's parking lot, where we stowed our backpacks, ate our fill at McGrath's Irish Pub, and were given an historical tour of the place by a congenial old fellow named Okey. After our stay we followed the white blazes across U.S. Highway 4 and made the climb up Pico Mountain to continue our journey.

On Hike 2 the white blazes brought me directly to the highway, which left me befuddled. I flagged a passing car for directions, learned that the trail had been relocated and that the Inn at Long Trail was now a half mile up the highway. Okey was there to explain what had happened, something about the trail being rerouted to bypass the ski slopes, which the old trail had crossed.

There was a blue-blazed trail now, he told me, blue blazes that followed the old white-blazed route.

So on Hike 3 I took that blue-blazed trail, dropping into the inn's parking lot as in old times and not feeling self-conscious in the least for missing some white blazes. That blue-blazed trail was, after all, the *real* Appalachian Trail. I would defy any purist to tell me otherwise.

Now on Hike 4 I was going in the other direction and found myself southbound turned-around, not even sure which direction to go at the highway. I plumbed deeply into my memory to recall Hike 2, turned to face south and asked myself, "Which way did I turn? It had been a sunny afternoon, so where was the sun then?" I worked it out. On Hike 2 the afternoon sun had been over my right shoulder. I'd turned left. This time I needed to turn right.

It was while plodding up the wet shoulder that I realized I had actually pitched my tent last night at the blue blaze junction that would have led me down to the Inn at Long Trail in a mile or less! Southbound turned-around. I had only ever made that as a climb so I didn't recognize it. I could have slept indoors last night, with ample food at the pub next door! I laughed at the irony. I didn't feel foolish, though, because I'd done it. I'd endured and I'd survived.

The rain came on with a vengeance as I reached the inn. I left my backpack under an eave then stomped in the foyer to leave as much of the wet there as I could. Once inside I looked for Okey. A woman at the front desk eyed me severely.

"Is Okey around?" I asked.

"No, he only works weekends."

"Really? He owns the place, doesn't he?"

She bore into me then with hard eyes. "No," she said huffily, "*I* own the place. Okey only helps out."

I was both addled and dumbfounded if the two can manifest side by side. "I'm sorry," I said, searching for sense in this new reality. "He's the only one I ever saw when I came here, so I thought he was the owner. He really knew the place. He showed me around twenty years ago, and told me a lot of things about the inn and the trail. This is my fourth thru-hike—" I stood a little taller, "—and my fourth stay. It's a tradition of mine."

"Well good for you," she said unimpressed, "but we're fully booked."

That took a moment to settle. The woman turned her attention to some ledgers as if my presence were an intrusion. "Aw, man," I muttered. "My streak is broken."

She shrugged without looking up, continuing her perusal of columned figures. I stood with abated breath, expecting her to look up at any moment and tell me that with my history she would *find* a place for me. She didn't.

Instead: "Well as I said, we're fully booked."

That was going to be the end of any further discussion of the matter. My shoulders slumped. My stomach growled. Breakfast was being served in the restaurant, the aromas of coffee and bacon limning the air. "Am I allowed to go in there if I'm not staying here?" I asked, forlorn.

"Sure, go ahead," she answered, eyes fixed on her ledgers.

So I wobbled into the restaurant, took a seat, and ate as much food as they could bring me in the thirty minutes before they closed out the breakfast service. Afterward, feeling marginally better inside although still grungy outside, I returned to the front desk, where the woman was still scanning her ledgers in deep concentration. Rain pounded against the windows. Lakes were forming in the parking lot. I discarded all decorum.

"Look, ma'am," I said. "I'm desperate here."

She looked up with withering annoyance. "I'm sorry but there's nothing I can do."

"Can you help me find some other place to stay around here?"

She nodded toward some brochures on a table. "You can look through those."

Would I could have. My eyes wouldn't focus, my reading glasses and phone were double-zipped outside in my backpack, and I didn't know the area anyway. "Ma'am, I need your help. Will you make some calls for me, some place close?"

To her credit, her features softened a bit at that. "Sure," she said.

She made a few calls, and after some minutes jotted a name and phone number on a slip of paper for me. "Killington Motel is not far. Steven says he'll hold a room for you."

"Thanks," I gushed in relief. "How do I get there?"

"There'll be a bus in a few minutes."

So, after the expiration of those few minutes, I was on a bus bound for Killington Motel, which was not more than a mile away but would have been a trial if I'd had to walk it in the cold rain.

Steven at Killington Motel was effusive and friendly. He got me checked in quickly, gave me an apple and a doughnut (which I devoured on the spot despite my big breakfast of less than an hour earlier), and showed me to my room, where I showered, fell back on the bed, and went right to sleep.

This was yet another nero, coming at the beginning of my big push for Mt. Katahdin and sending my goal of September 15 further into the realm of improbability. My next zero was to be in Norwich, Vermont, a couple of days away, where I had a mail drop waiting; and although I went through the motions later that day of hiking out the next morning, doing my laundry in the sink and resupplying at the convenience store next door, I felt a deep-rooted fatigue that no amount of food and comfort would amend. I was tired, just plain tired, resigned as I lay down that night that I was going to zero the next day. This wasn't an elective choice, this was an absolute physical imperative. One thought did humor me, though. The Inn at Long Trail had been fully booked. If I hadn't been southbound turned-around at my campsite the previous night I would have doggedly pushed on through the dark and rain, down the blue-blazed trail to the inn, where I would have been turned away and without the energy to do anything other than collapse in the parking lot. Matters, it turns out, often work themselves out for the better if we let them.

I awoke the next morning at the usual time, but lay late in bed because I simply couldn't summon the energy to get up. My chest felt hollow, my brain fuzzy, every bone like ballast. Zero number nine, I mouthed in disgust. I'd planned only five zeros for the entire hike. My body demanded otherwise, though. That was the reality. I wouldn't make Mt. Katahdin by September 15. I let that goal go, refocused on my situation, my physical condition, and what it would take to get through the Whites and the state of Maine. I would do what I had to do to finish the hike. That was the goal now, and only that. I would take a zero every other day if necessary.

It dawned a brighter morning. Soon I was limber enough to make my weary way outside, where I spread my tent in the sun to dry, along with my backpack and sleeping bag. By noon I felt strong enough to venture to Rutland for some supplies the convenience store didn't have. I took the bus, which runs back and forth regularly enough to inspire confidence, and returned to my room with supplies enough to see me to Norwich, as well as enough food and beer on hand to see me to the next morning. Breakfast biscuits were my new discovery on this hike. They were high-calorie, kept well, and were reasonably lightweight. I loaded these into my backpack then thoroughly cleaned the room. I'd told Steven that I would be leaving early and that when he saw the room it would be as if I hadn't been there at all, hoping this would even out some of the bad experiences with thru-hikers he had told me about.

I took off for the mile and a half road walk to the trailhead at five thirty the next morning, passing the Inn at Long Trail as it slumbered in the predawn. The weariness went with me, not completely exiled by my long rest. At Maine Junction I waved goodbye to the Long Trail, tempted as always to turn that way and see what was. I caught a cell signal on Quimby Mountain, so sent K-Bar a birthday text. I wondered where she was for her nineteenth birthday, and wished more than anything that I could have been there to celebrate with her, the way she'd been there in Tennessee for me.

There were a lot of climbs, which I took stoically. The trail was picayune in places, although not as muddy. Somewhere in there was the ladder down a rock face, not an obstacle so much as a novel break from routine. I pushed on and on, past Wintturi Shelter, where I spent the Fourth of July with The Dude and an Israeli girl on Hike 1, and where on Hike 2 I got up in the middle of the night to sleep on the ground because of all the snoring nobos. Next was Dana Hill, steeper than I remembered. It was four thirty by then, twenty-four and a half miles into the day. The rain came as I neared the top.

I hastily went off trail and found a place to pitch my tent, and got in before I was too wet. The rain drummed hard for half an hour then ceased as suddenly as it had begun. The sun came out, sending cheery rays through the dripping woods and sending me toward a decision. It was still early, Thistle Hill Shelter only seven and a half miles on, which would then set up a quick thirteen miles into Norwich, plenty of time to get in early, get my mail drop, and get the benefit, but my inchoate weariness warned me off. I'd make Norwich tomorrow regardless. I didn't need to push myself. What I needed to do was rest.

I set out in the dark in the morning, passing the tents of other thru-hikers who'd been caught in yesterday's rain. The day felt interminable, and this over terrain where I'd always made big miles, even on Hike 1. Norwich seemed farther away the closer I came to it. I stopped in to visit some trail angels in West Hartford. I'd met them on Hike 3. They lived in a house just off the trail route, and were generous with hot dogs and cokes. I learned from them that Hurricane Henri was even then bearing down on New England. People were evacuating low-lying areas, boarding windows and preparing for the worst. Thru-hikers, they told me, were getting off the trail en masse or else hunkering down where they were. A couple of them had already thrown down in the barn loft next door.

I gazed at the sky, which did have that peculiar, washed-out calmness about it, not even birds fluttering across my view. Norwich was only eight and a half miles farther on. I thanked them for the information and the trail magic, and got moving.

I reached Norwich Inn at three thirty and found it all but emptied. The lady at the front desk told me I'd been lucky, that they'd been fully booked but there'd been so many cancellations because of the hurricane that I now had the place practically to myself. She offered me a good discount, which encouraged me to ride out the hurricane there instead of in Hanover, New Hampshire, just across the Connecticut River. I loved Norwich Inn and had stayed there before. The elegant old place was hiker friendly and had its own brewpub, but it wasn't cheap. With the offered discount, I booked the next two days, long enough to recover my strength in their brewpub and ride out the hurricane at the same time.

Hurricane Henri didn't arrive at our latitude. Massachusetts took a lashing, but those of us in this part of New England went unaffected. On the very day that the hurricane was forecast to howl, I was out on the lawn behind Norwich Inn drying my tent under a bright, warm sun.

Zeros ten and eleven were my first (and only) consecutive zero days of the hike, and I made the most of them. My mail drop at the Norwich post office contained my cold weather clothing. The warmth of the day belied the need, but I knew that would change as soon as I climbed Mt. Moosilauke, the opening salvo of the White Mountains, and only a few days away. I now had neoprene gloves, waterproof socks, and a base layer from neck to ankles. The extra weight meant it was finally time for the kilt to go home. I packed that kilt into a box and gave it a sad goodbye. It had been my defining characteristic early in the hike, and it had its practical uses as a pillow and blanket, but I could no longer justify the additional weight.

Also in that mail drop was my third and last pair of shoes. The pair I'd bought in Front Royal had gone 777.5 miles, two hundred less than my first pair but these had taken on Pennsylvania. There was still some life left in them but I didn't trust them to hold together for what was to come, where my success if not my very life depended on good traction.

Those consecutive zero days also restored my energy and confidence. I ate continuously, so much that my shrunken stomach would ache after each sitting. I slept deep, nine or ten hours each night. My various pains waned. I washed and prepped my gear, everything clean and ready for the big push. New Hampshire was less than a mile away. This was it, the boogerbear out front of seventeen hundred miles, as if all else had been preamble. I needed my strength, and I needed every bit of resolve I could muster.

The trail would not be routine from here on, and it would not come easily.

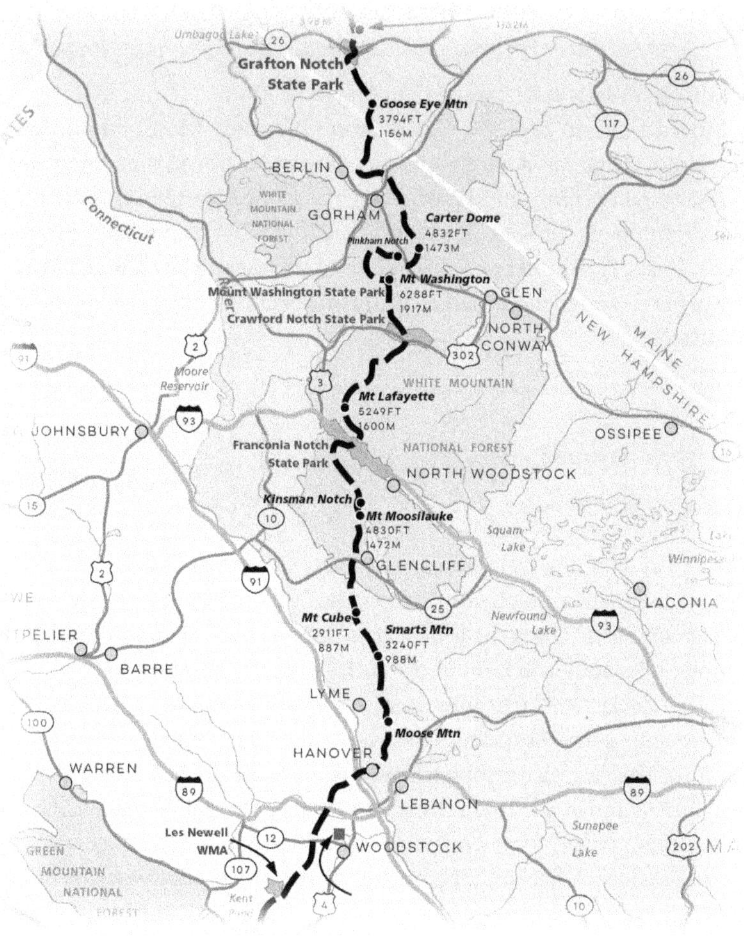

NEW HAMPSHIRE

160.9 MILES

WEDNESDAY, AUGUST 25, 2021

Mile 1775.3 - 25.8 Miles

Got the good early start I wanted, hiking by 5:00 a.m.

Moved fast and did 15 miles by noon. Crushed Moose Mountain, but then Holts Ledge was a hard climb and slowed me down; then Smart Mountain was a killer climb, and I mean tough as all hell going in this direction.

Caught up to Old School, who beat me to Fire Warden's Cabin. Too many nobos, so cooked dinner and pushed on to this stealth site a mile farther. I'll have a much better night here, I think, and get a good jump on the crowd back there.

THURSDAY, AUGUST 26, 2021

Hikers Welcome Hostel - 19.1 Miles

Woke up at 4:00 a.m. feeling fine, hiking by 5:30 in the dark.

Mt. Cube was a tough climb and ridge walk. Catching it early was wise. Made good miles. Met a thru-hiker named Lyric and hiked with him a while, talking philosophy and politics the entire time. He's a sharp kid.

Raced the last 4.5 miles into Glencliff, meeting the two "Tops" once again, who are nobos but were going sobo every time I met them, beginning back in Vermont. They have a car somewhere, and are leapfrogging in reverse. Decent guys, but a strange way to do the trail. Also met Dandelion again at the trailhead, and we talked for a while. Sweet girl. She gave me another cold beer. I couldn't visit with her too long because there were literally swarms of nobos behind me, all bunched up because of the hurricane, and I was afraid the hostel would fill up before I got there.

At the hostel, a smug guy named Fine has three sobo thru-hikes, and caretaker Varicose also has multiple hikes, although I couldn't quite link together his rambling stories. He has a chip on his shoulder about thru-hikers, and thinks the AMC is the greatest thing since LED headlights.

It rained earlier, but man it's hot up here in the bunkroom now. I'm soaking in sweat just lying here. But I did it! I beat my best time ever through that section. I'm resupplied for five days—man my pack is heavy now—and tomorrow, while all these people are still asleep, I'm going to set out to climb Mt. Moosilauke and do something I've never done before: I'm going to transit the White Mountains in one uninterrupted hike!

—

While Norwich, Vermont is uncommercially pretentious, it's sister city across the Connecticut River, Hanover, New Hampshire, is exactly the opposite, with the exception of the pretentiousness, which is an expected attribute of an Ivy League town. Hanover is the home of Dartmouth College, after all. There are high-end shops, cafes, movie theaters, pizza joints, fast-food chains, and convenience stores, most of which are absent in Norwich. I do appreciate Norwich for its quiet historicity but it's not a place to resupply, which is why I'd hoofed it into Hanover on the first day of my twin zeros.

The Appalachian Trail is blazed through Hanover, mostly skirting the college campus. There's a blue-blazed route to Robinson Hall on campus, the headquarters of Dartmouth Outing Club, which maintains the trail up to the top of Mt. Moosilauke. Thru-hikers can go to Robinson Hall (in non-Covid years) for information, free Wi-Fi, and lists of trail angels. Hanover is also where Bryson lived when he found the inspiration for and wrote his improbably popular book. Bryson has since repaired to England where he now lives undisturbed by unannounced thru-hikers calling at his door (at least as I've been told, I was never one of them).

Hanover is hiker-friendly for the most part, the way many families are friendly to the eccentric cousin at Thanksgiving, with food and sincere good wishes but not necessarily an invitation to stay the night. On Hike 1 a pair of fraternities allowed thru-hikers to sleep in their basements and use their kitchens and common areas. By Hike 2 these were gone, with nowhere else to stay in Hanover except a motel well out of town. It was the same on Hike 3, which is how I came to discover Norwich Inn. Now there's a hostel in Hanover. I didn't go there, having thrown down in Norwich, but it was gratifying to know it was there just the same. What I didn't learn until later was that the hostel was brimming with thru-hikers who'd piled in to wait out the hurricane that never came, a mini bubble that would soon be on the move.

I crossed the bridge over the Connecticut River at five o'clock in the morning, through a slumbering stillness uninterrupted by any urban intrusion, not even the clunk and beep of a garbage truck. No headlights flashed in my eyes or cast my shadow ahead, no distant sirens wailed. A Hanover patrol car sat stealthily in the median at the midpoint of the bridge, its bumper tapping the state line. I got the sense that the officer inside was asleep.

I continued on into town, passing darkened fraternity houses and apartments. The convenience store adjacent to the trail route wouldn't open for another hour. I'd hoped to stop in for breakfast and save what I had in my food bag, but wasn't willing to wait. I ate one of my own breakfast biscuits instead, then rounded the ball field and went up into the woods.

Moose Mountain came and went, a much tougher climb for a southbounder. I went over it with a cheery sense of achievement, dropped down to Hewes Brook, then at noon, after fifteen miles, began my climb of Holts Ledge, which was ridiculously steep, much worse than the southbound approach. What I'd gained going up Moose Mountain I gave back on Holts Ledge, chafing at my slowing pace.

The air was warm but not terribly hot, the sky mottled and mostly sunny. It wasn't the exertion that bothered me, but the slow pace. I'd set a goal, completely out of the blue, and a slow pace might rob me of it. In all of my hikes it had taken me at least two and a half days to hike the forty-three-odd miles to Hanover from Glencliff at the base of Mt. Moosilauke. The mountains in between were not the Whites by any measure but there were four major ones and they weren't easy. This time I wanted to do that section in a solid two days, making Fire Warden's Cabin on Smarts Mountain the first day, then over Mt. Cube to Glencliff the second day. I could then begin my climb into the White Mountains with the heady sense of having outperformed my younger self and with full confidence that I could do the same through what was to come.

If Holts Ledge was steep and frustratingly slow, Smarts Mountain was triply so. I scribbled on my AWOL page: *Good God Steep!* There were sharply canted ridge climbs, where traction was not guaranteed, and sections of near-vertical trail that were so eroded that a foot might slip back for every two steps of progress. Sweat came out of me in a rain of salt. If the weather had been poor, that climb would have been no less debilitating than Killington Peak had been. Nevertheless I grunted and slipped and scrambled and pressed on, a few feet at a time over a distance of 5.8 miles, finally reaching Fire Warden's Cabin at about six o'clock.

I'd gone by Old School earlier but his youth served him better on the climb so he beat me in. No one was in the cabin, which had sheltered me from cold, slashing rain on Hikes 2 and 3, and where on Hike 2 I came up with the idea for my novel *The Appalachian*. Tents occupied every available foot of flat ground between the cabin and through the woods to the fire tower. Old School found a place to string his hammock, hanging like ripe fruit above an adjacent tent (which is what we called hammocks in the grizzly country of Denali National Park, *hanging fruit*; while bivy sacks were known as *grizzly sandwiches*). I didn't want to stay in the cabin this time because I knew it would fill before nightfall, and worse still, continue filling *after* nightfall. Old School had told me about the bubble currently en route from Hanover. The site was overwhelmed already and would only get more so.

I brought out my stove and boiled noodles while I pondered what to do. A group of four southbounders drug in, one younger woman eyeing the scene in disbelief.

"There's no solitude here," she muttered in disgust to her friends. "Let's go."

I empathized too well. "You came on the Appalachian Trail for solitude?" I asked. This came out sounding sarcastic but that wasn't my intention.

"I'm a sobo, baby," she spat at me in derision, pounding her chest for emphasis.

They turned in a huff and took off down the trail. I felt bad. I'd meant only to comment on how crowded the trail had become these past years, and would have gone on to let her know that she'd finally find her solitude in Pennsylvania when the nobo tramline tapered to a trickle. I felt betrayed in a sense, my own tribe turning on me when their company would have meant so much. She was right, though. I looked around. Hikers sat or milled in colorful clusters, their bowls out. An acrid scent hung in the air. Something raucous was going on in the direction of the fire tower. It was all too much. I loaded everything back into my pack, said goodbye to Old School, and pushed on.

It was a dusky mile later when I found a nice stealth site. I set up in the quiet, spruce-tinted air, crawled into my tent and lay back with a sense of satisfaction. There *was* solitude on the Appalachian Trail if that's what you were looking for, and camaraderie too if that's what you wanted. You just had to decide which you needed the most in the moment and then hike to it. I'd made 25.8 miles that day, with a wonderful night ahead and Glencliff tomorrow. I'd fulfill my goal, there was now no question.

Taking Mt. Cube in the magic hour helped divert my attention from how steep the climb was. A mile into the three-mile climb, at the side trail to Hexacuba Shelter, I met a sobo and pulled up in surprise. She was a well-toned young woman, fair hair in a thick ponytail.

"Hey," I greeted her. "I don't usually see people this early."

"Yeah, well, that shelter's really crowded. I just wanted out of there."

"It was that bad?"

"Uh, huh. A bunch of nobos all got jammed up because of that hurricane."

I looked down guiltily. "I'm sorry to add to the crowding. You're going to run into another big bubble in a few miles. Same thing. The hurricane."

"Were you in it?"

"No, it didn't come this far north. I sat it out in Norwich. And the day was perfect. I'd be over Moosilauke by now if I'd just kept on going."

"Well, you're going to be there pretty soon anyway."

"Yeah."

She noticed the bill of my ball cap then, where I'd listed my thru-hikes with a black marker. "Ohmygod," she exclaimed, agog. "You've done this *four* times?"

"This is my fourth," I said. "My first three were southbound."

"So what's it like from here, then?" she asked. "Is it really all downhill after the Whites?"

I smiled tightly at that old saw. The Whites seemed ferocious because at that latitude their peaks were mostly above the timberline, and their trails had been routed in insanity. People would forget that the tallest peaks on the Appalachian Trail were down south, perhaps because those summits were forested and those trails were routed responsibly.

"I wish I could say it was," I replied. "But after what you've just done, nothing's going to seem hard to you, I promise. And congratulations, by the way. You're done with the Whites!"

"Thanks. And I guess I should congratulate you too–I mean for your summit."

"Well..." I stalled deprecatingly. "I've still got a long way to go, as you know."

"Yeah, but you've done it before so you know, too."

"I sure do," I sighed. "Well...happy trails. You have an incredible adventure ahead of you."

She smiled prettily. "Thanks. You too."

She took off, and I cast a long look up the side trail to Hexacuba Shelter. I'd visited it only once, on Hike 1. I chuckled at the memory, of being in there alone and wondering which of the many hexagonal walls I should park my back against. The shelters in Dartmouth Outing Club country were all unique in some way, the privies too, having been designed by architectural students at the college. I'd made a point of visiting every one of them on Hike 1. Since then I'd passed them by, reaching Fire Warden's Cabin the first day and then a hostel near Etna on the second, hiking into Hanover on the third. If Hexacuba hadn't been crowded I might have hiked in the three tenths simply for the nostalgia of it.

I continued on over Mt. Cube, and met a nobo named Lyric at New Hampshire Highway 25A.The trail route was confusing on the other side of the highway, with no obvious white blazes in sight, so we partnered up to explore a short way in each direction and up a gravel road as well. We eventually found the blazes, took off together, and our paces matched so well that we stayed together for quite a few miles.

Lyric was a teacher who taught at an underprivileged school. He had a light, wispy beard, an easy manner, and looked no older than twenty, although with his education and career he must have been in his mid to late twenties at least. His wife, he informed me, was also a teacher.

"So what's the deal with education these days?" I asked him. "I mean, my kids are grown so I haven't been involved in it for a long time. Everything seemed fine back then, but now all I hear on the news is how bad things are. I even heard that some schools don't teach cursive writing anymore. I mean, if you can't read cursive writing then you can't even read the Constitution!"

"It's worse than that," he said over his shoulder from a few paces ahead. "We don't teach grammar anymore either."

I pulled up short and gawped. "*What?* How can you not teach grammar? I mean, how can people get by without it? Grammar is like our operating system. Without it you can't understand the language."

"It's because we can't test for it," he answered grimly.

"What do you mean?"

We started up again, talking as we hiked.

"Everything is about testing now. If you have good test scores you get money, and if you have bad test scores you don't, so the school board only lets us teach subjects that are easily tested, like math. It's hard to do a quantifiable test on handwriting, or reading comprehension, or grammar, so they make us focus on things they *can* test for, so they can get the money, you know?"

"I don't get it. I thought Obama fixed all of that."

"Obama only made it worse. His *Race to the Top* was just *No Child Left Behind* on steroids. The testing got worse, and then the teacher evaluations–" he paused a step with a bitter look on his face, "–we have to get high test scores or else get fired, so what do you think teachers focus on, then? They focus on the tests, not on the students. I teach minority students in a poor school. The only way we get money is through test scores. And when it comes to grammar...well, you know there's a kind of ethnic grammar. If we try to correct it we're accused of racism."

"Omygod!" I exclaimed. "*Seriously?* That means all these kids are getting out of school with a different operating system, like Microsoft and Apple. In a few generations we won't be able to understand one another, and that'll only make it worse for them."

As an author, this was a visceral topic for me. There was a reason that English was the language of science, diplomacy, and aviation, which was partially due to the British Empire and America's ascendancy in the twentieth century but not completely so. A thousand years of scholarship and refinement had distilled English from its Latin, French, Norse, Gaelic, and Germanic roots into a coherent language that did away with gender cases, excessive accent marks, inverted verb or adjective order, and tortured syntax.

English made sense, and delivered unprecedented nuance through a vocabulary larger than that of any other language. And people knew this, which was why migrants from all over the world went to such desperate lengths to reach an English-speaking country. To teach anything less than proper English to students would inevitably endow them with third-world status even in the middle of modern America.

"I know." He shook his head sadly. "It's so bad my wife and I are thinking about quitting. It's one of the reasons I'm doing this hike, to figure things out, you know?"

"Yeah," I said soberly.

"I mean, the school board won't let us do anything, and the union gets in the way of anything positive. Get this: I know teachers who refuse to get the Covid vaccine, and the union backs them up. It's crazy."

"I know their kind," I said through gritted teeth. "They want all the benefits of society but none of the responsibility for it. If they'd been in a majority when I was a kid we'd still be dealing with polio and smallpox today. When I was a kid in school, they took us to one of those wards where all these kids who got polio were in iron lung machines. Believe me, when you see some shit like that you hold out your arm and say hurry up." I chuckled darkly. "The polio vaccine was on a sugar cube, but still."

"That's something my generation doesn't really know about—"

"Which is where history comes in—"

"Which we don't really teach anymore."

Good God this conversation was depressing, shocking as well but depressing because I intuitively knew that there wasn't a damn thing any of us could do about it, unlike those halcyon years of the sixties and seventies when we thought we could achieve anything. There were simply too many selfish interest groups, too much pandering, and too much greed. It's a mortal blow when an optimist is brought down a notch or two. I stumbled for something to say.

"Well, I'm sorry you're having to deal with all of that. You know, there's a lot of things young people do that I think is nuts, but I don't let it bother me. I know these old farmers back home who get so worked up over it that they about give themselves heart attacks. They get in a lather over that young girl congresswoman in New York, and the Muslim one and the rest, so I ask them why they even care. I mean, I disagree with a lot of that stuff too, but I tell them that we're not going to have to live in that world. We'll all be gone by then. Young people have to live in that world so young people should be making the decisions. I wouldn't mind if we passed a law that every politician over fifty had to leave office. Better yet, the world would probably be a better place if all us old guys just dropped dead right now."

Lyric laughed. "Well, I wouldn't go that far. I mean, you're pretty open-minded. It would be too bad to lose that."

"Thanks," I said dryly, "but most of the people in my generation sold out. I think it's probably better to be rid of all of us."

That conversation covered the distance to New Hampshire Highway 25C, where Lyric split off to meet up with some friends. I continued on over Mt. Mist, my thoughts in chaos, then dropped down to New Hampshire Highway 25 and Glencliff, nineteen miles done for the day. It was about two o'clock.

There was a trail angel in the parking area dispensing goodies to a few gathered thru-hikers. As I drew closer I saw that it was Dandelion.

"Hey Dandelion," I said cheerily as I approached.

"Hey. It's Solo isn't it?" she asked with a smile.

"Yeah."

"Here ya go, then." She tugged out a cold beer and handed it to me.

"Aw, man—thanks!"

It was not blistering hot, but hot enough that I relished that beer. Dandelion and I spoke for a while, indifferent to the other thru-hikers lounging nearby. She had spent time with the military in Germany so we were able to share some anecdotes of what it was like over there. After those restorative minutes I took my leave.

"I'd better get going," I said. "There's a big crowd of hikers not too far back and I want to get to the hostel before it fills up."

"Yeah, I heard," she said.

"Are you going to be here a while?"

"Yeah, I think so."

"Well, after I get checked in I might come on back."

"I hope you do."

With that I made the short three tenths walk up the highway to Hikers Welcome Hostel, where I'd stayed flush from my victory over the Whites on Hikes 2 and 3. During that short walk, the sky clouded over and let loose with a warm rain. I stepped inside and stamped off the wet. The place hadn't changed, except that this time there were a lot of thru-hikers in there. As a southbounder I'd never shared the place with more than a few others.

The caretaker came out, a wiry guy with a wiry black beard and a sarcastic manner whom I will call Varicose. He had a low opinion of thru-hikers. On my last thru-hike the caretaker had been a pleasant young woman named Dallas.

"Aren't you a thru-hiker, though?" I asked him. He looked like one.

His eyes rolled, I swear they did. "I've got two northbounds, a southbound as far as Harpers, the Long Trail up to mile—I couldn't catch that part—and then from mile—I couldn't catch that part either—some of the Benton MacKaye Trail and the Pinhoti..." and on and on with sections of trail I'd never heard of and which he recited so quickly and rotely that I couldn't really follow any of it.

"Okay then," I said, taking a breath for him. "Do you still shuttle to the store in the evening?"

"Yeah."

"Good, sign me up."

"Go sign yourself up," he said dismissively. "It's over there."

Sigh.

I went upstairs and claimed a bunk next to a couple of Southern ladies who were hiking I know not what, whether thru-hike or section they seemed unable to articulate. Rain pattered against the window but it was stifling hot in the bunkroom. I went back down into the cooler air of the common room, took a pizza out of the freezer and slid it into the microwave. There were six or eight guys lounging around, one of them a multiple thru-hiker named Fine, who had three southbound thru-hikes and was going north this time just like I was.

"That's awesome, man!" I gushed. "We're doing the same thing." What an incredible coincidence. I looked forward to an evening of talk with him, comparing notes, the years of our hikes, who we might know in common, and whether we might have met.

"Whatever," he said, and walked away. I shook my head as he went outside to sit at the picnic table under the canopy. Not everyone is personable, and some are less than that.

A moment later a young female thru-hiker came in.

"Are any of you Solo?" she asked the group.

"Yeah, that's me," I said.

"Dandelion left because of the rain, but she wanted me to give you this."

The girl handed me a beer, which went well with my pizza. Bless you Dandelion, I thought, hoping I might see her again but I never did.

Old School came in, and then a flood of others. The place filled up quickly. After the rain tapered off, tents began to pop up out on the lawn. Old School stretched his hammock between a couple of trees then we shared a load of laundry. Sitting at the picnic table under the canopy as the washing machine gurgled, conversations started up. There were maybe six thru-hikers at the table, one girl the rest guys. Fine wasn't among us. The White Mountains were the main topic, of course.

"So what are they really like?" I was asked.

"Not as bad as some people say," I answered. "The climbs out of the notch drops are pretty hard, but once you get on top you can make good miles, and get incredible views if the weather's good."

"What's a notch drop?" someone asked.

The White Mountains were where I added some additional vernacular. Variously through the mountain passes—called notches in that part of the country—where highways cut through, were egregiously steep descents, what I called *notch drops*. There were no towns on the trail through the Whites, but in each of those notch drops you could usually catch an easy hitch out for resupply or lodging, taking the Whites from one notch drop to the next, hitching out and then coming back the next morning for the equally egregious climb up the other side.

"But what about Mt. Washington?" someone asked.

"That's the tough one," I said.

There were twenty-six miles through that section between Crawford Notch and Pinkham Notch, with Mt. Washington in the middle, notwithstanding Mt. Madison and the rest, almost all of it above the timberline and exposed to the fiercest winds on Earth. I'd never come anywhere close to doing that section in one pull, although on Hike 2 Rocklayer had managed it by hiking through the night. I inevitably wound up at Lakes of the Clouds Hut on Mt. Washington, where I'd always been able to score a work-for-stay, then pushed on and out the next day. The problem this time was that because of Covid, work-for-stays had supposedly been suspended (that was not entirely accurate, as it turned out), which left thru-hikers with the unenviable choice of either hiking way down the mountain to the timberline to camp or else paying an exorbitant fee to stay in the hut.

"Damned Appalachian Money Club," someone spat.

I empathized with the sentiment. The Appalachian Mountain Club, or AMC, was formed in 1876 as a charitable organization and with the noblest of missions: to explore and conserve the White Mountains. They erected their first hut at Madison Springs on Mt. Madison in 1888, modeling it on the alpine huts of Europe. In 1894, the New Hampshire Legislature passed enabling legislation that empowered the AMC to own, acquire, and hold land in line with its mission, all with the best of intentions but they unwittingly created a future monopoly over the White Mountains and elsewhere.

Over time, the AMC established the hut system through the White Mountains, purchased a swathe of the Hundred-Mile Wilderness in Maine, as well as tracts in New York, New Jersey (hence the Mohican Outdoor Center), Massachusetts and beyond. By modern times, they managed campgrounds, visitors centers, restaurants, gift shops, outdoor activities, and hostels, all under the aegis of a 501 (c) (3) charitable non-profit organization that behaved more as a for-profit concessionaire than a charity. The fees they charged for a cold bunk in their unheated huts could exceed a hundred dollars, while a simple tent pad in a campsite might cost ten or fifteen dollars.

Thru-hikers could avoid all of this by stealth camping, but in that signature section between Crawford and Pinkham Notches, almost all at elevation on rocky Mars-like terrain, and subject to weather that could turn deadly in an instant, options were few and the monopoly won out, as it had for me at some point on every thru-hike thus far. The quota for work-for-stays might be full or the hut itself might be full, which could only foretell a bitter night on hard rocks or else a painful descent off the mountain and subsequent climb the next day. What thru-hikers despised was that the AMC provided few options beyond what money would buy, when a simple awning on the back of the huts would suffice. The AMC also performed poor trail maintenance, leaving one to wonder where all the money they raised from their several hundred thousand members went, notwithstanding the high fees the AMC charged for services.

On Hike 1 the white blazes in AMC country were so bright that I could follow them even through the mist-whipped rocky uplands, with blue blazes leading off to the easier trails that the weekenders used. By Hike 2 these blazes were fading and by Hike 3 they were mostly gone, replaced with confusing signs at trail intersections that listed historical names for trails, names that meant nothing to an Appalachian Trail thru-hiker. Bog logs were rotten and sections of trail were overgrown. Cairns sprouted like mushrooms, marking a confusion of intermingling trails, and my once-favorite shelter in the state of Maine, Cloud Pond, had been allowed to fall to ruin.

What made all of this bearable was the croo at the huts, who were mostly (but not always) young, idealistic, caring, and engaged. Many were thru-hikers themselves. They understood the rigors of the trail, and the man-made challenges of the White Mountains in addition to the natural ones. I'd met croo in the huts who'd stopped what they were doing to help me out of a bad spot, and who'd pushed the rules to help others. The couple of bad experiences I'd had, at Zealand Falls Hut on Hike 1 and Carter Notch Hut on Hike 2, were but outliers of the many, many exceptional experiences I'd had otherwise. No few of these croo understood the situation clearly. When I balked at the outrageous price of an Appalachian Trail bandana on Hike 1, the young guy behind the counter said with a hangdog expression, "Yeah, we suck."

Varicose had joined us while this conversation went on, growing ever more agitated at each word until he stood in indignation and pointed a trembling finger.

"You thru-hikers have it too easy," he all but hollered. "You're all lazy. You want the AMC to do everything for you. You show up and expect free food and a place to stay, and if they're full you bitch about it. The sobos get in at noon and take all the work stays when they've only been hiking for a couple of hours, and then a nobo comes in who's been hiking all day and there's no room so he bitches and blames the AMC."

The other hikers were quailing under this onslaught but I kept my eyes fixed on Varicose. I didn't agree with a thing he said, but I wasn't looking for a debate. Nothing I could say would change his mind, but would only bring on bad juju, and none of us needed that this close to the Whites. He continued his tirade, counting the beneficence of the AMC on his fingers as he went:

"If you get the thru-hiker pass, you only have to pay ten dollars to camp for your first night and only five dollars after that. And they'll give you two free baked goods and a free bowl of soup. *A free bowl of soup!* So don't say that the AMC doesn't do anything for you, you just want *everything* for free!"

I allowed a sardonic smile, remembering the old sign at the New Hampshire-Maine state line, long since gone. It read: *Welcome to New Hampshire, the ~~Live~~ Hike Free or Die State*. We didn't want anything from the AMC for free, we only wanted what the Appalachian Trail provided through its two thousand miles beyond those seventy-nine miles in the Whites, which was freedom from the *need* to pay for a place to sleep. And a free bowl of soup? How generous. Those hundred calories wouldn't go far to replace the five thousand calories it took to climb up for them.

Varicose sputtered off as if he'd soiled himself by speaking to thru-hikers, stabbing comments at the air as he went. The other thru-hikers around the table filtered uncomfortably away, leaving me alone with the girl, who might have been twenty or so. She had a pale, oval face, straight dark hair and a fragile expression.

"He makes me feel terrible," she said, scratching at the tabletop with a fingernail.

"What do you mean?"

"When he said that we're lazy and that we have it too easy. Do you think that's true?"

"No. There's nothing easy about the Appalachian Trail. Phones have changed it, that's for sure, but phones don't make the climbs any easier. So don't listen to him, just keep hiking your own hike."

Her expression darkened. "I don't think I'm a real thru-hiker anymore. I think maybe he's right."

My brows creased. "I don't understand."

"I—I skipped Vermont, so now I don't feel like I even belong here. I feel like I'm a cheater. But my friends got so far ahead that I couldn't catch up, so I had to skip to Hanover. I *had* too."

Her eyes were moist when they met mine. I knew how she felt, I truly did. The worst feeling on the Appalachian Trail, worse than being wet and filthy and bug bitten, was the feeling of being left behind.

"Look," I said. "Listen—you're a thru-hiker. This is *your* journey. So you skipped Vermont, so what? You've still climbed some really tough mountains. You've been sleeping in shelters and on the ground for months. You've lost all your weight, you're hungry all the time, you know what it's like to get into a rank sleeping bag, and you're going to climb into the Whites tomorrow. When you get to that sign on Katahdin, you're going to feel like you've done something impossible. You're not going to care about Vermont, but if it still bothers you, hell, you can always go back and do it. This is *your* journey, not somebody else's, and nobody has any right to tell you otherwise."

"Ohmygod," she sniffed. "Thank you! I feel so much better. I thought—you know—you've hiked so many times I thought you'd look down on me."

"No way. That's not how the journey works. You're going to crush this, I promise."

She smiled sweetly, some color in her cheeks now, and I went off to join the shuttle to the store for resupply. All that talk about the AMC, as well as Varicose's tirade, had conjured a plan that I wasn't sure was doable but I thought I might try just the same. Through every one of my hikes, I'd hitched out in the notch drops and gone into town for food and lodging. In a section here and a section there over the years, I'd had to pay to stay in the huts, credit cards accepted. On Hike 2 I'd paid seventy-nine dollars for a bunk in the AMC lodge in Pinkham Notch, and on Hike 3 I'd shuttled back and forth from Pinkham Notch to the hostel in Gorham. This time, though...if I could carry enough food maybe I could push all the way through the Whites, never leaving the trail, camping all the way, and giving no money to the AMC. It would be hard, the extra food weight in my backpack would be heavy, but by damn I was going to try!

FRIDAY, AUGUST 27, 2021

Mile 1812 - 17.6 Miles

I wanted Kins-man today but didn't even come close. Still, I made good miles.

Slept reasonably well, up at 4:00 a.m., ate two sandwiches, took a shower, and was hiking by 5:30.

Cool weather. Made a good climb up Moosilauke and got to the summit at 9:00 a.m., 30-minute break then started down. Into Kinsman Notch at 12:30, took a 15-minute break, then started the real climb. Really tough and slow-going. Seemed easier last time. Didn't get to Eliza Brook until 5:00 p.m., which means only 7.5 miles in 4 ½ hours! Pushed on one more mile and stealth-camped up in the woods.

I'm a little concerned because there's an active bear in the area. All food is hung in a tree, so I'll have to hope for the best. My food bag was so heavy that I broke a few branches until I found one that would hold.

So I didn't make Kinsman but I did do 17.6 miles over Moosilauke and then up here, not going out in the notch for the first time. So all in all it was a good day, and my goal to go through the Whites without interruption is still on.

SATURDAY, AUGUST 28, 2021

Mile 1828 - 16 Miles

These were 16 hard-fought miles.

Stayed in the bag until 5:30 a.m., broke camp and started climbing. Tough climbs. Overcast sky. Got a little bit of a view on South Kinsman, but not much. Cold and windy up there, too.

Made Franconia Notch at 12:30 p.m., then climbed for 1 ½ hours to reach the trail to Franconia Ridge, then climbed more and more and more. Clouds moved in on

On South Kinsman Peak

Lafayette, light rain and wicked cold wind. Wanted to push on to Garfield, but decided to stealth here and stay dry.

It will be a cold night.

SUNDAY, AUGUST 29, 2021

Mile 1844 - 16 Miles

Rained or splattered most of the night. Quite cold, and didn't sleep very well. Stayed in the bag until 5:30 a.m., tent wet inside and out.

More hellish climbs and cold, and no views early on. Got magic at Galehead Hut when the hut master (young woman) gave me pancakes and coffee to sweep out the dining room, and enough extra pancakes to carry out! 6 for dinner tonight.

Met a couple of nice girls, one named TB (Tiny Bladder) who gave me food at Zealand Falls Hut and packed out my trash for me, she hiking out to see her parents. The sun even came out for a while, but now at 6:45 p.m. it's starting to sprinkle.

Pushed to this stealth site at 5:30 p.m. My plan for Mt. Washington is still on depending on what the weather does. Supposed to be storms tomorrow. At any rate, I have once again beaten the rain to camp.

MONDAY, AUGUST 30, 2021

Lakes of the Clouds Hut - 14.1 Miles

A warmer night. Slept okay. Up at 5:00 a.m., hiking by 6:30.

Made fast time down to Crawford Notch. Started climbing at 8:30, a long, hard climb but not as bad as I expected. Got rained on, dried out in some brief sun, then got rained on again and soaked. Stopped at Mizpah Spring Hut for a break—couldn't yogi any food—then on. Arrived here at 4:00 p.m. Offered to lecture for dinner and a bunk, but hut master Jesse declined. He did give me free food and a place in The Dungeon, so after all this time I'll finally be staying down there.

I think it's going to be an awful night, crammed in The Dungeon with those other hikers, but I'm dry, warm, and fed, and I'll be in Pinkham Notch tomorrow. I have made my goal, straight through the Whites without interruption!

TUESDAY, AUGUST 31, 2021

Pinkham Notch - 15 Miles

The night was as bad as I was afraid it might be. Tossed and turned, couldn't sleep, and quite cold.

Waited until 6:00 a.m. to get up so as not to inconvenience China, Straight, or Timber, who proved a little too self-absorbed for good conversation last night. Didn't stick around for breakfast, just gobbled down a couple of energy bars and got moving at 7:00.

The rocks seemed worse than ever before and I don't know why. Mt. Washington was so windy and shrouded in fog that I had a hard time finding the trail. Confusing signs, so I climbed Mt. Adams by mistake. Didn't reach Madison Springs Hut until after 1:00 p.m., where I successfully yogied some food. Damn I was hungry. There was nothing left in my food bag except one energy bar.

Met a man on Mt. Adams named Matt, 43 yo and just finishing his 48 New Hampshire 4000' peaks. We hiked out together and then he gave me a ride into Gorham, where I threw down at the Quality Inn and will zero tomorrow.

Man, I went down hard twice today. I'm really beat up, but I pulled the Whites in 5 days and 4 nights!

WEDNESDAY, SEPTEMBER 1, 2021

Gorham, New Hampshire - Zero

Zero number 12. Saw Straight, who pretended not to notice me. Busy all day with laundry and resupply. Dried my tent in the parking lot, and got it in just before it started raining again. I've eaten a bunch and I'm still starving. Stocked up on breakfast biscuits and beer. I'm out of here in the morning.

—

I left out of Hikers Welcome Hostel to the snores of the others, three tenths to the trailhead through the gathering light and with a resurgent attitude. I *was* a southbounder on a northbound trail, all business, alone as I must be because I couldn't achieve what I wanted to achieve otherwise.

I climbed Mt. Moosilauke in the magic hour, and magic it was, mile after heightening mile of solitude and soft light, five and a half miles in all on an unpunishing trail maintained by Dartmouth Outing Club that gained almost 4000 feet of elevation. I reached the rocky and rounded 4802-foot summit at nine o'clock in a gale of a wind and under a fair sky. Peaks poked through clouds to the north in ominous invitation, seeming too far, too high, and too rugged to traverse but I would be climbing many of them over the next several days just the same.

Many thru-hikers don't include Mt. Moosilauke (pronounced moos-i-Lah-kee) in the Whites, believing that the real range doesn't begin until AMC country on the other side, but that's inaccurate. A glance at the trail profile shows a beast with a great humped back looming up the page and dwarfing those mountains to the south, with a treacherous 3000-foot drop into Kinsman Notch over a distance of 3.8 miles, which proceeds for a period on slippery granite aside a waterfall. Wooden steps have been riveted to the rock in places, winding down an otherwise unnegotiable steepness. Lives have been lost going up or down that side of the mountain. And in geological truth, Mt. Moosilauke *is* a part of the White Mountain Range, the southernmost peak as a matter of fact.

I had always dreaded a descent of Mt. Moosilauke's north side. On a climb you decide where to put your feet. On a descent gravity often decides for you. Climbing this as a southbounder, I could choose every step with caution. On previous thru-hikes I'd watched northbounders precariously picking their way down at angles that seemed impossibly steep, in which one wrong step might send them flailing into the chute of the waterfall, then to toboggan off the mountain. I'd advised hikers who were willing to flip-flop to take Mt. Moosilauke southbound for safety, especially in wet weather. What I found on my descent was that it wasn't as bad as it looked from below. I made it through safely and without difficulty, albeit on dry rocks. If it had been raining, that descent would have been a bit more intense.

I made it down to Kinsman Notch at twelve thirty, dropped pack and found a rock to sit on. This was it, the big decision. I had never crossed that notch on the same day, I'd always hitched out. To continue on up the other side would commit me to my plan. There would be no easy out if I got too tired, or if the weather turned, or if things just didn't go well.

My backpack weighed twenty-six pounds, light by the standards of many but mercilessly heavy by mine, loaded with twelve pounds of food, enough to see me through, or so I hoped. This wasn't a random number. Those twelve pounds represented roughly 32,000 calories. If I burned six thousand calories a day—quite possible considering the climbs I'd be making—and could get through the Whites in five days, then I would have two thousand calories left over, or about what my normal daily caloric intake was in routine life back home. It seemed an adequate buffer, and with room to treat myself to a few extra calories here and there.

I gave one last look around. The weather was fair, the temperature mild. The air smelled clean, scented with evergreen, and the sun was a benevolent beacon flickering through the trees. I shouldered my backpack. I could make out the trailhead across the two-lane highway, those few rocky steps before the woods consumed all. I'd never climbed that but I recalled the descent clearly because the Whites are not easily misremembered. I knew what was coming.

I swallowed hard and crossed the highway.

The initial climb out of Kinsman Notch gained about a thousand feet over the distance of half a mile, all on what was essentially a rock-clotted drainage rather than an actual trail. Lore had it that many of the trails in New Hampshire and Maine were actually old Indian trails, which followed the drainages, the quickest routes to the tops of the mountains where views were long and enemies could be spotted at a distance. That certainly made sense. The rocky routes of rushing rainwater were almost always the steepest, though—and required less trail maintenance, I might add—while there were ample other trails that led to the same peaks, the less punishing trails used by day hikers and weekenders, formerly blue-blazed when that was still a practice. The Appalachian Trail had been routed on the more difficult trails for reasons inexplicable, nevertheless that's where the fading white blazes went, and so did I.

My goal was to clear the Kinsman peaks that day, camping on the other side and with a relatively easy descent into Franconia Notch the following morning. This would take me a little more than eleven miles beyond Kinsman Notch, hand me twenty-eight miles for the day, and send me to sleep with an unrivaled sense of achievement. All of my experience should have advised me otherwise.

The climbs never really stopped. Even the descents were climbs, over piles of glacial rubble protruding from the downward grades. I managed a pace of a mile and a half an hour at best, often less. I burned through the day with excruciating slowness on a trail beyond picayune, and didn't reach the side trail to Eliza Brook Shelter, seven and a half miles on, until five o'clock. There was a dampness in the air, clouds crowding the sky. The light was low even at that latitude and in that season.

I wasn't going to stay in Eliza Brook Shelter. It was there on Hike 3 that I had to spoon with all those nobos. That story was humorous when told elsewhere, but in the moment I could still smell those guys, feel their rancid heat. I pushed on for a mile, climbing with Eliza Brook to my left and with dense steep woods to my right. When I could simply not push myself any farther I scrambled up into the loamy woods, stamped out a spot and pitched my tent. My food bag was so heavy I could barely pull it up into a tree, breaking branches on my first attempts. A sign at Eliza Brook had warned of a foraging bear in the area, something I'd never encountered in New Hampshire. My trekking poles were supporting my tent, so I lay inside with my bear spray near one hand and my knife near the other.

I drifted off quickly, not dissatisfied with my 17.6 miles. I'd crossed Kinsman Notch and I'd never done that before. It had been a hard day but a good day. I slept deep and well.

I topped South Kinsman peak in the magic hour, but all in a lowering gray that stole the sun and the sharper colors. I had my photograph taken on that peak, the horizon disappointingly close but my expression was ebullient. The Kinsman peaks were the first major challenge in the Whites and I'd crushed them. My confidence was high, the trail to come less intimidating.

I dropped down from North Kinsman peak toward Franconia Notch, about 3000 feet over five and a half miles, a mild grade as go the White Mountains but what loomed on the other side of the notch was either some of the best or some of the worst hiking on the Appalachian Trail depending upon the weather.

Here was another notch I'd never crossed on the same day. Flume Visitors Center was a mile east on a side trail, the towns of Lincoln and North Woodstock a few miles farther down the highway. On Hike 1 I'd walked up the highway to see the Old Man of the Mountain, the rocky outcrop high up Cannon Mountain that uncannily resembled a man's face in profile. This is the image minted on the reverse of the New Hampshire commemorative quarter. That face had endured through prehistory and into the present, known to Indians, Colonials, and Appalachian Trail thru-hikers alike, but it collapsed in May 2003, now to be seen only in photographs.

Down in the notch at noon thirty, I sat under the highway overpass and finished off an energy bar in three ravenous bites, the thousand calories I'd put in for breakfast having disappeared as quickly as they'd been delivered. I reached into my food bag for a jumbo honey bun, 480 calories of sugar but nothing as portable was more filling for a complaining stomach. I avoid dense sugary foods during the first two-thirds of each hike (and certainly won't touch the things at home), but in that final push, when there's no fat left in my body to salvage, the heavy dough and sugar-rush of a honey bun can fool my stomach and fuel me for at least an hour.

My fingers and lips were sticky now. I put the bun wrapper in my trash bag and noted with dismay how full that bag already was. Cars rumbled back and forth on the highway overpass, the light beyond the concrete as dull and lifeless as the concrete itself. The sky was a uniform gray, the ceiling so low that the mountains seemed no more than heavily wooded hills. I'd advised thru-hikers over the years to zero if that's what it took to get this next section in good weather. Franconia Ridge was up there, and in polarizing light offered perhaps the most magnificent views on the Appalachian Trail. I knew because I'd caught that ridge twice in weather that could inspire great poetry, and once when it seemed that Thor had brought Ragnarök to Earth.

I again had to question my goal. If I started that climb, my next out would not be until Crawford Notch, 27.7 miles away over peak after peak. I looked blankly in the direction of Lincoln and North Woodstock, where I'd stayed three times before. There was food and comfort there, and some damned good locally brewed beer. The hitch was easy from Flume Visitors Center, and it was still early in the day. I'd get the benefit.

I inventoried my food bag. After only a day and a half in the Whites I had already delved too deeply into that bag. I divided out ramens and honey buns and instant potatoes, separated them by the days I would eat them and saw plainly that there wouldn't be enough. I added energy bars and peanuts to the count, the convenient calories I carried in the belt pouches of my backpack. All told it still wouldn't be enough, close if I consumed them with discipline but not quite.

My mind railed. I *always* underestimated my food needs, and dammit I didn't know why. Everything had made such sense back in Glencliff, but those preparations now seemed so inadequate as to be laughable. I hardened my resolve, stood and shouldered my backpack. I would not stop—I would *not.* I wanted to do this, and I wanted it so badly that not even starvation would deter me. I took up my poles and began my climb.

I will say from experience that in great weather that climb is an inspiration, with view after breathtaking view, so much so that the steep rocky trail melts from memory, leaving only regal blues and rich greens and towering vistas. In poor weather it's a trial of endurance that would test someone a third my age.

One foot up, another foot up, into the low clouds where the gloom permeates the woods and haunts the imagination. The wind whipped up on the exposed ridge above Liberty Spring Campsite, damp and cold. There were dozens of hikers out in it, weekenders and day hikers, a few of them up from Greenleaf Hut, way down below on its prominent perch. Disappointment showed in every face as people trudged on and upward to the shrouded summit of Mt. Lafayette. Once I cleared that cloud-enclosed peak, the crowds thinned to none.

There was nothing beyond Mt. Lafayette for a day hiker. Rounding a wall of rock just off the summit, I could as well have stepped over the horizon and into the howling wilderness. The wind tore at me, piercing my rain shell and whisking away the voices of the day hikers behind me. The feeling was of being alone and bereft on a rocky sea, with nothing ahead but hunger and deepening darkness. Cold pinpricks of rain tapped a tempo on the bill of my cap. I wanted to make it to Mt. Garfield, another four and a half miles, but in that weather I couldn't conceive the ambition let alone summon it. I dropped down to the timberline and stealth camped as the first hard drops began to fall, sixteen miles for the day.

It was cold enough and wet enough that I risked firing up my stove inside the tent, perching it on a damp bandana and doubly careful not to knock it over. That would be a calamity beyond reckoning, but that stove warmed the inside of my tent so thoroughly and so quickly that I began to risk this each night and each morning from there to Mt. K.

I ate my ration, but then as my stomach continued to complain, I ate more. In cold combined with the climbs, my calorie burn must have been significantly higher than I'd assumed it would be, perhaps upward of eight thousand calories per day, which is an incredible deficit and clearly demonstrates the extreme exertion required by those climbs.

It was cold enough that night to test the limits of my down bag liner. I slept in my base layer and with a buff on my head but still I shivered through the small hours, reluctant to break the seal of meager warmth around me when the time came to get up the next morning. What I had in plenty was coffee, which I indulged well beyond my usual starting time. The rain had let up, at least there was that. When I got going at last it was at a lethargic pace through damp and cold and an otherworldly stillness broken only by echoing drips of water from the trees.

There was no view on Mt. Garfield, only the same sodden air. I paused at the side trail to Garfield Ridge Shelter. I had a history with that place and had used it as an important locale in my novel, *The Appalachian*. On Hike 3 I discovered that the old cabin had been torn down and replaced with a bright, brand new shelter, a nice building but with none of the historicity of the old one. I didn't feel a need to go in this time.

I continued down the mountain, my fingers numb and white, my face taut and pasty. I pulled in at Galehead Hut to warm up, eyeing the paying guests with envy as they poured hot coffee into bottomless cups. There were baked goods in baskets–everything I needed to revive myself was right there, a dollar or so for this, a dollar or so for that, not unfair prices at all but I'd made a commitment to myself. At last, stomach growling, I couldn't endure it any longer. I went up to the hut master, a young woman with an approachable expression, and asked her if there were any breakfast leftovers that I could save her from having to carry off the mountain.

This was a yogi technique that sometimes worked if you timed it right. There is no road access to the huts. All the necessary supplies, from pounds of flour and sugar to rolls of toilet paper, are hiked in by the croo, who wear Sherpa-like wooden pack frames to carry the load. Conversely, all rubbish is packed out the same way, from regular trash to food scraps to—ick—composted human waste. The croo use side trails for this purpose, trails not as strenuous as the Appalachian Trail but that's a relative comparison if you have a hundred pounds on your back and shoulders. The croo are, therefore, the heroes of the AMC, let me be clear. Diligent thru-hikers will always pack out their own trash—even offer to pack out some trash for the croo—and avoid using the privies if possible.

With paying guests coming and going, and weather that could turn from one hour to the next, delaying guests on their way, the croo inevitably prepare more food for some of the breakfast and dinner services than can be consumed. The cold and congealed leftovers then add to the weight that has to be carried out, which is why there's an incentive to dole out these leftovers to starving thru-hikers.

In my addled state I didn't get that hut master's name. She was pretty in that healthily young and vigorous way of outdoor people. Although her expression was approachable I still stepped forward with a note of apprehension. She led an enviable life in the clean air, panoramic vistas, and authentic reality of the outdoors, but at the same time she had to deal with the sometimes petulant paying guests and probably no few truculent thru-hikers. One can imagine the mobile frat party, and the impact it might have if it made it this far. It's difficult not to become jaded. I knew this from my time with the national parks.

I made my pitch, still damp and numb, and was rewarded with more than I could have anticipated.

"Sure, we've got leftovers," she said without any sense of ambivalence. "Tell ya what—I'll trade you if you'll sweep out the dining area."

I looked around. The breakfast dishes had already been cleared. About a dozen hikers lingered, sitting in groups at the long tables, talking and finishing their coffees. The floor wasn't that dirty.

"Sure—absolutely," I said as if saved—not *as if*, I *was* saved. "Which trash can do you want me to put the dust in?" What was swept off the floor wasn't tossed into the environment but was packed out as well.

"That one over there."

"Great. I'll get right on it."

"No, that's cool. Eat first. And get some coffee. You look cold."

I wondered in that moment if I could adopt her as a daughter. I poured a cup of hot coffee, which I sipped in ecstasy, the simple things magnified. Brief minutes later, she came out of the kitchen with a stainless steel pan of cold pancakes, perhaps as many as twenty.

"I'm sorry they're cold already," she said.

"Oh, gosh, I don't care," I said, and I meant it. My eyes were fixed on those pancakes, half of which, in my imagination, were already in my stomach.

"Eat all you want. I'll bring you some honey in a minute."

I fell on those pancakes like a coyote to a carcass, having to force myself to slow down. I had another cup of coffee—ohmygod no morning on the Appalachian Trail had ever been that sweet. I didn't stop until my stomach was so tight that I couldn't bend over. There were six pancakes left. I put those in a ziplock and smiled in satisfaction. No matter what—no matter the weather or the climbs—I would be eating well that night.

The hut master smiled knowingly when I returned the empty pan. "Thanks for helping us out," she said, and I think she meant it.

I found the broom and started sweeping, doing the most thorough job I could. When offered a work-for-stay or a work-for-food, thru-hikers should do their best to work hard and not just go through the motions. We are, after all, not only working for ourselves but also for thru-hikers yet to come.

She finally had to stop me. "That's enough, Solo," she said. "You worked hard and did a great job. Now go out and make some miles."

Yeah, I would have adopted her on the spot.

I pushed on over South Twin Mountain, not an easy climb, then dropped down that long, jagged descent past Guyout Shelter toward Zealand Falls Hut. The sun showed itself now and then as I lost elevation, from 5000 feet down to about 2500, revealing views of a valley floor dappled in light from individual rays. I pulled in at Zealand Falls Hut to water up, about nine and a half miles—and many hours—from Galehead Hut.

I met a pair of thru-hikers there, both young women, the most personable of whom was TB, whose name, she informed me in mild embarrassment, stood for Tiny Bladder. We laughed at that and struck up a conversation. She and her friend were about to set out on a side trail, where TB's parents would be waiting to take them into town.

"Look, I've got to get rid of some stuff," she said. She opened her food bag, which contained energy bars and chocolate bars, peanuts and crackers. "You want any of this?"

I didn't have time for Southern abstemiousness, other thru-hikers were sideling over at the mere mention of food. "Hell yeah!" I exclaimed, and I dug in, stuffing my backpack's belt pockets and then stuffing more into the front pouch.

"I'll pack out your trash for you if you want," she offered then.

"Really?"

"Sure. We're going to be out for a couple of days, so it's no problem."

My trash bag was now so full that I'd used it for a pillow. I handed it over, relieved to lose the bulk of it, said my grateful goodbyes and pushed on.

The trail proceeded on through a boggy area, with even a few intrepid mosquitoes still out and about. I squished and splashed, navigated moss-bearded bog logs, and after another four miles, as an evening rain began to spatter, I stamped out a stealth spot on a dry rise between two brooks a mile short of Ethan Pond Campsite. I spent a pleasant and expectant night despite the rain. It was warmer at that lower elevation, my stomach was full, I'd made sixteen miles again, and I would drop into Crawford Notch during the magic hour tomorrow.

Crawford Notch was the last challenge in the White Mountains, or rather, the second to last challenge. After that would come Mt. Washington, and then out to Pinkham Notch. This time I didn't hesitate, pause, or prevaricate. I crossed the railroad tracks and the road and continued up the other side without a hitch in my step. What I remembered about Crawford Notch as a southbounder was that I was glad I didn't have to climb it. The climb was 3000 feet up to Mt. Webster, this over a span of 3.3 miles. The worst of it, though, came in the first 2000 feet over a distance of about two miles, much of it hand-over-hand. I stowed my trekking poles and got after it.

You don't measure miles per hour in that kind of terrain, but hours per mile. At least the weather had cleared, a voluminous sky and glinting sun. There were storms in the forecast, though. Somewhere hours on and a couple thousand feet higher, the sun would be rubbed out as if by a divine hand, the winds would become gale-force, and day would turn to deathly cold night.

I stopped to down an energy bar or two whenever I could wedge myself between rocks. At that level of exertion I could actually feel those bars being digested, as if greedily, followed by the instantaneous surge of energy, every molecule consumed. Scatologically, there wouldn't be much left to give back.

I continued on and up, racing through my food the way I couldn't race through the trail. I thanked God it wasn't raining. I stopped at Mizpah Spring Hut after six and a half miles of this, too late in the day for any leftovers. The sun cast a few last lonely rays through gathering black clouds. Other thru-hikers were throwing down at the hut even though it was still relatively early. I pushed on.

My plan had been as simple as this, depending upon what the weather did: hike as close to Lakes of the Clouds Hut as I could, find a hollow between a couple of boulders, and wrap up in my tent as if it were a bivy sack. The night would be uncomfortable but not desperately so. I could then hike into Lakes of the Clouds Hut the next morning, try to yogi some leftovers, and then a few hours after that I would be out in Pinkham Notch and I would have done it!

The weather turned too quickly for that plan to work. Lakes of the Clouds Hut was only four and a half miles farther on, but in that terrain it might as well have been twenty. I wasn't a half mile beyond Mizpah Spring Hut when the sky went black and a frigid wind howled hard enough to numb my fingers in an instant. I hastily donned all of my cold weather clothing. The prudent thing to have done would have been to backtrack to Mizpah Spring Hut, but there was no lightening coming out of that sky, and it wasn't raining yet, so I pushed on. I'm glad I did but it wasn't easy.

The wind seemed to buffet me from all sides, with no main force to lean into. I was sometimes blown off my feet, finding tentative purchase on an adjacent boulder. It was not a boulder ballet through there but a boulder brawl. Fog streamed in, actually the swirls of clouds driven before the wind. I could no longer feel my feet, and my hands were useless. I couldn't sleep out in that, I would have to use the hut, no choice.

Through frigid miles I formed a new plan. Think about it, I said aloud to myself in repetition and rehearsal, my lips too numb to more than mumble the words: You're an 8000-miler, you're an author, and you're kind of old for this kind of thing. You have valuable insights, priceless insights even. You've written books about this in which Lakes of the Clouds Hut figures prominently. Who wouldn't be interested in that? You could offer to do a lecture—you did an ad hoc lecture before at Lakes of the Clouds Hut and drew a pretty large audience. They'd clapped afterward, for God's sake. So a bunk and some food in exchange for a lecture is not a hard ask. They'll probably be thrilled. It has to be this way because if the hut isn't doing work-for-stay when you get there, and if The Dungeon is already full, which it will be because it only holds six people, then there won't be anything else.

It was a good plan, I was sure of it. I rehearsed what I would say as I pushed on through the wind, quarter mile after interminable quarter mile over rocks and between boulders, desperate for Lakes of the Clouds Hut to materialize ahead.

The hut came into view at four o'clock, although my body swore it was eight or nine and the sky couldn't make a decision between night and day. I'd done 14.7 miles in nine and a half hours, an average pace of one and a half miles per hour which, in that weather and terrain, was phenomenal.

I stumbled in, dropped pack, and looked around, bewildered. The place was packed with people, mostly paying guests in clean designer outdoor garb, but on a bench against a wall sat a motley line of unmistakable thru-hikers.

I smelled food from the kitchen and thought I would faint. A grinning guy in an immaculate fleece vest and a rakish five o'clock shadow poured himself a cup of coffee and I almost did faint. I had to sit down, I had to rub my lips and work feeling back into my fingers. All the commotion was disorienting but the place was warm and that's all that mattered.

It took a while, maybe half an hour before I could articulate clearly enough to make my pitch. Now that I was there I felt the itch at the back of my neck, my plan seeming less certain if not preposterous. I approached a young woman at the desk.

"Could I speak with the hut master please?"

"You mean Jesse? Sure. Just a minute."

I leaned back and scanned the room, the dining room actually, the long tables populated with chatty guests. None paid me any notice, but the thru-hikers in their motley line had their eyes on me as if I had a card up my sleeve. It wouldn't do for them to hear any of this.

A young guy came out with a frown, mid to late twenties, not a thru-hiker, one can just tell.

"You wanted to speak to me?" he asked warily.

"Yeah. Can we go somewhere discreet?"

That drew a deeper frown. "Sure, let's go this way."

He led me down the hall and out the back door into the cold wind. I hadn't meant *that* discreet. I shivered where I stood, rehearsed my pitch one last time.

"So," I said, "I'm an 8000-miler, an author, and I'm sixty-three years old. Give me a bunk and some food and I'll give a lecture to your guests."

There, it was out. Jesse seemed bewildered, dipping his eyes in confusion as if studying the ground for an answer to a perplexing question.

"What?" he asked in incomprehension.

"Uh—" That wasn't the response I'd been expecting. I repeated my proposal in diminishing confidence. Jesse laughed when he got the gist of it.

"Man," he said, still laughing, "I thought you had a complaint or something. Wow. So look, I don't need any lecturers. We can take care of that ourselves, and one of our guys is a thru-hiker, too. So I can sell you a bunk or I can give you a spot in The Dungeon. And we have some leftovers. I can give you some of that, too, but that's all I can do."

"You still have room in The Dungeon?" I asked, torn between humiliation and salvation.

"Yeah. So I've got to get back in now. Just tell them what you want to do."

He turned then and went in, shaking his head and chuckling, and I stood in the cold feeling more humiliated than I could bear. After a moment's distance I followed on and spoke with the girl at the desk, who gave me a third of a pan of cold oatmeal and some walnuts to sprinkle on top. I didn't begrudge the viscous oatmeal, I ate every filling bite of it. I made an assumption based on nothing and poured myself a cup of coffee. After that feast I felt much better.

"Are you a thru-hiker?" a middle-aged and fetching woman in a black fleece vest asked me.

"Yes, I am."

"That's awesome!" she gushed. "Tell me about it."

Some of her friends sidled over. Soon there were eight or ten people gathered around my place at the table, enough that I had to stand to speak to them all. I shared a few anecdotes, the rigors of that day. I deliver my lectures extemporaneously, the way Asimov did, so those folks were getting the same thing they would have gotten in a more formal setting. When Jesse walked by with a harried look and a suspicious eye at me, I added loud enough for him to hear, "So I offered to do a lecture for you folks tonight but they turned me down. Sorry, but I've got to go stake out my place in The Dungeon now." I turned my back on their disappointed faces, gathered my things, and went out and around to The Dungeon.

I'd written about The Dungeon but I'd never actually stayed in it. I claimed a bottom bunk in it on Hike 1, but The Dude and Gentle scored us work-for-stays so I was able to sleep in the dining room that night (we slept on the tables back then, but perhaps the unhygienic implications of that were finally recognized because in later years we slept on the floor). There was a shelf of ice in The Dungeon on Hike 2, and on Hike 3 I didn't bother to go out for a look.

The Dungeon is pretty much what its name implies, a dank, dark cellar. It was built as an emergency shelter for winter hikers who might come along when the hut was closed, rumor held as a consequence of a hiker or hikers who froze to death one night. There are six tightly stacked wooden bunks in there, and nothing else. The door is heavy metal, and screeches when it's opened or closed. The hut's generator sits nearby, droning loudly and numbingly until they shut it off at about nine or ten o'clock.

There were three thru-hikers in there already, two girls and a guy. They had, of course, claimed the best bunks, and were throwing me resentful glances as if I had intruded into their private space. I looked up with a groan to a top bunk. Wet socks and underwear were draped along each rail. There was no way to escalade that bunk without stepping on wet and funky intimate clothing, a nauseous thought.

"Sorry," one of the girls said, and she moved a wet sock about an inch to the left.

I tossed my sleeping pad and bag up there, left my backpack huddled with the others against the spare space of a wall, then clumsily hauled myself up, already wondering how I would get back down and make ready in the early hours without disturbing everyone. It wouldn't be possible, so they would be waking at hiker sunrise whether they wanted to or not.

The wind howled outside, battering the door as if with conscious determination. The generator droned loudly enough nearby to numb my hearing. I laid my head opposite that wall in order to dilute the pummeling as much as possible. It was late enough by then that I doubted any other thru-hikers would show up, so it was just the four of us, bundled against the refrigerator-cold of The Dungeon but infinitely better off than being outside.

I worked hard to engage those three in conversation. All they would talk about were personal tribulations that were, without a doubt, profoundly significant in their lives but to me rang as common as rain. They never talked about the trail at all, no stories of their journeys or their adventures, as if the trail were an inconvenient side trip between coffee shops or bars or wherever else they vented their woes back home. I gave up on them after a time and tried to sleep.

I spent a miserable night but not because of them. Astoundingly, they were all very quiet once their eyes closed. It was the pounding of the wind, no less than a hurricane beyond that steel door, and a creeping cold. My sleeping pad scrunched and crunched at every brief movement of my shoulders or hips, translating through the hard wood of the bunks as if through the body of a guitar. I let the air out to spare the others but then the cold found me and seeped along my length. I lifted to shove clothes under my body for insulation, and banged my head hard on the low ceiling, falling back with stars in my vision.

I lay in frigid impatience until six o'clock the next morning, when the others began to stir. I waited for them to drag themselves up and out to the dining room, then hopped down and set to my own preparations. I had a kink in my neck that tugged into my right shoulder, which no amount of rubbing and popping would relieve. All I had left to eat were a few energy bars. I downed all but one, wearily shouldered my backpack, and took off at seven o'clock.

The air was eerily still, the wind seeming to have lost its nerve, but the fog was so dense that finding the proper trail away from the hut used up irreplaceable minutes. I pushed on into it, swallowed by the gloom after the first few feet. Mt. Washington's summit was only one and a half miles on and up from Lakes of the Clouds Hut, a cheery jaunt on a clear day but that's not what this was. It took me an hour to reach the summit, the Sherman

Adams Building materializing like a megalithic monster only in the last few feet before I reached it. There was a snack bar inside that would have gone a long way toward restoring me but the place didn't open until nine, and in that weather perhaps later yet.

I took shelter in the lee of the building, went for my last energy bar but then changed my mind. I still had thirteen and a half miles to go, with Mt. Jefferson and Mt. Madison in the way, followed by that long rocky descent of near 3000 feet. I would need that energy bar for later.

The wind had started up again, as to be expected on Mt. Washington, which has experienced the highest winds ever recorded on the planet. What was odd was that the fog seemed to be thickening even more, completely unaffected by the wind, as if the wind itself were the fog, or the fog the wind. I couldn't see more than a foot or two ahead, and this is not an exaggeration. I crossed the parking lot, the surety of its surface my only guide. The Sherman Adams Building was lost in the fog behind me, the way ahead gray right before my eyes. Somewhere across that parking lot would be the Cog Railway, and across it the trail.

The irony of rugged Mt. Washington is that there's an auto road to the top, as well as the Cog Railway. Were I so inclined I could follow that road all the way down and make the transit in a fraction of the time. Of course that's not what I was going to do. On Hike 1The Dude, Gentle, and I (and Gentle's dog Barney) made that interminable rocky climb together, hour after hour in a fractured landscape worthy of nightmares. The sky had been abundantly clear. That kept our spirits up but did nothing to ease the strain or our otherworldly senses of having been transported beyond our imaginations. When we cleared a last rocky crest, the railway and the road came suddenly and shockingly into view, lots packed with colorful cars in stark contrast to our miles and miles of dun granite, and people everywhere snapping photos. We were so displaced and disassociated that we felt we needed to flee from the chaos of it.

This time I was looking for that rocky crest but I couldn't see it. I couldn't see *anything*. I probed the edges of the parking lot, too afraid to step beyond it less I become lost in the fog. A white blaze would have shown even through that but there were no white blazes to follow anymore. I probed, found the Cog Railway, and risked venturing along its length a little way in each direction until I noted scuffed rocks at my feet, which had to indicate the trail. I crossed over, following the scuffed rocks. A cairn materialized ahead so I went that way. I could have been off on any side trail but I took my chances. At last a weather-beaten sign, tilting in the wind. I was on the Appalachian Trail, thank God for that.

The landscape was featureless, not only in the smothering gray, even in bright light it would just be rocks and more rocks, ridges and saddles and undulations. The cairns marked erratic paths, no white blazes left after a decade or more of blasting winds. I pushed on as if in an isolation tank, with no perception of time or distance. I perked up when the trail began a steep climb, which must have meant Mt. Madison. Somewhere ahead would have to be Madison Spring Hut and the possibility of food, or at least coffee. Dammit, I'd pay if I had to. My fingers were stiff, my feet numb. I was cold to my core and well on through.

I climbed.

How high and how long? I didn't know. The fog began to break as I went, though, revealing glimpses of sun-warmed rocks, and how was that possible? Where was the sun? Why wasn't it *here*?

I climbed, features gradually resolving: the rocks ahead, a lonely cairn, soon the flank of a mountain and a saddle up above where a solitary man stood. It was as if I'd found Friday's footprint in the sand, a sudden hearkening of hope. The man was coming down the mountain toward me. By the time we met, visibility had opened up enough to reveal a velvet saddle far below, a crossing of trails like lines on a map, and a pair of ant-like hikers making their way along.

"Hey dude," I said with peculiar joy. "Do you know if the hut's near here?"

"The hut?" he asked, clearly confused.

"Yeah, Madison Spring Hut. This *is* Mt. Madison, right?"

"No, man. This is Mt. Adams."

I fell back against a rock in disconsolate exhaustion. Mt. Adams was not on the Appalachian Trail. Without blazes I'd had to follow the cairns, which could mark any trail whatsoever and with no indication of where you were going. I'd gotten off on the wrong trail and I'd climbed a mountain for nothing, not even a decent view!

His name was Matt. He was a handsome guy, an airline pilot, forty-three years old and practically trembling with excitement. He was a peak bagger, and Mt. Adams completed his journey over the forty-eight highest peaks in New Hampshire. He'd completed this, furthermore, at the same age his father had been when his father passed away, and on the very date of his father's passing! I didn't have to sense what an important life moment this was for him, it was obvious in his animated expression. I congratulated him, and even though I wasn't in the best of circumstances right then, I sincerely meant it.

"The trail to Madison Spring Hut is down there." He pointed to the intersecting trails far below. "You just need to backtrack then turn right at that intersection."

I groaned, or moaned, I'm not sure which.

"I should be able to go over Adams and get there, though," I said. I looked up. The peak was *right there*. It felt foolish to climb a mountain and then not go over it.

"Yeah, you can do that. It might even be faster, but I'm not sure."

"Okay, then. Good to meet you bro." We bumped fists and went our separate ways.

I had a notion that from the top of Mt. Adams I'd be able to see the hut and could then navigate to it by sight. The fog had almost completely lifted, leaving in its wake a sunny and warmer day. When I reached the top, though, and with a view I could appreciate, I could not see the hut or any semblance of a trail down the other side. Now I felt doubly foolish. Always forward, never backward, but I saw no other way except to backtrack to a marked (albeit poorly) trail.

I caught sight of some curious blue lichen, stepped in for a closer look and realized that what I was seeing was the last flaking remnant of a blue blaze. Yes! I could make out another blue blaze ahead, and then another after that. It was the side trail to Madison Spring Hut, it had to be. So I took off following blue blazes, down, down, down, skirting cliffs in places, boulder ballet in others. A desultory cairn rose now and then but it was the blue blazes I followed, and they eventually led me to the hut.

It was one o'clock when I reached the hut, six hours to go seven miles. My stomach knotted painfully. There were no leftovers in the hut, no food except what I'd have to purchase. I was about to down my last energy bar when an older day hiker offered me a couple of his granola bars. I thanked him effusively and downed those bars in two bites or less. I watered up then, shouldered my backpack, and looked up with dread at the steep climb over Mt. Madison that began right there. I consoled myself that once over that peak it would be all downhill to Pinkham Notch, which was delusion. There would be false peak after false peak along that descent, boulder ballets and rock scrambles. These reentered my memory. It was probably faster to climb that mountain than go down it.

Before I could start out, Matt came sauntering in with a grin.

"Solo! You made it."

"Yeah. I found the old blue-blazed trail."

"Really? I didn't think you'd be able to see it anymore, that's why I went the other way."

"Well, it's there," I said sourly. "But probably not for too much longer."

Matt laid out his lunch, noted the look on my face and didn't need to ask. "Here, Solo," he said. "I'm hiking out and I've got a lot more food than I need."

I devoured the offered granola bars as well as a thick brownie, and could actually feel the sugar warming my blood. Matt's car was parked in Pinkham Notch. "You wanna hike out together?" he asked. "I'll give you a ride into town if you want."

I perked up at the serendipity of it. "Hell yeah," I said.

"Great."

We set out shortly thereafter. It wasn't two o'clock yet, and we had 7.8 miles to the bottom at Pinkham Notch. Matt wanted to be there by six so that his wife and kids wouldn't have to wait and worry, but he was dubious that we could do it.

"No," I said, glancing at my watch, "we'll be out by six. I promise you."

The climb up Mt. Madison went quickly but the rocky false summits on the way down were precarious. A misplaced step could lead to disaster. Matt had good skills on the rocks, outpacing me sometimes by a quarter mile, but when we finally reached the timberline I got out ahead. The trail was picayune with rocks and roots and boggy low spots, but I flew over that, my goal just a few miles ahead and man I couldn't contain myself. Matt panted to keep up.

"Do I need to slow down, dude?" I asked him over my shoulder.

"No, keep going. Keep pushing me."

"Okay."

I had *arete*, I was hiking light, my poles up and out the way Tri-Pad had taught me, joyous to be out of those mountain tracks and back on an actual trail. I felt as free as an untethered falcon. I leapt over rocks, skated off roots, hopped from side to side over the boggy areas without breaking stride, and then the trail finally caught up with my enthusiasm. I slid off a root and went down hard onto my right shoulder. The kink in my neck from that morning magnified into a sharp pain from below my ear to deep into my shoulder.

"Ow," I said, collecting myself. "Shit that hurts."

"Are you okay?" Matt asked as he came up.

"I'll live," I muttered. "Damn."

"I need a break anyway. Why don't we sit for a minute."

"Sounds good."

Matt shared out some granola bars, bless him, while I cocked my neck to the left and right trying to crack that kink, all with no success. It wasn't the old injury to my shoulder, it was a pinched nerve. A visit to a chiropractor would take care of it with a single pop, but where would I find one of those?

I paced it off, pushed the pain to the back of my mind, and we continued on, albeit at a slower pace. We arrived in Pinkham Notch at exactly six o'clock, both of us grinning.

"We did it!" he said. "Just like you said we would. I can't believe it."

"Well, I was pushing you pretty hard through a lot of that."

"And I'm glad you did. It helped me know what I can do. If I hadn't met you I'd probably still be a couple of hours back."

"Well, I'm glad it all worked out."

Matt drove me into Gorham, where I had him drop me at the first motel we saw, which was Quality Inn. I could have gone to one of the hostels but I wanted to be alone with my achievement and not expose it to any potential surly attitudes. We said our goodbyes, which were sincere and included a quick hug. I regretted later not getting his phone number.

I tried to yogi a beer from the desk manager while I was checking in, describing to her how rejuvenating a beer was after a long, hard day on the trail. I hinted and hinted at the stash of beers she probably had back there, replenished each day by the housekeepers. I gave her a wink as if only the two of us were privy to that knowledge but all I got in return was a nonplussed look. I had just given up the quest when a tall, bearded guy in line behind me handed me a cold beer, even better when the desk manager said I could drink it right there!

So it was an eventful fifteen-mile day, and the culmination of something I wasn't sure I could achieve. But I had—I had by God crushed the White Mountains in five days and four nights!

The next day was a guilt-free zero number twelve for me, well earned by my reckoning. I ate, and ate, and resupplied and did laundry. I lay through the later afternoon with pizzas and beers and breakfast biscuits, clean in every cranny and with gear washed and ready to go. Next would be the Wildcat Range and that god-awful climb out of Pinkham Notch.

I now had a major goal behind me. It was time to forget it and start again.

THURSDAY, SEPTEMBER 2, 2021

Mile 1884.1 - 10.4 Miles

My lowest mileage in a while, but I didn't get started until 9:00 a.m. I didn't stop out of exhaustion, but only because it was getting late and starting to rain.

Up at 5:30 a.m., ate a lot of breakfast, and talked to hikers for a while, including Running Bear, whom I hadn't seen since PA. She skipped a section to get here. Also saw Old School, who hadn't done the Whites yet.

Started hitching at 8:30. Caught a ride pretty quick from a one-legged guy named Hopper. He lost his leg in a military helicopter accident, pretty freakin' grisly.

The Pinkham climb took over three hours. Met a lot of thru-hikers today, including Lilac and Wheels. Nice kids. Lilac so resembled a woman named Nancy I knew years ago that Lilac could have been her granddaughter. I asked just in case—what kind of serendipity would *that* have been—but the two were unrelated. Some sun here and there, no rain until now. I'm pretty sure I won't be able to make Maine tomorrow after all. I just didn't go far enough today.

It's going to be a really cold night up here.

FRIDAY, SEPTEMBER 3, 2021

Rattle River Hostel - 10.1 Miles

Super cold overnight, perhaps in the mid-30s, plus some light rain. Slept not well but I did sleep some. Up at 5:00 a.m., hiking by 6:15 on wet rocks and through a chill wind.

Took the remaining peaks in the gloom of the morning, no magic hour to speak of, and no view from Mt. Moriah. Out at 12:30 p.m. and threw down at Rattle River. Saw Eric but did not recognize him. He didn't recognize me either, so we're even. Ghost sent out for pizza and beers, which we shared. He tried to crack my back for me, but it didn't work. I'm very tired and my neck and shoulder really ache.

SATURDAY, SEPTEMBER 4, 2021

Mile 1910 - 15.2 Miles

I didn't quite make Maine, but I came close. Just needed more daylight, pitch black by 7:45 p.m.

Slept incredibly well, didn't wake up once until 6:00 a.m. Spent the morning talking and drying out my tent. Bruiser, the 74-year-old I met in Shenandoah, is here on a flip-flop and hasn't changed in demeanor or subject matter.

Perfect weather, started hiking at 9:45. Lots of climbs and views, lots of mud and rocks. Passed Ghost—turns out he was the one who gave me the beer at the Quality Inn in Gorham, but I was so tired then that I didn't remember.

Pushed and pushed, shoulder and neck killing me, but as it got dark and started looking like rain I had no choice but to take the first stealth site I found and be grateful for it, which I am. It's going to be cold tonight, but hopefully not as cold as the Wildcats. There's an odd rumbling out there in the dark, no idea what it is, rocks contracting, maybe?

I'm not sure exactly where I am, but probably close enough to the state line that I'll regret not going on anyway. Oh well, I'll be in the state of Maine tomorrow regardless.

A day hiker could spend an entire Saturday going up and down the north side of Pinkham Notch, then return home that evening in such a rush of strenuous achievement that visits to the gym could be deferred for a month without any sense of guilt. Few are the day hikers, though, who take on that climb. There are other, easier trails for them to follow. I remembered that climb clearly, as a descent, of course, and wondered if I would be fooled by it as I had been by so many others: would going northbound be easier than it appeared during my southbound thru-hikes, the way Mt. Moosilauke had been?

No, it wasn't.

I caught a hitch back to Pinkham Notch at nine o'clock that morning from a Vietnam vet named Hopper who looked about as used up by life as a man can be but who was chipper and chatty just the same. It was a damp, cool morning, the road still slick from some rain overnight. Fog oozed down the shrouded mountains in wispy streams of gray, but every so often we would pass through a remarkably sunny patch, the reflection off the wet pavement painful in my eyes, only to be snuffed out a moment later as the fog closed back in.

The drive was about ten and a half miles. Hopper took it slowly with bald tires on slippery roads, so we had some time to talk. We were well on our way before I noticed that his right leg was missing. He noticed me noticing him, and explained: "Helicopter accident. It almost took my arm, too—you should see the scars—and it laid me open from breastbone to belly. One of the corpsmen said he could see my heart beating. Think about that, man, to actually *see* it. Holy crap."

I winced at the image. "Was it in the Nam?" I asked hesitantly.

"Naw, it was on base in California. Can you believe that shit? I thought I was in for a lucky ride during the Nam, but then that engine blew and the prop came flying off, and it found me better than any VC sniper could of—I need a cigarette. Keep your eyes on the road for a minute, would ya?"

He took a hand-rolling cigarette gadget from his dashboard, and as one-handed as Willie Nelson, rolled himself a perfect cigarette while keeping us steadily in our lane. He took a puff and continued: "So they put everything back in and sewed me up. Couldn't save the leg but they did save the arm even though it was just hanging by gristle. Something like that will kinda reset your life, you know?"

No, I really didn't, but I nodded anyway.

"Damn government, though—you can't get those idiots to do anything right. I went in for my check the other day—had to drive thirty miles because they wouldn't mail it to me—and here I was standing on one leg, the other one was—well, I'm not sure what they did with it but they didn't give it back, I'll tell ya that—well, it was *missing*, right? And the guy there tells me that without the right paperwork I can't prove I was disabled so he can't give me my check. Can you believe it?"

"Man that sucks." I'd heard stories like that one before.

"Yeah. So he says to go on home and the paperwork should come in the mail in a week or two and to come back then, and I tell him I can't pay rent, and he tells me that he's awful sorry but rules are rules and he has to follow 'em to keep us all safe. To keep us *safe?* What the hell does that mean? Would I be safe sleepin' out on the street because I couldn't pay my rent?"

I growled low in my throat. It was a phrase I despised but had infiltrated every bit of discourse, from political speeches to media commentary: *to keep the American people safe*. Not to protect us, not to defend us, but to keep us *safe*. I didn't need the government to keep me safe, I could take care of that myself. All I needed the government to do was ensure justice, and it could start by giving a disabled vet his damn check.

Hopper dropped me at the Pinkham Notch visitors center, then rattled on down the highway. I crossed over to the trailhead and paused before going on. The first mile would be flat, an innocuous opening to what lay ahead. The climb up to Wildcat Mountain Peak D would be about 2200 feet over two miles, much if not most of it hand-over-hand. I went ahead and stowed my trekking poles just to get it over with. There were so many Wildcat peaks that they had alpha designations, E, D, C, and A, which was the tallest of them at about 4500 feet. There was probably a Peak B out there somewhere too, perhaps on a side trail. In between each were craggy saddles, and then after Peak A would come a sharp drop into Carter Notch, then the climb over Carter Dome, almost touching 5000 feet, then over Mt. Hight, then over Middle Carter Mountain and North Carter Mountain, then over Mt. Moriah, and then finally a smooth 5.9-mile drop—what I call a *swoosh*—down to U.S. Highway 2 near Gorham.

The entire section covered 20.1 miles, with an AMC hut in Carter Notch, a campsite toward the other end, and some ski lifts on Wildcat Peak D, otherwise nothing. Along the way, side trails were slung like ropes from the various peaks, all of which probably required fewer calories to climb than the Appalachian Trail route did. On Hike 1 I entered this and felt enmeshed as if for weeks. On Hike 2 I stumbled soaked to the skin and obviously hypothermic into Carter Notch Hut, teeth chattering so uncontrollably that I couldn't form answers to the barrage of questions hurled at me, whether I wanted a work-for-stay or pay, when what I needed most—and was not offered—was a cup of hot coffee.

On Hike 3 I caught that section in astounding weather for the first (and only) time, and discovered along the way that the view from Mt. Hight actually rivaled if not surpassed the view from Franconia Ridge. I'd left out of Rattle River Hostel that morning at five o'clock, and dropped into Pinkham Notch at five in the afternoon, completing the entire section in twelve hours. The opening climb was easy for southbounders, though, and the drop into Pinkham Notch, although precarious, went much quicker than a northbound climb. I entertained no notion of doing that section in a day this time but if I could just get over North Carter Mountain, tomorrow would start with a quick, magic hour climb over Mt. Moriah followed by the swoosh to U.S. Highway 2 and Rattle River Hostel, which was right on the trail, bringing me in early enough to get the benefit.

That was the plan, but it didn't quite happen.

There was an invigorating moment on an exposed ledge about half way up when the sun came out and a majestic view materialized as if pixel by pixel, but then another bank of dense clouds rolled in and there stayed for the duration. I climbed hand-over-hand on mossy wet rocks. The moss actually provided some purchase. The lichen-encrusted rocks were as slippery as oil.

Younger thru-hikers passed me by, ambling agilely up as if gravity were no force to reckon with. Being passed by people leaves you with an odd sense of inadequacy. Monkey Man way back in Tennessee knew this. He said he enjoyed catching and passing other hikers regardless their age, that it gave him a sense of superiority. I dismissed being caught from behind as nothing more than a consequence of my age, but then a gray-bearded guy not too far from my years went by and I was forced to confront my frailties. Perhaps the climbs weren't as difficult as I believed them to be, just made so by whatever deficiency it was that existed in my physiology.

I came out onto Wildcat Mountain Peak D in a cloak of fog not quite as dense as Mt. Washington had been but close. A pair of young thru-hikers were there, Lilac and Wheels. Lilac had a heart-shaped face and a matching smile under a longish nose, and so resembled a woman named Nancy I knew once that I had to stop and gawk. Lilac could have been Nancy's granddaughter, so close was the resemblance. I questioned her as we took photographs in front of the misty Wildcat sign, and we determined that no, she was in no way related to the woman I'd known. We then partnered up to find the trail, which was hidden in the fog, then we continued on our way, the two of them pulling quickly ahead.

I stopped for a water break on the boulders around the lake in Carter Notch. The sun made a brief appearance and I stood in it, arms wide in its reassuring warmth. Thru-hikers went by me one after another, bound for the side trail to Carter Notch Hut. When the sun went away moments later, I went too, bypassing the hut.

The climb up Carter Dome was 1500 feet of wet misery. Mt. Hight barely offered views of the surrounding woods let alone anything beyond. Darkness began to descend with me into Zeta Pass, the wind cold and biting, and then some rain in icy splatters. I looked for a stealth site, found one and set up quickly ahead of a lazy gray drizzle. I had no idea where I was, just somewhere beyond Zeta Pass and not quite to Middle Carter Mountain, well short of my goal and with maybe an hour of light left, but I wasn't going to risk repeating my hypothermia of Hike 2.

There was a bog log just beyond my tent. I heard footsteps going over it and looked out to see Lilac and Wheels, who were pushing on undeterred by the cold rain. They must have gone into Carter Notch Hut, otherwise they would have been well ahead of me. Lilac, I knew, had Guthook, so I hollered out and asked her if she could tell me where I was. She paused and thumbed her phone under her rain shell, then told me that we were at mile 1884.1. So I was camping just two tenths from Middle Carter Mountain at an elevation of about 4500 feet, with only 10.4 miles behind me and about the same ahead tomorrow.

And at that elevation it was going to be a cold, cold night.

Inside my down bag liner, I wore every article of clothing that I carried, including my rain shell and with the hood over my head. It didn't freeze overnight but it must have come close. My breaths clouded the peak of my tent, but the cheery warmth of my stove set me on my way in good spirits the next morning.

That day was no different than the previous, cold, cloudy, wet. I trudged up and over the two Carter mountains first thing, then down and down past Imp Campsite, then up and up over Mt. Moriah, fully exposed to an excruciatingly cold wind and with no views at all, and then I was in the swoosh and it went fast. I walked up to Rattle River Hostel at twelve thirty, 10.7 miles done and still early enough to get the benefit.

The first thing I did after eating a bag of corn chips someone had left out on a table was to look for a chiropractor. The ache in my neck and shoulder was worse if anything, unfazed by the ibuprofen-acetaminophen cocktail that I'd learned from a sports doctor I'd met by chance back in Damascus all those eons ago. His prescription worked incredibly well for all the other pains to which I was prone, but not this one. All the chiropractors even remotely close saw patients by appointment only—no walk-ins—so that was that.

A tall, black-bearded thru-hiker named Ghost thought he might be able to help me. He hugged me around the chest, then lifted and shook me as if I were no more than a rag doll, which in my state and weight I probably resembled. This didn't help, though. Later I stood under a hot shower until my skin was pink, and that didn't help either, so I gritted my teeth and compartmentalized the pain, as I had done with my torn shoulder on Hike 3. Pain would now be part of my journey, there was nothing to be done about it.

Resupplied and rested, I set out late the next morning for the state of Maine. The sun shone that morning so I loitered at the hostel while my tent dried, and didn't get underway until nine forty-five. I only had 16.5 miles to traverse to reach Maine. How many times had I clobbered that many miles by mid-afternoon? I was certain that I would lay my head in the state of Maine that night. I was cheered by the thought, even more confident when I passed Ghost and a few other thru-hikers who'd left the hostel earlier that morning.

Ghost, as it turned out, was the guy who gave me the beer back In Gorham! I was embarrassed not to have realized it was him, passed it off as the fault of my aging eyes, and thanked him again for his kindness. I liked Ghost a lot, but never saw him again after that exchange.

Those sunny first few miles soon morphed into the brooding cold I'd been enduring since the Whites. My pace slowed in the cold and the mud and a few wrong turns down poorly marked side trails. The blazing was not good. I remembered with a laugh how Eric at Rattle River Hostel had sent his guys out with cans of white spray paint to correct this when I informed him about it on Hike 3. They'd marked the trail pretty well for the first couple of miles, but no one could have expected them to carry on this far.

And then there was the grade. That section was definitely faster and easier for a southbounder, resembling jagged downward steps when going in that direction. I ran low on daylight as I cleared Mt. Success, and with incipient rain in the chill air. I dove into the next stealth site and pitched my tent, 15.2 miles for the day and only a little over a mile left to the state line. So I would not lay my head in the state of Maine that night, but I would the next, and from then on to the finish.

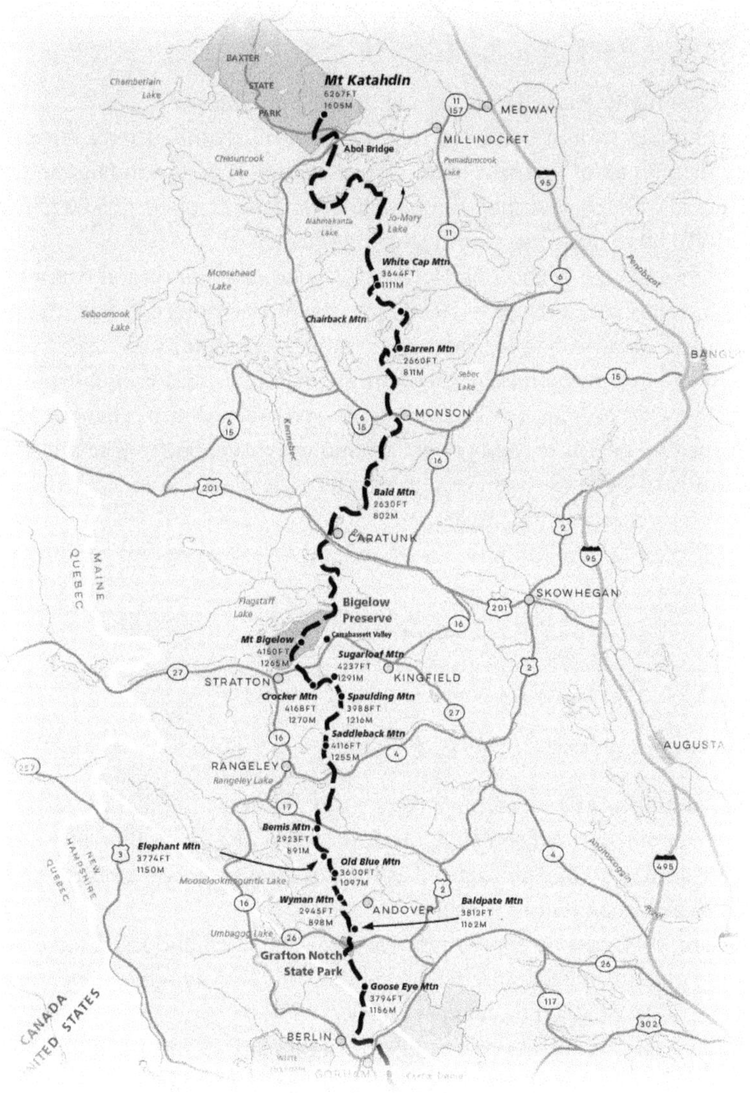

MAINE

281.8 MILES

SUNDAY, SEPTEMBER 5, 2021

Speck Pond - 11.3 Miles

Cold last night. Painful knees and shoulder but I did sleep.

Hiking by 6:15 a.m., crossed the state line shortly thereafter, a big muddy puddle after all of this rain. A tough day of climbs, slips, and falls, and then Mahoosuc Notch, and then climb Mahoosuc Arm. Got here at 5:00 p.m. and paid $10.00 to camp, no stealth sites anywhere.

Went through Mahoosuc Notch with Lilac and Wheels and had a much better time than in the past. Heavy gray sky but no rain so at least the rocks were dry. A damn bog log farther on sunk two feet into the muck when I stepped on it—really inexcusable trail maintenance—and then later I found that every other hiker I talked to had likewise fallen victim. That bog was so churned up by hikers trying to get around the rotten bog logs that it looked as if a herd of cattle had been driven through there, a shocking sight and grievous environmental impact.

My plan for the day was 7 more miles over Old Spec, but couldn't do it before dark.

MONDAY, SEPTEMBER 6, 2021

Grafton Notch - 4.6 Miles

Rained most of the night. Slept okay, up at 5:00 a.m., hiking by 6:15.

Wet, cold, decided to bail at Grafton Notch and go to Pine Ellis Hostel, where I am now. The rain started as soon as I got here. Food, resupply—I am very weary, impatient to finish.

Later on I gave up space in my room so that Wazi and sister Rage would have a place to stay because the hostel was full. They caught the rain on Old Spec, and Rage was full-on hypothermic.

I'm weary, weary, weary—tired, bone tired, used up and I don't know how I'll be able to go on or even if it's important to me anymore.

TUESDAY, SEPTEMBER 7, 2021

East B Hill Road - 10.3 Miles

Stayed up late last night talking to Wazi and Rage, so slept all the way through to 6:00 a.m.

Shuttled to the trailhead at 9:00, hiking by 9:30. Topped Baldpate two hours later in a howling cold wind but at least no rain, then out at East B Hill Road at 2:45 p.m. Caught a ride back to Pine Ellis with Wazi and Rage. Realized that I am burned out, so will do short miles tomorrow as well.

WEDNESDAY, SEPTEMBER 8, 2021

South Arm Road - 10.1 Miles

Sticking with Wazi and Rage, shuttled to the trailhead at 9:00 a.m., hiking by 9:10.

Got out ahead and made quick time. The Moody Mountain climb took an hour. I was out by 2:00 p.m., where Tim, a trail angel, was doing magic, beers and red Mainer hotdogs. My shoulder aches but might be a little better. Rain tomorrow, so another short day planned.

THURSDAY, SEPTEMBER 9, 2021

ME17 - 13.2 Miles

Shuttled early at 7:30 a.m., hiking by 8:10 and thank God!

This section was awful. We didn't get rained on but the trail was sloppy and slick. Rage went down and dislocated a finger, I mean the thing going at right angles to the knuckle. She snapped it back into place and soldiered on. Tough gal. I went down a few times, too, but only scrapes and bruises.

8 hours later we made it out, muddy, tired, bleeding. Gadget called me from Greasy Creek Friendly. It looks as if everything is going well down there.

I'm feeling much better, and tomorrow I'll get to see Steve at Hiker Hut! I've been looking forward to this for a thousand miles.

I have a cherished photograph that The Dude took of me at the Maine-New Hampshire state line on Hike 1. That photo was taken with a disposable Kodak, so the image is grainy and of low resolution, which actually lends a rugged historicity to the remoteness of that section of the Appalachian Trail more than two decades ago.

We'd gone through Mahoosuc Notch earlier, following bright blazes and right-angled arrows over, between, and under those massive boulders, with

The Dude sometimes having to help me drag my heavy and unyielding external frame backpack through the tighter squeezes. The weather was fair, as I recall. The trail was dry, the blackflies hadn't tormented us in a couple of days, and when we reached those signs we felt as if we'd escaped to freedom after a month interred in brutal Maine.

I say "those signs" because back then the state line was marked by two hand-painted signs, one for New Hampshire, which I have already described, and a blue one with white lettering for the state of Maine that read: WELCOME TO MAINE, THE WAY LIFE SHOULD BE. There was also a modern white AMC sign, which lacked gravitas in that setting. Today that modern sign is all that remains.

A large mud puddle filled the site this time, lapping against the big rocks we sat on to rest back then. It had rained overnight. The morning was damp and gray but not too cold. I noted the AMC sign, shrugged, then high-stepped around the edge of the puddle and continued on into Maine, this time with coursing excitement.

My mind was in this state: I was in *Maine!* I'd crushed the White Mountains and by God I'd crush Maine too. 280 miles or thereabouts at twenty miles per day—I had my hiker legs after all; this was what I'd been *waiting* for—and I would be on Mt. K in two weeks or less! I'd never gotten out of Maine in less than a month, but this time I'd race through it, free of blackflies and blowdowns, the autumn leaves turning and with blueberries along the trail, no snakes, no nettles, no poison ivy, just go, go, go. I flipped forward through my diary to mark the page and the day, then proceeded on at an easy step.

I went over Mt. Carlo and Goose Eye Mountain, a pair of jagged teeth leading down to Full Goose Shelter in its secluded notch. A quick climb over Fulling Mill Mountain would then send me down into Mahoosuc Notch, that boulder-crowded jungle gym known as either the most fun or most hated mile on the Appalachian Trail. Afterward I would go over Mahoosuc Arm and then Old Spec Mountain, and then the swoosh into Grafton Notch, up the other side to Baldpate Lean-to and I would pitch my tent, having escaped the AMC and now safely ensconced in Maine Appalachian Trail Club country. I could see every mile in my mind.

I pulled in at Full Goose Shelter for a rest, where I found Lilac and Wheels, as well as a clean-shaven and energetic nobo named Snazzy, who had a good disposition and an easy manner. He was in his late twenties or early thirties. His upper lip curled when he spoke, making his words seem to come from one side of his mouth. We all discussed the coming notch as we ate our snacks and energy bars. It would be easier to handle the packs and poles if we went through together, I suggested, and they accepted my advice. A pair of young women day hikers came in then, leading a dog, which proved that there was a shortcut side trail to the site somewhere but damn if I knew where it was. They brought out sandwiches and joined our conversation.

The day wasn't inspiring but it wasn't particularly bad. Snazzy noticed a small sign on a post across the way and went to study it. This proved to be a collection box for donations to the AMC.

"They've got balls asking for money," he grumbled as he came back. "They charge like hell for everything, and the trail's in terrible shape."

"Yeah, it is pretty bad," I agreed. "It didn't used to be like this. I don't know what the hell is going on, but I won't give them any money. I made it a point to get through the Whites this time without it and I pulled it off."

"Yeah, they suck," Snazzy added to that.

"We're AMC trail maintainers," one of the women flatly announced, startling us into scarlet shades of embarrassment.

"I'm so sorry," I said, wincing. "I didn't mean too–"

"No," she cut in. "You're right."

"What do you mean?" Wheels asked. He'd been silent thus far.

"Well, there are sections we want to work on but they won't let us," the woman explained.

"Why not?" Snazzy asked.

"They say they don't have enough money in their trail maintenance budget."

"*What!*" Snazzy blurted in incredulity.

"Yeah, they say they don't have it in their budget, so we do the best we can on our own. Do you remember the section up to [omitted to preserve anonymity]."

"Yeah," Wheels chimed in. "That was an awesome section."

"Well, we did all that work ourselves, even bought the paint with our own money. They told us not to paint blazes but we did it anyway. I don't think they even know."

We were all shaking our heads in disgust. This certainly wasn't MacKaye's vision. How had it come to this?

We thanked them for their dedication and hard work, then Lilac and Wheels took off. I followed soon after. Snazzy said he would be along shortly. I cleared Fulling Mill Mountain and dropped down into the notch, where I found Lilac and Wheels waiting.

"Where's Snazzy," they asked.

"He said he'd be along."

We waited fifteen minutes, Lilac and Wheels getting antsy, myself as well. Finally Wheels said, "Look, Solo–Lilac and I need to get going."

"Yeah..." I searched up the trail and saw no sign of Snazzy. The sky looked heavier now, as if rain might come at any time. "Okay, yeah, we'd better go."

The fractal chaos of Mahoosuc Notch has never seemed the same on any two of my thru-hikes. The boulders still sat where they had since the last glaciation but the surrounding trees and brush clothed them differently, like the same man in a suit and tie or in a farmer's overalls. This time the clothes were thick and green, and the blazes were threadbare.

We were confused almost from the outset. "I think we're in it," Wheels said.

"Yeah, we're in it," I confirmed.

"But I don't see any blazes," Lilac commented.

"We should be able to find something if we look around," I said.

"Don't you remember the way?" Lilac asked.

"No." I shook my head with a nostalgic smile. "It looks different every time. I even got lost in there on my last hike, started climbing up out of the notch thinking I was on the trail but it was a social trail someone had made, so I had to backtrack until I finally found an arrow kind of hidden by some bushes and then I took it from there. Let's look around. We'll find something."

And we did, a faint blaze that resembled a splotch of lichen from one angle and more of a rectangular shape from another. We found it as we three took position on separate boulders and then sort of triangulated on it. We continued on, sometimes spotting the next blaze on the other side of a chasm, which we either leapt or skirted. In places we would brace one another so that one of us could tenuously peer around a high corner for the next hint of a blaze, or else lie flat with two pairs of hands grasping a backpack as one of us shinnied out far enough to look over a ledge for an arrow down in the depths. It was possible, even easier, to transit Mahoosuc Notch without blazes, but Wheels and Lilac were adamant that we follow the blazed route as loyally as we could, and I agreed.

The sharp, cleaved gaps between the boulders did not threaten with bottomless falls. Most falls would be twenty feet or less, but the gaps had cracks and fissures and steeply canted angles, which could lead to fractured skulls and broken legs, or even worse, leave you wedged and trapped the way that guy up in Utah had been some years back.

We made leaps of faith in places, passed our backpacks and poles through the narrow cave-like openings at the bases of the larger boulders, hefting them hand-over-hand and then tugging them through one at a time. This went on and on for two hours. When we came out the other side, though, it didn't seem to have taken that long, an hour at most. Going through with

Lilac and Wheels made the transit fun as it had never been fun for me before. The rain held off, and that made it even better.

I stopped for a break at the base of Mahoosuc Arm, a 1700-foot climb out of the notch over a distance of a mile and a half. Again, there was a side trail somewhere. That climb wasn't entirely necessary, but what blazes there were said otherwise. Lilac and Wheels pushed on while I sat and contemplated the coming climb. Snazzy came out soon after, wearing a curled lip and a lopsided grin.

"That was awesome!" he exclaimed.

"So you had a good time, then."

"Oh, hell yeah."

"Sorry we didn't wait for you."

"That's cool. I really kinda wanted to do it by myself anyway. It's all good."

He pushed on as well. I sat for a few more minutes and then took off myself.

Mahoosuc Arm was not the grueling climb of a Pinkham Notch or a Crawford Notch, but it was long, steep, and time consuming. The day fled before me as I planted one foot and then the next, the air growing colder as I ascended, the saturated cloud layer coming closer. My rain shell was damp with dew when I reached the exposed top, icy pricks of rain striking my cheeks every now and then. Off in the misty distance, across a broad, boggy saddle, I could just make out Snazzy inching his way into the next stand of woods. I shivered. The landscape looked cold, desolate and lonely. I started down.

The high mountain bogs are deep pools of muck populated with grassy hummocks, dwarfed shrubs, and the odd island of granite. On Hike 1 I slipped off a bog log into one of these, experiencing terror as one leg plunged to the thigh. I lost my shoe while pulling back against a cloying vacuum, then spent the better part of an hour on my belly on the bog log fishing with my hiking staff to retrieve the shoe, pushing on afterward coated in black mud. It was my habit after that to test the bogs with my trekking poles whenever I went over the bog logs. Sometimes those poles would plunge below the murky surface in their entirety, what lay below nothing less than gooey quicksand. Think of the bodies found in the peat bogs of England and Scotland, some of those bodies a thousand years old or more; think what bodies might be discovered here one day, Indians of various periods, a French fur trader or two, and perhaps a stray thru-hiker.

So bog logs were important. I was crossing a long run of them, which lay over the bog like a crooked snake. Some were canted at angles, the result of the freeze-thaw cycle, while others might be rotten in the middle, requiring a slippery leap that could too easily end in misadventure. I planted a step on a next bog log, which unexpectedly plunged two feet into the muck, soaking my shoe and coating it in gunk and leaving me to jump and sprint ahead in a panic less the entire thing sink with me on it.

Some of the bog logs were too rotten to traverse. The hundreds if not thousands of thru-hikers who'd come before me had faced those same conditions. They'd leapt onto the grassy hummocks, using these as stepping stones across the bog, trampling the grass and destroying fragile roots in a widening circle. I had no choice but to do the same. I looked back when I finally reached the security of a granite surface and was shocked by what I saw. The bog looked obscene, like a great oozing wound. It would take decades for that to heal, and all for lack of essential maintenance. At a minimum, the trail could have been routed around the bog, staying on the more durable granite. The impression I had was that no trail maintainer had been up to take stock in a long time.

I entered the woods and began the climb up Old Spec Mountain. On the way would be Spec Pond Shelter and Campsite, which was an AMC site that cost money for a stay. On Hike 1 The Dude and I did a work-for-stay there, helping sift and transport composted human excrement in exchange for a free night in the shelter. The exchange was not worth it.

The day had gone too long for me to meet my goal, while the cloud layer was closer, thicker, and threatening. The air was chill, my breaths trailing in clouds behind me. I looked for a stealth site as I climbed but the terrain was too steep, too rocky. There was nothing, and I suspected there would be nothing ahead either, not in those dense woods, not on that steep mountain. Resigned and with a sigh, I went into Spec Pond Campsite for the first time in twenty years, paid my ten dollars and claimed a tent platform. The caretaker, a young woman, was pleasant and good-natured, which took away some of the sting. She gave me a tangerine, bless her. Lilac and Wheels were set up on the other side of the campsite. Snazzy, they told me, had pushed on, trusting to find a stealth site somewhere. I learned later that he'd pitched his tent near nightfall on the rocks atop Old Spec, anchoring his tent with stones, and had spent a wet, blustery, and freezing night.

I spent a not uncomfortable night myself, but my mental state was strained. From the morning to the night of that day I had gone from exultation to a worrisome depression. I'd only made 11.3 miles. Granted, Mahoosuc Notch had been in there, but still... And the cold–damn I was tired of the cold, and the wet, and climb after unforgiving climb. On a southbound thru-hike I would have been in the area of Hot Springs, North Carolina by then, in the full flush of Springer fever and about to turn on incredible miles.

But in this terrain I couldn't do it—and I wouldn't be able to do it, not as I had idealized. As it was, the closer I got to Mt. Katahdin the farther away it seemed. At my excruciatingly slow pace, it might migrate with the continents before I got there.

I roused myself lethargically the next morning and broke camp in the dripping darkness. It had rained sporadically throughout the night, letting up only an hour or so earlier. The trail wasn't running but intertwined roots acted as dams to form ankle-deep puddles, while overhanging evergreen limbs would loose their own chilling rain if bumped. I set out in the first light after six o'clock and made my climb, searching along the way for any stealth sites that might have been, and found none. So I'd made the right call, even though it didn't feel that way.

Eventually I was over the top, where on Hike 3 I'd met an intriguing young woman named Untitled under a warm, azure sky. This time the sky was leaden, the swoosh muddy and slippery. I couldn't take it at the speed I would have on a dry day. Slipping and sluicing down the mountain, my shoes saturated and my feet numb, I came to a realization: I'd had enough. Period. I decided to bail out in Grafton Notch, which would mean a nero of only 4.6 miles but so be it. I called Naomi at Pine Ellis Hostel and asked her to come get me.

I'd stayed at Pine Ellis Hostel in Andover, Maine three times before, although never from Grafton Notch, which was a rather long drive and would cost me some money for the shuttle. I didn't care—the hell with my rules. In that mindset, I would have followed a blue-blazed trail to Mt. Katahdin if one had existed.

Pine Ellis Hostel is a two-story Victorian residence now showing its years. There are private rooms to let upstairs, a bunkhouse out back, a detached garage to the side where the washer and dryer are located, and a covered porch up front. The rain started up just as I arrived. Naomi was the same caring soul she'd been last time, while Ilene Trainor, who owned the place, was aging although not appreciably during the three years since I'd last seen her. She and her husband Paul established Pine Ellis Hostel long before my first hike. I met Paul then, when I was in a similar dispirited state, and he gave me the advice I needed to keep going. I learned on Hike 2 that he'd passed away, another of the great trail legends gone. I wondered sometimes if there was a Valhalla for those departed trail warriors, a place for them to gather, break bread, and reminisce about old times on the Appalachian Trail.

I took a private room, wanting nothing more than to cocoon myself in quiet while I worked through my dispirited thoughts. I woodenly attended to my chores to get them out of the way, laundry &c. I hoofed to the store for food and resupply during a break in the rain, then returned to my room and fell back on my bed, rubbing at my aching neck and shoulder. There were three beds in the room, a waste of space for only me but again I didn't care.

That depression, which seemingly came from nowhere, was as deep as any post-trail depression I'd ever endured. I ran scenarios through my mind, weighed consequences: What if I quit? What if I skipped to Mt. K? Could I live with myself afterward? And who would know, really, unless I told them?

Well, I would know.

I had foregone beer at the store and had matriculated directly to boxed wine, which I sipped dispassionately, running through it all again as my head swirled. Without someone like Paul Trainor there to talk me down, how would I ever cope? A knock came at my door in the later afternoon, as rain began to once again splatter at the windows. Naomi stuck her head in.

"Solo," she said apologetically, "I'm sorry to bother you. We've got two thru-hikers downstairs who got caught in the rain on Old Spec. The hostel is full, though..."

She trailed off at that, leaving me not to wonder where she was headed. There were wet thru-hikers downstairs and nowhere else for them to stay. Dispirited though I was, I wasn't about to turn them away.

"Hell yeah, Naomi, send them up."

"Are you sure?"

"Sure I'm sure. I mean, there are two more beds in here that shouldn't go to waste."

She smiled. "Thanks, Solo. I'll send 'em up."

I heard bumping on the steep and narrow stairs, and then a pair of fifty-somethings came dripping in, a brother-sister team named Wazi and Rage. Wazi was robust and in reasonable spirits, but his sister Rage was not in a good way. She was hugging herself, shivering and shaking, her hair pasted against her pale forehead, her rain shell as wet as if it had just come out of a washer.

"Th-th-th-thank you so much," she chattered.

"Yeah, we really thank you for this," Wazi added.

Wazi was at a good body weight for that point in his hike, but Rage looked absolutely emaciated, her skin drawn and thin and no weight on her anywhere. She looked about the way I would have looked in similar circumstances.

"That's cool, guys, no problem—but you all need to drop your gear and get Rage in a hot shower."

"Y-y-y-yeah," she agreed.

They dropped sodden gear and got to it, leaving me alone for an hour while they showered and warmed up and made a dash to the store. They looked human when they got back, although Rage was still shivering. She handed me a box of wine, then pulled a blanket over her shoulders.

"That's for you," she said in a voice no longer tremulous. "I can't thank you enough for letting us stay in your room."

"Thru-hikers have to take care of each other," I said, blushing under the attention. "We always say you can get one more hiker in."

"Well, two this time," Wazi noted with gratitude.

They spread out their wet things and took inventory while I laid back and sipped wine. I learned that Rage was the older of the two by a couple of years and that she was a consummate marathoner, which is what actually accounted for her trail-thin physique. The thru-hike had been Wazi's idea, a journey he was prepared to undertake alone, but Rage had been intrigued and so had joined him even though she'd never done anything remotely like it in her life. She had a competitive drive that I recognized, competing more with herself than others. The siblings snapped at each other from time to time, making me laugh. I liked them both.

We shuttled back to Grafton Notch together at nine o'clock the next morning. My plan was to continue on as I'd intended, only this time topping Baldpate Mountain and camping somewhere in the vicinity of Moody Mountain that evening after eighteen or twenty miles. My heart wasn't in it, though, I knew that the moment I stepped out of the shuttle.

The sky was relatively clear, the air warm down in the notch. It wouldn't be a bad day of hiking but I looked forward to it with a dread I couldn't dissuade. In that moment I wanted to be nowhere other than home, sitting in my easy chair, staring deadpan at a television, and eating from sunrise to sunset. I wasn't going to make twenty miles, who was I kidding? I'd be surprised if I made twenty miles again, and now Mt. Katahdin seemed even farther away, short miles over mountain after brutal mountain when I wanted to be pulling thirties instead.

Rage and Wazi quickly got out ahead on the first rooty climb, while I trudged along with little ambition and even less motivation. Soon they were out of sight. The irony of Rage and Wazi's plight the previous night was that they had days ago reserved that very same room for the next several nights. Their plan was to slackpack the thirty-three-odd miles between Grafton Notch and Maine Highway 17, dividing it into three short sections and returning to Pine Ellis each night. This was simple to arrange because two roads cut through there, each a short drive from Andover: East B Hill Road, and South Arm Road. It was from South Arm Road that I traditionally hitched to Pine Ellis Hostel during a southbound thru-hike; and on Hike 2 I did essentially what Wazi and Rage were doing, albeit in the other direction.

I continued on and up. The climb wasn't that difficult and the trail was mostly dry by then, but I couldn't escape my darker thoughts. I was tired of the Appalachian Trail, no, I was *sick* of it. I wanted to be anywhere else, I didn't care, even *France* would be a relief. Mt. Katahdin kept receding, moving farther away with my every forward step, always on the horizon and never to be reached. It didn't help that I knew what lay in between, mountain after mountain, river fords and picayune trail, as well as my two Appalachian Trail boogerbears and the Hundred-Mile Wilderness withal. It exhausted me just to think about it, so much so that when I cleared the timberline on Baldpate's west peak, the wind frisky but the sun shining, and with the first substantial view I'd had in forever, I scarcely noticed. I saw only boulders and blazes, roots and rocks, a seemingly endless file of them from there to the other side of the world.

Across the woody saddle, I spotted the colorful specks of Wazi and Rage picking their way along a rounded ridge below the east peak, their distance from me seeming vast while really they were no more than half a mile away. The two were strong hikers, so perhaps I wasn't doing as badly as I presumed. The sight of them cheered me in an unexplainable way. I kicked up a step and went after them.

I didn't catch them until the top of the east peak, and only then because they'd stopped for a break. I approached them somewhat re-spirited, took out an energy bar and munched while I spoke. The idea had come to me during the climb up the east peak, the only question was whether or not they would go for it.

"So look, guys," I said, "whaddaya say I stick with you for the next few days? I'll shuttle back with you each day, and I'll kick in for the room."

I didn't tell them how desperate I was for them to agree, and I'm not sure what I would have done if they'd said no. Fortunately for me they actually seemed thrilled.

"Sure, Solo, of course," Rage said with a grin. "After what you did for us, it's the least we can do."

So we hiked out together after a short 10.3 miles. David, Ilene's son-in-law, was there to pick us up, as Rage and Wazi had previously arranged. David is an American Indian, a bit younger than me, who displays the same taciturn mystery and reticence as every Indian I've ever known. I first met him on Hike 2 when he'd stepped in to help out after Paul passed away. We'd shared no more than a dozen words between then and now but somehow his meaning always got through. I doubt anyone in the state of Maine knew the trail as well as David. Through shrugs and mumbles and penetrating gazes, he intimated that he'd hiked every mile of the trail in that part of the state, in each direction and many times more than once. I got the sense that he saw the trail as a living thing and, on deeper reflection, I guess it was.

We returned early enough to get the benefit and then some. I hiked the few blocks to Mill's Market and sat in their diner for a burger and fries, and then another burger and another mess of fries, and then, just for the heck of it, another burger and fries to carry back to the hostel.

I sat on the porch to eat my third burger in an hour, and talked with the other thru-hikers, some surly but most of them pleasantly disposed. I met one intense, bearded young guy named Mohawk, whose world-wide exploits were fascinating to hear. My four thru-hikes paled to what he'd done in the Himalayas.

I turned in early that night, in the same bed I'd occupied the previous night. Rage and Wazi came in later but I was sound asleep by then, my mind easing, my sleep dreamless.

10.1 miles the next day went in quick time through pretty weather. I got out ahead of Wazi and Rage and maintained that lead all the way to South Arm Road, stepping out of the woods at two o'clock and meeting a trail angel named Tim who was doing trail magic. He had beers and was grilling those peculiar but tasty red Mainer hotdogs. Some of the other thru-hikers were dubious of the red dogs, but I chewed those dogs with relish, one after another.

A shuttle from a hostel called The Cabin pulled up, the owner of the place, Honey, at the wheel. The Cabin was farther outside of Andover, a competitor to Pine Ellis, I guess, but there were plenty of thru-hikers to go around. I'd never stayed there—I'd never even been there—but thru-hikers spoke highly of the place, the same way I spoke highly of Pine Ellis. I introduced myself to Honey if for no other reason than to meet another trail person. She told me that Nimblewill Nomad was currently at her place, which made my heart speed up by two and a half beats or so. This meant that I was finally going to be able to meet the penultimate trail legend, but no, he'd already been through and would tomorrow shuttle toward Mahoosuc Notch and continue southbound. Honey offered to take me to The Cabin to meet him, and I just about accepted her offer, but then I thought no, I didn't want to intrude. Nimblewill Nomad probably needed his rest, and was doubtlessly being hounded by every thru-hiker in the place. I didn't want to add to that. I thanked her anyway, and missed my last chance to meet him.

Back in Andover, I went to Mill's Market and sat for another burger or two or more, now familiar enough in the place that the cooks didn't need to ask me what my order would be. I felt sated and satisfied. It was amazing what a regular diet of thick hamburgers could do. I gave a wry thought to Robbie back in Virginia, my promise to try to become a vegetarian. I apologized to him over the distance and then ordered another burger.

I had another blessedly restful night, and got up early with Wazi and Rage for our next section, this time the 13.2 miles to Maine Highway 17. That section didn't look bad at all on the trail profile, just Old Blue Mountain sticking up like a canine tooth, Bemis Mountain much less intimidating. I knew that section though, I remembered it well. I pulled straight through it on my previous thru-hikes, from Maine Highway 4 near Rangeley all the way to South Arm Road, where I then hitched out to Pine Ellis, 26.4 miles on those thru-hikes, so the shorter miles we'd planned for the day would surely go quickly.

David advised that we leave earlier than the usual nine o'clock shuttle, and further advised in spare words that we take the section southbound. Not for me, I told him, always forward, never backward, but I would pass on his thoughts to Wazi and Rage. They, too, were adamant. True north, they called it. Slackpacking was one thing but reversing direction was something else entirely. Rage asked me again why I wasn't slackpacking as well. I told her my rule, and besides, my loaded backpack wasn't too much heavier than their practically empty ones.

We set out at seven thirty under a heavier sky, taking to a trail that was tough from the outset. We stayed together through most of it, if only because we were each challenged equally by the trail conditions. David's advice had been well founded and my memory was inverted. Going northbound through that section was hell.

The trail was wet, boggy, slippery and heartless. We climbed and descended sections of canted wet granite that were so slick that we had to hug the trees along the verges to prevent ourselves from slipping and then shooting down as if on a playground slide, fifty feet here, thirty feet there—sometimes even a mere few feet were challenging, a ridiculously short drop but a broken ankle could still be the result of a slip. Going down those inclines was easy in dry conditions, with traction assured, but in the wet they were slides toward broken bodies. So many hikers before us had faced the same conditions that the trees along the verges were stripped of limbs and bark, many in the process of dying from the trauma.

We were muddy, scraped and bruised, making painstaking progress one tentative footstep at a time. Coming down a slide, where there was no choice but to take it on our behinds, Rage veered off her trajectory and slammed into a boulder right behind me. She wailed in anguish and I spun around, my palms scratched and cut, a clump of mud clinging stubbornly to the bill of my cap.

"Rage, what happened?" I asked in a panic. She lay in a heap at the foot of the slide. "Are you okay?" Wazi was up above, just sitting down for his own undignified slide.

Rage sat up with a face twisted in agony. I gave her a quick scan, saw no blood, no bones sticking out. "Just stay still," I told her. "Let me check you out."

She held out her right hand and looked at in in disbelief. Her middle finger was at an almost right angle to the others. Broken? I couldn't tell. Her face was blanching in shock. I had to get something to cover her hand, to get her eyes off it. I went for a bandana, and in that moment as I looked away she grabbed hold of that finger and yanked it straight. I heard the crack. Her cry was contained. Wazi reached us then, not sure what was going on. We bound her fingers and then I dug into my pharmacopeia for some vitamin I. She was trembling so much that she dropped the tablets into the mud. "Don't worry," I said. "I've got more," but before I could produce them she'd scooped the pills out of the mud and had popped them into her mouth.

Damn, that Rage was a tough gal. I inquired later and learned that she was married. Too bad.

It took us eight hours to traverse those 13.2 miles. After a final sadistic climb, we came out of the woods and onto Maine Highway 17 in a bitter wind and a light sprinkling of rain. Back at the hostel, showered and fed, I felt wonderful despite our travails that day, ready to get back to big miles.

My depression was completely gone. My only theory for the episode was that my body was so depleted of nutrients that it forced me to take action, as if two entities reside in each of us, as if something inside me knew that I would push myself beyond all reason so it messed with my mind to make me stop. Whatever the cause, neither depression nor self-doubt touched me again for the remainder of the hike. My drive was restored. I would push hard, I would push long, and I would achieve things I'd never achieved before.

And tomorrow, at last, I'd reach Hiker Hut near Rangeley, Maine and I'd be able to see my good friend Steve.

FRIDAY, SEPTEMBER 10, 2021

Mile 1977 - 17.5 Miles

Our shuttle left at 7:00 a.m., so I was up at 5:00 to make ready. Drizzling this morning but it stopped and the day became really nice.

Said my goodbyes to Wazi and Rage at the trailhead, then took off at 8:10, making quick time. Got to ME4 at 1:30 p.m., then went the three tenths up the road to see Steve at Hiker Hut. Steve crushed my heart. He didn't remember me, and was completely dismissive. "I see hundreds of hikers," he said, and he was full, and Freewind's flowers were gone. All of this really took the wind out of me.

I went back to the road, and decided not to go into Rangeley but to just go on and start this next section. On the way up I met Mountain Goat and Disco, whom I hadn't seen since Hot Springs! They'd flipped at Delaware Water Gap and were now hiking south from Mt. K. Seeing them again came as a comfort I can't explain, and really lifted my spirits after Steve.

Pushed on to here where I have stealthed. Mileage is approximate. Tomorrow Saddleback, and, yep, time for a boogerbear.

—

Coming off Saddleback Mountain on Hikes 1 and 2, I hitched into Rangeley, Maine to stay with Bob O'Brien at Gull Pond B&B. Bob was a fascinating old man, a deep conversationalist who could venture into diverse topics and explore them with the breadth and depth of an autodidact. Bob wasn't listed in AWOL on Hike 3. I learned later that he'd passed away, another place setting at that Valhalla trail table.

There was, however, a newer hostel listed in AWOL on Hike 3, Hiker Hut, which was only three tenths up the highway from the trailhead. I'd just spent a particularly trying pair of days among the Crocker, Sugarloaf, Spaulding, and Saddleback peaks in which I'd endured abominable weather and had, for the first time ever for me in the state of Maine, been crowded into a shelter with reeking nobos, whom I was told were known as *early* nobos, or *winter* nobos. I'd never heard of such before, and prior to then had never encountered a nobo bubble sooner than Hanover, New Hampshire. I was low on patience, stamina, and daylight when I finally emerged onto Maine Highway 4, where I turned right toward Rangeley, hoofed the three tenths to Hiker Hut, and met Steve.

I noted as I went down Hiker Hut's long twining driveway that there was something unique about the place, something familiar and exotic at the same time, all immersed in a stilling serenity. The motif was Tibetan, I learned, which explained all. The outbuildings had that rustic oriental look about them, as if they belonged in the snowy Himalayas. There were flower beds, pathways, and a gurgling stream below. Just above through a screen of trees was the highway, whose sounds of rumbling traffic seemed much farther away than they were, as if truly beyond a lost horizon. I was entranced.

Following the path, feeling as if I were in a state of grace, I sighted a man up a ladder doing repairs to a roof.

"Hey there. What can I do for you?" the man asked from on high without looking away from his work.

I still had the reek of nobo on me, and felt disgusting in my own skin. "Hot shower, hot food, cold beer," I answered wearily.

"Okay then," he said, stowing his hammer and climbing down. "Let's go."

It was June 7, 2018, and this was Steve.

What followed was a whirlwind of activity in Rangeley, a hot shower at the YMCA, food and beer at a local pub, and resupply up the street, Steve carting me to each in his battered old red pickup, then waiting while I did what I needed to do.

Steve was a half year shy of my age. He was my height and my build, with a long, clean-shaven face, narrow eyes, and short brown hair going gray and receding above his temples. We didn't get back to his hostel until well after dark, a deep cold settling in. He had built the place with his own hands, setting it up completely off the grid. I was the only thru-hiker there, bundled in the bunkroom under one of Steve's flannel sleeping bags. I was comfortable enough, but then Steve came in with a battery powered heater, which he set up next to my bunk. I was reassuringly warm in minutes, and spent one of the most peaceful and satisfying nights I'd ever spent on the Appalachian Trail.

Steve was up as early as I was the following morning, ready with hot coffee, the aroma of scrambled eggs frying in a pan. I wandered around the property in the enchanting dawn light, a lavender sky above, the gurgling stream, bird song, the steam from my coffee warming my face, a sense of eternal peace coming with every sight I saw and every breath I took. That was the morning of my sixtieth birthday. The news of this excited Steve, who was himself soon to join the roll-call of sexagenarians.

I decided to zero. It just felt right. Steve and I ate our scrambled eggs, sipped our coffees and talked. I told him my story, he told me his, of difficulties earlier in his life but he'd found his calling in India, where he journeyed every winter to help the poor children over there. He was a practicing Tibetan Buddhist, the first I'd ever met and I was intrigued. I felt a comfortable connection to Steve. I told him about Freewind, the young man whose ashes I carried. I thought Steve's gardens would be a worthy place to scatter some of Freewind's ashes but wasn't sure how Steve would take to the notion. "Freewind," he said distantly. "*Freewind*...I love that name." And then he turned his narrow eyes to mine and said with the soberest expression, "I'd be honored."

Later that day, Steve's girlfriend Kathy arrived with some dahlias they were going to plant in front of the bunkhouse. Steve wanted me to sprinkle some of Freewind's ashes in every hole Kathy dug for the flowers, so that, as he said, "Every hiker who comes here will know Freewind."

Steve burned incense, chanted and rang a bell as I sprinkled Freewind's ashes, Kathy coming in behind to plant the flowers. It was a moving ceremony, and when it was done I felt as if I'd been true to Freewind and that Steve had adopted Freewind's spirit into that place. Steve and I stood for a photo afterward, our arms over each other's shoulders, looking as much like brothers as two previous strangers could.

Later in the afternoon, Steve cooked me that birthday dinner of spaghetti with enormous meatballs. We sat and sipped beers and watched the stream flow in the twilight. Steve invited me to India, he called me his brother, and I felt as if I were.

I wrote about Steve and his Hiker Hut in my book *More Notes from the Field*, and sent him an autographed copy. I mailed him my Springer Mountain summit photo, and we spoke on the phone a couple of times. The Covid pandemic interrupted my plans to surprise him in India, but here I was now, a scarce three years later, thru-hiking the Appalachian Trail once again and soon to be reunited. I couldn't suppress my excitement.

I took to the trail with Wazi and Rage that morning. It was a splendid morning following some earlier rain, cool but not cold. The sky was clear, the sun bright on my face, and the air smelled as clean as Arctic snow. I said my goodbyes to the siblings, along with my thanks. They were heading to a hotel in Rangeley after that section, while I was going to throw down with Steve at Hiker Hut. We might not see each other again, and when I pulled out quickly ahead of them, reenergized and hiking once again with *arete*, I was pretty certain we wouldn't.

I made a quick 13.2 miles over one of the most forgiving sections of trail in the state of Maine, coming out onto Maine Highway 4 at one thirty. I didn't break step, but turned left this time and scooted the three tenths up the road to Hiker Hut.

Everything looked more or less the same as I proceeded down the driveway. I noted a couple of tents back in the woods, and a rick of firewood under a blue tarp. Of course there would be other thru-hikers here this time, but that didn't matter. I followed the path to the buildings. A young thru-hiker came out of the bunkhouse and threw me an incurious look. I ignored him, looked for Freewind's garden, and my heart fell. The flowers were gone, the garden choked with weeds. But then, I thought quickly, Freewind's flowers would not have survived their first winter. Steve had probably replanted that garden several times since then.

I looked ahead to the main cabin, to the picnic table out front where Steve and I had once sat for breakfast, then went to the table and dropped my pack. A woman in a face mask came around the corner. "Can I help you?" she asked quizzically.

I couldn't make out the face behind the mask, but it had to be Kathy. I smiled warmly. "Hey Kathy, it's Solo," I said, walking toward her. The masked woman did the Covid back-step, two steps backward for every single step I took toward her, as if the virus might be leaping from me like lice. I frowned and pulled up short. "You *are* Kathy, right?"

"No," she said, taking one final, cautionary step back. "Kathy's not here anymore."

"Oh, no," I said in dismay. "Is Steve here, then?"

"Yeah, he's here."

She made no move, no motion, no gesture.

"Well, uh, can I see him?"

"I'll go find out."

She went up into the main cabin while I waited with a sudden creeping sense of wrongness about the situation. I heard voices inside, a back and forth, one of the voices in the brusque timber of a man. The masked woman—who never offered her name—came out. "He's busy but he'll be out in a minute."

"Did you tell him it was Solo?" I asked with a descending sense of disassociation.

"Yeah." She stood there behind her mask.

"I know Steve," I said to her, oddly feeling as if I needed to defend my legitimacy, my right to be there. "I stayed with him three years ago. We scattered some of Freewind's ashes in that garden." I pointed, although she didn't follow the gesture, just kept her cautious eyes on me.

A man stepped out, but this man wore a beard that hid every feature I would recognize.

"Are you Steve?" I asked tentatively.

"Yeah," he answered in a begrudging tone. I brightened just the same. After all, I looked different, too. Once he recognized me he would grin and hold out his hand and the few years since June 2018 would evaporate to nothing and everything would be just like it was then.

"Hey Steve, it's Solo."

"Who?"

"It's *Solo*." I found myself pleading for some reason. "You know me. We scattered Freewind's ashes right there."

"I see hundreds of hikers," he said dismissively, as if brushing lint off a sleeve. My face fell. My heart thudded above my navel. And then he asked with derisive impatience, "What do you want?"

I simply could not understand what was happening. "I wanted to see you again," I said shakily. A knife was pushing up from beneath my ribs, but surely at any moment he would remember it all and we would embrace. "I thought I would stay with you tonight."

"We're full," he said, and walked off. Those were the last words he spoke to me. If John[3] back in Pennsylvania had broken my heart, Steve in Maine had crushed it.

I sat numbly at the picnic table, tried to process it all but couldn't. A lip trembled. The masked woman still stood there. "We were friends," I said abjectly in her direction. "We scattered Freewind's ashes—there was a ceremony..." I trailed off, remembering it all, comparing it to now and nothing fit, nothing held place, nothing made sense. "He called me *brother*," I said to her with glistening eyes and a look that must have held anguish.

"I'm sorry," she said, "but we're full. You can probably get a hitch into Rangeley from the top of the driveway, that's where the rest of them do it."

She turned and left, and I sat as heavily as an overloaded backpack, my senses muted, my sensibilities ground and cubed like a cut of raw beef. I stood finally, shouldered my pack and plodded back up to the highway. I looked right toward Rangeley, where perchance I might be able to meet up with Wazi and Rage, but then felt a rush of disgust and betrayal so overpowering that I turned left for the trailhead instead, walking woodenly along the highway.

We were *friends*. He'd called me *brother*. He'd invited me to *India*—I kept a photo of the two of us on my *desk!*

Excuse me for a minute—

—okay, I just shredded that photo.

I took to the trail. The trail was the only escape, the only thing *real*. Steve was a fraud, must have been from the beginning. I ground my teeth, cursed, and charged up the mountain. *Don't use anger*, I mouthed to myself, which was a mantra so oft repeated during my second thru-hike that I'd used it in my novel, *The Appalachian*. Don't use anger on the trail, I repeated over and over again on that hike, after run-ins with surly nobos in their multitudes. Stay calm, I would remind myself. The trail isn't about anger, it's about escaping anger, but now I *was* angry, and that anger powered me up the mountain, mired in a miasma of misanthropy and ready to lash out.

Two thru-hikers were coming down the trail toward me, sobos I assumed, my own tribe, so I tempered my hostility. As we pulled close, one of them beamed.

"Damn, it's Solo!" the beaming guy exclaimed.

I focused hard, and this time my eyes really were failing me, but a face resolved and by God if it wasn't Mountain Goat, with Disco two steps behind!

"Mountain Goat...and Disco. Ohmygod!" I couldn't believe it! The last time I'd seen them was in Hot Springs as they set out for their pub crawl in Asheville. The coincidence was astounding. "What are you guys *doing* here?"

"We flipped at Delaware Water Gap," Mountain Goat explained.

Disco stepped forward. "Solo, it's *so* good to see you," he said, and the moist look in his eyes confirmed that he meant it.

We took some minutes to catch up on what had happened during the months and miles since Hot Springs. Hagrid had to get off the trail, they told me. Cinderella and Groot were still on a northbound path, but way back. Mountain Goat and Disco were afraid that it was getting too late in the season so they'd flipped. Like me, they'd lost their tramily, but at least the two of them had stayed together. They were excited to learn that Ultra Burn and K-Bar were still on the trail and that they would probably meet up with both of them soon.

We said our goodbyes eventually, which brought an unexpected pang. Reconnecting with them somehow dampened what had happened with Steve, reassuring me that there were, indeed, authentic people on the trail. And age lends you a certain pragmatism about relationships. You can't lose a friend you never really had.

I continued up and on, my anger abated. I took a stealth site in the timberline below Saddleback peak and set up for the night, seventeen and a half miles for the day and my first boogerbear coming tomorrow. I wasn't worried about that boogerbear, not now.

The way I felt right then, that boogerbear should be worried about me.

SATURDAY, SEPTEMBER 11, 2021

Mile 1993 - 16 Miles

Really cold last night and this morning. Got an early start at 6:15 a.m., then caught cold wind and fog on Saddleback, cleared out by Saddleback Junior, and then came the long slog and climbs. I pushed and pushed to get here so I could get a good jump on tomorrow and get well ahead of that mobile frat party back at Spaulding Mountain Lean-to.

SUNDAY, SEPTEMBER 12, 2021

Stratton, Maine - 11.9 Miles

Cold this morning, but on the way by 6:15 a.m. Tough climbs, but also some sections where I could move fast. No views at all, just clouds and mist.

Made it out by 1:30 p.m. There was trail magic at the trailhead, ruined by the mobile frat party. Caught a ride to Spillover Motel. Stratton Motel has apparently closed.

Well, I did it but I'm pretty tired. The people here went up the road to the store and brought me a bottle of wine—yes, a bottle, not a box. Nice folks and a nice place. I'm going to zero tomorrow and hope the weather improves before I go into the Bigelows.

MONDAY, SEPTEMBER 13, 2021

Stratton, Maine - Zero

Zero number 13. Really sore this morning, stiff. That was a hard push I did, but faster than ever before. Take that, boogerbear.

Did laundry and resupply. Ran into that damn mobile frat party again. What dicks. 11:00 a.m., chores done. The weather for tomorrow is looking good.

TUESDAY, SEPTEMBER 14, 2021

Mile 2022.8 - 11.9 Miles

Up early feeling well. Food, then caught a lucky hitch. Hiking before 8:00 a.m.

Went on alone for a good while, then looked back to see Rage coming up! Thought I had lost them. They had a hostel set up for tonight and tried to get me in, but the place was full. We hiked together to Avery Peak in astounding weather, first time ever for me. Take that, boogerbear #2! Arrived here at 5:00 p.m. and pitched my tent. I had more miles in me but it's getting dark so much earlier now, and heavy clouds were moving in.

WEDNESDAY, SEPTEMBER 15, 2021

Caratunk, Maine - 19.1 Miles

It did not rain overnight so I awoke to a dry tent, not cold either.

Hiking by 6:05 a.m., a little hard to see. Pushed it hard to make the Kennebec ferry by 2:00 p.m., slowed by a scary fall that cracked my neck. For a few minutes there I was afraid I was paralyzed, but I did not lose sensation and all seemed to be well.

It became a wet day, although I never got rained on per se, just sprinkles and mist and heavier rain behind me. Made it to the river at 1:15 p.m., plenty of time for the canoe ride across. Rob was the operator, nice guy and he knows his stuff. Took a room at Eric's Sterling Inn, with dinner and beers at Northern Outdoors. Damn if the mobile frat party hasn't caught up to me again. I've got to get out early tomorrow and lose those dicks.

THURSDAY, SEPTEMBER 16, 2021

Mile 2061.5 - 19.6 Miles

Four months on the trail. Slept deep and soundly, up at 5:30 a.m. for coffee.

Lingered at Sterling Inn talking to Eric, who did remember me, so I didn't get to the trailhead until 9:00. Great weather today. Despite the late start and the climbs, I had a good day. Found this stealth site at 5:30 p.m. The mileage is approximate. Regardless, Monson tomorrow in 13 miles or thereabouts.

FRIDAY, SEPTEMBER 17, 2021

Mile 2078.6 - 17.1 Miles

Damn cold this morning. Up at 4:45 a.m., hiking in the dark by 6:00.

Met up with Nick of Time (Nick), who wound up being a great guy also trying to outrun the mobile frat party, and here I thought he was one of them. We hiked together all the way to Monson, pushing past the blue blaze and on to ME15, his idea and I'm glad I went with it. He resupplied in Monson and then hitched out. Great weather, but I pushed it too hard today and I'm worn out.

At Shaw's, Poet and Hippy Chick are not here so I dealt with Hambone and Nugs for check-in and resupply. And the mobile frat party has damn shown up. So I will head into the 100-Mile tomorrow morning and see what I can do in there this time.

—

The thirty-two-odd miles between Maine Highway 4 near Rangeley and Maine Highway 27 near Stratton contain the last section of the Appalachian Trail to be completed, which was accomplished by the Civilian Conservation Corps in 1937 and is marked by a bronze plaque embedded in a rock face just off Spaulding Mountain and seemingly in the middle of nowhere. That section also contains the two-thousandth mile for northbounders, which is crossed coming down North Crocker Mountain. Those thirty-two miles are home to eight peaks of over 3000 feet, with five of those near 4000 feet or more. It's a rugged section of Appalachian Trail, probably even in good weather but I wouldn't know—I've never had good weather through there.

On Hike 3 I sat in Stratton, Maine for three days waiting for the weather to improve before I could begin my climb of 3000 feet up North Crocker Mountain. I wasn't half way up the flank of that mountain when the favorable forecast turned to spitting ice and freezing rain, but on into it I climbed, fetching up wet and frozen late in the day at Spaulding Mountain Lean-to, where I was soon thereafter overrun by that first-ever nobo bubble that I'd encountered in the state of Maine. The hike out the next day over Poplar Ridge and the Saddleback peaks was just as cold, just as wet, and just as trying, and then I met Steve, and, well, you know.

Hike 2 went similarly, just as wet although not quite as cold. I shivered alone in Spaulding Mountain Lean-to that time, pushed on with chattering teeth the next morning, and then, in a surreal reversal seemingly from one step to the next, stumbled over the broad hump of Saddleback Mountain in a heat and humidity worthy of the Atchafalaya in August. I was so hot and so dehydrated so quickly that I couldn't make it off the mountain that day, which was my fiftieth birthday. I wound up camping with those Mainers who were fishing on Eddy Pond, then hiked out to stay with Bob O'Brien the following day.

The Dude and I had a likewise difficult time in there on Hike 1. It took days to get across, in shivering cold and wet at the beginning, and in stifling heat and humidity at the end. The climbs were the hardest we'd encountered yet, not including Mt. K, which has no analog on the Appalachian Trail. My stove blew up along the way. New blisters formed and blackflies swarmed. I later described those thirty-two miles as the toughest section of the Appalachian Trail, bar none. I've revised that somewhat, weather and direction certainly play a role, but that section is tough either way. It was one of my boogerbears. I set out on the frigid morning of September 11 from my camp at mile 1977 to change that.

I had camped near or at 3000 feet, well within the timberline and sheltered from the wind, but that night was cold, really cold. I counted my good fortune that it hadn't rained, otherwise I would have been reprising Hike 3 albeit in the other direction.

The wind caught me the moment I cleared the timberline, gusting gale force and in a fog to rival the Mt. Washington of however long ago it had been. I stepped quickly back into the shelter of the timberline and donned all my clothing: base layer, waterproof socks, neoprene gloves, a buff on my head, my ball cap on that, and then the hood of my rain shell cinched tightly to prevent my ball cap from blowing off the mountain and down into Rangeley.

I resumed, buffeted this way and that and making progress no quicker than it seemed those Mt. Everest climbers do when seen from afar. The trail profile shows a smooth first hump up Saddleback Mountain, but it's not smooth at all. There are rolling ridges along the way, like giant folds of dough, seldom more than ten or so feet high but traversing these requires some zigging and zagging along natural inclines that act as ramps. In the spring sun of a beautiful and temperate day, topping these would probably be a tremendous amount of fun. I wouldn't know.

At least there were blazes, which shone phenomenally white even through the fog, so getting lost was no concern. At a high point that I presumed to be the top, I braced into the wind and stood for a deep look into the fog. On a clear day I would be able to see Rangeley to my left and far below. Somewhere in the vicinity, a blue-blazed trail used to lead down there, perhaps still did but I saw no evidence of it.

Not too far along, I dropped into the col between Saddleback Mountain and The Horn, that pommel of granite that gave the mountain its name. Into the shelter of the trees down there, I stopped for a break to let my hearing recover in the calmer air. The numbing effect of the continuous roar of wind in my ears was akin to walking along a busy interstate highway for hours and then stepping under an overpass where traffic noise was muted. Sounds were suddenly sharp again, the swish of evergreen boughs, the trickle of water–I even heard the chirp of a bird, which was probably the loneliest bird on the mountain just then.

Soon I went over The Horn, exposed to the fury of the wind once more, then dropped into the col between it and Saddleback Junior and stayed in the trees for a while. My pace picked up through there. While climbing the steep, wooded flank of Saddleback Junior, my ears still muzzy from the buffeting earlier, I heard a branch snap behind me and I spun around with my trekking poles up and ready to stab. A young, smug-looking nobo shouldered past me without a word.

"Hey bro, say something next time!" I hollered at his back. Those words didn't even draw a shrug, he just kept up his climb and was soon out of view.

Atop Saddleback Junior, the wind had died down to a deathly still, although the sky remained heavy and with a foreshortened view. I made my way down the mountain and into the cover of the trees. The trail was wet and muddy. A procession of feet had churned that mud into cloying wallows. I stayed out of it as much as I could, hopping from rock to rock. I arrived at Poplar Ridge Lean-to after a few miles of this, where I went in for a break and found the guy who'd passed me earlier sitting there and rubbing his bare feet. His shoes sat next to him, caked in mud.

"Hey man," I announced as I came in. He neither answered nor looked at me. I dropped pack and sat across the way from him, looking up into the shelter, remembering exactly where my stove had blown up twenty years earlier, noted the rock I'd cracked my head against when I was blown backward off the porcupine step. A thru-hiker named Inchworm had died in the area a few years before my Hike 3. Someone had mounted a memorial sign for her inside the shelter, which I now noted, with disgust, was missing and probably decorating the wall of some morbid collector's garage. That level of disrespect is hard to stomach.

I put some calories in while watching that nobo rub his feet. I tried to make conversation with the guy but pulling teeth was not an adequate metaphor. His feet were pruned and bone white, which served him right for churning up the puddles and mud. "I've got some diaper rash cream that'll help," I offered. He mumbled something. "What's that?" I asked.

"I use coconut oil on my feet," he said, still not looking at me. Coconut oil? I'd never heard of such but I guessed it could work. It would give his feet a savory sweet smell as well, like a sunny day at the beach, or a pina colada. To each his own, but not for me.

I continued to throw comments, about Inchworm, the missing memorial sign, my misadventure at Poplar Ridge Lean-to, none of which drew a glance of interest. I did learn that his name was Condom, or perhaps Condominium, it was hard to tell from his disinterested mumble. Condom was clean-shaven and wore a funny hat. He didn't look dispersonable, but he obviously was and I'd had enough.

"See ya," I said while hoping otherwise. I shouldered my pack and got out of there.

Ahead was Spaulding Mountain, six miles of scrambling climb up to about 4000 feet. I thought I'd pull in short of that at Spaulding Mountain Lean-to. The day was not gone but it wasn't particularly inspiring, all dripping gray and gloom and with no views in the higher reaches. I'd make it out tomorrow just the same, so I settled on Spaulding Mountain Lean-to as my goal, the reek of those Hike 3 nobos coming back as clearly in my memory as a bout of ptomaine.

I was going on, up and up, cocooned in the effort and strain when something rustled right behind me and I spun around with my trekking poles up and ready to stab. It was Condom—again—and again unrepentant. He shouldered past me while I stood agape at his behavior.

I continued up, digging hard with my poles, and then I heard another sound behind me and I spun around with my poles ready, and a swarthy bearded guy went by, as equally unconcerned that he'd about been skewered. "What is it with you guys?" I asked his retreating form, receiving no more of an answer than had come from Condom.

A brief ray of sun lit Spaulding Mountain Lean-to when I arrived. I heard voices as I approached, so I pulled up in the screen of the woods to listen before I went in.

"Are the others coming?" a voice asked.

"Yeah, they're back there."

"Good."

It was Condom and his swarthy buddy, and worse still, apparently more were on the way. I backed out of there, took to the trail, and pushed hard over Spaulding Mountain, coming down the other side and now the day had gone long. I stealthed in the cold and wet near the bronze plaque, sixteen miles done and hopefully far enough ahead to stay ahead of what I feared was a mobile frat party.

There was actually some timid sun the next morning, which delivered a truncated magic hour before the clouds and mist took over once more. I made quick time over Sugarloaf Mountain, or rather along its flank. There are ski runs atop the mountain, and a ski hut that The Dude and I stayed in on Hike 1, but this time—and in that weather—the six tenths side trail to the summit was uninviting.

I dropped down, down, down to Caribou Valley Road, then began my climb of South Crocker Mountain, 2000 feet over two miles, pushing myself hard for fear that the mobile frat party would swarm around me during that slow climb. I made the top—still no view—dropped into the col and then topped the north peak—still no view—and then I was in the swoosh to Maine Highway 27 and Stratton, a little over five miles away, not yet noon and at a pace I thought would insulate me from the mobile frat party. I was almost out—almost—when someone cleared his throat right in my ear and I spun around, startled, and it was Condom, who pushed on past without a word.

Dammit!

I made it out minutes later to find that someone was doing trail magic in the parking area. There were camp chairs set out, all of which were occupied by thru-hikers, one of them Condom and one of them Swarthy Guy, who must have blue-blazed out somewhere because I hadn't seen anyone all day save for Condom. The group was cackling and cracking beers, and about as inviting as a scorpion's nest. I hustled across the parking lot and then across the road, my thumb out and praying for a quick hitch. The sun made an appearance and suddenly it was hot. An older man—who must have been sponsoring the trail magic—saw me and waved me back over. I tried to pretend I didn't see him but he was adamant, so I trudged back in defeat.

It turned out that the man was the father of one of the girls present, who was herself a member of the mobile frat party. Her mother was there also. They beamed at their daughter's accomplishment so far, although I doubted they understood the nature of her tribe. I ate chips and drank an offered beer. The dad introduced me to his daughter, who shrugged and turned her attention back to her buddies, none of whom acknowledged my presence with even a meeting of eyes. Once I'd spent what I thought was an appropriate amount of time, I told the dad that I needed to get out and get a hitch. He offered to drive me, leaving the mother to tend the kids, so I made my escape from the mobile frat party.

The dad explained along the way that they were following their precious daughter, staying in motels and then meeting up with her at the road crossings, a most excellent example of platinum blazing.

Stratton Motel, where I'd stayed three times, was either out of business or between owners. There'd been new owners on every one of my stays so this was nothing new. The mobile frat party was staying at a hostel somewhere in the area, so I had the dad drive me to Spillover Motel just out of town, which thankfully had a room available.

I drug in and did my chores, and only afterward took the time to appreciate my achievement. The weather had been awful, the mobile frat party had been annoying, but I'd made it out by one thirty, 11.9 miles for the day and my best time ever through that section. I'd slain a boogerbear, and now it was time to slay another one.

The Bigelow Range was next, and was also my next boogerbear. On each of my three previous thru-hikes, I left out of West Carry Pond Lean-to and started the day in pleasant weather under fair skies. The first significant climb of the day on those thru-hikes was to the flattened top of Little Bigelow Mountain at 3000 feet, followed by a mild descent and then a tough climb up to Avery Peak at 4000 feet. On each hike I had exceptional views from Little Bigelow Mountain, and on each hike the weather closed in while I was making the climb to Avery Peak.

I was on Little Bigelow Mountain with The Dude on Hike 1. We started up Avery Peak together under a puffy blue sky, but along the way the sky blackened and opened up with a hammering rain that turned the trail into a torrent in minutes. Wet and wind-lashed, the last I saw of The Dude was from a distance at the stone lookout tower up top, which had been boarded over, the sanctuary within just a taunt. He was beating on the boarded-over door, desperate to get inside, and then the rain and furious wind obscured my view and I proceeded on, mostly on hands and knees.

It was hours later, near dark and over a procession of storm-battered peaks, before I reached the only shelter there was, the Horns Pond Lean-tos. I dove in with gratitude only to find that the force of the wind and rain was blowing the storm directly into the open front of the shelter. I spotted a caretaker's wall tent across the way, no caretaker currently in residence, so I let myself inside and I dried out, and I felt guilty about it but I did leave that place as clean as I found it, along with an apologetic note. I met up with The Dude at Stratton Motel the next day, where I had my 43rd birthday celebration. The Dude told me that he'd become so disoriented up on Avery Peak that he'd just rolled up in his tarp out in the open and had spent the night on the cold hard rocks.

Hike 2 went almost identically except this time I was alone. The storm blew up at about the same time on the same climb and with the same fury. The lookout tower up top was still boarded over, still taunting with the sanctuary it could have provided. The Horns Pond Lean-tos were still open to the brunt of the storm, and the caretaker's wall tent was still unoccupied, so I let myself in once again.

On Hike 3 I expected it. I watched the black clouds gather as I climbed toward Avery Peak, could actually see the wall of rain racing toward me, with a half slice of clear blue sky behind me. If anything, that storm was worse than the previous ones had been. I was on hands and knees before I even reached the lookout tower, which was still boarded and still taunting. I pushed on a little way to Bigelow Col, where the fury of the storm forbid me to go farther. There was a cabin in the col, but boarded and locked. I fought desperately to pull the boards off a window, but whoever had done the work had done it well. I tried to pry the padlock off the door with a trekking pole, my skin stinging from the pummeling rain, but without success. Eventually I rolled up in my emergency bivy sack, lying on the cabin's narrow and exposed front step to stay above the water, and spent a less than comfortable night.

In summary, my every transit of the Bigelow Range had been during a furious storm. I'd never seen the view up there, and had no concept of what it might be like on a fair day and under a gracious sky. The Bigelow Range was for me, absolutely, a boogerbear.

This time might be different. The weather forecast was inconclusive but seemed to indicate that late-day storms would lash the peaks tomorrow, clearing the day after tomorrow when a high pressure system pushed through the area. Waiting it out meant I would have to take a zero, but the chance to have an actual view from Avery Peak made a zero worthwhile. It might also give the mobile frat party a chance to get ahead, which was worth a zero on its own.

I idled through my thirteenth and final zero day of the hike, saw to my chores early on then hoofed it up the road to the gas station for lunch. There was a diner inside the gas station, with everything on offer from eggs and pancakes to burgers and fries. I ordered a double plate of eggs and pancakes then settled in at a Formica table to replenish some of the calories I'd given up during the past few days. Local people came and went, dressed for work in flannel and Carhartt, paying for their gasoline or walking out with large cups of coffee. A bell on the door clanged as each came in, and again when they left. I dug into my eggs, liberally sprinkled with hot sauce. I use hot sauce anyway—the hotter the better—but on the trail just about everyone does, the best and lightest-weight way to turn bland trail food into something palatable.

The bell clanged, and then again in a series, clang, clang, clang, clang... I looked up from my food and there was Condom, and Swarthy Guy, and maybe four or five others. They piled up against the counter and overwhelmed the poor woman taking orders, picking things up, tossing them back, fiddling with everything and leaving disarray in their wake. They swarmed to the few tables, unapologetically jostling me as they pushed and shoved their way in. I stood in frustration with my plate and retreated to a corner to finish in hurried bites, and then I got out of there.

The weather was fair down in the notch, warm, a partly cloudy sky, but none of that could predict what was going on at elevation. Still, I questioned that zero, fought the urge to just take off and go. The sky blackened in the later afternoon, and then the rain came, along with a chilling wind. It would have been brutal at elevation, no less than I'd experienced every other time, so I'd made the right call and I was grateful for it.

It was cold in the morning but the sky was a heaven of blues going brighter. I caught an early hitch and was making a magic-hour climb by eight o'clock. The climb was not difficult going northbound, a little over 2000 feet over 4.3 miles, more of a swoosh on a southbound thru-hike.

I was alone on the mountain, and under a sky that could draw tears at its purity. And my God there were views—so many views, clean rich greens, sharp granite peaks, and dotted lakes below like drips of blue ink. This was what I had never seen, what had been hiding in storm clouds for twenty years. It was as if a magic gate had opened in a tempest, spilling light and hope into the turbulent darkness and I'd stepped through it.

I stopped on South Horn at near 4000 feet to take in the majesty of the view. Not a cloud smudged that polaroid sky. The sun was an immaculate yellow orb, and the air was clean and fresh and a touch cool. I turned my face into this, closed my eyes and just let it fill me. A sound down the trail broke that reverie, and I turned to see Rage coming up and wearing a grin.

"Hey Solo."

"Rage! I wondered if I'd ever see y'all again. Where's your brother?"

"He's behind me somewhere. I was just so jazzed by this weather that I took off."

"It's amazing, isn't it?"

"Maybe my best day on the trail so far."

"Mine too, I think."

Wazi caught up soon after, and then we went together along the ridge to Bigelow Mountain's west peak, gawping at the view. People have told me that I hike too fast to appreciate the views, to which I've always countered: "When you're hiking you're *in* the view." And we were, superimposed against a vast blue sky trimmed with granite and green. We stopped on Avery Peak for photos, all of us taking it in for the first time.

It was, as a Kiwi I'd met years ago in Scotland would say, *magic*.

We started down, went over Little Bigelow Mountain and then the swoosh to East Flagstaff Road and past Little Bigelow Lean-to. Wazi and Rage were going to shuttle out from there to a hostel for the night. Rage had reception up on the ridge so she'd made a call to see if she could get me a bunk in the hostel, but the place was full. I wasn't disappointed, though. The day was too exceptional for that, and there were still some hours of daylight left. Their driver gave me a beer and then we all said our goodbyes, that time for the last time. I stayed in touch via text but I never saw either of the siblings again.

Pushing on, I stopped at mile 2022.8 after almost eighteen miles and pitched my tent at a campsite on East Flagstaff Lake, a pretty place with sandy beaches and a sunset over the water and I was completely alone with all that beauty.

It was magic.

A blanket of heavy clouds filtered in past sunset, bringing with them the musty smell of rain. Those clouds held their load overnight, though, because I awoke to a dry tent and warmer air. I was on the way by a little after six o'clock, poking along at first in the low light. Dawn came so much later now, and dusk so much earlier, those previous twelve or fourteen hours of daylight now reduced to nine at best. I marveled at this. On a southbound thru-hike it would be spring now, the sun up at four thirty and not down until nine or so, which is where the southbounder definitions of *hiker sunrise* and *hiker midnight* come from. Similar conditions are experienced in the spring by northbounders down south, but not as extreme as at these latitudes.

I needed an early start that day because the Kennebec River lay nineteen miles ahead. The Kennebec is a broad although shallow river that would not be difficult to ford if not for the dam upstream, which might do an unannounced release as a hapless thru-hiker was making his way across. Hikers had drowned crossing the Kennebec, which was why the ATC provided a ferry service and practically begged thru-hikers to use it. The ferry was a canoe with a single operator in that season, who called it a day at two o'clock. In other words, missing the ferry meant that I would have to sit idle on the south bank until the next day, either that or ford, which I really didn't want to do. So I needed to make nineteen miles by two o'clock. The trail through there is mostly flat although picayune as hell, so there was no guarantee that I could do it.

I started moving fast as soon as there was enough light to reveal the treacherous roots and rocks. And I moved, never stopping once for a break. Mist began to fill the woods, and then some light sprinkles, not enough to soak me but enough to make everything damp and slippery.

I was exceeding a three mile per hour pace, dodging rocks and roots, leaping over puddles, and soon suffused with *arete*. All my senses were on the trail ahead, anticipating the hazards, adjusting for them before I reached them, never breaking stride. I felt a hard-driven urgency to make that ferry. I did not want to waste a good part of a day waiting on the south bank, and I did not want to ford the river, but I decided that I would ford if I had to because all of a sudden I was determined to rest my head on the north bank of the Kennebec that night come what may, and I became so subsumed into that goal that nothing else was acceptable.

The miles dissolved through the day, damp, the threat of heavier rain behind me. I ate energy bars as I moved, ripping them open with my teeth and pausing for breath between each chew. Had I ever pushed myself this hard? I couldn't say.

I made my way up a hillock of evergreens, the trail littered with needles, which are terribly slippery when wet. My feet would go out from under me but I would catch myself with my poles, powering on and taking the slips in stride. The problem with evergreen woods, especially spruce and hemlock with their short needles, is that all those seasons of fallen needles fill the cavities between the snaking roots, creating the illusion of a solid surface.

You know you're on this when your footfalls thump and sound hollow. The going becomes spongy. Sometimes a foot will suddenly plummet into a camouflaged crevasse of roots. If you're lucky you can yank it out and keep going, and if you're not lucky you might break an ankle.

I was moving fast, making a low climb through this, noon or thereabouts, two hours left and still some miles away when my left trekking pole plunged as if into a cavern and I went over hard onto my left shoulder, which impacted against a high root and whiplashed my neck to the side, cracking loud enough to startle some birds and terrify me. Never had I heard such a violent sound come from my body.

I lay there in the wet needles, too afraid to move. In my mind I could visualize a dislocated third cervical vertebrae, the bone pushing against my spinal cord and I knew what that would mean, it would mean paralysis from the neck down, about as awful a fate as one can imagine, especially if, like me, you'd known someone who suffered this. I could have cried at the injustice of it.

Gradually, little by little, I moved a finger, and then a toe, and then all of my fingers and all of my toes. Everything seemed to be working. I risked moving my head, ever so slightly. I felt no pain, no numbness. I risked turning my head the other way and felt no danger there either. Eventually I took a breath and pushed myself into a sitting position, probed the back of my neck for a bulge but everything seemed to be where it belonged. I got to my feet, shakily, stood there and went through all of the movements again just to be sure. Everything seemed fine, and then I noticed that the pain I'd been carrying in my neck and shoulder since Pinkham Notch was gone! I smiled knowingly then. What the trail had done was give me a traumatic spinal adjustment that went further than any chiropractor would have ever dared. My pain was gone, and remains so to this day.

Both of my trekking poles were bent. I straightened them as well as I could against my knee, then turned back for the trail and got to it. I emerged onto the gravelly bank of the Kennebec at one fifteen, plenty of time to make the ferry and I knew it but I couldn't stop until I had my hand on the canoe and my salvation was guaranteed. The canoe and operator were on a spit of gravel beyond a shallow inlet across the way. I didn't break stride but raced toward them, splashing across the inlet and coming up on the operator as if he were a quarterback and I defensive lineman.

"Whoa there," he said, holding out his hands. "You made it. *You made it.* Drop your pack and rest a minute. You're okay, you made it."

I stayed at Sterling Inn outside of Caratunk, Maine that night. I knew the owner, Eric, from Hike 3, and was pleased that he remembered me. Sterling

Inn is an historic old lodge that Eric and his son have spent years restoring. Our talks on Hike 3 were all about the challenges of maintaining an old house, and continued on Hike 4 as if no time had passed in between. He shuttled me to Northern Outdoors for food and beer, where I was horrified when the mobile frat party came swarming in, even more horrified when I learned that some of them were staying at Sterling Inn.

Back at the inn, they took over, of course, flopping on every couch and chair in the common room, bogarting the television, cackling and chattering and raising a din. I retreated to my room, where I endured their raucous noise until well after hiker midnight.

The next day started out gray and cool. I lingered longer than was wise talking to Eric, but then at nine o'clock felt the pressure of the awakening mobile frat party so I got moving. I quickly put the seven miles between Caratunk and Pleasant Pond Mountain behind me, alone through all of that, but as I began my climb of Moxie Bald Mountain a youngish bearded guy in an off-red hat went by me, signaling that the mobile frat party was loose and catching up.

I went over Moxie Bald Mountain under a fair sky and with some rewarding views, but didn't linger. They were back there somewhere, and one of them was even ahead of me. On the other side of Moxie Bald Mountain was Moxie Bald Lean-to. That was where I assumed the mobile frat party would throw down for the night so I pushed on hard, a mile past the lean-to and in diminishing light, where I stealth camped aside a little brook. As I was settling in, the guy with the off-red hat went by. How I'd gotten ahead of him was a mystery—perhaps he'd taken a break on Moxie Bald Mountain—but now I had one of them ahead of me and the rest possibly coming as well. By absolute dark no other hikers had gone by so I slept feeling secure save for the one, 19.6 miles closer to Monson, Maine and the Hundred-Mile Wilderness.

I didn't dally the next morning but got to it even before there was enough light to see. I was only a mile ahead of the mobile frat party. Sure they would probably sleep until nine o'clock but with their youth they might catch me just the same. I'd given them the opportunity to get out ahead of me back in Stratton but that hadn't worked, so now it was up to me to get out ahead of—and hopefully stay ahead of—them.

It was a cold morning, but dry. The twinkling dawn hinted at a pretty day to come. My plan was to go 13.8 miles to the blue-blazed side trail into Monson, where I would then stay with Poet and Hippy Chick at Shaw's Boarding House, resupply, then head into the Hundred-Mile Wilderness the following morning. The trail would be mostly flat, although picayune in places and with two fords to make, the west and east branches of the Piscataquis River;

nevertheless I still expected to get in early enough to get the benefit and also spend some time with Poet and Hippy Chick.

I stayed at Shaw's Boarding House on Hike 1, where I met the proprietor, Keith Shaw. Keith was a gravelly old Mainer, the real deal, authentic in every bone. I was in bad shape when I met him. He fed me, talked wisdom, and sent me on my way with renewed confidence a couple of days later. "At least Solo knows how to read," he would say with a gravelly chuckle to any available audience. "The sign says *Maine* to Georgia, not the other way around. Do you know the difference between a pond and a lake?" That question would make his rheumy eyes glitter. "If you can swim across it without drowning it's a pond." He said this with an infectious mirth and a bite of tongue. I really liked that old man.

By Hike 2 Keith Shaw had passed away, taking his seat at that Valhalla trail table. The boarding house was being managed by a pair of ladies who did their best to preserve Keith's traditions but who seemed worried about the future of the place. I spent the night there with a northbounder named Trek, a retired military guy who'd been yo-yoing the trail since 2003. I have often wondered what happened to him.

Shaw's Boarding House had new owners on Hike 3, Poet and his wife Hippy Chick. They were off at Trail Days when I came through so I wound up staying with Rebekah at Lakeshore House, where I was treated like royalty because I was their first thru-hiker of the season. Poet and Hippy Chick were back before I departed Monson. I went to meet them and discovered, astoundingly, that I'd met them before, on Hike 2 when they were doing their northbound thru-hike. I remembered their trail names clearly. We puzzled where we had met, which I suspected was at The Mayor's house in Unionville on that rainy night. I looked forward to seeing both of them again. Rebekah, I learned later, had sold Lakeshore House.

So I took off that morning excited to be reunited with friends. After a mile or two I crossed a gravel road, and off to the side of it, just breaking camp, was the guy in the off-red hat. I was surprised when he waved me over.

"I saw your tent last night," he said as he loaded his backpack.

"Yeah, I saw you go by."

"That was a nice spot. I wish I'd gotten there first, but this one was oaky, too."

"Yeah, well, uh..."

"My name's Nick of Time, but people call me Nick."

"I'm Solo."

"Good to meet you Solo." We bumped fists.

Nick seemed friendly, not like the mobile frat party at all. I asked him about this.

"What?" he said with an ironic laugh. "I'm not with those guys. I can't stand those guys. I've been trying to get away from them for days. They stopped at Moxie Bald Lean-to, so that's why I pushed on last night."

"Really?"

"Yeah."

So we wound up hiking together, each at a brisk pace for the same reason, to stay ahead of the mobile frat party. Nick, it turned out, was thirty-four years old and had earned a PhD in environmental engineering or the like. He was a fascinating guy, and our conversations about ecology and sustainability went deep, especially as regarded the missing moose in Maine. I hadn't seen a moose since Hike 2. I was told on Hike 3 that moose calves were quite literally being exsanguinated by ticks, and that the moose had moved farther north to escape them. Global warming was probably the culprit. Neither of us had seen a moose so far, and I wouldn't see one all the way to the end of the hike. This was astounding because on Hikes 1 and 2 moose had been everywhere. I'd even been chased by them a couple of times.

The day went quickly. I pushed hard to stay up with Nick, and had the feeling that he could have left me behind at any time. He stayed with me though, and I was glad to get to know him. Soon we were across both branches of the Piscataquis and at the blue-blazed junction to Monson.

"I want to push on to the road and hitch in from there," he said.

I debated this in my mind. That would mean 3.3 more miles to Maine Highway 15 and then a hitch back to Monson, while the blue-blazed trail would get me into Monson in only 1.8 miles. More than that, I would then be able to hike out in the morning and not have to rely on a hitch or shuttle.

"But you'd be doing almost four miles there and back," Nick countered, "or a little over three now. That's a good head start for tomorrow, and you know those other guys are going to take the blue blaze. And besides, they say getting a hitch out of Monson is easy."

He was spot on. "Yeah, let's go for it," I said.

We hiked the quickest three miles I've ever hiked, emerging onto Maine Highway 15 less than an hour later, where we caught a hitch almost immediately. We split up in Monson, Nick to get some food and resupply, and me to Shaw's Boarding House. Nick's plan was to hitch out afterward and push on into the Hundred-Mile Wilderness. The day was perfect, and it was still early enough to make significant progress into the Wilderness but I wanted to see Poet and Hippy Chick, so Nick and I bumped fists and said our goodbyes.

Shaw's Boarding House was overrun with thru-hikers. I knew a few of them, including Old School, who'd pink blazed to catch up to a girl, who had herself not arrived yet. We laughed at the comedy of it. It was good to see Old School again. He took my novel, *The Appalachian*, off a shelf in the common room.

"Is this you, Solo?" he asked.

"Yeah."

"Wow." He walked off in thought, flipping pages as he went.

I went into the kitchen where I met the caretaker, a big, gentle, and saintly patient thru-hiker named Hambone. The first thing he did when I introduced myself, before a tour or any lecturing, was hand me a beer. "You need this, I know," he said with a wink. "I'll show you around when you're ready." My mind raced all the way back to The Tuna in Virginia, and how he'd failed at this simplest of gestures. Hambone was a real thru-hiker and knew how to properly treat other thru-hikers.

I took a private room just in case the mobile frat party showed up. To be trapped with them in the bunkroom would have been a Faustian level of agony. Poet and Hippy Chick were, to my disappointment, out doing shuttles and not due to return until late in the evening. Hambone said he would let them know I was there, but I waved that off. "Naw," I said, "when they get back they'll want dinner and time with their kids. It's cool. I'll see them in the morning."

Rested and resupplied for the Hundred-Mile Wilderness, I watched out the window as the mobile frat party trickled in by ones and twos and then the entire group. Under Hambone's crossed arms and no nonsense gaze, they behaved themselves. I turned in at dusk, sated after a big meal at Lakeshore House and with a food bag that weighed as much as the one I'd climbed Mt. Moosilauke with.

Tomorrow was it, the Hundred-Mile Wilderness; and after that, Mt. Katahdin.

SATURDAY, SEPTEMBER 18, 2021

Mile 2091.5 - 15.9 Miles

Had a good day and a bad day. Slept very well, up at 5:30 a.m., packed and showered, big breakfast, Poet straightened my poles, then gave me a ride to the trailhead.

Hiking by 9:00, a late start and a slow trail later on. Never saw another hiker after I left the others at the trailhead, so I think I've finally escaped the mobile frat party. I wonder how far Nick got yesterday?

Sun for a good part of the day. Light rain later made everything slippery. Went down and cut my right wrist on a sharp rock, a long and deep cut up into my palm.

Stealthed here on the Barren Ledges at 5:30 p.m., wanted Cloud Pond but it was getting too dark to make that climb. So short miles and a wound, but otherwise I feel okay.

SUNDAY, SEPTEMBER 19, 2021

Mile 2113.5 - 19 Miles

This was a tough day, really cold in the morning, and a lot of slow, picayune trail. I pushed myself to exhaustion but finally got ahead of my Hike 3 miles. At least the weather was nice.

I'm not moving as fast as I expected, so will probably need 5 or 6 days to finish. The trouble is, I didn't bring enough food. I've done it to myself again!

MONDAY, SEPTEMBER 20, 2021

Mile 2137 - 23.5 Miles

I had hoped to do the 100-Mile in 4 days. I now know it won't happen because I don't have the strength to do a 41-mile day through this. Alt plan is 25 tomorrow, then 15 to Abol Bridge, get food (I'm almost out), then go 9 more to one of the campgrounds if they're not full. Otherwise stealth. Summit on Thursday.

It was the coldest yet this morning, hard to get going but I was hiking by 5:45 a.m. A few mountains early on, Gulf Haggis, Hay, White Cap, and Little Boardman. Afterward the trail flattened and I made 3 mph, but too late to make big miles for the day. Threw down here at 5:30 p.m. I'm wiped out.

Met a man on White Cap named Papa Van Winkle, who gave me some granola bars! I had eaten all of mine and was getting worried. Now I just might make it to Abol Bridge without passing out from hunger.

TUESDAY, SEPTEMBER 21, 2021

Rainbow Stream Lean-to - 26 Miles

A big day and I feel every mile of it. Not as cold this morning, hiking by 5:30 a.m.

Made quick time on a fast trail, 3+ mph, but then slowed by roots and rocks and some climbs. Went down once and cut my leg. Also out of food and worried about that. Yogied a bagel from some section hikers, and some peanut butter from Keebler (nobo), then ran into trail magic at mile 15 or so. Hot dogs, beers, cookies—those folks saved me. One of the girls was Rebekah's step daughter and remembered me from Hike 3!

Pushed on over Nesuntabunt, a hard slog. Wore me down. Popped a 5-Hour Energy to keep going.

A guy and gal in the shelter, Roman and Princess. Keebler came in later. The copy of *The Appalachian* I left in the shelter on Hike 3 is sadly gone.

Thank God I'm out of this tomorrow. The end is so near, but still a few miles to go and hurdles to jump.

WEDNESDAY, SEPTEMBER 22, 2021

Katahdin Stream Campground - 24.9 Miles

Josh—Loves Star Wars and Bruce Campbell movies.
Ben—Loves rum and 4wd trucks.
Both from W. Mass.

Not as cold, up early, hiking by 5:30 a.m. Not as fast through there as I remembered. On Rainbow Ledges I met up with—of all people—Mighty Mo! She flipped at Pinkham Notch and was now going south, still looking tough as ever. It was good to see her.

I was out of the 100-Mile by 11:00 a.m., not the 4 days I'd wanted but since I got out before noon I think 4 ½ days is honest. Bought food and supplies and beers at the store, then pushed on into Baxter State Park. The ranger at the kiosk was gone until 2:30 p.m., so I went on into Baxter without registering.

Very slow on picayune trail, much worse than I remembered but the season probably had something to do with it. Didn't reach Katahdin Stream until 3:30 p.m., all campsites full. I got my permit from Wendy and was prepared to stealth somewhere up the Hunt Trail when Ben and Josh invited me to share their campsite. They gave me beers, cornbread, and chili, as well as a lot of good conversation. I lucked out and I know it.

In the tent at 7:30 p.m. Intend to start up Mt. K before sunrise.

I couldn't have asked for more.

I am very lucky today.

—

There are signs on either end of the Hundred-Mile Wilderness that variously proclaim, depending upon which direction you're going:

> CAUTION - THERE ARE NO PLACES TO OBTAIN SUPPLIES OR GET HELP UNTIL ABOL BRIDGE 100 MILES NORTH. DO NOT ATTEMPT THIS SECTION UNLESS YOU HAVE A MINIMUM OF 10 DAYS SUPPLIES AND ARE FULLY EQUIPPED. THIS IS THE LONGEST WILDERNESS SECTION OF THE ENTIRE A.T. AND ITS DIFFICULTY SHOULD NOT BE UNDERESTIMATED.

This is a warning that would give anyone pause. On Hike 1, and to a lesser extent on Hikes 2 and 3, Maine's Hundred-Mile Wilderness was alike the darkest Congo. On that first hike I loaded up at the Abol Bridge Store with all the food I could carry, gulped, and then took my first trepid steps into the heart of darkness. But today that remoteness is an illusion, a bit of romantic history. With smart phones and satellite trackers, hikers can now (and from what I heard at Shaw's, many do) slackpack the Hundred-Mile Wilderness, shuttling out on graded private roads to spend their nights at Shaw's. Poet and Hippy Chick also provide a service in which they stash five-gallon pails of food and supplies at strategic locations within the Wilderness. Hikers who indulge in this service shoulder lighter backpacks and never have to worry about running out of food.

Several times during this transit of the Hundred-Mile Wilderness, I encountered nobos who were slackpacking southbound in order to catch the shuttle back to Shaw's. Once again I had to ask myself what their hikes were all about. While I do hike by my own strict rules, I am no purist; nor am I a pretentious ass hat, as one defensive hiker wrote after reading my Killington Peak field notes. (That's an awesome pejorative, by the way.) I'm not trying to invalidate anyone's hike, I'm simply a veteran of an earlier era trying to understand what these cobbled hikes mean to people. Are these folks on journeys of discovery, pushing their limits to reveal and refine their inner characters, or are they simply checking an extreme sport off their lists? Regardless their motivations, their smart phones have robbed the Hundred-Mile Wilderness of its Congo-like mystery. Their hikes are, if not necessarily easy, at least less challenging. Perhaps Varicose at Hikers Welcome Hostel had made a good point after all.

This was all moot to me in the end because I was going to go old-school through the Hundred-Mile Wilderness, and relive as much of that earlier mystery as I could.

I slept soundly that night at Shaw's and was up well before dawn the next morning, where I found Poet in the kitchen brewing coffee and warming up the stoves in preparation for Shaw's famous and voluminous breakfast. He greeted me right away but with only laconic enthusiasm. I didn't expect to be greeted as if I were a celebrity, but then, well, yeah, I kinda did. I was the only thru-hiker there who'd stayed with Keith Shaw, the only one who'd met Poet and Hippy Chick during their thru-hike in 2008, the only one whose books were on the shelves in the common room, and the only 8000-miler currently on the premises. Surely all of that spoke for itself.

After a few contemplative sips of the coffee Poet handed me, I took a moment to step back and think it through. Poet and Hippy Chick had made Shaw's Boarding House into a sprawling, boisterous operation. In addition to the old Victorian house, they'd added a bunkhouse, laundry room, and a camp store. They'd introduced shuttle services and the other things, and had managed to do all of this while raising their kids and remaining true to Keith Shaw's traditions as well as incorporating their own. That they had the stamina to keep up with it all was astounding, so I stepped out of my pique to admire their efforts, and when Poet served Shaw's bounteous breakfast to what must have been forty or more thru-hikers, I dug in with gratitude and awe.

Poet took the time during what was obviously a hectic morning to straighten my trekking poles and replace a worn tip. The morning was rising prettily around us, thru-hikers coming and going through all their own preparations, pelting Poet with questions as he pulled my bent trekking pole against his knee. I envied his reserve. I know I couldn't have duplicated it. I wanted nothing more than to get together with him for some long conversation, but circumstances wouldn't allow it. I would have to come back some day, in the off season when he wasn't busy, or perchance I'd see him at Trail Days once the Covid situation settled down. I looked forward to either outcome.

In a raucous scramble, six of us loaded into Poet's SUV for the first shuttle to the trailhead. The members of the mobile frat party were wandering around, rubbing their eyes as if they'd just awoken. I had a feeling I wouldn't see them again, and that proved to be true.

Poet drove us to the trailhead at nine o'clock, where I stood with the group for a photo even though I didn't know any of them. I dodged up into the woods and got a move on while they all lingered and chitchatted. The weather was perfect, clear, dry, and neither hot nor cold. I raced through those first few miles, putting so much distance between us that none of them ever caught up to me.

I moved out quickly from the trailhead not to outpace the others but because I'd set a new goal for myself: to complete the Hundred-Mile Wilderness in four days. On Hike 1 I caught a serendipitous ride out to Shaw's after five days when a game warden came along just as I'd convinced myself to quit. It took me nine days to get through on Hike 2, interrupted on Jo-Mary Road when I ran out of food and scored a lucky hitch back to Millinocket with a fisherman. It took me eight days on Hike 3, through the harshest early-season hiking conditions I'd ever encountered, with deep snow on White Cap Mountain, biblical blackflies, and miles of tangled blowdowns. As a northbounder this time, with trail legs and the season as my ally, I was certain I could make twenty-five miles per day. I didn't achieve that but I came close.

It went at first better than I could have hoped. The weather was remarkable, the trail not savage in the least. I followed a jagged profile that stays near 1000 feet for fifteen miles, on trail that was picayune in places but on sure feet because conditions were dry. This was a Hundred-Mile Wilderness I could only have dreamed of, the main reason to go northbound. I cherished every mile until it began to rain later in the day. The trail I'd been taking almost effortlessly suddenly morphed into a beast with sharp teeth. Mt feet went out from under me and I went down, impacting an incisor of a rock that sliced my right hand from wrist to palm as cleanly as a kitchen knife.

That cut was deep, splattering blood all over the offending rock. My hands were too dirty for any bandage to adhere, so I washed out the cut as well as I could with water from my bottle, bound my hand with a bandana (the red one), and pushed on at a much slower pace.

The day gave up on me at the base of Barren Ledges, 15.9 miles into the Hundred-Mile Wilderness, and three-odd miles short of my goal at Cloud Pond Lean-to. I'd covered the nineteen miles between Cloud Pond and Main Highway 15 on my last hike, through smothering humidity and suffocating blackflies. But the southbounder days of late spring are longer than the northbounder days of early fall. To reach Cloud Pond I would have to climb over Barren Mountain in the dark, which I wasn't prepared to do, so I stealth camped in a soft, grassy open space below the Ledges and closed out my first day in the Hundred-Mile Wilderness.

Shivering in the deep cold of the next morning, my usual breakfast wasn't enough to stir my metabolism. I doubled the calories in the urgency of the moment while trying not to notice what this would lead to farther up the trail. I was on my way in the not-quite light, the cut on my palm warm and throbbing even as my fingers were cold and numb.

The trail was damp from yesterday's rain, but that morning rose clear and comfortably warm. That next section was tough, not in significant elevation but in a jagged roller coaster that made the one in Virginia seem trivial: Barren Mountain, Fourth Mountain, Third Mountain, Columbus and Chairback, all compressed together into a distance of ten and a half miles, followed by a rocky descent of Chairback Mountain that was reminiscent of Lehigh Gap; and then the first major ford of the Hundred-Mile Wilderness, the west branch of the Pleasant River.

Depending upon the season, the Pleasant River can resemble the Kennebec in its wide and shallow sweep. It was sedate this time, while last time it raged and just about flushed me to my fate downstream. A group of section hikers was huddled on the north bank, gazing disconsolately at the expanse of water before them. I paused only long enough to remove my socks. I ford rivers sockless but in my shoes. My shoes then dry over the next few miles, and afterward I stop to put my dry socks back on.

The river fords in Maine are rocky and slippery beneath your feet, too easy to slip and tumble and then be washed downstream. Going across barefooted can be precarious. Many thru-hikers wear their camp shoes through the fords. I don't carry camp shoes, not anymore. They're just something else to have to keep up with, and I found that I really didn't need them. Those section hikers observed wide-eyed as I crossed, as if I were performing some kind of miracle. They peppered me with questions once I got across. I explained my system, they each sat to remove their socks, and then they safely waded to the other side, giving me an appreciative wave as I turned and resumed the trail.

After Pleasant River the trail began a gradual climb of six and a half miles to Gulf Haggas Mountain. I didn't make it quite that far. I pulled in below Carl A. Newhall Lean-to after nineteen miles and stealth camped for the night.

I could be thankful for the weather, and I was. In rainy conditions those nineteen miles would have been the worst cursing misery imaginable. They were strenuous just the same, demanding calories at a rate I should have anticipated but for some reason hadn't. I inventoried my food bag that night with concern. I thought I would be fifty miles in by then, while I'd managed barely thirty-five. I had no room for denial—not only was I not going to be able to go through the Hundred-Mile Wilderness in four days, I was also not going to have enough of food. It was as simple as that.

Up before dawn, I hiked out into another freezing morning, working with greater diligence to ration my food but the terrain forbid that. Gulf Haggas Mountain, Hay Mountain, and then White Cap Mountain, with the first views of Mt. Katahdin off in the distance. The exertion was such that I couldn't stay out of my food bag. I ate guiltily but I had no choice, no other way to fuel those climbs. I started counting calories as I hiked, and laying alternate plans, one of which was to reach Jo-Mary Road and hitch out for more food. But no—no, no, no! I would not interrupt this hike. What if I stumbled across one of those secreted five-gallon pails from Shaw's, I wondered. Was I capable of raiding someone else's food? I feared, in that honest place in back of my mind, that I might be.

I made the summit of White Cap Mountain under a picture-blue sky, with views north to the anvil-top of Mt. Katahdin, seeming much closer than seventy-three miles away. More relevant in the moment, though, was Abol Bridge and its camp store at fifty-seven and a half miles away, the end of the Hundred-Mile Wilderness. I looked into my food bag with despair, trying to figure out how I could allocate two ramens and three pouches of instant potatoes over that distance. These represented calories I could easily down in half a day but would now have to sustain me for possibly three days. They wouldn't be nearly enough, and later, when my blood sugar crashed, I would hike slower yet, compounding the problem.

I sat in the mountain-top sun of a day that had become pleasantly warm, running mileages through my mind, searching for any scheme that would split those fifty-seven and a half miles into something I could do with the calories I had remaining. My stomach knotted painfully. All of my convenient calories were gone, no peanuts, no energy bars, no nothing. My two ramens could be breakfast for the next two mornings, I supposed, with two of my three pouches of instant potatoes to bribe my stomach those nights, and perhaps the third pouch to serve as snacks along the way. I could boil that last pouch, divide it evenly into ziplocks then eat them cold as I went, perhaps just enough of a tease to keep me moving.

I knew better, of course. My energy would crash. I would push myself as I always did but my pace would slow so much that I'd spend at least one full day without food. This would not be fasting as we might comfortably do at home, but the expenditure of thousands and thousands of calories with nothing to replace them and no body fat left to salvage. It would be forced starvation, nothing less, and even a single day of that could be destructive in the Hundred-Mile Wilderness. Perhaps then I should just down all my calories at once and push hard for a forty-mile day, keep going after dark, just push and push until those calories were spent and then drag through the final seventeen miles on willpower alone.

Such are the thoughts when you set a goal you refuse to give up on, puzzle pieces that won't fit together in any combination but you insist that they try. It wouldn't work, I knew it wouldn't work. I could no more hike forty miles in a day and over that terrain than I could have when my food bag had been full. I was going to have to hitch out at Jo-Mary Road, about seventeen miles farther on, no choice. The trail would flatten after Little Boardman Mountain, those last miles would go quickly.

It was while ruminating on that unpalatable solution that a middle-aged man named Papa Van Winkle came up the trail and sat down on rock nearby. We talked while be broke out his lunch. He was section hiking with his son, who had fallen behind. They were to meet on White Cap Mountain and then push on together.

My stomach rumbled emptiness while I watched Papa Van Winkle eat. I felt light-headed, a bit dizzy. At last I threw off all dignity and just asked him outright: "I'm out of food. Do you have anything you can spare?"

"Sure I do," he said, not in the least taken aback. "I always pack too much."

It seemed that his problem and mine were exactly opposite. He handed me a couple of granola bars, which I slobbered down like a hungry hound, some of the wrapper as well. He sat back in amazement watching this. The sugar coursed through me in an instant. Suddenly I could locate the back of my mind again.

"Man, you *are* hungry," he said. "Here, take a few more."

I ate one more on the spot, and now with a functioning brain, saved the other two for later. Those were enough calories to get me moving again. I gave Papa Van Winkle my most profound thanks, then headed down the mountain, my confidence restored by a few hundred calories.

I forded the east branch of the Pleasant River, went over Little Boardman Mountain, and then I was into that flat run toward Jo-Mary Road. I pulled up just short of the road and stealth camped, twenty-three and a half more miles done and committed now to staying the course I'd set for myself. Just a few hundred calories is all it had taken to completely reorder my thoughts. Amazing. I was now within forty miles of Abol Bridge. If I could just make Rainbow Stream tomorrow I could then push on to Abol Bridge the following morning for a five-day transit of the Hundred-Mile Wilderness, not the goal I'd set for myself but still faster than I'd ever crossed it before.

And I was okay with that.

I ate potatoes and ramen for dinner that night, and then potatoes and ramen for breakfast the next morning. When I took off at about five thirty I had only one pouch of potatoes and one granola bar left in my food bag.

It was a warmer morning, the weather continuing fair. I had been lucky with the weather, not wanting to even contemplate how bad off I would have been otherwise. I was still going to run out of food, but the coming section was mostly flat all the way to Abol Bridge. The granola bar, I decided, would be lunch. I would then go to sleep hungry, have the potatoes for breakfast the next morning, and then just get through the remaining miles as well as I could. It all hinged on whether or not I could reach Rainbow Stream Lean-to at twenty-six miles away. This would put Nesuntabunt Mountain behind me, with only the Rainbow Ledges ahead, the last climb on the Appalachian Trail before Mt. Katahdin. If I could separate those two climbs with a night's sleep in between, I was positive that I could maintain the energy to go all the way.

Jo-Mary Road is a dirt road used by loggers and fishermen—and now by shuttle drivers. I stepped across it within minutes of breaking camp and then enjoyed a magic hour in the low Maine woods beyond. There were bog logs in places, footbridges in others, ferns and moss and a lot of marsh and spongy forest floor, but in that season there were no biting bugs, none at all. I had only imagined walking across Maine without the torment of blackflies but my imagination hadn't gone far enough. It was wonderful, so wonderful. Without realizing it I entered into *arete*, making a pace on that mostly level trail that left miles behind me unnoticed. The calories, though...I ate my last granola bar before ten o'clock and now I had nothing left save the single pouch of instant potatoes, which had already been designated as tomorrow's breakfast.

Somewhere around Potaywadjo Spring Lean-to, after about nine miles, I began to grow faint. My pace faltered, my head spun, and I had a hard time catching my breath. It was then that I encountered some elderly section hikers. One of them, a woman, guessed my state before I even said anything. "Here," she said, "take my bagel. You need it more than I do."

It was one of the smaller bagels but I would have been grateful for a crumb. I ate it ravenously, flushed it down with water, thanked her and kept moving. It was all urgency now. I could actually feel that bagel metabolizing through my system, giving me a spike of energy that couldn't last so I had to make the most of it, I had to make as many miles as I could before I crashed again.

About five miles later, just past Nahmakanta Stream Lean-to, my body had metabolized every atom of that bagel. I began to flag again, my pace slowing, my stride not as steady—and then I met Keebler, a young nobo who wore an elf-like hat. He gave me a peanut butter cup, and again my energy surged.

I thanked him and took off. Maybe, just maybe, I might make it yet. What I learned on that day was just exactly how far a set amount of calories would take me. A couple of miles later, coming up on the side trail to Nahmakanta Lake, that peanut butter cup now speeding its way out of my system, I heard voices ahead in a camping area right off the trail. By then I felt as if I'd established a pattern: yogi some calories, push on a few miles, yogi some more calories...with luck I might be able to hopscotch all the way to Abol Bridge on a palmful of calories every hour or so. I turned toward the voices hoping for nothing more than to yogi a single granola bar. What I walked into was full-blown trail magic.

They were a group of younger folks out for some fun on the lake, local people for the most part, and with the presence to know that thru-hikers would be passing by in their dozens. To that end they'd brought magic, a lot of it: hot dogs, beers, snack bars, cookies, and a table of condiments from relish and mustard to hot sauce and mayonnaise. It was as if the wealthiest feast of a medieval king's court had been whisked into the woods by Merlin. I didn't have to yogi anything, they insisted.

I put down six hot dogs in quick succession, paused for a pair of beers, then put down two more. Ohmygod, this was beyond largesse—this was absolute opulence! Some chocolate-chip cookies kept my mouth busy for a minute, then I sheepishly returned for more hot dogs. The guy filled my plate without annoyance, only a smile. "Eat up," he said. "That's why we brought all this."

Other thru-hikers came in, along with Keebler. We laughed at my desperation of an hour earlier, and I was sure to let him know that without his peanut butter cup I might not have made it this far for hours, if then. One of the young women was Rebekah's stepdaughter. She remembered me from my stay at Lakeshore House on Hike 3. "I'm the one who cooked you that pot roast," she reminded me with a grin. "Are you ever not starving?"

I grazed for an hour, my stomach now a hard ball in my belly. In other circumstances a nap just then would have been perfect, but I still had eleven miles to go and it was now past two o'clock. I pocketed a few extra snack bars, gave thanks that included naming after them any future children I might produce, then pushed on fully restored, renewed and triumphant. The food in my belly would last until tomorrow. Nothing could stop me now.

I cleared Nesuntabunt Mountain eight miles later, downing an energy drink to keep my pace up. I'd done nineteen miles by then and I was feeling it. As I climbed some stone steps up the mountain, I absently noted the stone step I'd slipped off of on Hike 2, which accounted for the brace I had to wear on my right ankle. But that was old history. This was new history.

Those energy drinks work! From there I flew, past the cataract jumble of Pollywog Gorge, over Pollywog Stream and then to Rainbow Stream Lean-to, where I arrived at sunset, twenty-six miles for the day and I'd never have made it if not for the kindness of others. Rainbow Stream Lean-to plays a profound role in my novel *The Appalachian*. I left a copy of that novel in the shelter on Hike 3, and jumped in eagerly now to see if it was still there. It wasn't. I hadn't really expected it to be. At a heavy 750 pages, I doubted that anyone would have carted it off. I looked to the fire ring and assumed that the ashes I saw included those of my novel.

There were two section hikers in the shelter, a middle-aged man named Roman and a young woman named Princess. Roman was gregarious and weathered, with a faraway expression that hinted of a past life. Princess was red-haired and perky. She noticed my inflamed palm and insisted on tending it. After wiping my palm with alcohol, then daubing the cut with something akin to super glue, she applied a clean bandage and secured it with surgical tape. I still wore that bandage atop Baxter Peak, and the cut healed cleanly with only a thin scar.

I pitched my tent that night on a rise above the shelter. The breeze was sighing and cool, the stars like flecks of crystal. I was still so full from the trail magic that I didn't need to open my last pouch of instant potatoes. Those potatoes went up Mt. Katahdin with me and reside in my kitchen cupboard today.

I left in the dark at five thirty. Roman roused as I got underway. "Good luck, Solo," he said from the dark depths of the shelter. "And congratulations."

"Thanks, Roman."

I hopped the rocks across Rainbow Stream (there used to be a log bridge), made a quick rooty climb, then pushed hard for Abol Bridge just fifteen miles away

I found *arete* before the sun rose, and climbed up to the Rainbow Ledges in the magic hour. The sky was graying somewhat, occluding Mt. Katahdin in the distance, but the air smelled clean and fresh, the breeze cool but not cold. I met a group of three hikers going southbound, then pulled up with a start when I recognized one of them as Mighty Mo with her orange backpack.

"Mighty Mo!" I exclaimed, unexplainably pleased to see her again.

"Solo," she smiled, her former reticence residing aside the trail somewhere. "It's great to see you again."

"What are you doing here?"

"I flipped at Pinkham Notch. I just didn't want to take any chances, you know?"

"Yeah, I get it. So you've already summited?"

"Uh, huh. So when are you going up?"

"It has to be tomorrow. The weather's supposed to get bad on Friday."

"I heard."

"Did you do the Hunt Trail both ways?"

"No, we came down the Abol Trail."

One of her hiking partners, a middle-aged man, stepped up and interjected, "And I felt like we took our lives in our own hands coming down that."

"Really?"

"Yeah. It might be shorter than the Hunt Trail, but the rocks are steeper. Going down them was terrifying."

This was disappointing news. I'd hoped to use that trail myself so that I wouldn't have to backtrack on the Hunt Trail—always forward, never backward—but I didn't think it was worth risking what he described. It was probably better to climb the Abol Trail, where you could decide where to plant your feet and not abdicate that to gravity, but the white blazes weren't on the Abol Trail, they were on the Hunt Trail.

We said our goodbyes and then I sprinted on over picayune trail, maintaining a quick pace and passing the sites of some of my misadventures on Hike 1. I stepped out of the woods and onto the Golden Road at eleven o'clock, crossed the bridge, and hustled into the store for a beer and some food. I'd done it! Not in the four days I'd hoped, but four and a half days was close enough. But I still had nine more miles to go, through Baxter State Park to Katahdin Stream Campground.

There were a half dozen hikers lounging around the front of the store. "So what's up?" I asked them as I sipped my beer.

"We're stuck here until tomorrow morning," one of them told me.

"Why?" I asked in confusion.

The hiker explained, his frustration evident in his tone: "You have to register at the kiosk about a half mile up the road. The problem is that all the campgrounds are full, and if you don't have a campsite reserved they won't let you in—so we have to camp here and then line up at the kiosk at six in the morning to reserve a campsite, and we have to do that because they won't let anybody go up the mountain after ten in the morning, and, well, that's still nine miles away so you'd have to do that in less than four hours and then climb the mountain all worn out, so we have to camp here today then camp there tomorrow then go up the mountain the next day—if the weather's good. It's all fucked."

I took that news with a tight jaw. I'd been hearing rumors about this for weeks, and had been worried about something like this for longer than that. Southbounders didn't encounter the crowding that northbounders did. This was not something I'd ever faced. I had tried to solidify my knowledge beforehand, but getting accurate information had proved ridiculously futile, with the various websites posting contradictory information, and with various rangers citing different lines each time I called. And the trail telegraph was worse than anecdotal, salted with exaggeration along the way.

I went in for another beer, a few honey buns, and enough energy bars to get me up the mountain and back.

"Where are you going?" that hiker asked me as I took off up the road.

"I'm going to Mt. Katahdin," I replied over my shoulder, and I meant it. Stealth or otherwise, I was climbing that mountain tomorrow.

It wasn't yet noon. There was a note on the kiosk, the ranger out doing his rounds until two thirty or so. Even this far into the hike, burning daylight was still almost unendurable. I powered past the kiosk and took to the trail, running scenarios through my mind in case a ranger accosted me. I was on a day hike, I could say; or I was meeting someone at Katahdin Stream Campground; or better yet, I had a shuttle scheduled to pick me up at the campground and bring me back tomorrow—all of which were reasonable excuses, and none of which I intended to do. If it came to it I would stealth camp and then stealth up the mountain itself. I would not be deferred, not now. I'd come too far to have my patience tested.

As it turned out, all of my concerns were unnecessary.

The trail through Baxter State Park was picayune and plodding, as if placed that way on purpose to slow my progress. The roots were tangled and constant, the trail scalloped and spongy along the ponds. Somehow I kept up a good pace and didn't fall. I walked into Katahdin Stream Campground at three thirty through an ominous chill wind and under a filling sky, four hours to do nine miles.

In a bid to keep my ascent of Mt. Katahdin legal, and with Plans B, C, and D close at hand in case things didn't go my way, I went into the ranger station to formally register, where I met Wendy, a young, helpful, and achingly sincere park ranger. She explained the procedure to me, contradicting some of what that thru-hiker at Abol Bridge had told me. Yes, the campgrounds were fully booked, and yes, I would have to hike out and then back if I couldn't find a campsite, either that or shuttle to Millinocket, which had been my backup Plan B lie if this didn't work out. No, I was not going to shuttle to Millinocket or hike back to Abol Bridge. I was going to stealth, but I didn't have to. Wendy pointed to some campers across the way. "They've only got two people in a six-person site. I bet they would let you camp there if you asked them."

I thanked Wendy and went on over to meet Josh and Ben, thirtyish guys from Massachusetts who were out for a long weekend. Ben, a lover of rum and 4WD trucks, said he came every year to spend a few days going up and down Mt. Katahdin. His friend Josh, who was totally into Star Wars and the films of Bruce Campbell, had joined Ben this time. Both were doing trail magic, passing out beers and energy bars as if they had an endless supply.

"Pitch your tent right there," Ben pointed. "Do you like chili and cornbread?"

"Hell yeah!" My mouth was already watering.

"It'll be ready soon," Ben said to that.

Full of chili, cornbread, beer and rum, and with my tent set up against the coming night, I was in thru-hiker nirvana. Those thru-hikers at Abol

Bridge would now be in their tents just beyond that dusty road, wasting away the day because of some misinformation that had propagated word-of-mouth. Three of them would have been welcomed at this site, and there were other sites around that were half empty. They all could have come in if they'd taken the risk.

We talked around the campfire as nightfall took us, Josh in awe that in the 90s I'd attended a cast party for a Bruce Campbell film. We disagreed about which was the best Star Wars movie. I said it was *Empire Strikes Back*, while he claimed it had to be *Revenge of the Sith*. Ben just observed, sipping rum with a knowing smile.

I turned in early, excitement coursing along my skin. In many ways this resembled my southbound thru-hikes, where I would turn in for the night at Neel Gap, waking at three thirty in the morning for a climb in the dark over Blood Mountain and the thirty-mile race to Springer Mountain. This time I didn't have thirty miles to hike, just 5.2 very difficult miles, but I would be up early just the same, starting up Mt. Katahdin in the dark.

I didn't need an alarm clock. I told myself to wake up at four o'clock and that's when my eyes popped open. I ate two honey buns, broke camp and was on the darkened trail by five o'clock. Ben and Josh were asleep in their tents, Ben telling me last night that they would be gone before I got back down the mountain. I regretted not being able to say goodbye to them, to thank them one last time.

The first couple of miles of the Hunt Trail go quickly, and then the trail shoots up and the pace slows. I cleared the timberline as daylight came up, a gray dawn but with a high ceiling. Snazzy, whom I hadn't seen since Old Spec, went by me, offering premature congratulations with the sparkle of excitement in his eyes.

I pushed on into the hand-over-hand section, stowed my trekking poles and got to it. This is a dangerous section. I'm not aware of any fatalities having occurred there but there must have been some. The rocks can be slippery, with leaps of faith that can be redirected mid-flight by sudden gusting winds. There are squeezes, narrow ledges, and a precarious piece of sweating rebar with which to lever yourself over an eight-foot wall. A slip there could break a leg; a slip elsewhere could mean a plummet into the timeless and unyielding rocks below.

At last I cleared the hand-over-hand section and got into The Gateway, a long, wind-exposed ridge. The mountain at that elevation was socked in, damp, cold, and gusting. I leaned into the wind and pushed on with numbed feet; finally The Tableland, the trail running like an icy stream. On and on, cairns rising from the gloom, moisture spraying off my rain shell in the wind, and then, after a little less than four hours of struggle and a little more than four months to reach it, the sign appeared through the fog and I was there.

I went to the sign, dropped to my knees, touched it reverently with numbed fingers, and was almost blown over by a gust. After a few moments of reflection in which twenty years and 8000 miles raced through my mind as one, I went around an outcrop to get out of the wind, where I found Snazzy, irrepressible excitement shining in his eyes.

"We did it! We did it!" he grinned.

"Yeah, we did," I said in excitement and weariness, both.

Snazzy took my summit photo, buffeted by the wind and with moisture condensing on the camera lens. Other hikers arrived, one of them Old School. He enlisted Snazzy for his own photo, dropped trou and everything else and climbed up on the sign stark naked in that freezing wind but with a wide grin.

"Damn, Old School," I hollered incredulously. "Shit, bro." I was freezing just standing there, while Old School's wang was in the wind.

Afterward, in moods gone melancholy and as crowds of thru-hikers arrived, Snazzy went down Knife's Edge, Old School went down the Abol Trail, and I retraced my route down the Hunt Trail.

Working my way through the maze of rock in the hand-over-hand section, I caught up to Preacher and Winston. Preacher was perhaps in his forties, friendly and gregarious, and in the process of climbing the highest peak in every state. Mt. Katahdin was his 38th. Winston was from Virginia, a strapping young man, eighteen years old, just out of high school and grappling with some major life decisions. He and Preacher had met on the climb and had gotten on well so were hiking together.

I stayed with them on the way down, shared stories in the heady afterglow of achievement, and learned that Winston had his Jeep parked at the campground. I asked him if he could give me a ride to Millinocket and he said sure, no problem. He would be pulling out anyway, on his way back to Virginia, and there's no route out that didn't go through Millinocket so it wouldn't be an inconvenience at all. I breathed a sigh of relief. I could have hitched out and probably wouldn't have had any difficulty getting a ride, but it's always nice when a sure thing comes along.

Back at Katahdin Stream Campground, much warmer and with even a spot of sun, I said goodbye to Preacher, Winston went off to fetch his Jeep, and I spotted Old School sitting on a picnic table looking for his own ride out.

"So do you think he'd give me a ride out, too?" Old School asked hopefully. He was in a rush to get back to Shaw's, where that amorous adventure finally awaited him.

"Maybe," I said. "We'll just have to ask."

Winston's Jeep was so full of camping gear and supplies that there was hardly enough room for me.

"Sorry," he told Old School. "I would but there's no room left."

Old School deflated. "I can squeeze in the back," he said in desperation.

There was everything but a kayak in the back of that Jeep. I looked on dubiously as Winston agreed to try. The two rearranged a few things, Old School shoehorned himself in with his knees bent against the backpack in his lap, but he was in, so off we went.

It's twenty-five miles or thereabouts from Katahdin Stream Campground to Millinocket. By the time we got there my stomach was growling and I could hear Old School's doing the same in the back. I offered to buy beers and burgers for both of them, so we went into a diner across the street from Ole Man's A.T. Lodge. Winston was too young to drink, and Old School didn't have his I.D. with him, so I was the only one who could celebrate with a beer. For Old School and Winston, the burgers were celebration enough.

Afterward, Old School got himself up and ready for a complicated hitch back to Shaw's, which was too far out of the way for Winston to drive him. Old School came in for a goodbye hug, which surprised me at first but then seemed to fit perfectly in that moment of post-trail elation. We would probably never see each other again, so I returned his hug and felt a bit wistful at our parting.

The A.T. Lodge was fully booked so Winston drove me to a nearby hotel.

"So what's next for you?" I asked him before I got out.

"I've got to figure some things out," he said. "I'm gonna take the long way home and camp as I go. I need to be alone for a while, I can think better that way. Who knows, maybe I'll hike the A.T. too, you know, alone the way you did."

It was embracingly warm in Winston's Jeep. I lingered, and thought, the silence between us expectant.

"You know," I told him, "this was my fourth thru-hike, and four is enough. I'm not doing this again, so your trail name will now be Solo until someone comes up with something better. Do us proud."

His eyes widened in surprise, and then they misted.

"I will," he promised, earnestly shaking my hand at the honor. "I will."

EPILOGUE

TUESDAY, SEPTEMBER 27, 2021

Smith County, Tennessee

I got home tonight at about 9:00 p.m. The place looks better than last time. Vince and his kids did a great job keeping the place up while I was away. There's still a lot of work to do out there, though, to get everything ready for fall and winter.

It's serendipity—or else a tremendous coincidence—that I got home on the 27th. That date has popped up a lot on my hikes, and surely represents something to come.

I'm starving, but I absolutely will not eat anything right now. It's like I told them all early on, you have to control your hiker hunger or you'll balloon up in a matter of weeks, and getting that weight back off is nigh impossible save for another Appalachian Trail thru-hike.

Right now I weigh 146 pounds, about what I have weighed at the end of every thru-hike. I intend to put on no more than 14 pounds, which will return me to the proper weight for my age and height. I'll do this not by dieting, but by eating a maximum of 2400 calories per day. The FDA says that this is the proper amount of daily calories for my age and activity level. I'm going to do it just like I did last time: I'll divide those 2400 calories into twelve equal portions and snack on them throughout the day to still the hunger pangs. When this isn't enough I'll chew on my knuckles if I have to. After a couple of weeks the hunger pangs will settle down, and after a month my body will adjust. I'll then be able to add extra calories until I bring my weight up to about 160 pounds, then I'll resume the 2400-calorie maximum from then on, eating healthily, of course, with no refined sugar, very little salt, and even less processed food.

I'll also start the light weight training again so that I can get my muscle tone back and prevent those 14 pounds from going straight to fat, because let's face it—every extra calorie thru-hikers eat once they finish the trail goes straight to fat unless they take measures to prevent it. This regimen worked well after Hike 3, giving me a physique I didn't even have when I was a teenager. It's much easier to tailor your body when you've lost all your body fat. There's got to be some science behind this, but I've never come across it in my books. At any rate, I know from experience that losing weight is terribly difficult unless something like a thru-hike comes along. After Hikes 1 and 2 I gained 50 pounds or more—all going to fat—and it happened so quickly! I could not get that weight back off until my next thru-hike, and then finally after Hike 3 I decided to do something about that weight gain once and for all. The Appalachian Trail gave us these bodies like a gift. It would be a shame to waste the effort.

SATURDAY, OCTOBER 23, 2021

Smith County, Tennessee

Today is a month since I summited Mt. Katahdin. A month before summiting, I'd been taking that Hurricane Henri zero in Norwich, Vermont and with all that would come afterward—deep time, lifetimes.

Things are finally falling into shape here on the farm, but the weeks have raced past, leaving me feeling cheated of time. The Appalachian Trail is tough, often brutal, but the trail is life at a time-elongating pace in which each second leaves an imprint, in which each second is lived and felt. The seconds are a blur back home, fleeing from memory. Their loss, I think, is the reason some of us go back again and again.

I've received summit photos from everyone now. Ultra Burn met a girl named Happy Feet after we split up. They summited together under a clear blue sky and above a pure white sea of cloud. Ultra Burn had his smile back. He found his hike, and of that I'm pleased and proud.

K-Bar summited on a day as clear as spring water, the far horizon falling away along the curve of the Earth. She looked more mature than her nineteen years, confident, and bar-the-door ready to do it again! A few short months later, in May 2022, she set out to thru-hike the Pacific Crest Trail.

And then Rocky and Switz on a likewise clear day, and Matador sitting atop the sign with a look of quiet victory. Mohawk made it up in the same furious weather I endured, baring his chest against the elements as if daring

K-Bar and Pink Panther

Greasy Creek Friendly Gadget and Cee Cee

Me on Mt. Katahdin

Mohawk on Mt. Katahdin

Dips on Mt. Katahdin

K-Bar

Ultra Burn and Happy Feet

Rocky and Swift

Matador on Mt. Katahdin

Nimblewill Nomad and K-Bar

Freewind

Katahdin to match the Himalayas, while Dips poignantly knelt to the irreconcilable emotions of the moment, her journey just beginning.I miss them all.

SATURDAY, NOVEMBER 20, 2021

Smith County, Tennessee

Ultra Burn and Happy Feet visited me today. It was all I could do to hold myself together. They both looked well, happy, and looking forward to larger lives. Ultra Burn's smile–it had been so long since I'd seen it, years in trail time, a little over four months in normal time.

We compared hikes, of course, and I didn't mean to brag but it just came out that way. I made my best and fastest thru-hike ever, 131 days and with uninterrupted transits of both the White Mountains and the Hundred-Mile Wilderness, far outperforming my younger self at ages sixty, fifty, and forty-three.

They gave me a ball cap with my four thru-hikes listed on the bill, and with a fifth hike as yet undated, and I wonder–I have to wonder: What might I be able to do when I'm seventy? Or when I'm eighty?

Perhaps I might just head on back when I'm eighty-three and see if I can't break Nimblewill Nomad's record.

Back on the Farm - Happy Feet, Ultra Burn, and me

ABOUT THE AUTHOR

Kirk Ward Robinson, a four-time Appalachian Trail thru-hiker, was born and raised in south Texas and has since lived in every continental American time zone. He is an inveterate hiker and cyclist, which is how he prefers to travel and explore the world. His wide-ranging career has included roles as a chief operating officer, bookstore manager, stagehand, bicycle mechanic, and executive director of an educational non-profit organization in cooperation with the National Park Service. Robinson has been twice named to Kirkus Reviews' *Best Books*: in 2012 for *Life in Continuum*, and in 2015 for *The Appalachian*. He earned five stars from Foreword Clarion Reviews for his novel *The Latter Half of Inglorious Years*.

These days he maintains a small ancestral farm in the hills of Tennessee. *www.kirkwardrobinson.com*

Lightning Source UK Ltd.
Milton Keynes UK
UKHW012102121022
410372UK00004B/273

9 780999 604281